FURTHERING

How should we reflect theologically about culture? Tim Gorringe presents a threefold, and interrelated, reflection organized around culture, power and mission. First, Gorringe interrogates culture through contemporary cultural studies but also through the contribution of the great eighteenth century theologian, J.G.Herder. He concludes by considering the question of cultural imperialism. Second, Gorringe asks where power is located in culture, and how the Church relates to that, arguing that the central theses of liberation theology are far from dead. The third part turns to questions of mission, asking whether this is morally feasible in a culturally pluralist world and considering the implications of Samuel Huntington's notorious thesis of the 'clash of civilizations'. Gorringe argues that mission is in fact a vital part of a respectful multicultural society.

For Jean-Marc Éla and Aloysius Pieris
Teachers of the Universal Church

Furthering Humanity

A Theology of Culture

T.J.GORRINGE
University of Exeter

ASHGATE

© T.J. Gorringe, 2004

Published by
Ashgate Publishing Limited
Gower House
Croft Road
Aldershot
Hants GU11 3HR
England

Ashgate Publishing Company
Suite 420
101 Cherry Street
Burlington, VT, 05401-4405 USA

Ashgate website: http://www.ashgate.com

British Library Cataloguing in Publication Data
Gorringe, Timothy
  Furthering Humanity: A Theology of Culture.
  1. Christianity and culture. I. Title.
  261

Library of Congress Cataloging in Publication Data
Gorringe, Timothy
  Furthering Humanity: A Theology of Culture/Timothy Gorringe.
     p. cm.
  Includes bibliographical references and index.
  1. Christianity and culture. 2. Multiculturalism—Religious aspects—Christianity. I. Title.
  BR115.C8G66   2004
  161–dc22   2003063793

Reprinted 2005

ISBN 0 7546 4031 0 (hbk)
ISBN 0 7546 4032 9 (pbk)

Typeset by Tradespools, Frome, Somerset
Printed and bound in Great Britain by MPG Books Ltd, Bodmin, Cornwall

Contents

Preface

Any book has complex origins, and this is no exception: in the first instance in teaching undergraduate courses in theology and culture; more importantly in seven years in India struggling to come to terms with Tamil language and culture; in many years of appreciative reception of the cultural materialism represented by the likes of Raymond Williams, Stuart Hall and Terry Eagleton; in an even longer interest in the thought of Johann Gottfried Herder which was probably sparked by the essay in Barth's *Protestant Theology in the Nineteenth Century*; in a passion for the folk tradition mediated by A.L.Lloyd who once, communist that he was, came to sing for my middle class church group, and by Ewan MacColl and Peggy Seeger. Those names date me, but I remain unrepentantly committed to the socialism which inspired their understanding of popular culture.

The book and the courses from which it comes, represent an attempt to bring all this together within a Christian theological perspective. Doubtless it is 'another kind of failure', but if so I ask my critics to address the issue of culture and power, and culture and empire, better than I have done. The absence of anthropology will strike many as strange. I began with it, but the need for political analysis took me further and further from much of what passes as anthropological reflection on culture. Experts in cultural studies will doubtless find the theology strange, and theologians will raise their eyebrows at the cultural studies. I am sorry if I disappoint both parties but this is my last and I must stick to it. I am sure it is not the only path into the theological future but I am equally sure it is one of them.

Tim Gorringe
Exeter
Easter 2003

PART I
CULTURE

In modern society, it is not enough to occupy factories or confront the state. What must also be contested is the whole area of culture, defined in its broadest, most everyday sense. The power of the ruling class is spiritual as well as material; and any 'counterhegemony' must cary its political campaign into this hitherto neglected realm of values and customs, speech habits and ritual practices.

Terry Eagleton

Chapter 1

The Long Revolution

Human beings, says Clifford Geertz in a famous image, are animals suspended in webs of significance they themselves have spun.[1] 'Culture' is the name for those webs. It is what we make of the world, materially, intellectually and spiritually. These dimensions cannot be separated: the Word is necessarily flesh. In constructing the world materially we interpret it, set values on it. To talk of values is to talk of a culture's self-understanding, its account of its priorities. The everyday world, the built environment, rituals, symbols, ideals and practices all rest on these values. At the end of his discussion of cultural imperialism John Tomlinson remarks that the failure of modernity is a specifically cultural one, namely the inability to decide what people should value, believe in, and what sense they ought to make of their everyday lives.[2] 'Values set down final standards for desired social relations, individual modes of behaviour, social and political structures, life-goals and ideals for the individual and the collective self. Furthermore, they also bind people's feelings and guide their moral judgement.'[3] Culture, we can say, is concerned with the spiritual, ethical and intellectual significance of the material world. It is, therefore, of fundamental theological concern.

The Meanings of 'Culture'

The metaphorical application of the tilling of fields – agriculture – to the cultivation of minds is ancient and obvious. Cicero spoke of the *cultura animi* in a phrase picked up in the Renaissance by Thomas More and Francis Bacon amongst others.[4] The idea of the 'cultivated' person is a variant of this metaphor, denoting the end result of a process. The familiarity of the noun 'culture' tends to obscure this older, active, use of the word but it is important to remember it. For one thing the reference back to agriculture reminds us that 'culture' cannot be separated off from economics, and that different modes of production are bound up with different cultures. The decisive significance of the experience of work and ways of life in shaping culture is reflected in the differences between peasant, industrial, working class, managerial and now

---

1 C.Greetz, *The Interpretation of Cultures* London: Fontana 1993 p.5
2 J.Tomlinson, *Cultural Imperialism* London: Continuum 1991 p.169
3 T.Meyer, *Identity Mania: Fundamentalism and the Politicisation of Cultural Differences* London: Zed 2001 p.71
4 Cicero, *Tusculan Disputations* 2.5 (13) For More and Bacon see R.Williams, *Keywords* London: Fontana 1976 p.87

postmodern cultures, reading postmodernism, with Frederic Jameson, as 'the cultural logic of late capitalism'.[5] This connection is especially important today in the light of the ecological crisis, when culture as a way of life organized around infinite growth is turned against culture as the nourishing of life in all its fullness.

The idea of culture as cultivation highlights the fact that culture is *process*. For Raymond Williams this process 'has no particular end, and ... can never be supposed at any time to have finally realized itself, to have become complete'.[6] This is a warning against ideas that this or that culture might have arrived at 'the end of history' but it also uses language which is implicitly eschatological, and, as we shall see later in the chapter, Karl Barth believed that eschatology was the theological category under which culture had to be discussed. To say that culture has no particular end is not to imply that it is aimless. Theologically understood, culture is the name of that whole process in the course of which God does what it takes, in Paul Lehman's phrase, to make and to keep human beings human. Culture in this sense is, under God, 'the human task'.[7] Process means change, and change involves both success and failure, golden ages and ages of iron, periods of creativity and periods of decadence.[8] If ethics is the conversation of the human race about its common project, canvassed more importantly in histories, gospels, plays, novels and soap operas than in the treatises of moral philosophy, then it is this discussion which seeks the criteria by which we decide what is success and what is failure. Once again ethics, the question of value, is integral to the question of culture.

The origins of the word 'culture' in agricultural processes are recognized in some respects in an opposite way in the 'organic' notion of culture, which emphasizes the importance of 'roots'. Trees and plants, even of very common species, change subtly from region to region depending on their soils. They have diverse ecologies and need time to put down roots. So, the metaphor implies, human beings need to attend to their roots, an idea developed famously by figures as different as Simone Weil and Alex Haley.[9] As

5   S.Latouche, *The Westernization of the World* Cambridge: Polity 1996 p.41 Latouche defines culture as 'the response human groups make to the problem of their social existence'. He argues that the separation of culture from economics originates in Plato's split between matter and spirit. This split means that whilst we 'respect cultures' the process of economic development which destroys cultures is left intact.

6   R.Williams, *Resources of Hope* London: Verso 1989 p.37

7   The phrase is Barth's but he qualified it by saying that the task is the response to God's Word. K.Barth, *Theology and Church* London: SCM 1962 p.337

8   Cf Raymond Williams: 'The human energy of the long revolution springs from the conviction that men can direct their own lives, by breaking through the pressures and restrictions of older forms of society, and by discovering new common institutions. This process necessarily includes both success and failure ... We tend to absorb the successes and then to be pre-occupied by the hard knots of failure. Or as we approach the failures, to see if anything can be done, we are distracted by the chorus of success.' *The Long Revolution* Harmondsworth. Penguin 1965 p.375

9   Simone Weil writes: 'A human being has roots by virtue of his real, active and natural participation in the life of a community which preserves in living shape certain *particular* treasures of the past and certain particular expectations for the future ... Every human being needs to have multiple roots.' *The Need for Roots* London: Routledge 1958 p.41 my italics

exemplified in the regionalism of someone like T.S.Eliot it signals the truth that cultures cannot be bought off the peg, or be created overnight, but grow slowly, find expression in cuisines and building as well as music and poetry, and to that extent are literally 'rooted in the soil'. Here we have the origin of the understanding of culture as a 'way of life'. This sense of cultural process, which remains close to the agricultural metaphor, remains vital, even in an 'age of migration'. Some of the difficulties of multiculturalism, explored in the final chapter, stem from here. At the same time the organic metaphor alone is inadequate for there is, as has always been recognized, an irreducible tension between nature and culture:

> From the beginning of recorded time culture has been an extraordinary achievement, a heroic imposition on nature or natural tendency. Culture takes on nature, as a cultivator does the soil ... there is also, we might say, a human soil to be made fertile. But this transition from *humus* to *homo* includes a testing, by the gods or man himself, of human nature, which may encourage its autonomy or forge a link between culture and domination.[10]

The idea of 'heroic imposition' here ought to ring some alarm bells in the light of the ecological crisis. A cultivator does not 'take on' the soil. She or he *cultivates* it, which is a very different matter, implying learning what is possible and what is not, responding to local conditions of soil, climate and so forth, learning to irrigate in ways which do not cause erosion, which do not cause problems for my neighbour downstream. Domination, the model for capitalism since at least 1492 and the arrival in South America, is the antithesis of culture and sooner or later spells its death. At the same time there is a transition from *humus* to *homo*, a testing, the emergence of the arts by which we nurture life, in the course of which the relationship between nature and nurture is constantly renegotiated.

In the eighteenth century the word acquires the various senses with which we are now familiar, rather differently in Germany, France and England. German borrowed French 'cultur', but, according to Norbert Elias, the term was mobilized by the rising bourgeoisie to refer to the *result* of 'cultivation', and turned polemically against mere 'civilization', looking back to an earlier distinction between courtly manners and true virtue. 'On the one hand, superficiality, ceremony, formal conversation; on the other, inwardness, depth of feeling, immersion in books, development of the individual personality.'[11] *Kultur*, as it came to be spelt, is indissolubly linked to *Bildung*, education, the formation of the person by the study and practice of poetry, philosophy, music and so forth. This marked a clear difference from the French and English concept of civilization which could refer to political, economic and social facts,

---

10 G.Hartman, *The Fateful Question of Culture* New York: Columbia University Press 1997 p.172
11 N.Elias, *The Civilising Process* Oxford: Blackwell 1994 p.16 Kant distinguished between the idea of morality, which was properly part of culture, and the application of the idea in a concern for honour and decency which 'amounts only to civilizing'. I.Kant. *Ideas on a Universal History from the Point of View of a Citizen of the World*, quoted by Elias, ibid p.7

and which quickly acquired a plural form, to distinguish the ensemble of these around the world.[12]

Schleiermacher in 1799 marked an enthusiastic adoption of the new concept by theologians when he published his famous manifesto addressed to '*die Gebildeten*', the cultured, amongst the despisers of religion. These were those who had leisure to immerse themselves in philosophy and the arts and who, in doing so, were doing that which was truly religious, cultivating a sense and taste for the infinite. The cultured have arrived, through the union of knowledge and feeling, at the awareness that there is nothing in their own nature which is not a work of the World Spirit. 'In virtue of this feeling, all that touches their life becomes truly a world, a unity permeated by the Divinity that fashions it.'[13] Here religion and culture have become almost indistinguishable. It was self-evident to him that the working class had no leisure for this and could not therefore lead in either religion or culture.[14]

This development is by no means the whole of the German story, as we shall see shortly, but it had momentous consequences. The concept of *Kultur* became definitional of German life and the First World War was fought, from the German side, as a struggle between culture and barbarism.[15] The results of twelve years of German fascism plunged this self-understanding into the abyss and postcolonial critics have generalized such critique to Western culture as a whole. 'When the native hears a speech about western culture,' wrote Fanon, 'he pulls out his knife ... The violence with which the supremacy of white values is affirmed and the aggressiveness which has permeated the victory of these values over the ways of life and thought of the native mean that, in revenge the native laughs in mockery when Western values are mentioned in front of him.'[16]

The contrast between 'culture' and 'civilization' made in Germany was not made in France where, as Elias shows, the contrast between true and false civilization could have the same meaning as the German contrast between culture and civilization. The term *civilisation* came into common currency in the early 1770s in France to express the aspirations of the reform movement in French high society and the hope that 'the improvement of institutions, education and law will be brought about by knowledge'.[17] The role the

---

12   Elias, *Process* p.4

13   F.D.E.Schleiermacher, *Speeches on Religion to its Cultured Despisers* 2nd edn tr John Oman New York: Harper 1958 p.70 Daniel Bell is indebted to these late eighteenth century understandings of culture in defining it as the realm of sensibility, of emotion and moral temper, and of the intelligence which seeks to order these feelings. *The Cultural Contradictions of Capitalism* London: Heinemann 1976 p.36

14   Schleiermacher asked his 'despisers': 'Do you seriously expect me to believe that those who daily distress themselves most toilsomely about earthly things have pre-eminent fitness for becoming intimate with heavenly things, those who brood anxiously over the next moment and are fast bound to the nearest objects can extend their vision widest over the world, and that those who, in the monotonous round of a dull industry have not yet found themselves will discover most clearly the living Deity?' *Speeches* p.12

15   Elias, *Process* p.7

16   F.Fanon, *The Wretched of the Earth* Harmondsworth: Penguin 1967 p.33

17   Elias, *Process* pp.38–39

philosophes, and especially Voltaire, played in its emergence meant that from the start it was polemically opposed to superstition and theological ignorance.

The emergence of the term 'culture' in England was, unsurprisingly, tied more closely to the industrial revolution. Raymond Williams' 'long revolution' comprises the interrelated processes of industrial change, democratic empowerment and widening cultural access – the extension of learning, literacy and advanced communication to all groups rather than to the few.[18] It is the huge social, economic and political changes of this period which force the issue to prominence.[19] The development of the idea of 'culture', Williams had already shown in *Culture and Society*, was in many ways a protest against the inhumanity of industrial capitalism. 'Culture', in the sense of high culture, was both a critique of much that was happening and 'a mitigating and rallying alternative'.[20] Williams linked it with key changes in the words 'industry', 'democracy', 'class' and 'art'. He could have added that 'religion' was another term which acquired a new sense at this time, and as part of the same process, as Schleiermacher classically shows.[21] When Calvin wrote his *Institutes of the Christian Religion*, he expounded the creed but, as Barth shows in a careful exposition, the word 'religion' slowly acquired first independence and then priority in the seventeenth and eighteenth centuries.[22] Schleiermacher, in the name of religion, valorized individuality, inwardness, feeling as the antithesis to dogma. His contemporaries, the Romantic poets, did exactly the same thing for the lonely and cultivated individual, beginning that process by which culture sought to take the place of religion.

That Elias' account of the development of the term *Kultur* in terms of depth, inwardness and education is only half of the story is shown by the crucial work of one of the great Enlightenment dissenters, Johann Gottfried Herder. In an argument to which Schleiermacher must have been indebted he is one of the first to draw attention to the importance of different cultures. 'Nothing is more indeterminate than the word "culture",' he wrote, 'and nothing more deceptive than its application to all nations and periods.'[23] Anticipating what today we would call subcultural theory he recognized that differences in occupation, social class and religion generate different cultures.[24] For him every culture

---

18   Williams, *Long Revolution* p.11
19   Cf Homi Bhaba: 'Culture only emerges as a problem ... at the point at which there is loss of meaning in the contestation and articulation of everyday life, between classes, genders, races, nations.' *The Location of Culture* London: Routledge 1994 p.34
20   R.Williams, *Culture and Society 1780–1950* Harmondsworth: Penguin 1961 p.17
21   'The period of the 16th–18th centuries', wrote Karl Barth, 'was in its own way a great period, when European man resumed the powerful offensive which had been made by Graeco-Roman antiquity, beginning to discover himself as a man, his nature, his possibilities and capacities, humanity. The discovery of "religion" belonged ... to the same movement.' K.Barth, *Church Dogmatics* I/2 Edinburgh: T&T Clark 1956 p.293
22   Barth, *Church Dogmatics* I/2 pp.284–291
23   J.G.Herder, 'Reflections on the Philosophy of the History of Humankind', *Sämtliche Werke* ed B.Suphan Hildesheim: Olms 1877–1913 vol 13 p.4 Schleiermacher explores the importance of different cultures in Speech Five.
24   Herder, 'Reflections', *Werke* vol 14 pp.34–35

represents a different embodiment of the divine Spirit and therefore to eliminate cultures, or to preach the superiority of one over another, is to fly in the face of divine purpose. Here the notion of culture as a way of life, implicit in the organic idea, is extended to the variety of human cultures. This sense of cultural otherness is clearly part and parcel of increased trade and travel, merchant capitalism and the beginnings of European colonialism. Herder's theorization of it, in turn, stimulated that interest in different cultures which finds expression in the social and cultural anthropology of the nineteenth century. E.B.Tylor's *Primitive Culture*, published in 1871, gives us the classic definition of culture as a way of life: 'Culture or Civilization, taken in its wide ethnographic sense, is that complex whole which includes knowledge, belief, art, morals, law, custom and any other capabilities and habits acquired by man as a member of society.'[25]

Over the past two centuries Christian reflection on culture, driven by the needs of mission, has been mostly preoccupied with the relation between the gospel and 'non-Christian' cultures (it is, of course, an open question whether any culture can be 'Christian'). Herder, however, raises the question of culture relating to class. Might it be that the cultures of different classes were as opaque to each other as those of different regions of the world? Writing as a socialist in the wake of the Second World War, and in response to T.S.Eliot's ruminations on class and culture, Raymond Williams was exercised by the possibility of a common culture, a 'free, contributive and common process of participation in the creation of meanings and values'.[26] What he got was cultural populism, a shift in the balance of cultural power which is by no means self-evidently positive. The questions raised here will be the theme of the third chapter.

As already noted, the principal distinction in discussions of culture is between 'culture' as a whole way of life, and 'Culture', as literature and the arts, as in the 'culture' pages of the newspapers. With our greater awareness of subcultures this today has to be complemented by recognition of culture as identity, as in 'the culture of East Devon beekeepers' or of Iranian mullahs.[27] The use of the word to identify leading traits in society has also become

---

25 E.B.Tylor, *Primitive Culture: Researches into the Development of Mythology, Philosophy, Religion, Art and Custom* Gloucester (Mass): Smith 1958[1871] p.1 Tylor was dependent on G.F.Klemm's *General Cultural History of Humankind* published between 1843 and 1852. Williams argues that the sense of culture as a way of life is to be found in the whole discussion from Coleridge to Carlyle. *Culture and Society* p.229

26 Williams, *Resources* p.38

27 Immanuel Wallerstein puts the issue of subcultural identity in terms of personal traits. Thus while all persons share some traits with all others, sharing universal characteristics of the human species, all persons also share other traits with only some others, and all persons have still other traits which they share with no one else. 'When we talk of traits which are neither universal nor idiosyncratic we often use the term "culture".' 'Culture as the Ideological Battleground of the Modern World System' in M.Featherstone(ed) *Global Culture* London: Sage 1990 p.31 In an exasperated aside, however, in response to the accusation that he does not give enough prominence to culture in his analysis, Wallerstein remarked: 'Culture is a non science invented for us by nineteenth century social science. We must surmount this trinity of economy, polity, culture.' Ibid p.65

general, as in the 'culture of silence', the 'culture of complaint', the 'culture of narcissism' and so on. These are not subcultures, but significant cultural trends.

At the heart of all these accounts of culture is the question of *meaning*. In one way or another we are dealing at every level with questions of meaning and value. This fact was recognized in the semiotic understanding of culture proposed by Geertz whose 'webs' cannot be analysed but only interpreted and described. Culture, for him, denotes 'an historically transmitted pattern of meanings embodied in symbols, a system of inherited conceptions expressed in symbolic forms by means of which men communicate, perpetuate, and develop their knowledge about and attitudes toward life'.[28] It is 'the shared repertoire of practices, symbols, and meanings ... the space of signifying practice, the semantic ground on which human beings seek to construct and represent themselves and others – and, hence, society and history'.[29] This understanding of culture has extremely important implications for our understanding of mission, and of the relation of Church and culture generally. It runs the danger, however, of losing sight of the unity of the whole cultural process, of the necessary interconnectedness between culture as a way of life and culture as cultivation, a danger shared by those who restrict culture to sensibility.

Culture as a Christian Theme

This outline of the recent discussion makes clear that whilst 'culture' may be a noun of recent provenance, the issues raised are immemorial, as any reading of Scripture shows. The Bible is probably not far out in suggesting that culture wars have been with us from the very beginning. The conflict between Cain and Abel is a conflict between agricultural and pastoral societies, different ways of life, and its end result, according to the authors of Genesis, is the founding of urban civilization. Three different cultures, then, appear right at the start of the scriptural narrative, all marked by violence. Territory, land, is bound up with culture from the start, signified in the promise to Abraham. Largely edited during the 'exile' the biblical narrative already conjures with the question of diaspora: What does it mean to sing the Lord's song in a foreign land?

The four hundred year conflict between Yahwism and the culture of Canaan is prepared by Moses' acculturation in Sinai and his adoption of the Kenite God, YHWH. This conflict is focused most dramatically in the story of Elijah and the prophets of Baal. The role fundamental values play in culture is illustrated by the fact that it centres around different accounts of what is ultimate and therefore different understandings of the norms of human behaviour. No cultural pluralist, Elijah wants to create a unified culture.

---

28   Geertz, *Interpretation* p.89
29   J. and J. Comaroff, *Of Revelation and Revolution* vol 1 Chicago: Chicago University Press 1991 p.21

Canaanite society he stigmatizes as idolatrous: elevating sexuality and power as ultimates in a way inconsistent with the God of the poor. At the end of his revolution he is told that there will remain 'seven thousand which have not bowed the knee to Baal, whose mouths have not kissed him' (1 Kings 18.18).

That the struggle did not end with the slaughter he initiated is witnessed endlessly by the eighth century prophets, and by their executors, the Deuteronomists, who anticipate Spengler by two and a half thousand years in their theory of the decline of Israel. They propose a vision of cultural purity which demands political autonomy for its realization, and boundaries which are non-porous – a sort of fence down the West Bank. No such luck. Culture wars were renewed after the exile, in the struggle between a Hellenism which was hegemonic around much of the Mediterranean and a Judaism which rejected central tenets of what this hegemony counted as truly human, a contest which gave rise to the Maccabean revolt.

Curiously these issues are very muted in the gospels, though Ched Myers reads Mark in terms of a conflict between a culture of purity and honour on the one hand, and a culture seeking to overturn these distinctions in the interests of the poor and marginalized on the other.[30] Unlike the conflicts with Canaan, or with the Hellenists, however, this struggle was fought out, as the stories make clear, by those who read the same texts and shared most of the same assumptions. Reflection on the implications of Jesus' stand, however, quickly generated new culture wars as we see in the story of Stephen (Acts 7), and more densely and provocatively in Galatians.

Of course 'Yahwism' did not mean the selfsame thing from Moses to the Maccabees, but in the 'parting of ways' between Judaism and Christianity, in the last four decades of the first century, it acquired a set of definitions, clarified by the diaspora imposed by Rome after AD 130, which enabled its survival 'amongst the nations' for two thousand years. Making transmission by birth the norm, its reality was bound up with ethnicity but also by storytelling. 'Next year in Jerusalem,' said each family at Passover. Without a homeland the Jewish community nevertheless continued to dream of home, a land whose geography and topography they knew intimately from the scriptures which nourished their corporate life. Until 1948 they were the primary example of the possibility of cultural survival, and the maintenance of cultural identity, without a homeland – and Hannah Arendt opposed the creation of the Jewish state precisely because she believed that homelessness was what allowed Jews to escape ethnocentrism.[31]

The new religion which developed from Jesus put to sea on the ocean of universal culture – the implication of the symbolically complete list of Acts 2. The strains of that decision are already evident in the letters of Paul. When it comes to sexual conduct some of you, he writes to the Christian group in Corinth, behave even worse than Gentiles! (1 Cor 5.1) They probably were

---

30   C.Myers, *Binding the Strong Man* Maryknoll: Orbis 1988
31   H.Arendt, *The Origins of Totalitarianism* New York: Harcourt Brace 1973

Gentiles, but for Paul they were a 'new people', standing in both continuity and discontinuity with existing Israel.

The problem of how to position oneself as a Christian, *vis-à-vis* the dominant culture, remained a pressing question for centuries. In the middle of the second century the converted teacher of philosophy, Justin, found the need to evolve a theology which would allow him to go on venerating Socrates as someone from whom you still had to learn. Harnack, at the end of the nineteenth century, characterized the theological development of the following centuries as 'acute hellenization', a form of syncretism. His remedy was a return to the 'simple gospel', considered by opponents to be a baptism of Bismarckian social norms and therefore no less syncretistic.

Harnack's thesis has never commanded universal assent, and indeed in some respects it did not apply to Tertullian, at the end of the second century, who insisted that Christians refuse to compromise with any occupation, even any world view, which might question the sole lordship of Christ. When he asked, 'What has Athens to do with Jerusalem?', 'Athens' stood for the hegemonic intellectual culture, the reigning plausibility structure, of the Mediterranean world.[32] Even after Constantine made the empire Christian this question did not immediately go away. The first nine books of Augustine's *City of God* ask what, if anything, we can take from 'the greatness which was Rome'. He is far less accommodating than Justin was but, as the sense of Christianity being set in the midst of an alien culture faded, the dominant tension came to be seen as existing less between Christian and non-Christian cultures and more between this life and the next. This Augustinian understanding, deeply pessimistic about all human achievement, was to dominate the Church for at least a thousand years. At the same time, both the northern missions to the Slavic and Scandinavian peoples, and the encounter with Islam, raised the issues of struggle with different cultures, only this time from a position of political (though by no means always superior) power.

Just as we cannot assume that there was a culturally homogenous entity called 'Yahwism', so we need to remember that 'Christendom' is an umbrella term for a number of loosely related cultures. Perhaps more crucial than the creed in medieval Europe was the growth of the cities and of trade from the eleventh century onwards, made possible by the relative peace which followed the endless raids and invasions which had marked European history from the third century on. Class tensions, we know, were marked in this society, but it is probably still true that there were a good many aspects of culture which were shared across the classes, and across the regions of Europe from Scandinavia to Warsaw to Vienna to southern Italy, between, say, 1100 and 1500.

When it is claimed that Christianity provided the seed-bed for modern Europe it is this period which is in mind.[33] In providing the framework of law and of values, in providing a common narrative which gave coherence both to

---

32 The question mark by Tertullian refers to his dependence on various forms of Greek philosophy, especially Stoicism.

33 T.S.Eliot is one of the strongest proponents of this view. In a postwar lecture he argued that 'the common tradition of Christianity has made Europe what it is ... I do not believe that the

the round of the seasons and to individual life, Christianity deeply informed the culture of everyday life, whilst through the religious orders it dominated culture in the sense of learning and of art. In this sense the cultural struggle of the first to the fifth centuries was absent, though the seeds of a new struggle were all around. The growth of the cities was coterminous with what we call 'the Renaissance', whose green shoots are already clearly visible in the twelfth century, and whose political side was a vehement hostility to theocracy. Anticlericalism was rife at all levels of society and, when joined to the rediscovery of classical humanism in the fifteenth century, began to suggest that Christianity and culture were not coterminous after all. Lutheranism posited two kingdoms, Church and state, operating according to rather different principles, but otherwise the Reformation as such did not emphasize the distinction between Christianity and culture. What drove a wedge between the two were the religious wars of the sixteenth and seventeenth centuries, producing a disgust which found expression in the savage critique of the dark ages of superstition voiced classically by Voltaire.

As we have seen, it was precisely at this moment that the term 'culture' emerged. We saw how, with both Herder and Schleiermacher, religion was at first understood as an integral part of culture, something associated with the Romantic emphasis on interiority and the connection between inner development and meaning and value. In the course of the first half of the nineteenth century, however, the religious emphasis weakened and was replaced by what was in effect a metaphysics of subjectivity and imaginative process. 'Culture was at once the secularisation and the liberalization of earlier metaphysical forms.'[34] In a development which I shall explore in the following chapter, culture became a substitute for religion.

Christ and Culture

Richard Niebuhr provided a famous, if rather ahistorical, typology for understanding the interaction of Christianity and culture in *Christ and Culture*, published in 1951. Within a few years of the book's appearance, notes John Howard Yoder, 'the terms suggested, and the classification of various typical positions which it proposed, had become the common coin of contemporary thought, not only among specialists in Christian ethics, but in many other circles as well'.[35] For this reason we have to give it particular attention.

---

culture of Europe could survive the complete disappearance of the Christian Faith ... If Christianity goes, the whole culture goes.' *Notes towards the definition of Culture* London: Faber and Faber 1948 p.122

34   R.Williams, *Marxism and Literature* Oxford: Oxford University Press 1977 p.15

35   Yoder says of *Christ and Culture*: 'Few single works of contemporary theology could compare [to it] for popularity going beyond theological circles, for enormous formative impact upon the way other people think, and for great "holding power".' J.H.Yoder, 'How H.Richard Niebuhr Reasoned: A Critique of Christ and Culture' in G.Stassen et al(eds) *Authentic Transformation* Nashville: Abingdon 1996 p.31

The lectures which gave rise to the book were delivered in 1949, near the beginning of the emergence of the world order, or disorder, in which we presently live. The Berlin airlift was under way, and the world lay frozen into two polarized political ideologies. The position of a significant part of the Church with regard to this development was made clear when the Vatican, which had been able to make a Concordat with German fascism, announced excommunication for anyone practising or preaching communism. Senator McCarthy began his hearings the next year. President Truman announced his plan to bring 'underdeveloped' nations up to the level of the developed, initiating the so-called 'development decade'. All over the world former colonies were claiming their independence. There was, then, a strong sense of world reconstruction. In this context Niebuhr was concerned with the values which would underpin such reconstruction, values which he found in the Christian gospel.

In his understanding of culture he drew on the work of American social anthropology, and defined culture, or civilization – for he does not want to distinguish between the two – as the 'total process of human activity' and the total result of that activity.[36] We cannot define its essence, but we recognize that it is social, a form of human achievement, and constitutive of values which articulate the human good. The idea of the kingdom of God is just one amongst many such values. Because 'culture' describes everything we do as humans it is irreducibly plural and 'lays its claim and authority' on every person. The question Niebuhr posed was how the Christian should respond to this authority and claim. The criterion was provided by 'the Jesus Christ of the New Testament' who defines the gospel, and who, in turn, exercises authority over Christians.[37] There are, then, two authorities and the task is to map their relationship. To this end he proposed a fivefold typology which, despite extensive discussion and critique, has survived the fifty years since its first airing. Niebuhr's work has survived as well as it has partly because it is well nuanced, and therefore resists crude caricature. He recognizes that he is proposing 'ideal' types, which no historical individual perfectly exemplifies, and further that the positions shade into one another. Nevertheless he wants to suggest that Christian responses to culture fall into oppositional, conformist, synthetic, dualist and conversionist modes.

The first letter of John in the New Testament with its warnings against 'the world' and 'the lust of the flesh, the lust of the eyes, and the pride of life', and Tertullian and Tolstoy in the later tradition, illustrate a stance of 'Christ against culture', where the gospel calls into being what is later called an *oppositional* culture. This stance, Niebuhr felt, was necessary but inadequate. Though we recognize the contribution of monasticism and Protestant sectarianism, instantiations of this view, the real reform of culture was accomplished by more moderate voices. The historical record is, therefore, against the antagonistic response to the wider world. Methodologically it is

36   H.R.Niebuhr, *Christ and Culture* New York: Harper and Row 1951 p.32
37   Niebuhr, *Christ and Culture* p.12

impossible because human beings cannot exist outside culture. Radical Christians are caught in a double bind, making use of the culture they ostensibly reject. Theologically this type of position supposes that revelation stands outside culture, which is impossible, and it tends to suggest that sin is found in culture and not amongst the elect, generating thereby a sectarian Church which exists for itself rather than for the world. It is also inadequately Trinitarian, failing to establish a proper relation between Christ and Creator, and therefore tending to Manichaeism.

The polar opposite stance is that of Christ understood as fulfiller of culture. No biblical support for this view is suggested, but Niebuhr might, perhaps, have turned to Wisdom. In the tradition Ritschl and Harnack, but also the Christian socialists Shailer Matthews and Ragaz, exemplify this view. Niebuhr is noticeably as hard on those who are attracted by Marxism or socialism as on those who identify the gospel with bourgeois society. The strength of the *conformist* stance is that it makes the universal meaning of the gospel clear and does justice to all those aspects of Christ's work which affirmed the body, or the culture, of his day. Its weakness is a tendency to appeal to cultural elites, to overvalue 'reason', to underestimate sin, and therefore to end up with some kind of self-reliant humanism. It too fails to give an adequate account of the relation of Christ and Creator.

Niebuhr's third category, 'Christ above culture', describes the attempt to take the middle view, what he calls the *synthetic* position. Thomas Aquinas is the main exemplar, a monk who served a Church which was the principal guardian of high culture in its day. (This is one of numerous occasions when Niebuhr slips between the anthropological sense of 'culture' and the notion of 'high culture'.) Aquinas' idea that God is the law in Godself; that creation manifests 'natural' law; and that good positive law aspires to echo this, is the perfect example of the middle way. In the classical formulation, grace does not destroy nature but perfects it. The danger is that this view tends to absolutize the relative and reduce the infinite to a finite form. What was manifestly 'natural' for Thomas is not for us, and it now seems that agreement as to what is natural cannot be reached. There is also an endemic tendency for the middle way to graduate towards cultural conservatism and to institutionalization.

Luther and Kierkegaard are taken to illustrate a fourth position, of Christ and culture in paradox. Where the Christ against culture paradigm takes its stand against culture in general, this position is more concerned with the question of the divide between God and human beings. The Church is corrupt as well as culture; piety may be as sinful as passion. The *dualist* recognizes that she or he, too, belongs to a culture which is corrupt. The danger with this position is that the relativization of all human works can lead to antinomianism on the one hand, and to cultural conservatism on the other. There is no necessary link between law and grace.

The final category is that of Christ as the 'transformer of culture', exemplified by the rather unlikely combination of Augustine and F.D.Maurice, and this position is clearly Niebuhr's preferred option, despite his disavowal of any one 'right' answer to the problem. It is the only one of the types to which the objections are not stated. The *conversionist*, so called, takes creation seriously, as well as atonement, and has a more sanguine view of its possible redemption here and now. The position has, in Niebuhr's view, a more positive understanding of history as the story of God's 'mighty deeds'. History is read as the story of the dramatic interaction between God and human beings. It underlies a practice of responsible engagement which nevertheless recognizes that the kingdom is quite different from anything we create. Augustine, read, like the Augustine of Radical Orthodoxy, without the anti-Pelagian treatises, is seen not to reject the cultural tradition he has inherited, but to transvalue it, to redirect, reinvigorate and regenerate it.

For all its popularity, this typology is nevertheless full of problems. I have noted that Niebuhr tends to elide the anthropological notion of culture with that of 'high culture'. As soon as you do that the typology starts to fracture. Tertullian, for example, was the most brilliant Latinist of the Western tradition, and we simply need to mention Tolstoy's name in this connection to indicate the problem. Those who come from the 'counter cultural' tradition very often do so precisely in view of their knowledge of, and even commitment to, the high culture tradition. Conversely, those representing the 'Christ of Culture' position may sometimes avow a populism which finds the high tradition profoundly problematic. In short, as soon as we nuance the idea of culture we find the need to develop a richer understanding of the engagement of Church and culture than Niebuhr's typology allows. As Yoder puts it, every morally accountable affirmation of culture discriminates:

> The cultural stance of the Christian church according to the New Testament will ... not be a matter of seeking for a strategy to be applied uniformly, either accepting or rejecting ... all of 'culture' in the same way ... Some elements of culture the church categorically rejects (pornography, tyranny, cultic idolatry). Other dimensions of culture it accepts within clear limits (economic production, commerce, the graphic arts, paying taxes for peacetime civil government). To still other dimensions of culture Christian faith gives a new motivation and coherence (agriculture, family life, literacy, conflict resolution, empowerment). Still others it strips of their claims to possess autonomous truth and value, and uses them as vehicles of communication (philosophy, language, Old Testament ritual, music). Still other forms of culture are created by the Christian churches (hospitals, service of the poor, generalized education, egalitarianism, abolitionism, feminism). Some have been created by the Peace Churches (prison reform, war sufferers' relief, international conciliation).[38]

Such discrimination makes Niebuhr's global use of the category of culture impossible. At any given point any Christian might want to invoke all of Niebuhr's categories to describe their relation to the dominant culture.

A further problem relates to the broad brush nature of Niebuhr's examples. He notes that probably all fail to exemplify their case exclusively. This is indeed the case, and some, like the Gnostics, or Augustine, perhaps hardly exemplify it at all. So vague is his typology that it cannot be falsified.[39] He makes his case modestly but all this does is to underline the view that any conviction that truth

---

38 Yoder, 'How Niebuhr Reasoned' p.69
39 Yoder, 'How Niebuhr Reasoned' p.51

can be known and can lay upon us definite claims which we must unequivocally obey is naïve.[40] To say that there is no one right answer is to canonize pluralism. His preferred 'conversionist' paradigm by 'being inclusive and pluralistic, fitting to the Ivy League graduate school culture, makes it precisely the best view after all'.[41]

Niebuhr consistently points out that the positions he critiques are inadequately Trinitarian, but, given his starting point in the Jesus of history, this is true for his own work. His central preoccupation is with discipleship to the historical Jesus, and with avoiding any implicit or explicit Manichaeism, any failure to honour creation. However, given the need to understand culture through the categories of Wisdom, Logos or Spirit, exemplified equally by the Wisdom tradition, Justin, Hegel, and the missionary theologians (!), a satisfactory theology of culture must be more full-bloodedly Trinitarian than that. The absence of a Trinitarian perspective perhaps accounts for his individualistic understanding of the Church which, again, has failed to learn from Herder's insistence that everything, and everyone, is related, and that culture has to be understood in terms of those relations. The Church as a body has almost no place in the argument for Niebuhr. The 'conversionist' paradigm which he favours has what Yoder calls a 'vacuity about moral substance' which follows on from the failure to define criteria or lines of direction for change.[42] What is meant by transformation is so inadequately defined that it is virtually indistinguishable from the Western doctrine of progress.[43]

For all of these reasons this immensely influential typology has to be dropped, to be replaced not with an alternative typology, but with a more complex mapping of the interrelation of gospel and culture. Before giving an account of that mapping I will – to stay with the metaphor – first set out its orientation.

The Long Revolution

'Man is the most ignorant creature when coming into the world,' wrote Herder in his *Essay on the Origin of Language*, 'but immediately he is apprenticed to nature in a manner in which no animal can be.':

> It is not only that one day teaches the following, but also every minute of the day teaches the next, and one thought the following. It is an essential trait of the human mind, to learn nothing for one moment only, but to connect everything with what it already knew, or to store it up for future associations ... At no single moment can he be said to be the whole man, rather, he is always in a state of development, of progress, of becoming ... We are always growing out of childhood, however old we may be; we are always in motion, restless and dissatisfied. The essence of our life is

---

40 Yoder, 'How Niebuhr Reasoned' p.52
41 Yoder, 'How Niebuhr Reasoned' p.82
42 Yoder, 'How Niebuhr Reasoned' p.43
43 Yoder, 'How Niebuhr Reasoned' p.53

never fruition, but continuous becoming, and we have never been men until we have lived our life to the end.[44]

What drives this process? To talk of Christ as the transformer of culture is to point to the role the gospel or mission plays in the process, and this takes us to Raymond Williams' notion of the 'long revolution' which I have taken as the title for this chapter. For Williams it referred to that complex of economic, political and cultural changes which began in the late eighteenth century and which had delivered manifest goods for the working class from which he came. Wedded to no Promethean doctrine of inevitable progress, he nevertheless remained committed to the possibility of a more humane, more just and more fulfilling future, and he looked to socialism to deliver it. In the light of the centrality of culture to both the biblical and Christian narratives, I want to suggest that the long revolution does not just refer to the developments since the late eighteenth century but might, as Herder suggests, be a way of viewing human history as a whole, what he calls, in a fascinating series of 'letters', the 'furthering of humanity'.

To suggest this raises at once a number of spectres. Is it not simply to resurrect the Whig idea of history, the notion of inevitable progress? From our perspective we are only too well aware that there is no such thing. In 1981 Alasdair MacIntyre invoked the memory of the European dark ages, and we need to be reminded of this. During the first European dark ages, wrote Jacques le Goff, 'artistic taste underwent a regression and so did morals ... not only did the old stock of peasant superstitions re-emerge, but all the sexual perversions ran riot and acts of violence turned nastier'.[45] Cultural pessimism smacks of Manichaeism but on the other hand there are only too many instances of cultural collapse, and the way in which a rapacious capitalism threatens both the planet and the survival of local cultures means that we cannot rule out the idea of 'a new dark ages'.

Again, is not the suggestion that the gospel plays a key role in such progress both historically very questionable and ultimately a piece of idealism? To respond to these doubts I turn to a rather unlikely source, an article Karl Barth wrote on 'Church and Culture' in 1924. In the most recent edition of the encyclopaedia *Religion in Geschichte und Gegenwart* he found definitions for culture as, 'the sum of the aims proceeding from human activity and in turn stimulating human activity' or 'the idea of the final goal and the totality of norms by which human activity should be guided'. If these are our definitions, he says, 'the Church could only speak negatively and polemically on the significance of culture. The two entities would not only exist on different levels, but on mutually exclusive levels, as truth and error.'[46] Why should the Church

---

44   Translation in F.M.Barnard, *Herder on Social and Political Culture* Cambridge: Cambridge University Press 1969 pp.156–157
45   J.le Goff, *Medieval Civilization* Oxford: Blackwell 1988 p.32 A.L.Kroeber had already made much the same observation, tracing its roots back to the Hellenistic period in *Anthropology* New York: Harcourt Brace 1948 p.285
46   K.Barth, 'Church and Culture' in *Theology and Church* London: SCM 1962 p.337

view 'this so-called culture with horror, as an impossible fantasy and an idol'?[47] The answer we expect is the Augustinian one that without grace humankind can do no good thing, so that the best virtues of good pagans are nothing but splendid vices. The answer we get is somewhat different. The task of culture, according to Barth, is the realization of our humanity – a definition suggestive of Herder's idea of the 'furthering of *Humanität*'.[48] The problem is that we exist as soul and body, spirit and nature, and we have to bring these into unity. Spirit must mould nature, and nature actualize spirit. Because we fail to do this 'Christian preaching ... has met every culture, however supposedly rich and mature, with ultimate sharp scepticism.'[49]

From these remarks I take three fundamental points for any theology of culture. First, I read the mutual moulding of nature and spirit as a reference to the significance of the incarnation for any such theology. The implications of such a formation can, of course, follow from the method of what we have learned, from Raymond Williams, to call 'cultural materialism'. Thus Williams noted in 1961 that:

> We have got into the habit, since we realized how deeply works or values could be determined by the whole situation in which they are expressed, of asking about these relationships in a standard form: 'what is the relation of this art to this society?' But 'society' in this question, is a specious whole. If the art is part of the society, there is no solid whole, outside it, to which, by the form of our question, we concede priority. The art is there, as an activity, with the production, the trading, the politics, the raising of families. To study the relations adequately we must study them actively, seeing all the activities as particular and contemporary forms of human energy.[50]

Where Williams has 'art' we can also put 'religion' or 'theology', but Christians should have been familiar with this from the intrinsic logic of their own position. The inseparability of material and mental, base and superstructure, is what John had in mind in the opening words of his Gospel. The 'Word' – teaching, doctrine, story, narrative, reason or cause – became *flesh*, not as an adventure, an avatar, a brief encounter, but as an account of how it might be possible to talk about God in a world where the powerful wash their hands of inconvenient decisions and the poor are crucified, and where there is nothing whatsoever, no knowledge and no revelation, which is not mediated by the body. 'Flesh', as John spells out in some detail in the course of his meditations, means culture – food, the world of symbols, the way in which we cherish bodies. The gospels rather prominently highlight the connection between culture as metaphor and culture in its original sense as the reproduction of life through farming. Jesus feeds the five thousand; his first word to Jairus is to give his daughter something to eat; his parables are about sowing and harvesting, banquets, feasts, the need to obtain a loaf when the shops are shut; he shares table fellowship with his disciples and with the outcast. All this dependence on

---

47   Barth, 'Church and Culture' p.338
48   J.G.Herder, 'Seventeen Letters on the Furthering of Humanity', *Werke* vol 18
49   Barth, 'Church and Culture' p.339
50   Williams, *Long Revolution* p.61

physical culture becomes Culture – spirit, training in perfection – through Word and sacrament, so that John characterizes Jesus as 'the bread of life'. That food plays such a central part in the Christian dispensation is no accident for food is a vital aspect both of culture as a way of life, and as an expression of high culture.[51]

We have got used to separating economic and political questions, questions of survival, from questions of ethics and aesthetics, but 'culture' is precisely the marriage of all of these, unity without confusion or division of Word and flesh. Barth read this out of the anti-dualism of Christian theology. 'The term *culture*,' he wrote, 'connotes exactly that promise to man: fulfilment, unity, wholeness within his sphere as creature, as man, exactly as God in his sphere is fullness, wholeness, Lord over nature and spirit, Creator of heaven *and* earth.'[52] This means that the questions about justice, questions of entitlement, broadly speaking, political questions, cannot be divorced from culture. When Barth speaks of fullness and wholeness here he is basically invoking the idea of justice as *shalom* of the Old Testament, which we shall explore in the seventh chapter.

Second, Barth argues that the gospel meets every culture with 'sharp scepticism'. I shall show in a moment that that was not his final word, but it points to what the liberation theologians called the 'eschatological proviso', the fact that no culture embodies the kingdom. In Barth's terms it is torn between nature and spirit, in other words marked by antagonism and the fact that reconciliation has not been reached. A theology of culture has to address this antagonism and alienation and think through ways of addressing it. In conventional theological terms this is the problem of sin and redemption. The crucifixion of Jesus is a reminder of the barbarism which Walter Benjamin found attached to any monument of culture. It warns us to pay attention to the dark side of cultural history.

How was it possible, George Steiner asked, in reference to Eliot's *Notes towards the definition of Culture*, to write a book in 1948 and say nothing about the Holocaust? 'How was it possible to detail and plead for a Christian order when the holocaust had put in question the very nature of Christianity and of its role in European history?'[53] The question applies *a fortiori* to Niebuhr, but we can extend it, and put it into the indicative: we cannot write a theology of culture without taking account of the Church's collusion with imperialism,

---

51 Gilles Luneau pointed this out when French farmers were jailed for protesting about McDonald's: eating, he said, 'is an intimate, daily activity, a source of pleasure, a means of survival, and a critical aspect of the way in which we relate to the earth. Food has its rituals in every culture, creed, religion and philosophy. Wheat, maize and rice are more than just crops. They are the outcome of the fusion of sun, water and soil. In eating, humans inscribe themselves in the cycles of the universe, and this is far more profound and basic than just making money. Wheat was growing long before coins were cast.' J.Bové, *The World Is not for Sale* London: Verso 2001 p.xii T.S.Eliot agreed with him in this, describing the decline of culture in Britain as marked by indifference to the preparation of food. *Notes* p.27 On this position the renewed interest in cuisine in Britain over the past twenty years is a sign of cultural renaissance but this is surely debatable.

52 Barth, 'Church and Culture' p.343

53 G.Steiner, *In Bluebeard's Castle* London: Faber and Faber 1971 p.34

patriarchy and racism. Whilst Lamin Sanneh is right that the agenda of
Christian theology cannot be set by Western guilt, nevertheless there is a bland
ignoring of these facts which borders on indecency. For, whilst there are still
those for whom arguments against the existence of God centre on 'science',
today the most cogent arguments are precisely those which inspired the
hostility of Voltaire: the history of the Church. We cannot play Pangloss in
respect of these facts.

Scepticism, however, is not the last word. Barth argued that because God is
the Lord of the entire created process culture can be a witness to the promise, a
reflection of the light of the incarnate Logos. Whilst there is no place for a
sanctifying of cultural achievement, *à la* Schleiermacher, 'there is even less
place for a basic blindness to the possibility that culture may be revelatory, that
it can be filled with promise'. Thus, 'The Church ... will be alert for the signs
which, perhaps in many cultural achievements, announce that the kingdom
approaches.'[54] Culture, then, has a sacramental, or signifying, role.[55]

Culture, as a way of referring to the shaping of human society in body and
spirit, is instinct with promise. Herder put this well in his ironically titled, *Yet
Another Philosophy of History*:

> No one lives in his own period only; he builds on what has gone before and lays a
> foundation for what comes after. Thus speaks the analogy of nature, the pattern of
> God eloquent in all his works; obviously mankind must be similar. The Egyptian
> could not have existed without the Oriental, nor the Greek without the Egyptian; the
> Roman carried on his back the whole world. This indeed is genuine progress,
> continuous development, however little it may prosper the individual! Becoming on a
> grand scale! History may not manifestly be revealed as the theatre of a directing
> purpose on earth – of which our shallow histories boast so much – for we may not be
> able to espy its final end. But it may conceivably offer us glimpses of a divine theatre
> through the openings and ruins of individual scenes.[56]

We are even warier of talk of providence today than was Herder but the
question we have to put is whether it is possible that, if God exists, God's
existence could be 'of no effect' (Rom 3.3, 4.14). This question applies to the
Augustinian reading of history, for which the main point is not the overall
story but the redemption of the saved from the *massa damnata*. To think like
this is to deprive history of a purpose, in fact to make history non-history.
Since persons are shaped by their contexts, and understand themselves and
their projects within the framework of ongoing events, this would also make
the affirmation of individual teleologies problematic. In fact what happens is
that every individual life is viewed in the context of eternity rather than in
terms of the role played within the historical narrative as a whole. There is a
good reason for this, for most people who have ever lived have been pawns
rather than great players, and might well feel they had contributed nothing to

---

54   Barth, 'Church and Culture' p.344
55   Compare Terry Eagleton's dictum that 'Art defines what we live for, but it is not art for which
we live.' T.Eagleton, *The Idea of Culture* Oxford: Blackwell 2000 p.64
56   Translation from Barnard, *Herder* p.188

the larger process. On the other hand the biblical narrative is framed within a historical promise – 'in you shall all the nations of the earth bless themselves' (Gen 12.3) – and the Church has understood the incarnation as God's engagement with the historical process.

The mission of the Church follows from the mission of the Son, and was understood from the first as a matter of urgency. This is not because, as the New Tribes Mission chronicled by Norman Lewis believe, only those who profess the doctrine will be 'saved', but because the historical process has such significance for God that God is prepared to die in the midst of history for its redemption. The idea that it is only individual sinners who are saved is irredeemably individualist, as Schleiermacher realized when he described sin as 'in all the work of each and in each the work of all'. From the point of view of redemption 'culture is the limit set for men, on the other side of which God himself, in fulfilment of his promise, makes all things new'.[57]

Thirdly, eschatology, as we have already seen, is a key category for the discussion of culture. It means that culture, as formed reality and real form, is the process of becoming. Barth wrote his essay on culture during the Weimar republic, and was only too well aware of the possibility of cultural decline. Theologically, however, he turned his face against any cultural pessimism. The Church confronts society with eschatological anticipation:

> Not with an undervaluation of cultural achievement, but with the highest possible evaluation of the goal for which it sees all cultural activity striving. Not in pessimism, but in boundless hope. Not as a spoilsport, but in the knowledge that art and science, business and politics, techniques and education are really a game – a serious game, and game means an imitative and ultimately ineffective activity – the significance of which lies not in its attainable goals but in what it signifies.[58]

Eschatology, then, construed as a theology of hope, and grounded in the resurrection, is one of the main keys to any theology of culture.

In its attempt to map the relations of gospel and culture this book falls into three parts. Culture, in a number of related senses, is the theme of the first part. In the second chapter I pursue the theme of the relation of religion and culture, and consider the impact of Barth's critique of religion. How are religion and culture to be distinguished? What kind of relationship do they have? If religion is unbelief, where does that leave culture? One of the key figures in this discussion, Matthew Arnold, also raises the question of the relation of high culture and popular culture. Whereas in the early decades of the twentieth century high culture could be taken for granted as a norm, today cultural populism has reversed these priorities. Mediating between high and popular culture is folk culture which draws on what Lewis Mumford considered the origin of ethics, peasant culture. To the best of my knowledge this has scarcely

---

57 Barth, 'Church and Culture' p.347
58 Barth, 'Church and Culture' p.349

received any theological attention and I turn to it here in the third chapter, in this respect continuing the emphasis on the vernacular in *A Theology of the Built Environment*.[59] Such cultures are everywhere in retreat in the face of 'modernity'. I consider the impact of modernity, and the discourse of cultural imperialism, in the fourth chapter. In each chapter, and throughout the book, I am in dialogue with work in cultural studies and social science, outlining arguments in these disciplines before attempting a theological response. In this I follow the methodology of liberation theology which insists that, if we understand the implications of the incarnation properly, then social analysis is an essential prologue to theological reflection.

The second part of the book is concerned with power – an aspect of culture which Niebuhr's typology largely ignores. I consider power through the related ideas of ideology and hegemony, and through a consideration of cultural politics. The fifth chapter considers the nature of ideology, and asks whether Christianity necessarily functions as an opiate. I turn from here to hegemony and correct an imbalance in my earlier treatment of this theme by emphasizing the need to construct counter hegemonies.[60] The losers in any hegemony are identified by race, class and gender, a fact emphasized by liberation theology over the past thirty years. I turn to this discussion in the final chapter of this part of the book.

The final part of the book is organized under the theme of mission, or alternatively, the inescapable cross cultural aspect of the Church's life. One often reads that the Church today is growing fastest outside Europe. Not so often remarked is that this fact arises from Western colonialism. I consider the implications of that fact in the eighth and ninth chapters. Following on from that I address Samuel Huntington's thesis about the clash of civilizations, and ask how that affects Christian mission, before turning, in chapter eleven, to the issue of mission in a multicultural society. If it is true that mission is of the essence of the Church, how can it be understood alongside the 'respect for difference' which is close to the heart of contemporary ethical discourse?

In approaching culture in this threefold way I hope to do justice to the fact that it cannot be discussed sensibly outside of economic and political realities, of colonialism and neo-colonialism. Equally, as the superscription to the first part, from Terry Eagleton, indicates, there are inescapable questions of meaning, direction and purpose which theology brings to the overall cultural discussion.

---

59   T.J.Gorringe, *A Theology of the Built Environment* Cambridge: Cambridge University Press 2002

60   T.J.Gorringe, *Karl Barth: Against Hegemony* Oxford: Oxford University Press 1999

Chapter 2

Religion, Faith and Culture

The gospel, I have argued, plays a key part – indeed, according to Christians *the* key part – in the 'long revolution' through which God makes and keeps human beings human. But the gospel only exists institutionally – through Churches, sects and communities, through monasteries, seminaries, faculties of Theology. Institutions have to survive amongst the bulks of actual things; they are part of culture. As such they take on the colouring of the culture of which they are part, adopt the ruling ideas of the age, make historic compromises and lose their utopian energy.

For some, we have seen, religion and culture are one and the same and the truth of this position is that they are indeed inextricable. Inextricable but not identical? If not identical, how do we distinguish them? How does religion bear on culture? What happens when culture colonizes religion? Can an appeal to 'faith' over against the institutional forms of religion be sustained? It goes without saying that there is no one answer to these questions. Religion and culture were related in one way in the first three hundred years of the Church, when it was marginal, reluctantly tolerated and occasionally persecuted; in another way still under Constantine; in another way still under Charlemagne; in yet another way in the high middle ages – and so on. The period of closest relationship was probably not, as many suppose, between the eleventh and the fifteenth centuries, but under Protestant Erastianism. Enlightenment hostility to religion is partly born from reaction to the religious wars and religious persecution, but in its radical guise perceives that it is only too useful to the magistrate.

It is the tail end of this period, the period which most closely shapes our own, which I want to examine and I will do so through the work of three of the most seminal writers on the relation of religion and culture within the Anglo-Saxon tradition: S.T.Coleridge, Matthew Arnold and T.S.Eliot. It is true that the world even of Eliot has passed away, as we shall see, but their influence on the discussion has been so profound that we cannot go round them, but only through them. For all three, 'religion', by which they mean Christianity, is a positive category, and I test their accounts of the relation of religion and culture through Barth's sharp critique of culture Protestantism before returning to the theme of religion, culture and the long revolution.

Religion, Culture and Politics: Coleridge to Eliot

Coleridge and a 'National Church'

Coleridge's last publication, *On the Constitution of Church and State*, is dismissed in a paragraph by his most recent biographer, but has exercised an extraordinary influence on thought about the relation of religion and culture since its appearance in 1830.[1] Coleridge was prompted to write it by proposals for Catholic emancipation. He supported these but shared fears about conflicting loyalties which had been part of Protestant stock in trade since the late sixteenth century and which are of importance in understanding what today is referred to as 'Islamophobia'.[2] The issue forced him to think through the basis for a national Church, and what its relation might be to the Church universal. The latter was 'no state, kingdom, or realm of this world ... but ... the appointed opposite to them all collectively – the sustaining, correcting, befriending opposite of the World'.[3] The Christian Church 'has no Nationalty [*sic*] intrusted to its charge. It forms no counter balance to the collective heritage of the realm.'[4] This Church cannot be a national Church without forfeiting the very name of Christian, and exists in every state in the form of public communities. It has no visible head, or sovereign, or any single source of universal power.

What we call the national Church, by contrast, draws strength from the Christian Church but is not the Church. Coleridge offers a version of the biblical metaphor of the olive tree. The Christian Church is the olive tree, said to fertilize the surrounding soil and improve the strength and flavour of the vines in its neighbourhood. The national Church is the vine, and the state the tree which supports the vine.[5] The function of the national Church can be understood by dividing the state, as in medieval France, into three estates, the third of which is the intellectual class, which he called a clerisy. The clerisy comprises all denominations and all faculties – lawyers, doctors, musicians, architects, natural scientists, but also theologians. Some of this group would remain at the universities, but the majority would be distributed throughout the country so that no person would be without guide, guardian and instructor.[6]

Coleridge followed Kant in distinguishing between civilization and culture. The former:

> is itself but a mixed good, if not far more corrupting influence, the hectic of disease, not the bloom of health, and a nation so distinguished more fitly to be called a

---

1   Richard Holmes devotes not quite fifteen lines to it in *Coleridge: Darker Reflections* London: HarperCollins 1998

2   Between the end of the sixteenth century and the end of the nineteenth century anti-Catholic sentiment was fuelled by the idea of divided loyalty. Fears about the role of the Jesuits, a sinister intellectual force committed to the overthrow of the Protestant monarchy and the restoration of Catholic hegemony, can be compared to the fears today concerning militant Islamic groups. In his excellent discussion of the Muslim Umma S.Sayyid does not see that the closest analogy to the Umma is the way the early, and then the post-Tridentine, Catholic Church understood itself. 'Beyond Westphalia: Nations and Diasporas – the Case of the Muslim Umma' in B.Hesse(ed) *Un/settled Multiculturalisms* London: Zed 2000 pp.33–50

3   S.T.Coleridge, *On the Constitution of Church and State* ed T.Colmer vol 10 of the *Collected Works* London: Routledge 1976 p.114

4   Coleridge, *Constitution* p.117

5   Coleridge, *Constitution* p.56

6   Coleridge, *Constitution* p.43

varnished than a polished people; where this civilization is not grounded in cultivation, in the harmonious development of those qualities and faculties that characterise our humanity. We must be men in order to be citizens.[7]

The job of the national Church, then, is essentially educational. Through cultivation it secures and improves that civilization 'without which the nation could be neither permanent nor progressive', ensuring the conjunction of law and liberty, civilization and freedom. It supplies the vision without which the people perish. Its charge is to make a given national civilization of lasting worth to the human race. The national Church both requires and is required by the Christian Church for the perfection of each:

> For, if there were no national church, the mere spiritual church would either become, like the papacy, a dreadful tyranny over mind and body, or else would fall abroad into a multitude of enthusiastic sects, as in England in the seventeenth century. It is my deep conviction that, in a country of any religion at all, liberty of conscience can only be permanently preserved by means, and under the shadow of, a national church – a political establishment connected with, but distinct from, the spiritual church.[8]

That this is a fairly precise description of the Anglican establishment is hardly a coincidence and of course represents something of the enthusiasm of a convert given the Socinianism of Coleridge's youth.

In the education offered by the national Church theology occupied the key role because it was 'the root and trunk of the knowledges that civilized man, because it gave unity and circulating sap of life to all other sciences, by virtue of which alone they could be contemplated as forming, collectively, the living tree of knowledge'.[9] Theology, in Coleridge's understanding, embraced the interpretation of languages, the conservation and tradition of past events, history, logic, ethics, 'the determination of ethical science, in application to the rights and duties of men in all their various relations, social and civil', and first philosophy, the doctrine of ideas. It played a key role in making us 'men before citizens'. Culture as formation, in other words, comes before polity and, in Coleridge's view, is a prerequisite for polity.

It is clear that Coleridge's views are shaped by the peculiar form Christendom took in England, with a state Church which nevertheless allowed an effective separation of powers. His idea of a national Church, of a clerisy involving all disciplines, might be thought to be at best an analogy to what he calls the spiritual Church were it not for the fact that when he wrote all Fellows at the two English universities were clergy, and clergy provided distinguished economists, natural scientists and philosophers, as well as theologians. Theology, in fact, did not exist as a separate discipline in these universities. Questions arising from a majority non-Christian population had not yet arisen. His understanding of the relation of religion and culture is part utopian vision

---

7 Coleridge, *Constitution* p.42
8 S.T.Coleridge, *Table Talk vol 1* ed C.Woodring London: Routledge 1990 p.482 (31 May 1834)
9 Coleridge, *Constitution* p.47

of the extension of universal education, in a society where it was confined to the few, but partly an astute recognition of the role the institutional Church played in forming the national culture, a role which, he failed to see, was deeply problematized by the realities of class and by the Church's effective 'option for the rich'.

Arnold: Faith and Culture

Matthew Arnold's *Culture and Anarchy*, published in 1869, probably the most celebrated account of the relation of religion and culture in English, drew on these seminal ideas of Coleridge. The profound melancholy of two of Arnold's most famous poems, *Dover Beach* and *Stanzas from the Grand Chartreuse*, has suggested to later generations that Arnold was an agnostic, and a century after his death non-realist theologians adopted the famous phrase from the former poem, 'the sea of faith', to describe their movement. But this would have horrified Arnold. When Colenso was impugned for questioning the historical veracity of the Pentateuch Arnold surprised his liberal friends by attacking him. Colenso's views on Scripture were, if anything, more conservative than Arnold's, but Arnold's objection was that Colenso left ordinary people nothing to live by. Arnold's view was, as Trilling puts it, 'For those who cannot reason out what is right, religion lays down the path; for those who cannot find an abstract ethical basis for their action, religion provides the code.'[10] This might seem patronizing, but, as Raymond Williams reminds us, Arnold was an untiring advocate of popular education and, in intention at least, an avowed egalitarian.

Politically Arnold was a convinced liberal, with all the strengths and weaknesses of that position. An accomplished Germanist, he believed that Goethe was the most revolutionary force in modern Europe through his habit of questioning all taken for granted certainties. 'Nothing could be more really subversive of the foundations on which the old European order rested; and it may be remarked that no persons are so radically detached from this order, no persons so thoroughly modern, as those who have felt Goethe's influence most deeply.'[11] Heine, who described himself as 'a soldier in the Liberation war of Humanity', was another enthusiasm, and reckoned by Arnold one of Goethe's true followers.

On the other hand, the 'anarchy' Arnold opposed to culture was working class pressure for democratic reform – the demand that the (male) industrial proletariat should have the vote. When this led to rioting Arnold embarrassed himself by citing his father's views on what ought to be done with rioters in a draft for what became the first chapter of *Culture and Anarchy* published in the *Cornhill Magazine* in 1867. His father's reaction to riots in the 1820s had been that the rioters should be flogged and the ringleaders flung from the Tarpeian rock. When the book was published two years later he left this out and, as

10   L.Trilling, *Matthew Arnold* New York: Columbia University Press 1949 p.213
11   Cited in Trilling, *Matthew Arnold* p.207

Raymond Williams remarks, 'We must give him the credit of his second thoughts.'[12] In another *cause célèbre*, the trial of the Governor of Jamaica for the murder of African workers, Arnold likewise took the Governor's side. So Arnold's most famous phrase, 'sweetness and light', had its decided limitations.[13] On the other hand, his leading idea was that, in the new conditions of democracy, force must give way to rational persuasion.

Religion plays a central part in Arnold's life and work. As the son of Thomas Arnold of Rugby Arnold had been trained, in Lionel Trilling's words, 'to every sober virtue in one of the most pious households of England, taught everlastingly that life was serious'.[14] Arnold was far from an orthodox Anglican, but he was no agnostic either, and religion was not a matter purely of political convenience. On the contrary, it met the needs of 'three-fourths of our being'.[15] In an atmosphere where anti-Popery demagoguery could still stir up riots, and where the union of Calvinist Christianity and capitalism seemed to rule the roost, Arnold felt the need to right the boat. Disestablishment was under debate, and the Preface to *Culture and Anarchy* is a defence of the establishment of the Church on Coleridgean lines in terms of what it contributed to the education of the community. He urged SPCK to republish Bishop Wilson as an example of someone who commended religion (by which he meant Christianity) as common sense.

Arnold argued that an established Church which could produce men like Hooker and Butler had 'done more to moralise and ennoble English statesmen and their conduct than communities which have produced the Nonconformist divines'.[16] Being in the mainstream of human life is what contributes to our total spiritual growth rather than commitment to 'any speculative opinion'. Sectarianism, in Arnold's view, breeds narrowness of mind, and it is this which he opposes. The newspaper *The Nonconformist* had asked how the atheist Huxley proposed to cure 'all the vice and hideousness' visible at Epsom on Derby Day. 'I confess I felt disposed to ask the asker,' Arnold replied:

and how do you propose to cure it with such a religion as yours? How is the ideal of a life so unlovely, so unattractive, so incomplete, so narrow, so far removed from a true and satisfying ideal of human perfection, as is the life of your religious organisation as you yourself reflect it, to conquer and transform all this vice and hideousness?[17]

12   R.Williams, *Problems in Materialism and Culture* London: Verso 1980 p.7
13   Arnold reminds us that the phrase is taken from Swift's *Battle of the Books*, where it represented the triumph of ancient over modern culture.
14   Trilling, *Matthew Arnold* p.21
15   M.Arnold, *Literature and Dogma* London: Smith and Elder 1900 p.230 The vision of the God of righteousness 'meets the wants of far the largest part of our being, of three-fourths of it, yet there is one-fourth of our being of which it does not strictly meet the wants, the part which is concerned with art and science; or in other words with beauty and exact knowledge'.
16   M.Arnold, *Culture and Anarchy* London: John Murray 1920 p.xiii
17   Arnold, *Culture and Anarchy* p.20

Muscular Christianity, he felt, produced narrow and twisted personalities, immune to the real joy of life.[18]

In response to another, similar, stab at what Arnold called the Philistines, Williams remarks that it is itself a vulgar response to a perceived vulgarity and justifies the charges, brought at the time, of priggishness and spiritual pride.[19] Perhaps so, but Arnold was, as he acknowledged, speaking as a Pharisee of the Pharisees, and he is attacking the religion in which he himself had been brought up. In this book Arnold argued that such religion needed to be leavened by culture, by which he meant 'a pursuit of our total perfection by means of getting to know, on all matters which most concern us, the best which has been thought and said in the world'.[20] Arnold was an Inspector of Schools, and he had a high view of the redemptive possibilities of education. His enthusiasm for German *Kultur* meant that he had interiorized the tradition of *Bildung*. From the founder of the Prussian University system, Wilhelm von Humboldt, he took the doctrine that 'the true end of Man ... is the highest and most harmonious development of his powers to a complete and consistent whole'.[21] What he proposed was a compact between religion and culture, in which the one contributed moral earnestness and the other 'sweetness and light':

> Religion, the greatest and most important of the efforts by which the human race has manifested its impulse to perfect itself – religion, that voice of the deepest human experience – does not only enjoin and sanction the aim which is the great aim of culture, the aim of setting ourselves to ascertain what perfection is and to make it prevail; but also, in determining generally in what human perfection consists, religion comes to a conclusion identical with that which culture – culture seeking the determination of this question through all the voices of human experience which have been heard upon it ... likewise reaches. Religion says: The kingdom of God is within you; and culture in like manner, places human perfection in an *internal* condition, in the growth and predominance of our humanity proper, as distinguished from our animality.[22]

Religion and culture, then, share the same goal. The task of both is, in the words of Bishop Wilson, 'to make reason and the will of God prevail'. Both aim at perfection and salvation. Both culture and religion are inward realities and both insist on development: 'Not a having and a resting, but a growing and a becoming, is the character of perfection as culture conceives it; and here, too, it coincides with religion.' Finally, both religion and culture refuse to be understood individualistically:

> Perfection, as culture conceives it, is not possible while the individual remains isolated. The individual is required, under pain of being stunted and enfeebled in his own development if he disobeys, to carry others along with him in his march towards

---

18   Arnold, *Culture and Anarchy* p.xv
19   Williams, *Culture and Society* p.125
20   Arnold, *Culture and Anarchy* p.viii
21   In his *Sphere and Duties of Government*. Cited in Trilling, *Matthew Arnold* p.260
22   Arnold, *Culture and Anarchy* p.8

perfection, to be continually doing all he can to enlarge and increase the volume of the human stream sweeping thitherward.[23]

Culture goes beyond religion in thinking of perfection as the 'harmonious expansion of all the powers which make the beauty and worth of human nature', whereas religion concentrates on the moral element.

Arnold subscribed to the view, which he found in Heine, that Western culture was a synthesis of Hellenism and Hebraism. Arnold proposed a harmonious marriage of the two, in which, however, Hebraism (morality) would always be the senior partner. Written as one of his children lay dying, the closing paragraph of Arnold's preface to *Culture and Anarchy* firmly prioritizes faith:

> The intense and convinced energy with which the Hebrew ... threw himself upon his ideal of righteousness, and which inspired the incomparable definition of the great Christian virtue faith – the substance of things hoped for, the evidence of things not seen – this energy of devotion to its ideal has belonged to Hebraism alone. As our idea of perfection widens beyond the narrow limits to which the over-rigour of Hebraising has tended to confine it, we shall yet come again to Hebraism for that devout energy in embracing our ideal, which alone can give to man the happiness of doing what he knows.[24]

What culture added was the emphasis on harmonious perfection, 'developing all sides of our humanity'. Those who cultivate only religion 'have developed one side of their humanity at the expense of all others, and have become incomplete and mutilated men in consequence'.[25] To Hebraize is to sacrifice all other sides of our being to the religious side. Hebraism concentrates on morality, Hellenism on intellect, on seeing things as they are. It was not just working class riots but religious intolerance which led Arnold to the view that an advocacy of Hellenism was what was wanted. Those who would transmit this gospel would be Coleridge's clerisy, the universities, the parochial pastorate and the local schoolmasters. In the forty years since Coleridge wrote it had become much clearer that education should be state funded, and of this Arnold was a passionate advocate.

T.S.Eliot felt that 'the facile assumption of a relationship between culture and religion' was the most fundamental weakness of Arnold's argument.[26] We may feel that this is the pot calling the kettle black, but in any event the argument of *Culture and Anarchy* is misunderstood if it is read apart from *Literature and Dogma*, which was, in Arnold's lifetime, far and away his most successful book, going through three impressions in a fortnight and quickly selling more than 100,000 copies. In the first book all the weight is on the role of culture; in the second, it is on religion. We cannot forget, says Arnold, that the Muse of righteousness is far more real and far greater than the Muse of art

23 Arnold, *Culture and Anarchy* p.9
24 Arnold, *Culture and Anarchy* p.xxxvi
25 Arnold, *Culture and Anarchy* p.xi
26 Eliot, *Notes* p.28

and science. The latter is the Muse of the gifted few, but the former is the Muse of the work-day, care-crossed, toil-stained millions of men – the Muse of humanity. *Literature and Dogma* was written 'to win sure grounds for the continued use and enjoyment of the Bible' precisely for these millions – in other words, to answer the problem raised by Colenso.[27] Convinced that the advance of science would make belief in miracles impossible, and Church dogma incredible, Arnold advocates 'the natural truth of Christianity', and seeks to present a Christianity free from dogma, consisting in 'the inward feeling and disposition of the individual himself'. He rightly objected that much contemporary theology presented a picture of God as an 'infinitely magnified man', and in the first edition parodied such a being as an infinite version of Lord Shaftesbury. He put in its place, 'the Eternal Power, which is not ourselves, which makes for righteousness'.[28]

God is not, as the Calvinists teach, a righteous judge, but 'the element in which we live and move and have our being, which stretches around and beyond the strictly moral element in us, around and beyond the finite sphere of what is originated, measured, and controlled by our own understanding and will'. Our faith in God rests not on metaphysical proofs but on 'a moral perception of a rule of conduct not of our own making, into which we are born, and which exists whether we will or no'.[29] Science tells us that God is 'the stream of tendency by which all things fulfil the law of their being'. We cannot prove that there is a personal first cause but we know by experience that there is that beyond ourselves which makes a moral life possible.[30] Arnold understands that a moral life is not possible on the basis of the command. It is religion which helps us find 'the energy and power to bring all those self-seeking tendencies of the flesh, those multitudinous, swarming, eager and incessant impulses into obedience to the central tendency'. But what is religion, and how does it differ from ethics? The difference is one of degree. Religion is ethics heightened, lit up, by feeling. The true meaning of religion, therefore, is 'morality touched by emotion'.[31] The fount of this emotion is 'boundless devotion to that inspiring and affecting pattern of self-conquest offered by Jesus Christ'.[32] At the heart of the New Testament, for him, is the *epikeia* (2 Cor 10.1 usually translated 'gentleness') of Christ, which Arnold translates as 'sweet reasonableness'. The method and temper of Jesus is sweet reasonableness and the 'immense capacity for ceaseless progress and farther development' in Christianity is to be found in this method and temper.[33]

Much of Arnold's argument sounds decidedly eighteenth century, a return to the deism of Tillotson and Clark. Before we jump to that conclusion, however, we should consult what was perhaps his best piece of theological writing, the

---

27   M.Arnold, *God and the Bible* London: Smith and Elder 1884 p.5
28   Arnold, *Literature and Dogma* p.190
29   Arnold, *Literature and Dogma* p.92
30   Arnold, *Literature and Dogma* pp.188, 190
31   Arnold, *Literature and Dogma* p.16
32   Arnold, *Culture and Anarchy* p.92
33   Arnold, *Literature and Dogma* p.225

essay on 'Bishop Butler and the Zeit Geist'. Arnold often cites Butler with respect, but here Arnold subjects that reasoning to exemplary contextual analysis and shows that Butler in fact subordinated the gospel to the *Zeitgeist*, faith to philosophy. 'After reading the *Analogy* one goes instinctively,' he wrote:

> to bathe one's spirit in the Bible again, to be refreshed by its boundless certitude and exhilaration. 'The Eternal is the strength of my life!' 'The foundation of God standeth sure!' – that is the constant tone of religion in the Bible. 'If I tell you the truth, why do ye not believe me? – the evident truth, that whoever comes to me has life; and evident, because whoever does come, gets it'.[34]

That is the evidence to constrain our practice which is offered by Christianity. It is almost, dare one say it, the strange new world of the Bible, and it is this, his love for the Bible, which is actually the heart of Arnold's faith. The 'literature' of *Literature and Dogma* is not an anticipation of the 'Bible as literature' movement, but the recognition that Scripture is narrative, and works through metaphors, and the claim that to turn these into dogma is to ossify and falsify them, and to make them unbelievable. Arnold is fully convinced that the Bible contains the word of life. He is as saturated in the biblical text as Bunyan, which is why his writing still has the power it does. In answer to the question why we should study the Bible rather than other books his answer is that the 'Power, not ourselves, which makes for righteousness' 'is *revealed* in Israel and the Bible, and not by other teachers and books!'[35] 'To the Bible men will return, and why? Because they cannot do without it. Because happiness is our being's end and aim, and happiness belongs to righteousness, and righteousness is revealed in the Bible.'[36]

The problem here is what Arnold understands by righteousness. At the end of the day Arnold does not break through to the 'strange new world of the Bible' because he cannot hear the prophetic critique for his own times. Like many liberals his generous sentiments regarding human equality could be easily upset by what he took to be manifestations of anarchy, whether by black slaves in Jamaica or by the working class in Hyde Park. Though his love for Scripture is what gives his writings their force and resonance he represents a form of culture Protestantism for which 'Christianity' is reduced to ethics and ethics is about decency. He did not hear what many of his contemporaries heard, the cry of outcast London, nor did he see what some also saw, the injustice of colonialism. His reading of Scripture remained constrained by a bourgeois captivity.

Eliot and a Christian Society

T.S.Eliot took up Arnold's themes half a century after his death. Where Arnold was a signed up liberal, Eliot was deeply conservative, though in the patrician

---

34 M.Arnold. *Last Essays on Church and Religion* London: Smith and Elder 1877 p.139
35 Arnold, *Literature and Dogma* p.185 italics Arnold's
36 Arnold, *Literature and Dogma* p.197

and cultural sense which was opposed to industrial capitalism. A lifelong follower of Charles Maurras, he described himself as 'classicist, royalist and Anglo-Catholic'. At the same time he took the view that the Church could not align itself with any political wing because 'Conservatism is too often conservation of the wrong things; liberalism is a relaxation of discipline; revolution a denial of permanent things.' The radio broadcast in which that remark was made was given in 1937 on the topic of 'Church, Community and State'. There was, he said, an irreconcilable antithesis between Church and world and no permanent *modus vivendi*, no policy of live and let live, was possible. The Church's business is to interfere with the world. To accept two ways of life in the same society, one for the Christian and another for the rest, would be for the Church to abandon its task of evangelizing the world.[37] The political task of the Church was profound scrutiny of society, asking the question: 'to what depth is the foundation of our society not merely neutral but positively anti-Christian?'[38] The task of the Church was not to propose specific schemes for improvement, but much more to say what was wrong:

> What is right enters the realm of the expedient ... But the church can say what is always and everywhere wrong. And without this firm assurance of first principles which it is the business of the Church to repeat in and out of season, the World will constantly confuse the right with the expedient.[39]

From T.E.Hulme Eliot had learned that it was the doctrine of original sin which marked off the classical from the romantic view of human beings and which therefore lay at the root of most other divisions in social and political thought. Acceptance of this doctrine coloured all his political thinking.[40] When he said that the mission of the Church was to affirm, to teach and to apply true theology and to put the question of the meaning of human life and 'the end of man', it was this aspect of orthodoxy, especially, that was in mind.

These thoughts were somewhat expanded in the lectures which were published as *The Idea of a Christian Society*. The year was 1939, and the letters columns of the newspapers were full of discussion of what was happening in Germany, and the question of whether it amounted to a new paganism. Eliot acknowledged that British society was 'neutral' with regard to religion but believed that in so far as it retained a positive ethical basis this basis was Christian. A society has not ceased to be Christian until it positively becomes something else, he argued, and the choice before it was Christianity or paganism. Over against those who drew a comfortable distinction between

37   T.S.Eliot, *The Idea of a Christian Society* London: Faber and Faber 1939 p.92
38   Eliot, *Idea* p.95
39   Eliot, *Idea* p.97 Cf Hugh Montefiore's argument that cultures are characterized by 'root paradigms', assumptions about the fundamental nature of the universe, humankind, or the way in which people behave, which are so deeply held by the members of a society as to be essentially unquestioned by them and that it is these 'root paradigms' which are subjected to Christian critique. H.Montefiore(ed) *The Gospel and Contemporary Culture* London: Mowbray 1992 p.2
40   K.Asher, *T.S.Eliot and Ideology* Cambridge: Cambridge University Press 1998 p.36

Britain and Germany Eliot argued that capitalism constituted a *de facto* paganism. The problem of living a Christian life was set:

> by our implication in a network of institutions from which we cannot dissociate ourselves: institutions the operation of which appears no longer neutral, but non-Christian. And as for the Christian who is not conscious of this dilemma – and he is in the majority – he is becoming more and more de-Christianized by all sorts of unconscious pressure: paganism holds all the most valuable advertising space.[41]

To organize society on the basis of private profit leads to both deformation of humanity and the exhaustion of natural resources and 'a good deal of our material progress is a progress for which succeeding generations may have to pay dearly'.[42] Adapting social ideas to such a society was simple expediency and a surrender of faith. Profit could not be acknowledged as a social ideal, nor exchange value prioritized over use value. Nor could one plead ignorance of economic principles, because that would be to surrender the primacy of ethics.[43]

What was the answer to this problem? It was the formation of a Christian society in which there would be a unified religious–social code of behaviour. This would be effected by a radically revised version of Coleridge's clerisy. The Christian community as a whole was not in a position to provide such a society. Its belief was largely unconscious. In a paragraph reminiscent of Schleiermacher's reflections on the incapacity of working class life for true religion, Eliot wrote:

> For the great mass of humanity whose attention is occupied mostly by their direct relation to the soil, or the sea, or the machine, and to a small number of persons, pleasures and duties, two conditions are required. The first is that, as their capacity for thinking about the objects of faith is small, their Christianity may be almost wholly realised in behaviour: both in their customary and periodic religious observances, and in a traditional code of behaviour towards their neighbours. The second is that, while they should have some perception of how far their lives fall short of Christian ideals, their religious and social life should form for them a natural whole, so that the difficulty of behaving as Christians should not impose an intolerable strain.[44]

---

41 Eliot, *Idea* p.22
42 Eliot, *Idea* p.61
43 These ideas were developed by Daniel Bell in *The Cultural Contradictions of Capitalism* London: Heinemann 1976. Bell argued that one can see structural sources of tension in society between a social structure (primarily techno-economic) which is bureaucratic and hierarchical and a polity which believes, formally, in equality and participation; between a social structure that is organized fundamentally in terms of roles and specialization and a culture which is concerned with the enhancement and fulfilment of the self and the 'whole' person. These contradictions generate the social conflicts expressed ideologically as alienation, depersonalization, the attack on authority and so on. Ibid p.14 The loss of the Protestant ethic meant that only hedonism remained. 'The lack of a transcendental tie, the sense that a society fails to provide some set of ultimate meanings in its character structure, work and culture, becomes unsettling to the system.' Ibid p.21
44 Eliot, *Idea* p.29 Asher points out the resemblance between the Christian community and Plato's artisans, most human when they exercise a steady temperance. Asher, *Eliot* p.90

Leading the *hoi polloi* should be a 'Community of Christians' from whom one would expect 'a conscious Christian life on its highest level'. It would include both clergy and lay people 'of superior intellectual and/or spiritual gifts'. Their identity of belief and aspiration, their background of a common system of education and a common culture, will enable them to mutually influence each other and collectively form the conscious mind and conscience of the nation.[45] Thus a Christian *society* might be formed – not a Christian *state*, for the Christianity of the state is only a reflection of the Christianity of the society which it governs. The argument for Christianity was not, as it might be construed in Arnold, because it provides a foundation for morality. Rather, the necessity of Christian morality follows from the truth of Christianity. 'It is not enthusiasm, but dogma, that differentiates a Christian from a pagan society.'[46]

Between this lecture and Eliot's other major intervention on religion and culture, *Notes towards the definition of Culture*, published in 1948, came the completion of *Four Quartets*, Eliot's greatest achievement. *Burnt Norton* had been written in 1935; *East Coker* followed in 1940, *The Dry Salvages* in 1941 and *Little Gidding* in 1942. They form a stark contrast with Arnold's melancholy, his sense of:

> Wandering between two worlds, one dead,
> The other powerless to be born.

The difference is clearly formed by Eliot's strong Anglo-Catholic faith. On the one hand the poems are antiseptically free from optimism:

> I said to my soul, be still, and wait without hope
> For hope would be hope for the wrong thing; wait without love
> For love would be love of the wrong thing; there is yet faith
> But the faith and the love and the hope are all in the waiting.

On the other hand the poems weave together creation and redemption, a profound sense of historical continuity held together by the necessary repetition of the agricultural year, reaching back to the most primitive times; the sense of a continuing struggle in which it is not always possible to tell which side is the side of the angels. Yet the repeated 'England' of *Little Gidding*, with its references to the Blitz, is without doubt a recognition of a culture, a historical memory and sense of tradition, which is worth fighting for, a moment of that embrace of time by eternity which means that, as Julian of Norwich saw, 'All shall be well.' There is the sense of an England, largely rural, reaching back in unbroken continuity into the mists of time, a place where religious truth has been struggled for and known, a culture which withstands barbarism. The *Quartets* are a minefield of interpretation, but I agree with Denis

---

45   Eliot, *Idea* p.42
46   Eliot, *Idea* p.59

Donoghue that they stand in direct connection with the earlier essay. 'Eliot's hope,' he writes:

> is to clear a space, or if necessary to take over a bombed-out area, and there to build a new life of the spirit; to realize 'the idea of a Christian society' ... The redemption of time will be his theme, his case, but he will have to resist a Manichean force within himself which is notoriously subversive; it doesn't really believe that time can be redeemed.[47]

This Manichaean element – actually the trace of Manichaeism which Augustine always retained – is overcome by understanding the *via negativa* as ultimately positive.

The pamphlet which followed the war, *Notes towards the definition of Culture*, is of course a step down, not just from poetry to prose, but from great profundity back to the correspondence columns of the postwar newspapers. Where Arnold is in danger of assimilating religion to culture, Eliot, in this second pamphlet, is in danger of doing the reverse. He takes over the social anthropologists' understanding of culture and transposes it to religion. 'Religion is the whole way of life of a people, from birth to the grave, morning to night, and even in sleep, and that way of life is also its culture.'[48] In his view a culture cannot be preserved in the absence of religion and vice versa, but what he means by 'culture' here is art, as we see from the following remark that to judge a work of art by religious standards, or a religion by artistic standards, ought to come to the same thing.[49] This elision between culture as a way of life and culture as art and learning marks the whole discussion. The necessary relation of religion and culture meant that even the purest theological issue has cultural consequences, as the career of Athanasius, somewhat implausibly celebrated as one of the great builders of Western civilization, shows.[50]

---

47   D.Donoghue, 'T.S.Eliot's "Quartets": A New Reading' in B.Bergonzi(ed) *Four Quartets: A Selection of Critical Essays* London: Macmillan 1969 p.232

48   Eliot, *Notes* p.31 Jacob Burckhardt believed the same thing, asserting that religion is a prime condition of any culture deserving the name, and hence may coincide with the sole existing culture. *Force and Freedom* New York: Meridian 1955 p.165 The relation of religion and culture is glossed by Nicholas Lash in his assertion that religion has no content of its own: 'It is the content of politics, ethics and art; of law, economics and physics – of whatever it is that constitutes the "project" of human existence in the world of nature.' *A Matter of Hope* London: Darton, Longman and Todd 1981 p.287

49   Before the war Eliot was prepared to commit himself to the view that civilization could not survive without Christianity. The passage is close enough to MacIntyre's argument at the end of *After Virtue* to suggest subconscious borrowing: 'The World is trying the experiment of attempting to form a civilized but non-Christian mentality. The Experiment will fail; but we must be very patient in awaiting the collapse; meanwhile redeeming the time: so that the Faith may be preserved alive through the dark ages before us; to renew and rebuild civilization, and save the World from suicide.' T.S.Eliot, *Selected Essays* New York: Harcourt Brace 1932 p.342

50   This was a view which seems to have been shared by Paul Tillich who believed that religion as ultimate concern is the meaning-giving substance of culture, and culture is the totality of forms in which the basic concern of religion expresses itself. 'In abbreviation: religion is the substance of culture, culture is the form of religion ... Every religious act, not only in organized religion, but

Eliot saw that the total identity of religion and culture would mean 'an inferior culture and an inferior religion'. 'A universal religion is at least potentially higher than one which any race or nation claims exclusively for itself: and a culture realising a religion also realised in other cultures is at least potentially a higher culture than one which has a religion exclusively to itself.'[51] He did not want to affirm the identity of religion and culture, but rather their dialectical interplay, in which they were both identical and different, and to express this he proposed using the term 'incarnation'. Almost certainly, he has in mind the Chalcedonian definition, according to which the two natures are united 'without confusion, without change, without division and without separation'.[52] It is in this sense, then, that he wants to propose that culture is the *incarnation* of the religion of a people.[53]

This is an odd definition given his notorious description of English culture as, 'Derby Day, Henley Regatta, Cowes, the twelfth of August, a cup final, the dog races, the pin table, the dart board, Wensleydale cheese, boiled cabbage cut into sections, beetroot in vinegar, nineteenth century Gothic churches and the music of Elgar'.[54] Eliot realizes the oddness of the suggestion that horses and dogs are part of English religion, but does not see that it calls into question the identity in difference of religion and culture. For whilst no one will dispute that bishops in gaiters are part of culture, to argue that Derby Day and the dog track are part of religion is so to redefine religion as to make it incompatible with faith. This is true even given the most careful Chalcedonian glossing of his definition to the effect that religion and culture are identical on the unconscious level, but different on the conscious level. Eliot was perfectly well aware of the dehumanizing possibilities of religion, of the possibility that 'elements of local culture – even of local barbarism – may become invested with the sanctity of religious observances, and superstition may flourish instead of piety' so that people *slip back* to a primitive unity of religion and culture.[55] Given his organic, regional and intergenerational vision of culture it is difficult to see how this is going to be avoided.

The danger he is most concerned about, however, is not barbarism but social disintegration, the breakdown of communication between a culture's constituent groups, and it is easy to see why. Eliot thought culture could be

---

also in the most intimate movement of the soul, is culturally formed.' *Theology of Culture* New York: Oxford University Press 1959 p.42 Eliot was influenced, as he acknowledges in his Preface, by Christopher Dawson, who argued that all great civilizations grew out of religions, rather than the reverse. It followed that 'a society which has lost its religion becomes sooner or later a society which has lost its culture' and he illustrated the dire consequences by the decline and fall of Rome. It was 'impossible to exaggerate' the dangers when once social life has become separated from the religious impulse. *Enquiries into Religion and Culture* London: Sheed & Ward 1933

51   Eliot, *Notes* p.31
52   This seems to me more enlightening than Peter Ackroyd's suggestion that Eliot has in mind 'some kind of Bradleyan unity to which we may aspire but which we can never reach'. *T.S.Eliot* London: Hamilton 1984 p.291
53   Eliot, *Notes* p.28
54   Eliot, *Notes* p.31 Nothing could make clearer Eliot's distance from the present.
55   Eliot, *Notes* p.71

understood on the level of the individual, the group and of society as a whole, provided one realized that these levels were mutually interdependent. In his view the survival of groups, or classes, was essential for the health of society. 'The universality of irritation is the best assurance of peace ... a country which is too well united ... is a menace to others.'[56] What is important is the way in which these groups relate. As he put it in a postwar broadcast:

> The culture of a poet will be somewhat different from that of a politician; but in a healthy society these are all parts of the same culture; and the artist, the poet, the philosopher, the politician and the labourer will have a culture in common, which they do not share with other people of the same occupations in other countries.[57]

His apocalypse is a situation where religion, philosophy and art no longer inform each other and where 'the vestige of manners may be left to a few survivors of a vanishing class who, their sensibility untrained by either religion or art and their minds unfurnished with the material for witty conversation, will have no context in their lives to give value to their behaviour'.[58]

What Eliot senses but does not face is the reality of class conflict. A healthy culture needs different classes, he argues, and in some respects they form subcultures (a term he may have invented), but in order to avoid societal meltdown they must have a culture in common. This problem set the agenda for the young Raymond Williams. 'The making of a society,' he wrote, 'is the finding of common meanings and directions, and its growth is an active debate and amendment under the pressures of experience, contact, and discovery, writing themselves into the land.'[59] If we talk of culture as a 'whole way of life' then we must mean 'common meanings, the product of a whole people', shaped out of a contest and ongoing negotiation between individual and group meanings. But can we have a common culture between antagonistic groups? This question has been raised not just by class but by race, ethnicity and religion – something seventeenth century Europe knew only too well. Eliot's view that the 'common tradition of Christianity ... has made Europe what it is' is problematized by the fact that religion is politicized, as we see in Northern Ireland or the Balkans.

The pre-war Eliot is clearer-sighted about the necessary distinction of religion and culture. The intervening war, and the rhetoric of the struggle of good against evil, of a democratic muddling through as opposed to Auschwitz, has muddied the view. Further, in the *Notes* Eliot forgets the contradiction between capitalism and an organic society which he set out so forcefully in the earlier publication. He is therefore caught by the paradox that the class society he commends can only be created by the economic system he detests.[60] It makes the realization of his organic society impossible.

---

56 Eliot, *Notes* p.59
57 Eliot, *Notes* p.120
58 Eliot, *Notes* p.26
59 Williams, *Resources* p.4
60 Williams, *Culture and Society* p.237

All three of these authors write against the background of the Anglican establishment, an Erastianism where toleration of other Christian denominations, and finally of Jews, had been slowly and painfully negotiated over three centuries. None of them quite identify religion and culture. Both Coleridge and (the pre-war) Eliot preserve some space for the prophetic function of the Church, whilst Arnold makes the Christian ethic, mediated by Scripture, the lead force in culture in a pairing with the *epikeia* of Hellenism. All three conceive of the Church's influence on culture primarily in terms of education. How significant the Church was as a cultural force between the sixteenth and twentieth centuries remains a difficult historical problem but it is certain that if education remains the major strategy for political change, it cannot expect to exercise even the influence it did in the first half of the twentieth century in the currently secularized state of society. All three authors represent in different ways the taming of religion which one might expect in an Erastian state. I turn, therefore, to the most vehement protest against that taming, that of Karl Barth.

The Critique of Culture Protestantism

Karl Barth's theological revolution began in his turn against culture Protestantism, the identification of religion with high culture, or sweetness and light. In his view, the support of the Churches for the First World War revealed its bankruptcy. We can apply to it some words of Alasdair MacIntyre, who noted that any situation in which an ideology has no problems of conflict with philosophy or human or natural science is characteristically a sign, not that the ideology in question has triumphantly solved the intellectual problems of the age, but rather that that ideology has become empirically vacuous.[61] If we change 'ideology' for 'theology', here, then we have to grant that liberal theology had far too few problems with its age. Barth saw that the Christianity of the European nations was little more than a form of polytheism, an idolatrous harnessing of the deity to national agendas. It was this perception which led to his attack on 'religion' which, we saw in the last chapter, had been Protestantism's favoured way of talking about Church and gospel for more than a century.

Seeing the need to break the cultural captivity of the Church, Barth proposed to talk of faith and the gospel rather than of religion. Unlike the latter, the gospel exists not to give comfort but to witness to the power of the God who raises the dead. 'It is the alarm cry, the fire bell, of a coming new world.'[62] Deeply attracted by Christian socialism for some years, Barth had turned against it as yet another form of culture Christianity. Jesus comes:

---

61   A.MacIntyre, *Against the Self Images of the Age* London: Duckworth 1971 p.7
62   K.Barth, *The Epistle to the Romans* 2nd edn tr Hoskyns Oxford: Oxford University Press 1933 p.38

not to change anything, not to improve the flesh through morality, to transfigure it through art, to rationalise it through science, to overcome it through the Fata Morgana of religion, but to proclaim the resurrection of the flesh, the new human being who recognizes herself in God, because she is made in God's image (Ebenbild), and in whom God recognises Godself since God is her pattern (Urbild).[63]

The response to this proclamation is faith. Faith is 'respect before the divine incognito, love of God which is conscious of the qualitative distinction between God and human beings, God and the world, affirmation of the resurrection as the turning point of the world, affirmation of the divine No! which brings us to a shuddering halt before God.'[64]

Of the three authors whose account of the relation of religion and culture we have considered it is Eliot who explores most deeply the position of God in the relationship and he does that, in his poetry, by an appeal to the apophatic tradition. Perhaps there was no other option without turning poetry into propaganda. For Barth, however, faith is not just difficult in a secularizing world, as it is for Arnold, but an 'impossible possibility', a phrase intended to contradict what liberal theology regarded as only too self-evident a human possibility.[65] Faith is set over against religion because the latter, which means bourgeois Christianity, represents the domestication of the gospel. In his commentary Barth translates Paul's 'nomos', law, by 'religion'. Just as there is a necessary tension, a dialectical relation, between law and gospel, so is there with religion. What he calls the 'criminal arrogance of religion' has to be been done away with.[66] He agrees with Marx that religion functions as an opiate, underwriting human illusions.[67] In religion human beings seek to master their world, and make themselves finally secure – perhaps even through Eliot's *via negativa*. God, however, cannot become the prisoner of any human programme, is not part of any totality, and can therefore only be spoken of through paradox.

Paradox is what for Barth takes the place of the *via negativa* at this stage in his writing. To speak of God is not to speak of religion because this is the place where human beings bolt and bar themselves against God. Just where people believe they are raising themselves above common lusts and failings, precisely there, in religion, do they find themselves on 'the highest summit in the kingdom of sin' – a proposition it is not difficult to substantiate from the gospels.[68] It is no accident that 'the odour of death' hangs over these summits. Religion does not liberate us, 'indeed it imprisons us more surely than anything else'.[69] It is the 'working capital' of sin. The boundary of religion is 'the line of death which cuts between what is possible with human beings and what is possible with God, between flesh and Spirit, time and eternity'. An irrepressible

---

63 Barth, *Romans* p.277
64 Barth, *Romans* p.39
65 Barth, *Romans* p.138
66 Barth, *Romans* p.37
67 Barth, *Romans* p.236
68 Barth, *Romans* p.242
69 Barth, *Romans* p.276

bourgeois reality, it refuses to die. 'Enough, it must die, and in God we are free of it.'[70]

The reader of this charge cannot fail to ask whether Barth is returning us to the individualism of Kierkegaard, the lonely Jeremiah self-estranged from the Church whose attempts to bring about change must be by prophetic critique and not the slow process of education. And can the prophet exist without religious institutions in the background? Surely not. Barth concedes these points. There is a dialectic. *We have no option but to be religious.* 'What else can we honestly do than be – religious people, repenting in dust and ashes, wrestling with fear and trembling that we might be blessed and, if we have to take a position, taking that of adoration.'[71] We have no option but to cultivate religion, to reform and revolutionize it. But: 'the more consistently we are involved in religion the deeper the shadow of death which lies over us'.[72] Why? Because it is religion which faces us with the reality of sin, death and the knowledge that we do not know God, of our radical otherness with respect to the Creator.[73] It is the worst enemy we have – apart from God. Precisely for this reason we have to stay with it, to remain in solidarity with the Church, fully aware of the antithesis between Church and gospel.[74]

It is a tremendous piece of internal critique – a warning to the faithful not to presume on their piety (Schleiermacher, with his valorization of *Frömmigkeit*, is in the background). To believe in God, Barth insists, cannot mean a quiet conscience but only an unquiet one.

Barth developed the critique more than fifteen years later, no longer as the Red Pastor but as the Professor. As we saw in the last chapter, he argued that religion became a basically cultural term in the seventeenth and eighteenth centuries. Once again his concern is the liberation of the Church from the Babylonian captivity of 'Christendom', of a culture which takes the gospel for granted. He had developed the themes of the two Romans commentaries in terms of the contrast – not of reason and revelation, but religion and revelation. He argued that when the two are regarded as comparable spheres religion assumes a distinct and autonomous existence and, as a refusal of God's self-offering, this is equivalent to unbelief. Religion is the attempt to anticipate what God does in revelation. 'In religion man bolts and bars himself against revelation by providing a substitute, by taking away in advance the very thing which has to be given by God.'[75] The Bible is not a book of religion. 'From first to last it is the proclamation of the justifying and sanctifying grace of God':

> Sin is always unbelief. And unbelief is always man's faith in himself. And this faith invariably consists in the fact that man makes the mystery of his responsibility his own mystery, instead of accepting it as the mystery of God. It is this faith which is

---

70   Barth, *Romans* p.238
71   Barth, *Romans* p.252
72   Barth, *Romans* p.255
73   Barth, *Romans* p.250
74   Barth, *Romans* p.333
75   Barth, *Dogmatics* I/2 p.303

religion. It is contradicted by the revelation attested in the New Testament, which is identical with Jesus Christ as the one who acts for us and on us. This stamps religion as unbelief.[76]

Religions can and do die. They have a fundamental non-necessity. They peter out in either mysticism or atheism. 'The real crisis of religion can only break in from outside the magic circle of religion and its place of origin, i.e. from outside man.'[77]

It is this need to get outside the cultural totality which remains the key to Barth's attack but the change in context problematizes it. On the one hand, this volume of the *Dogmatics* was part of the struggle with fascism, where ideologues like Rosenberg were proposing new paganisms, religions of blood and soil. On the other hand, Barth also situated himself in the two thousand year old Christian discussion, and this involved relations with the great non-Christian religions. As opposed to the two Romans commentaries, where it is quite clear that 'religion' means Christendom, in this more systematic context other religions are in view and these too, like an assimilated Christianity, are rejected as unbelief. Barth retains the dialectic in this later account of religion, but in doing so effectively makes an exception for Christianity in his account of the religions. Christian religion is, he says, the sacramental area created by the Holy Spirit, in which the God whose Word became flesh continues to speak through the sign of his revelation, and the existence of human beings created by the same Holy Spirit, who hear this God continually speaking in revelation.[78]

As an account of the relation between the great religions this position of Barth's is quite inadequate. He needs the correction of theologians like Aloysius Pieris who insist on the need to learn from the great Asian religions. He, too, recognizes the need for dialectic because every religion is at once a sign and a countersign of the kingdom of God, a potential means of either emancipation or enslavement.[79] However, for Pieris all the great religions are fundamentally languages of liberation: all have a dream of a different future at their origin which looks back to the liberation of their founding moment. Though they can be corrupted by ideology they have a built-in mechanism to discern the enslaving and emancipating character of ideologies and to disengage themselves from even a helpful ideology when it has ceased to be helpful.[80] In the case of Christianity this is a return to the axial principle of 'justice to the oppressed people' which is the canon within the canon of the Hebrew Bible. All religions, then, are fundamentally positive and function as a memory of an absolute future, or a utopia which guides us towards the future.

This is an important correction to Barth, but it, too, is inadequate, especially in the face of the rise of murderous and deeply dehumanizing fundamentalisms, as Marc Ellis has demonstrated with regard to Judaism and Christianity, and

---

76 Barth, *Dogmatics* I/2 p.314
77 Barth, *Dogmatics* I/2 p.324
78 Barth, *Dogmatics* I/2 p.359
79 A.Pieris, *An Asian Theology of Liberation* Edinburgh: T&T Clark 1988 p.88
80 A.Pieris, *Fire and Water* Maryknoll: Orbis 1996 p.104

Chetan Bhatt in relation to Hinduism and Islam.[81] Barth saw the inadequacy of the Enlightenment critique of religion as superstition (though this category of critique cannot be altogether abandoned) and tried to get at the heart of what is potentially dehumanizing about religion. In this respect his critique retains its power but it needs to be read against the rise of fundamentalism, which began in Christian America at the beginning of the twentieth century, but has now embraced all major religions. The liberative de-centring which religion ought to provide is, in fundamentalist formations, subverted by the appeal to divine authority. In this case human actions cannot be criticized because human agency is displaced by Godly inspiration, thus legitimizing virtually any atrocity.[82]

Secular liberalism in the West has found itself all at sea in critiquing such fundamentalism, wrong-footed by the potential confusion with racism and cultural supremacy. As Chetan Bhatt puts it, 'We are not expected to criticize religion as we would any other discourse. Naïve relativism demands that we cannot attack its superstitions, its falsehoods, its brutalities and its profanities ... If the Enlightenment has taught us anything, it is surely that we have absolutely no reason to do so.'[83] He is right, but what we learn from Barth is that an internal critique of religion in terms of idolatry is possible, which I shall take up in Chapter 5. Pieris' description of religion as 'a discourse of liberation' *tout simple* is unsustainable. Instead, we need the kind of dialectical reading that Bas Wielenga proposes, writing out of India (where, in 2002, Hindu fundamentalists engaged in ethnic cleansing of Muslims in Gujerat). He argues that Christians need to affirm that in popular religion which is life giving and retain the critique of religion 'wherever and whenever it serves structures of domination and forces of death'.[84] Barth's critique of religion, we should never forget, began with the complicity of the institutional Church in Europe with mass murder.

Religion, Culture and the Long Revolution

For Arnold, writing in 1867, religion and culture contribute more or less equally to the long revolution of humanization – an idea savagely challenged in the footnotes to *Das Kapital*, published in the same year. Half a century later, with millions dead in the trenches, Barth with an almost equal savagery sought to tear up the whole synthesis between religion and culture which Arnold or Harnack classically represent. Half a century on again, with the advance of secularization in Europe, high culture has come to substitute itself for a fading sense of divinity and transcendence, as Terry Eagleton points out. In the

---

81 M.Ellis, *Unholy Alliance: Religion and Atrocity in our Time* London: SCM 1997; Chetan Bhatt, *Liberation and Purity* London: UCL 1997
82 Bhatt, *Liberation* p.106
83 Bhatt, *Liberation* p.271
84 B.Wielenga, 'Liberation Theology in Asia' in C.Rowland(ed) *The Cambridge Companion to Liberation Theology* Cambridge: Cambridge University Press 1999 p.60

absence of God it is what provides us with our moral credentials.[85] Culture, like science, has no need of the hypothesis of God. In the light of this challenge, and of Barth's attack on culture Protestantism, how ought we to think of the place of the gospel in the long revolution?

In the first place, religion and culture are, of course, inextricable. As a human reality, using words and symbols, religion only exists in cultural form. As Barth recognized, we can no more speak outside of culture than we can jump out of our own skin. This means that the danger of cultural assimilation or colonization is permanent. At the end of the twentieth century Lamin Sanneh finds the Western Church still trapped in cultural captivity, 'reduced to a mock rehearsal of society's agenda, gaily adopting the language of rights and justice in place of truth and repentance, and perforce capitulating to the litigious ideology of individual preference and group conflict'.[86] In the journal *Christian Century*, for example, a counsellor describes the Church as a 'well organized psychiatric unit marked by acceptance and tolerance; equality; commitment to honesty; meaningful rituals; and mutual helpfulness'. This, says Sanneh, is 'the kind of white middle-class massage parlour that mainstream Protestantism has been threatening to turn into'.[87] The tendency to see the Church in terms of individual healthy mindedness, as a selfhood that is vulnerable to bouts of low self-esteem, is light years removed from the Church as a fellowship of faithfulness to God's promises; and the tendency to explain all human relations in terms of power relations assumes an absolute moral autonomy for human partiality, the fragmented particularities that constitute our differences, and sees encounters between groups essentially as forms of hostility. We are left with human relationships as basically non-negotiable lines of suspicion and antagonism.[88] Effectively, Sanneh says, the Western Church remains culturally assimilated, and as such does not have a gospel to proclaim.

Can the Church be part of culture and yet not culturally assimilated? All Barth's methodological labours were devoted to trying to show that despite the necessary cultural form the 'Wholly Other', that which is not a member of this or any universe, can find speech within, engage with, human culture without being subsumed by it. It is, as Eliot also saw, the paradox of incarnation. In Lamin Sanneh's words, Christianity is not culture, but it is not other than culture.[89] As opposed to the distinctions of Niebuhr's typology we have a dialectic where the gospel, always imperfectly represented in the Church, always disrupts the cultural task precisely in the attempt to forward it. Barth expressed this in terms of the doctrine of reconciliation. The kingdom of Christ stands 'in the midst of enemies'. Nevertheless reconciliation is a fact and this means that faith is lived out 'as the proclamation of the righteousness of God in the valley of death'. From this point of view culture is the law in reference to which the justified and sanctified sinner practises faith and obedience. The

---

85 Eagleton, *Idea* pp.64, 2

86 L.Sanneh, *Encountering the West* London: Marshall Pickering 1993 p.212

87 Sanneh, *Encountering* p.220

88 Sanneh, *Encountering* pp.221, 223

89 Sanneh, *Encountering* p.53

promise implicit in creation is here law, command, the command to be human, a task which has to be actualized. 'The standard for such distinctions is always unity, the destined character of man, that man find himself as a whole.'[90]

One way in which the Church resists assimilation, remains Coleridge's 'befriending opposite of the world', is indicated by Raymond Williams' distinction between dominant, residual and emergent forms of culture. Religion belongs to the second category. What is residual is not archaic, the subject only of archaeological interest. It is something which has been effectively formed in the past but is still active in the cultural process. 'Thus certain experiences, meanings and values which cannot be expressed or substantially verified in terms of the dominant culture are nevertheless lived and practiced on the basis of the residue.' Organized religion is predominantly residual but within this there is a significant difference between some practically alternative and oppositional meanings and values (absolute brotherhood, service to others without reward) and a larger body of incorporated meanings and values.[91] The importance of this can be illustrated by Joel Kovel's argument (from a secular standpoint) that the Bruderhof in the United States offer a space from which resistance to global capitalism may cogently be built.[92]

This challenge is especially important given the tendency in the contemporary West for culture to usurp the place of religion. Terry Eagleton agrees with Williams that this is to lay on it a burden it cannot bear for when the arts are forced to stand in for God they crumble from the inside.[93] In the contemporary secularized West, he argues, we are caught in a double bind for culture is fatally enfeebled once it comes adrift from its roots in religion, but clinging to those roots means consigning itself to irrelevance.[94] The West ideally requires a version of culture which would win the life-and-death allegiance of the people, and the traditional name for this is religion. The rhetoric of the 'empire' or 'axis' of evil is an attempt to command this allegiance in the name of civilization, culture and every other positive value. However, as Eliot argued in *Idea of a Christian Society*, the invocation of stable religious values is undermined by the promulgation of a savage capitalism which respects neither God nor man, not to mention the planet.

In contrast to both Arnold and Eliot, Eagleton wants high culture to be put in its place, since it cannot alleviate the primary problems of the new millennium – war, famine, poverty, disease, debt, drugs, environmental pollution and the displacement of peoples.[95] Another form of culture, culture

---

90   Barth, 'Church and Culture' p.346
91   Williams, *Marxism and Literature* p.122
92   J.Kovel, *The Enemy of Nature* London: Zed 2002 p.190ff
93   Eagleton, *Idea* p.16 Williams notes that culture as a substitute for religion is a very doubtful quantity, especially when it is taken, as so often, in its narrower sense. He cites Newman's comment that if virtue is a kind of beauty, the principle which determines what is virtuous is, not conscience, but taste. *Culture and Society* p.134
94   Eagleton, *Idea* p.67
95   Eagleton, *Idea* p.130 Lamin Sanneh agrees, arguing that to recognize that there is no escape from culture is a different matter from saying that culture is all we have. Valorization of culture

as radical protest, is concerned with these problems. This has its specifically Judeo-Christian form in prophecy, and in contemporary theology this accent is sounded most consistently by liberation theology. A socialist, Eagleton remarks elsewhere, is someone who is endlessly astonished by the injustice which marks human societies. Liberation theology in the same way begins from the situation of the oppressed and marginalized, discerning God in the command to end such oppression.

One of the problems with the elision between the two main senses of culture, as a way of life and as creative achievement, is that it leads us to think of culture as inherently positive. But all cultures are deeply marked by imbalances of power on gender, racial and class lines, structured so that some strata of the population remain at the bottom. Barth is right that if we are to talk of 'revelation', something which we cannot derive from our culture but which is set over against it and critiques it, then it has to address these injustices. What has been left out of reflection on culture, said Barth, at the close of his reflections:

> is the insight that all Christendom and its relation to culture depends entirely upon hope; that the difference between reconciliation and redemption is a fundamental difference, and so also is that between reconciliation and creation. Upon the knowledge of the limit depends also the knowledge of the promise and the law.[96]

In these remarks he anticipates the recasting of eschatology in terms of hope which Moltmann undertook in response to Ernst Bloch. Hope has to be the eschatological dimension of liberation theology because the alternatives are fatalism, despair, or acquiescence with the status quo.[97] If we say that religion (Christianity, the gospel) is part of culture but cannot be identified with it without remainder, then hope is that remainder. The source of hope is extrinsic to the system as a whole, and Christians understand it as bound up in the story of the life, death and resurrection of Christ. To say, with Barth, that culture is constituted under the sign of hope is to say the injustices which deform each and every culture cannot be final, cannot be accepted as destiny. There is a 'strange new world' towards which culture is directed, the theological symbol for which is the kingdom. Rather than culture as destiny, this, according to the gospel, is the destiny of culture, reached by the long revolution, the journey from bondage to freedom.

---

follows loss of faith in religion and leaves us with cultural fundamentalism, culture as the source of ultimate values. This is a role which he, like Terry Eagleton, believes it cannot sustain. It leaves us with inadequate grounds for value judgements and for recognizing truth. Prophetic religion cannot be content with the postmodernist project of cultural deconstruction as the arbiter of truth, or with value engendering as definitive of vocation, even if in either case culture must schematize and mediate the gospel and values express its truth claims. Without a sense of transcendence, he suggests, there is no escape from self-centredness. *Encountering* p.229

96   Barth, 'Church and Culture' p.354

97   Cf J.B.Libanio, 'Hope, Utopia, Resurrection' in I.Ellacuria and J.Sobrino(eds) *Mysterium Liberationis* Maryknoll: Orbis 1993 pp.716–728

Chapter 3

The Quality of Culture

I have argued that religion and culture can be neither separated nor identified. The prophetic dimension of religion, represented today most clearly by liberation theology, puts insistent questions to high culture about its involvement with unjust power. Equally, Arnold's counter question to religion is concerned with bigotry and narrowness of vision. To press this dialogue further we need to consider the issues Arnold classically raises for us about the relation of high and popular culture.

Despite the variety of uses of the word 'culture' noted in the first chapter, it is probably still true that if I say of someone that they are 'cultured', or 'interested in culture', it means they spend their time at the Opera, reading poetry or visiting art galleries. This presents a problem for the Church and marks a deep ambiguity in its approach to culture. On the one hand, the Church is committed to the poor. This does not mean that it is eager to do good for the poor, the 'almshouse culture' of the twelfth to nineteenth centuries. As the liberation theologians have taught us, we learn from Scripture that God has a commitment to the poor which is far deeper than that. Thus the Salvadorean theologian Jon Sobrino writes: 'the Spirit of Jesus is in the poor and, with them as his point of departure, he re-creates the entire Church'. He goes on:

> If this truth is understood in all its depth and in an authentically Trinitarian perspective, it means that the history of God advances indefectibly by way of the poor; that the Spirit of Jesus takes historical flesh in the poor; and that the poor show the direction of history that is in accord with God's plan ... For this profound reason I maintain that the Church of the poor is not a Church for the poor but a church that must be formed on the basis of the poor and that must find in them the principle of its structure, organization and mission ... This means that the poor are the authentic theological source for understanding Christian truth and practice and therefore the constitution of the Church. The poor are those who confront the Church with its basic theological problem and with the direction in which the solution to the problem is to be found.[1]

To be true to this insight would seem to mean that the Church would need to cherish popular culture, culture of the people. However, when we look at the history of the Church, at least over the last five hundred years, there seems to be, by contrast, an elective affinity between the Church and 'high' culture. The Church has attracted great painting, music and architecture. Moreover, at the heart of the Church's faith is the view that human beings are called to

---

1 J.Sobrino, *The True Church and the Poor* London: SCM 1984 p.93

perfection. 'Be perfect [*teleios*] even as your Father in heaven is perfect' (Mt 5.48).

Matthew Arnold's definition of culture as 'a study of perfection' was not factitious. Culture, we saw in the first chapter, is fundamentally about values. Arnold urged the need for culture on his contemporaries because he wanted to amend their values, to change the spiritual ethos of his society. No culture embodies the values of the kingdom. All embody profound injustices and all need radical change. When we talk about means for growth and change we come to education, which has been one of the Church's major concerns from the beginning. If our concern is the long revolution, then we need to remember that, as Freire insisted, that revolution is 'eminently pedagogical'.[2] As soon as we come to education, in turn we come to curriculum, and to 'the best which has been thought and said'.

Theological imperatives seem to pull in opposed directions, therefore. To investigate this dilemma we need to look at the tensions between popular culture and high culture, and to consider questions of value and education.

High Culture

It is in the last quarter of the eighteenth century that the word 'culture' (translating *Kultur*) was acquiring what I have argued is its dominant sense, and the one with which we are most familiar, as identical with art, music and philosophy. It 'refers essentially to intellectual, artistic, and religious facts, and has a tendency to draw a sharp dividing line between facts of this sort, on the one side, and political, economic and social facts, on the other'.[3] Thus when Paul Tillich came to elaborate a 'theology of culture' what he meant was 'the great works of the visual arts, of music, of poetry, of literature, of architecture, of dance, of philosophy'.[4] This list at once calls to mind the myriad works of 'high culture' spawned by Christian faith and theology, the great cathedrals, the mass settings and Chorales, the canon of Western art from the eleventh to the twentieth centuries, the poetry of Donne, Herbert and Milton, of Edwin Muir and R.S.Thomas.

Further back, the marriage of Christianity and Platonism from the second to the fifth centuries was also a marriage to high culture in the sense of a permanent commitment to the view that human beings have a duty to nurture the soul, that knowledge and virtue are one, and that education therefore has a key role in the forming of human beings. In *The Republic* Plato argued that since reason alone could not save us, education, by which he meant training in art, music and poetry, was essential to development of a mature human being, capable of distinguishing between right and wrong and therefore playing their part in civic life. The contribution of Platonism to Christianity in its adoption

2 P.Freire, *The Pedagogy of the Oppressed* Harmondsworth: Penguin 1972 p.43
3 Elias, *The Civilizing Process* p.4
4 Tillich, *Theology of Culture* p.46

of these views has been permanent. As we saw in the first chapter, the assertion that the gospel and culture belong together has been taken for granted since Schleiermacher, and by all his theological heirs, all of whom assume 'culture' to mean high culture.

The development of the idea of *Kultur* was, as we have seen, bound up with the rise of the middle class in Germany, and its self-differentiation from the court on the one hand and the proletariat on the other. There are a number of strands in this development, not all necessarily pulling in the same direction. There is Kant's contrast of culture and civilization, where 'culture' means the achievement of moral autonomy, the ability to think freely without tutelage. Though this is widely criticized today we have to remember its context was resistance to a highly repressive Prussian state. There is the emphasis on the truth of 'feeling', which involved a challenge to conventional morality, as both Schleiermacher and Goethe show. We should also not forget that Schleiermacher, as the translator of Plato, achieved for German what Jowett did for English fifty years later. Platonic views of education fed deeply into the newly found understanding of culture. There is an emphasis on the importance of inner harmony for which, according to Fichte, *Kultur* is 'the last and highest means to that end'.[5] There is Hegel's doctrine that in the self-unfolding of Absolute Spirit religion was the penultimate rung of a ladder which ended in philosophy. This both bound religion into high culture and subordinated it to wider cultural norms. And finally, and most important, there is the enshrining of *Bildung*, formation, in the Prussian educational reform of Wilhelm von Humboldt.

In Britain these ideas were mediated above all by Matthew Arnold, the apostle of high culture to those he called Barbarians and Philistines, as well as to the Populace. Standing broadly within the Platonic tradition, culture is, in his famous definition, 'a pursuit of our total perfection by means of getting to know, on all matters which most concern us, the best which has been thought and said in the world'.[6] Contrary to what is often said culture, for Arnold, is not elitist or a status symbol, 'an engine of social and class distinction, separating its holder, like a badge or title, from other people who have not got it'. It is motivated both by love of knowledge and by a moral and social passion for doing good and it is impossible while the individual remains isolated. For him 'the men of culture are the true apostles of equality'. In line with what he had learned from German romanticism Arnold understood culture as 'a study of perfection, and of harmonious perfection, general perfection, and perfection which consists in becoming something rather than in having something, in an inward condition of the mind and spirit'.[7]

Arnold's context was, of course, rather different – that of an aggressive laissez faire capitalism which preached 'every man for himself', deeply anti-intellectual and wedded to pragmatism, empiricism and 'faith in machinery'.

---

5 Hartman, *Fateful Question of Culture* p.213

6 Arnold, *Culture and Anarchy* p.viii

7 Arnold, *Culture and Anarchy* p.10

Where *The Times* valorized English freedom to do what one likes Arnold insisted that 'culture indefatigably tries, not to make what each raw person may like the rule by which he fashions himself; but to draw even nearer to a sense of what is indeed beautiful, graceful, and becoming, and to get the raw person to like that'.[8] When people insisted that it was coal which made England great Arnold pointed them to the achievements of Elizabethan England, not based on economic success. We have seen that Williams reproves Arnold's sneer at the way of life, and the reading habits, of the Philistines. Fair enough. But Arnold's point was that the boast of this entrepreneurial class was that wealth proves the truth of their philosophy. He was endeavouring to show the necessity for a broader and more generous view, and in his context he was surely right.

Arnold's aim was the extension of culture, in this sense, to the whole population. It might be said that Arnold's greatest triumph was to help shape that ethos which led to the founding of the BBC by Reith, who defined it in 1924 in terms of the rejection of commercialism, the extension of availability of programmes to everyone in the community, the establishment of unified control over broadcasting, and the maintenance of high standards.[9] Perhaps, however, 'triumph' is too positive a word, for the BBC has consistently proved more popular with upper middle class than with unskilled audiences and has been accused of cultural paternalism, despite its adoption of a much more populist agenda in its newer channels.[10] Making 'the best which has been thought and said' available to all would be thought by some to be elitist in its definition of the good, though, as I shall argue later in the chapter, some such notion is implicit in any idea of education. The accusation of elitism was not helped by the position of F.R.Leavis and his followers. 'In any period,' Leavis tells us, 'it is upon a very small minority that the discerning appreciation of art and literature depends':

> It is (apart from the cases of the simple and familiar) only a few who are capable of unprompted, first hand judgement. They are still a small minority, though a larger one, who are capable of endorsing such first-hand judgement by genuine personal response ... The minority capable not only of appreciating Dante, Shakespeare, Baudelaire, Hardy ... but of recognising their latest successors constitute the consciousness of the race (or a branch of it) at a given time ... Upon this minority depends our power of profiting by the finest human experience of the past; they keep alive the subtlest and most perishable parts of the tradition. Upon them depend the implicit standards that order the finer living of an age, the sense that it is worth more than that, this rather than that is the direction in which to go. In their keeping is the language, the changing idiom upon which fine living depends, and without which distinction of spirit is thwarted and incoherent. By 'culture' I mean the use of such language.[11]

---

8   Arnold, *Culture and Anarchy* pp.11–12
9   J.B.Thompson, *Ideology and Modern Culture* Cambridge: Polity 1990 p.225
10 Thompson, *Ideology and Modern Culture* p.257
11   F.R.Leavis, *Mass Civilization and Minority Culture* cited in C.Jenks, *Culture* London: Routledge 1993 p.100

This is Eliot's cultural vanguard with a vengeance. As is often pointed out, Germany had such a class, and it did very little for it in either 1914 or in 1933 and what followed. It was especially in Germany that the centrality of high culture to Christian theology became an axiom of Christian theology for more than a century. The renegade theologian Feuerbach described culture in Fichtean terms as 'nothing else than the exaltation of the individual above his subjectivity to objective universal ideas, to the contemplation of the world'.[12] Even after the carnage of the First World War the great Church historian and liberal theologian Harnack could insist that God must be understood on the basis of culture, on the basis of knowledge gathered by culture, and on the basis of ethics, if culture and one's own existence were to be protected against atheism. The First World War was fought, we remember, to protect German culture against the barbarism of England and France. In response to this the theologian Karl Barth and the socialist Rosa Luxemburg were at one. Both understood the war as a reversion to barbarism. 'The triumph of imperialism leads to the destruction of culture,' said Luxemburg:

> sporadically during a modern war, and forever, if the period of world wars that has just begun is allowed to take its damnable course to the last consequence. Thus we stand today, as Friedrich Engels prophesied ... before the awful proposition: either the triumph of imperialism and the destruction of all culture, and, as in ancient Rome, depopulation, desolation, degeneration, a vast cemetery; or, the victory of socialism, that is, the conscious struggle of the international proletariat against imperialism, against its methods, against war.[13]

Barth for his part replied to Harnack that the culture he defended could be instantiated in the statements of the war theologians of all countries: '*These* statements can definitely not be considered as the "preaching of the gospel". Whether they *protect* culture and the individual "against atheism" or whether they *sow* atheism, since they come out of polytheism, would remain an *open* question in each case.'[14]

There is no evidence that Walter Benjamin knew of this exchange, but we cannot but be reminded by it of the famous sixth thesis on the philosophy of history which he wrote in 1940, fleeing from the Nazis. Benjamin saw history as the story of the victors, who carry the spoils in their triumphal procession. These spoils are called cultural treasures, and a historical materialist, Benjamin noted, 'views them with cautious detachment':

> For without exception the cultural treasures he surveys have an origin which he cannot contemplate without horror. They owe their existence not only to the efforts of great minds and talents who have created them, but also to the anonymous toil of

12 L.Feuerbach, *The Essence of Christianity* New York: Harper 1957 p.132
13 R.Luxemburg, 'The Junius Pamphlet' (1916) in *Rosa Luxemburg Speaks* ed M.Waters New York: Pathfinder 1970 p.269
14 H.M.Rumscheidt, *Revelation and Theology: An analysis of the Barth–Harnack correspondence of 1923* Cambridge: Cambridge University Press 1972 p.30

their own contemporaries. There is no document of civilisation which is not at the same time a document of barbarism.[15]

This applies *a fortiori*, we may add, to theology and Church. It highlights the central difficulty in seeking to discriminate between good and bad in culture: that 'judged on the basis of the historical record, high culture is no more or less patriarchal and racist than mass culture'.[16] This is not to say, however, that the values high culture stands for can be abandoned, a point I shall return to below.

Popular Culture and Mass Culture

'Cultural action,' says Freire, 'either serves domination (consciously or unconsciously) or it serves the liberation of men.'[17] I began this chapter by recalling the Church's option for the poor. We now have to consider whether this might involve an option for what today is called popular culture. We shall consider some attempts to distinguish popular culture and mass culture, but it is true that they have called forth the same critique and the same defence.[18] There is, of course, a contrast between the untutored masses and the educated or noble which goes back to the very beginnings of Greek philosophy.[19] The term 'mass', however, Raymond Williams has shown, acquires new resonance at the industrial revolution, bound up with the actual increase in population, the growth of the great industrial cities, of the factory system, and of the union movement.[20] From the start it was polemical, as in Burke's famous assertion that learning was being 'trampled under the hooves of the swinish multitude'. 'Masses' was a new word for 'mob' and Williams rightly protests that there are no masses but only ways of seeing people as masses. None of us thinks of ourselves as part of 'the mass'. 'Masses are other people.'[21]

The word 'popular', on the other hand, from its ancient use as 'of the people' and therefore culture actually made by the people themselves, comes also to designate inferior kinds of work (popular literature, popular press) and work setting out to win favour (popular entertainment).[22] The idea of popular

15   W.Benjamin, *Illuminations* London: Fontana 1973 p.248

16   J.Naremore and P.Brantlinger(eds), *Modernity and Mass Culture* Bloomington: Indiana University Press 1991 p.13

17   Freire, *Pedagogy* p.146

18   An example of the difference between popular and mass culture is the attempt of the British newspaper *The Mirror*, in April 2002, to re-brand itself as a serious popular newspaper in distinction to other tabloids.

19   Patrick Brantlinger traces this history in *Bread and Circuses: Theories of Mass Culture as Social Decay* Ithaca: Cornell University Press 1983 Plato, Herodotus and Aristotle all share the view that 'the many' are irrational or bestial; that they tend to be unruly and potentially revolutionary; and that excellence is rare and noble while evil and inferiority are common Ibid p.59

20   Williams, *Culture and Society* p.287

21   Williams, *Culture and Society* p.289

22   Williams, *Keywords* p.237 Ewan MacColl recalls Hugh MacDiarmid's refusal to allow that folk songs might be great poetry. In his own view, 'When it comes to dealing with the real world,

culture may, Williams surmises, follow the 1870 Education Act which brought into being a new mass public, 'literate but untrained in reading, low in taste and habit'.[23] This, certainly, was the view of the historian G.M.Trevelyan, who, when the popular press was whipping up fear of 'the yellow peril', rather feared 'the white peril', the masses nurtured on penny dreadfuls. 'How does it concern our culture,' he wrote:

> that Shakespeare, Milton, Ruskin, in times gone by wrote in our language, if for all the countless weary ages to come the hordes that we breed and send out to swamp the world shall browse with ever-increasing appetite on the thin swollen stuff that commerce has now learnt to supply for England's spiritual and mental food?[24]

This critique is what we would call today elitist, and appeals to 'the best that has been thought and said', but Cecil Sharp's friend, Charles Marson, claimed, from a rather different position, that 'nothing indicates more terribly the state to which the capitalist system has brought us than the contemptible, puerile and wearisome trash of our modern music-hall productions'.[25]

At the end of the First World War Spengler distinguished between a *Volk* and a mass. The latter showed 'uncomprehending hostility to all traditions representative of Culture (nobility, church, privileges, dynasties, convention in art and limits of knowledge in science)'. These developments betokened 'the definite closing down of the Culture and the opening of a quite new phase of human existence'.[26]

The phrase 'mass culture' came into common use in the 1930s in response to the mass movements of fascism, and the effects of propaganda campaigns and films. Totalitarianism was the context. The critique of mass culture can be fairly evenly documented from both left and right. In Spain in 1931 Ortega y Gasset, faced with the rising tide of fascism around Europe, noted that 'The characteristic of the hour is that the commonplace mind, knowing itself to be commonplace, has the assurance to proclaim the rights of the commonplace and to impose them wherever it will.'[27] T.S.Eliot's friend, the conservative historian and cultural critic Christopher Dawson, felt that 'mechanized mass culture' threatened the freedom of the personality by the pressure of economic forces, and sacrificed higher cultural values to the lower standards of mass civilization.[28] Eliot himself believed that 'a mass culture will always be a substitute culture'.

---

the world in which people live, work, love and die, the traditional song-makers and singers are ... far superior to their classical counterparts.' *Journeyman* London: Sidgwick and Jackson 1990 pp.281–228 If we grant this it has important implications for liberation theology's approach to culture and education.

23   Williams, *Culture and Society* p.295
24   Cited in Naremore and Brantlinger(eds), *Modernity and Mass Culture* p.7
25   Cited in D.Harker, *Fakesong* Milton Keynes: Open University Press 1985 p.179
26   O.Spengler, *The Decline of the West* London: Allen & Unwin 1932 pp.33–34
27   J.Ortega y Gasset, *The Revolt of the Masses* New York: Norton 1957 p.18
28   Cited in Brantlinger, *Bread and Circuses* p.105

It was not right wing critics, however, who gave classical shape to the critique of mass culture, but two refugees from the Frankfurt school, Theodore Adorno and Max Horkheimer, writing in America in 1944. For them the growth of a 'culture industry' spelled the death of culture. 'By subordinating in the same way and to the same end all areas of intellectual creation,' they wrote:

> by occupying men's senses from the time they leave the factory in the evening to the time they clock in again the next morning with matter that bears the impress of the labour process they themselves have to sustain throughout the day, this subsumption mockingly satisfies the concept of a unified culture which the philosophers of personality contrasted with mass culture.[29]

For Adorno and Horkheimer mass culture represented the paradox that Enlightenment became anti-Enlightenment, technical progress served simply to further mass deception. People who sing the praises of technology forget that those who control it are those with the greatest power over society. The stunting of imagination and spontaneity are implicit in the very nature of the media themselves (they were thinking of sound films). The great artists have a native distrust of style whereas 'What Dadaists and expressionists called the untruth of style ... triumphs today in the sung jargon of a crooner, in the carefully contrived elegance of a film star, and even in the admirable expertise of a photograph of a peasant's squalid hut.'[30] As soon as culture becomes a common denominator it comes within the sphere of administration. 'Formerly, like Kant and Hume, they signed their letters "Your most humble and obedient servant", and undermined the foundations of throne and altar. Today they address heads of government by their first names, yet in every artistic activity they are subject to their illiterate masters.'[31] Art becomes alienation. 'Light' art (and the BBC, of course, had a 'Light' programme) is the social bad conscience of serious art. The bread which the culture industry offers is the stone of the stereotype. It is an instrument of the self-derision and alienation of human beings.[32]

Much of the complaint against popular culture is bound up with commercialism. With the development of the gramophone, radio and the cinema, remarks Michael Pickering:

> An expanding commercialism is evident and ... new material became in time increasingly accepted and consumed in terms directed by the market, as a passion for a particular song would be succeeded by another, in a commercially dictated process

---

29   T.Adorno and M.Horkheimer, *Dialectic of Enlightenment* London: Verso 1979 p.131

30   Adorno and Horkheimer, *Dialectic* p.130

31   Adorno and Horkheimer, *Dialectic* p.133

32   Milan Kundera agrees. In *The Unbearable Lightness of Being* Sabina had thought that only in the Communist world could musical barbarism reign supreme. 'Abroad, she discovered that the transformation of music into noise was a planetary process by which mankind was entering the historical phase of total ugliness. The total ugliness to come had made itself felt first as omnipresent acoustical ugliness: cars, motorcycles, electric guitars, drills, loudspeakers, sirens. The omnipresence of visual ugliness would follow.' M.Kundera, *The Unbearable Lightness of Being* London: Faber 1984 p.93

where each phase of gratification prepares the way for its own supersession and replacement in like or superficially dissimilar kind.[33]

These kinds of complaints, however, go much further back and, as Raymond Williams has pointed out, the first authentically mass form of communication was the printed book. Thus we find Wordsworth in 1799 deploring 'the craving for extraordinary incident and the thirst for outrageous stimulation' created by the rapid spread of communication and the quickening pace of life, so that 'the works of Shakespeare and Milton, are driven into neglect by frantic novels, sickly and stupid German Tragedies, and deluges of idle and extravagant stories in verse'.[34]

Can popular culture and mass culture be distinguished? Stuart Hall and Paddy Whannel felt that the typical art of the mass media was a corruption of popular art. 'Mass art often destroys all trace of individuality and idiosyncrasy which makes a work compelling and living, and assumes a sort of de-personalized quality, a no-style. The personal element then becomes detached – a way of marketing the personality of the artist.'[35] In popular art there was still genuine creativity, but 'In mass art the formula is everything – an escape from, rather than a means to, originality.'[36] They cited the television pianist Liberace, who confessed:

> My whole trick is to keep the tune well out in front. If I play Tchaikovsky I play his melodies and skip his spiritual struggles. Naturally I condense. I have to know just how many notes my audience will stand for. If there's time left over I fill in with lots of runs up and down the keyboard.[37]

The idea that the audience will only stand for 'so many notes' is what distinguishes mass culture from popular culture which, by contrast, does not patronize its audience but is prepared to make demands on it. Hannah Arendt made the distinction in terms of the reduction of culture to entertainment and therefore the alignment of culture and consumption.[38]

Hall and Whannel wrote before television ownership reached saturation point. Within a decade 97 per cent of households in Britain owned a set. Numerous reports, usually in the United States, have taken a pessimistic view. In 1958 a report spoke of 'evidence of decadence, escapism and insulation from the realities of the world' on US television and predicted that 'If we go on as we are, then history will take its revenge and retribution catch up with us.' Another commentator maintains that the need to make money means that 'the lowest common denominator is catered to'.[39] In 1972 the US Surgeon

---

33 M.Pickering, *Village Song and Culture* London: Croom Helm 1982 p.177

34 Cited in Bell, *Cultural Contradictions of Capitalism* p.85

35 S.Hall and P.Whannel, *The Popular Arts* London: Hutchinson 1964 p.68

36 Hall and Whannel, *Popular Arts* p.69

37 Hall and Whannel, *Popular Arts* p.70

38 H.Arendt, 'Society and Culture' in *Culture for the Millions?* ed N.Jacobs Princeton: Van Nostrand 1961 pp.43–53

39 Both cited in Brantlinger, *Bread and Circuses* p.251

General's report on 'Television and Growing Up' concluded that televised violence leads to social violence. Ten years later a second government report reached the same view, and the same conclusions were reached by another report in 2002.[40] Marshall McLuhan successor at New York University, Neil Postman, cites studies which found that 51 per cent of viewers could not recall a single item of news a few minutes after viewing a news programme; 21 per cent of TV viewers could not recall any news item within one hour of broadcast.[41] He delivers what he calls 'the Huxleyan warning':

> What Huxley teaches is that in the age of advanced technology, spiritual devastation is more likely to come from an enemy with a smiling face than from one whose countenance exudes suspicion and hate. In the Huxleyan prophecy, Big Brother does not watch us, by his choice. We watch him, by ours. There is no need for wardens or gates or Ministries of Truth. When a population becomes distracted by trivia, when cultural life is redefined as a perpetual round of entertainments, when serious public conversation becomes a form of baby-talk, when, in short, a people become an audience and their public business a vaudeville act, then a nation finds itself at risk; culture death is a real possibility.
>
> Huxley believed with H.G.Wells that we are in a race between education and disaster, and he wrote continuously about the necessity of our understanding the politics and epistemology of media. For in the end, he was trying to tell us that what afflicted the people in Brave New World was not that they were laughing instead of thinking, but that they did not know what they were laughing about and why they had stopped thinking.[42]

A Muslim critic of Western culture like Ziauddin Sardar agrees with this assessment. Western backpackers seek culture in non-Western destinations, he argues, because culture has disappeared in the West and been replaced by talk shows. What is increasingly seen in art galleries, watched in theatres, read in novels, is trivial, banal, ephemeral. 'The serious, the complicated, the strenuous, the enduring, the profound are not just conspicuous by their absence but are also feared and shunned.'[43]

This is, to be sure, far too sweeping, but these authors are responding to a huge shift in the cultural dominant. The culture which was led by the market, 'the charts' and 'the top ten', only possible in the wake of the affluent society, came to define popular culture. What now became hegemonic was not 'high culture' symbolized by Reith's BBC, with its public service ethos, and its assumed role as guardian of public morals and as educator, but 'cultural populism'. This valorizes plebeian culture at the expense of high culture. High

40   Brantlinger, *Bread and Circuses* p.80

41   N.Postman, *Amusing Ourselves to Death* London: Methuen 1986 p.156

42   Postman, *Amusing Ourselves to Death* p.168 John McGrath, from a left wing perspective, agrees. *The Bone Won't Break* London: Methuen 1990 pp.146–148 In 2002 a BBC programme on 'Great Britons' drew up its list through a popular poll and ended up with either media personalities or people who had recently featured on television programmes. *Private Eye* 1066 1.11.02

43   Z.Sardar, *Postmodernism and the Other* London: Pluto 1998 p.134 Sardar teaches at Middlesex University. This seems a very odd assessment of cultural life in London in the last decade of the twentieth century as it boasted a multitude of events, in every art form (and not just Western art either), which were serious, strenuous and profound, and very often oppositional.

culture is elitist, conservative, snobbish, moralizing, paternalist. Popular culture is rooted in the ethos of the working or lower middle class, progressive, indifferent to status, non-judgemental in morals, tolerant of difference. The Church has suffered directly as a result of this cultural shift, being perceived as moralizing, judgemental, middle or upper class and out of touch. Attempts to create 'alternative worship' suffer both from a perception that they are cult-like, but also from the fact that they are not alternative at all, but an attempt to accommodate the cultural dominant.

An early manifesto of the new hegemony was Paul Willis' *Profane Culture*, a study of the motor bike and hippie cultures of the late 1960s. Willis found in these groups a cultural creativity lacking in elite groups, and, in what was to become a new cliché, a streetwise critical determination not to be fooled:

> Because they are surrounded by plastic ersatz and the detritus of the bourgeoisie, there is for all that a more desperate need not to be duped, but to find meaning and potential within what they find – they have nothing else. And in certain respects their eyes are clearer. For all the shit, there is a freedom in the market, on the streets, in the pubs and dance halls. And what is provided cynically for the profit of others and not for the benefit of the individual at least avoids certain kinds of moral over-rides.[44]

The sneer at 'moral over-rides' is characteristic of the new populism. Culturally, in Britain, 'posh' accents became a social liability (they were dropped by the BBC), and dressing down ('grunge') became fashionable. Popular culture quickly became defined in terms of 'meanings, pleasures and identities'. For a conservative like Daniel Bell hedonism is a world of make believe in which one lives for expectations, for what will come rather than what it is. 'It is no accident,' he wrote in 1976:

> that the successful new magazine of the previous decade was called Playboy and that its success – a circulation of 6 million by 1970 – is due largely to the fact that it encourages fantasies of male sexual prowess. If ... sex is the last frontier in American life, then the achievement motive in a go-go society finds its acme in sex. In the 1950s and the 1960s the cult of Orgasms succeeded the cult of Mammon as the basic passion of American life.[45]

But like it or not, 'pleasure' is the new cultural dominant, centred on the body and its 'meanings'. For a popular culture theorist like John Fiske such pleasures are intrinsically radical, designed either to shock the bourgeois, or to resist structures of domination especially those internalized ones of 'the discipline over self and others that those with power attempt so insistently to exert'.[46] There was now an acknowledgement and even glorification of the vulgar: 'the popular pleasures and transgressions of the carnivalesque tradition of the common people. Here there is no dignity, no humanistic ideals, no cultivation and improvement, no *Bildungsprozess*, sweetness or light, only the

---

44 P.Willis, *Profane Culture* London: Routledge & Kegan Paul 1978 p.5
45 Bell, *Cultural Contradictions* p.70
46 J.Fiske, *Understanding Popular Culture* London: Routledge 1989 p.69

egalitarian right to be different – of otherness, to remain the other in its own inchoate terms.'[47] The difficulty for a Church committed to the priority of the poor could not be stated more sharply.

By 1989 Michael Denning could tell us: 'Mass culture won; there is nothing else.' 'We have come to the end of "mass culture"; the debates and positions which named "mass culture" as an other have been superseded. There is no mass culture out there; it is the very element we all breathe.'[48] Under capitalism all culture is mass culture and there is now very little cultural production outside the commodity form. This applies to religion as to everything else, both in the sense that we can shop around for our religious commodities, but also in the sense that leisure comes to take on the aura of the sacred.[49] This is Williams' point about 'masses' and mass culture, but a point made by assimilation. 'There are no masses' because we are all masses. To this position Terry Eagleton responds that it is a culturalist error to take television, supermarket, and life style as definitive of late capitalist experience and to 'pass in silence over such activities as studying the bible, running a rape crisis centre, joining the territorial army and teaching one's children to speak Welsh'.[50] John McGrath argued similarly that there were many cultural fora, from pubs to drama groups to church groups to folk clubs, in which popular culture remained the site of 'an ongoing struggle' pitched against populism.[51] It is this culture, popular but not populist, which I now want to reflect on. For want of a better term I shall call it 'folk culture'.

Folk Culture

It was Herder who put the term 'folk culture' on the intellectual map. Herder pointed away from the universalizing culture aspired to by the *philosophes* and towards the priority of local cultures. He was interested in the culture of a whole people (*Kultur des Volkes*) and not just of its intellectuals, believing that each *Volk* had its own distinctive form of expression, in language above all, but also in song, dance, drama and so forth. At this stage folk culture and popular culture were one and the same, and it was this culture which was in mind when Tom Paine insisted that 'the people' must be the ultimate source of true learning or culture. Herder's perspective is pre-industrial. His folk culture is a product of that rooted society, predominantly a peasant culture, but still organically related to 'the town' through markets, which I mentioned in the first chapter. It is the culture of dialect, of different traditions of building, of the cultivation and processing of food, of myriad differences on the micro level.

47   Featherstone, *Consumer Culture and Postmodernism* London: Sage 1991 p.136
48   M.Denning, 'The End of Mass Culture' in Naremore and Brantlingert(eds) *Modernity and Mass Culture* p.257
49   Featherstone, *Consumer Culture and Postmodernism* p.113
50   Eagleton, *Ideology* London: Verso 1991 p.39
51   McGrath, *The Bone Won't Break* pp.62–65

This is one strand of what we mean by 'folk culture' and in mainland Europe, and in social anthropology, it continues far into the twentieth century. There is, however, another strand. Herder was an enthusiast for James Macpherson's Ossianic poems, and was initially taken in by these. The general enthusiasm with which these were greeted in Europe marked a reaction to classicism and the start of the Romantic interest in the small and humble, and therefore in the peasantry. The way for it had been prepared by the tradition of pastoral which ran right back to Theocritus, and which was a powerful influence on English poetry because Virgil's Eclogues and Horace's Odes were standard texts in European schools.[52] This tradition contrasted the simplicity and security of rural life with the falsity and danger of the court – a tradition powerfully reiterated by Shakespeare. Rousseau's 'noble savage' took his place in this tradition, and the next step, to the noble peasant found on one's very doorstep, was not difficult. In Britain what are now called 'folk' songs and dances had been collected and retailed for bourgeois audiences from the 1660s onwards.[53] At first they were simply retailed as national songs and dances, but already by 1723 Allan Ramsey's *Scots Songs* included material which illustrated 'the peculiarities of the lower orders' (a euphemism for bawdiness) and by the end of the century the contrast between unspoiled peasant and superficial town was taken for granted.[54]

In English (though not in German) the meaning of 'folk', however, quickly began to change. In mainland Europe it was, and to some extent still is, linked to national enthusiasms, and composers like Dvořák, Bartók and Vaughan Williams all drew heavily on 'folk music' for inspiration. By the middle of the nineteenth century in Britain, however, the word 'folk' had come to characterize the peasantry rather than the urban proletariat, and a way of life that was passing.[55] The English term 'folk-lore' was coined by W.J.Thoms, one of the founders of the Folk-Lore Society, in 1846 to refer especially to 'popular antiquities'.[56] As the century wore on the movement to collect the old traditions, songs and dances, already more than a hundred and fifty years old, became more consistent and attempted, at any rate, to be more 'scientific'. Dave Harker has illustrated the sheer fantasy involved in much of the middle and upper class folk song collecting, and the extent to which traditions were treated, as they were treated in the colonies, as property.[57] He demonstrates the extent to which the collectors found what they wanted to find and ignored the extent to which

---

52 See on this R.Williams, *The Country and the City* London: Hogarth 1985 chapter 3

53 Harker, *Fakesong*

54 Harker, *Fakesong* pp.10, 25

55 This is the point of Pickering and Green's objection that 'The "folk" have never existed. There have only ever been people called the "folk" by others existing socially and culturally outside of those groups so designated' in M.Pickering and T.Green, *Everyday Culture: Popular Song and the Vernacular Milieu* Milton Keynes: Open University Press 1987 p.13

56 Williams, *Keywords* p.136 Georgina Boyes draws attention to the way in which Tylor's work on primitive culture was taken up by British folk-lorists, who characterized folk traditions as 'survivals' from a primitive past. *The Imagined Village* Manchester: Manchester University Press 1993 p.8

57 Harker, *Fakesong* p.159

'folk song' was simply popular song – very often dominated by music hall, as the songs of the Copper family illustrate.[58] The collectors did not want to know this: for them 'the folk' represented an older and purer England. The composer Sir Hubert Parry, well known to those who attend that artefact of high culture, choral evensong, can be their spokesman. Noting that music was 'of the greatest service in refining the less prosperous classes and keeping them out of mischief', he nevertheless insisted that it had to be the right kind of music:

> This becomes most painfully evident if any collection of folk-songs of Ireland or Scotland or England or France or Germany or Russia be examined, and compared with the music in which the same sections of society delight in our time. The folk songs, which were once the prerogative and the pride of the people in its widest sense, are characterised by the purest beauty, by a simplicity, sincerity, tenderness, playfulness, innocent gaiety, healthy vigour; while the modern tunes, in which even the little country urchins wallow as soon as they can toddle, represent all the brazen affrontery, the meanest grossness, and the most hideous and blatant repulsiveness which our queerly compounded humanity is heir to. The people who wallow do not know that what they are wallowing in is degrading.[59]

What emerged from the work of great collectors like Sabine Baring-Gould – Church of England parson, JP and landowner – and Cecil Sharp, was the identification of folk tradition with the pre-industrial – and all the other changes of Williams' 'long revolution'. Cecil Sharp and his Somerset parson collaborator Charles Marson expressed it thus:

> The clapperings of the steam-binder have killed [folk song] from the harvest field; the board school master, a perfect Herod among the Innocents, slays it in the children by his crusade against all dialect but his own ... The purveyors of cheap harmoniums, singing evangelists with their unspeakable songs and solos, choir masters with their doggerel for Sunday and their clap-trap for the penny-reading, all prey upon the persecuted and forsaken remnant. Folk-song, unknown in the drawing-room, hunted out of the school, chased by the chapel deacons, derided by the middle classes, and despised by those who have been uneducated into the three R's, takes refuge in the fastnesses of tap-rooms, poor cottages and outlying hamlets. It harbours in the heathen kingdoms and the wilder parts. It comes out very shyly, late at night, and is heard when the gentry have gone home to bed, when the barrack-room has exhausted its Music-hall menu.[60]

Industrialization, universal education, evangelical Christianity, church choirs, music hall – these are the enemies of the folk tradition. If you valorize the folk tradition, therefore, you must seem to be against these things. F.R.Leavis and Denys Thompson felt the same way. What we have lost, they claimed, is the organic community with the living culture it embodies – the influence of the *Gemeinschaft–Gesellschaft* distinction is strong in most of these complaints. At the heart of it all is new technology. 'Folk-songs, folk dances, Cotswold

58   Bob Copper, *A Song for Every Season* London: Heinemann 1971
59   Sir H.Parry, *Style in Musical Art* London: Macmillan 1924 p.112 quoted in Pickering, *Village Song* p.50
60   Cited in Harker, *Fakesong* pp.179–180

cottages and handicraft products are a sign of something more: an art of life, a way of living, ordered and patterned, involving social arts, codes of intercourse and a responsive adjustment, growing out of immemorial experience, to the natural environment and the rhythm of the year.' It was machinery, they argued, which had destroyed the old ways of life, and prevented the growth of new in virtue of the constant change involved.[61]

In many respects they were right, of course. The nostalgia was not simply middle class, as Flora Thompson and Laurie Lee, both from 'peasant' backgrounds, make clear. Industrialization and urbanization were felt as both loss and gain by those they affected and there is no reason to think that those informants who told Baring-Gould or Sharp that everything had been different twenty, thirty or forty years before were making things up, nor to doubt their assessment that in some respects things were 'better' then. No doubt singing, storytelling and mumming traditions were affected, and some worthwhile patterns of peasant community lost. In their hatred of what capitalism had done to popular culture Sharp and Marson were not simply expressing an alienated middle class nostalgia but giving voice to a mood widely felt at the time, as G.M.Hopkins' *God's Grandeur* classically portrays. William Morris, too, famously said that 'Apart from the desire to produce beautiful things, the leading passion of my life has been and is hatred of modern civilization.'[62] The problem in the Sharp and Marson, or Leavis and Thompson, retrospective was in the failure to recognize the unjust and sometimes downright cruel exploitation which also characterized that old order, the overlooking of the extent to which mechanization represented a relief from 'useless toil', and the failure to see the extent to which unionization represented real gain.[63]

Folk culture and popular culture become differentiated towards the end of the nineteenth century with the advent of mass forms of communication. Michael Pickering argues that the crucial changes are twofold. First, a move from the amateur and local performer to the star performer; second, the increasing commercialization of performance and thus the move from cultural expression to cultural commodity.[64] We can add to this the enormous change represented by 'mechanical reproduction' in that music could now be enjoyed at any time, in the home, and did not require getting together with others, nor the acquisition of skill. These changes happened, of course, across Europe, but they had delayed impact in countries which kept a large peasantry. England (as opposed to Scotland, Wales and Ireland) was peculiar in the extent to which it lost its peasantry – the Great War was the *coup de grâce*.

In Germany the use of *völkisch* ideas by the Nazis cast a deep shadow on folk traditions, but in Britain and the United States a new round of the collecting of songs and traditions began after the Second World War, and this spawned the

---

61   F.R.Leavis and D.Thompson, *Culture and Environment* London: Chatto and Windus 1964 p.1

62   W.Morris, *The Earthly Paradise* in *The Collected Works of William Morris* London: Longman 1910–1915 vol III p.3

63   Boyes shows how the search for social consensus, over and above class division, drove much of the early folk revival. *Imagined Village* pp.32, 36, 65

64   Pickering, *Village Song* p.167

'folk revival' of the 1950s and 1960s, a largely urban movement, and linked to new forms of 'leisure'.[65] A.L.Lloyd, Ewan MacColl and others put the emphasis on urban and industrial folk song, rather than on agriculture, in conscious reaction to the pastoral image cultivated by Sharp. At the same time, as Harker has shown, though they came from the polar opposite end of the political spectrum to Sharp, they made many of the same assumptions about the nature of folk music. In any event this revival was quickly overtaken and outflanked by what has come to be known as 'pop' music – popular, but not 'of the people' in the sense that it was claimed the old folk music had been.

As the energy and enthusiasm of this revival ran out, scholarship became increasingly sceptical about some of the claims gathered around the idea of 'the folk'. For Michael Pickering the term 'folk' conveys many unfortunate assumptions, including:

> unverified suppositions of unspecified longevity for specific features of oral tradition ... assumptions of an exclusive sense of rusticity ... isolation from urban/industrial ways and forms ... a lost organic community ... communal origins (rather than intermeshed processes of communal and individual re-creation) of such features of popular culture as song and dance ... a canonical purity of 'folk' song ... constricting definitional conditions; and so on.[66]

Many of these dubious claims were present in the Ossian fraud, and have thus been around since the discovery of 'folk' music. At the same time it is important not to throw out the baby with the bath water. Whilst it is now agreed that what we call folk song was always a living tradition, integrating new material all of the time, that it had determinate authors rather than being simply an 'emerging' common culture, and whilst much of the tradition may be relatively recent, it is hard to doubt that some of it is very ancient indeed. We know this is true of some carols, for instance, and a song like 'Tam Lin' almost certainly contains very ancient material.

Much of the sociological discussion of the significance of folk culture, which denies any distinction between folk and popular culture, is guilty of an extreme Anglocentric and metropolitan bias.[67] This discussion assumes that folk culture is the predecessor of popular culture, and disappears into it, but it remains true at the beginning of the twenty-first century that 'folk music', not designated as such, but simply as music traditionally enjoyed by the majority of the people, is a cultural dominant in most parts of the world.[68] In the Baltic

---

65   There were links to fascism in the British revival, but they never became dominant. Two of the leading members of the postwar revival were both members of the Communist Party. Boyes, *Imagined Village* p.162

66   Pickering, *Village Song* p.20 Many of these false ideas are reproduced by Fiske, *Understanding Popular Culture* p.173

67   So, for example, Jim Collins, *Uncommon Cultures: Popular Culture and Postmodernism* London: Routledge 1989 p.18

68   Folk music enjoys far more airtime on Scottish or Irish radio than it does in England, for instance, where it has been virtually scheduled out altogether. This is in marked contrast to the early days of BBC broadcasting. Boyes, *Imagined Village* p.144

states folk music in Herder's sense – as music expressing Latvian, Lithuanian or Estonian identity as opposed to their domination by other cultures reaching back at least six hundred years – was vital in 'the singing revolution' of 1988 to 1991, and remains a vibrant expression of local culture.[69] The same may be said of countries like Greece or Turkey, where an indigenous music has not been swallowed up by Anglo-American popular music, and for much of Asia, Africa and Latin America.[70] Speaking of the shift of intellectual sensibility in Brazil between the 1950s and the 1980s, a shift which embraces the move of liberation theology as well, Osiel writes:

> the shift … from the fifties to the present could be crudely summarized as one from a negative to a positive view of popular culture. The intellectuals once perceived in the religious and recreational practices of the poor the very antithesis of what they sought for their country's future. The theologians saw doctrine, deviation and paganism. The liberal politicians saw illogic and unreason. The Marxists saw alienation and false consciousness. The social scientists saw particularism and ascriptiveness. All four saw superstition. Now they find spontaneity, communality and authenticity in the culture of the poor, values which should not be sacrificed for the falsely found universalism of [Western modernity].[71]

One of the great failures of liberation theology has been, in its concentration on class, to miss out on the question of ancient, indigenous cultures, with Aztec, Mayan, Misquito or other roots, and this proved a devastating weakness. The hostility to false universalism and the return to particularity implies precisely a new sensitivity to folk traditions. If we take a global view, therefore, and not a view centred in London, New York and California, what has come to be called 'folk culture' remains a cultural dominant. Even in England it is going too far to speak of this culture as 'shell-like and empty within',[72] for the culture associated with the second revival continues to maintain important values as a form of what Williams calls 'residual culture'. It is this category of residual culture which I want to develop. By it is meant an active factor within cultural process which is neither elite nor driven by consumerism. As Christopher Lasch notes, contemporary cultural criticism should not only attend to mass culture and the tradition of debate about it but should also examine:

---

69   This was explored in a series of programmes made by the BBC and broadcast from 18 to 22 February 2002 called 'Baltic nights'. The claim was that some Estonian folk song was 'thousands' of years old. At the same time we would not describe these cultures as 'folk cultures'. The English word is now too wedded to the sense of 'pre-industrial' for that.

70   In his report on Bangladesh Jeremy Seabrook cites a Bangladeshi informant who says: 'The fundamentalists provide programmes for the young. They have networks all over the country. And the Western interests are also busy, promoting their values through satellite dishes, pop culture, and consumerism. Bangali culture must be protected, against the attack by fundamentalism on one side and Western culture on the other, not to mention India and its cultural junk. Our hope is among the poor. Most cannot afford TV. They still live Bangali culture and it lives in them.' *Freedom Unfinished* London: Zed 2001 p.55

71   Cited in Featherstone, *Consumer Culture and Postmodernism* p.140

72   Pickering, *Village Song* p.164 The workers' theatre associated with John McGrath and 7/84 also represented continuities with this culture.

the persistence of allegedly outmoded forms of particularism ... that have not only
proved resistant to the melting pot but continue to provide people with the
psychological and spiritual resources essential for democratic citizenship and for a
truly cosmopolitan outlook, as opposed to the deracinated, disoriented outlook that
is so often confused, nowadays, with intellectual liberation.[73]

Dangerous as it may be to forge alliances with cultural conservatives I believe
both that worldwide what I am calling folk culture has precisely these resources
to offer and that within the West the Church almost uniquely embodies such
resources, precisely because it lives by tradition and embodies in its liturgical
life so many aspects of the older culture.

This is particularly true for folk music which, even in England, 'remains
modestly alternative in motivation to the realization of profit, and alternative
in experience to mass market consumption'. As Pickering and Green put it:

> it preserves an area of cultural activity and experience that is different to mass
> market consumption. It involves, in a divergent process, working on and with what is
> consumed, conserving older material that is of no current interest to the market, or
> creating new material that is likewise commercially unviable at the time of
> production.[74]

The difference in content from what has come to be called 'popular' music can
also be noted. In addition to songs about erotic love, there are also a great
many work songs, story ballads, political songs, protest songs, and religious
and ceremonial songs.[75] Harker notes (sympathetically) the left political slant
of the second revival, but far from that being a function of popular front
politics we might rather ask, as Dalit activists have asked in India, whether this
form of song does not preserve many forms of popular protest against the
dominant political and social order not tied to the policies of any political
party.[76] In this respect the relative commercial failure of folk song is a blessing,
for it is not subject to the constraints which commercial success imposes. In
general 'folk song' seems to have maintained an oppositional stance *vis-à-vis*
both elites and the capitalist market economy.[77]

For the theological relevance of this discussion I appeal once again to the
notion of residual culture. Of course it is interesting that the question of

---

73   Cited in Pickering and Green, *Everyday Culture* p.34

74   M.Pickering and T.Green, 'Towards a Cartography of the Vernacular Milieu' in Pickering
and Green *Everyday Culture* p.3

75   Ewan MacColl asks of folk clubs: 'Where else can you hear people singing songs made up by
farm labourers, sailors, weavers, coal-miners and others, 100 or 500 years ago? Where else can you
go and hear a song made up yesterday about an incident reported earlier on the media? At which
other kind of entertainment does the person sitting next to you suddenly get up and sing a song?'
Journeyman p.298 Bert Lloyd defended folk song against fellow communists who argued that there
could not be folk song in a capitalist society by arguing that folk-lore was essentially 'an everyday
affair'. Boyes, *Imagined Village* p.201

76   T.Appavoo, *Folk Lore for Change* Madurai: TTS 1986

77   Think, for example, of figures like Dick Gaughan, Leon Rosselson and Eric Bogle. In Britain
it is hard to think of a right wing folk singer, though of course folk music was mobilized by the
Nazis, and supports various unsavoury regimes elsewhere in the world.

theological relevance would not have arisen had we been talking about 'high' culture. As I have already argued in the first chapter, and in the introduction to this chapter, culture is about values. 'Folk' culture, I have argued, both preserves spiritual values which are in danger of being swamped by a consumer culture and remains significantly committed to non-celebrity, local performance. To the objection that it has virtually died out my reply is that this is not true for most cultural traditions, and secondly that, even in England, where the folk tradition has withered probably more than any other country, it retains deep roots. The fundamental theological significance of the folk tradition is to be found in the spirituality and values it preserves, especially when these have been saturated with the gospel, as is the case in much of Europe and North America. It is also true, however, that it survives in an important way in specifically Church contexts.

Michael Pickering points out that Methodism and Evangelicalism, in different ways, had enormous consequences for popular culture, and argues that ultimately they served not to liberate but to 'bind with briars'.[78] That judgment is surely too global. For many centuries, at the parish level, folk music and church music were virtually indistinguishable. The disappearance of the old village musicians, memorialized in Hardy's *Under the Greenwood Tree*, and the embourgeoisment of church music through the Royal School of Church Music in England, did not eliminate hymn singing. In some cases, as in Percy Dearmer's *English Hymnal*, the influence of the first wave of interest in folk music was strong, and hymn singing remains a practice which, in its combination of old and new material, and in its congregational or popular basis, remains close to a 'folk' tradition.[79]

In this respect, whilst there is much to deplore in current church music, there is also a modest return to the old church band, and this is to be welcomed. Just as the Bruderhof offer a base from which alternative regimes to capital may be imagined, so the continuing and living tradition of congregational music making offers a 'modest alternative' to the dominant capitalist-centred entertainment tradition, and it is no accident that the best material emerges from those areas, like Scotland, where the distinction between folk and popular was never fully made.[80] We should also reject the patronizing attitude with which folk culture in all its dimensions was often regarded, recognizing with Simone Weil that much of it was quite simply 'superb'.[81]

To return now to the opening remarks of this chapter. If it is true that 'the poor show the direction of history that is in accord with God's plan' then this surely indicates that the enthusiasm of Dearmer and others for the folk tradition was not mistaken. When every criticism of the romanticization of this tradition has been allowed it remains true that we hear the voice of the marginalized in this tradition as we hear it nowhere else before the advent of

---

78 Pickering, *Village Song* p.164
79 This is conceding Harker's point that folk songs have from the start been selectively collected and presented.
80 Thinking especially of John Bell, and the production of *Common Ground*.
81 Weil, *Roots* p.84

blues music. Both the celebration of ordinary life, and the protest against the injustice of a tyrannical social system, are theologically significant if the premises of liberation theology are granted. With great richness and depth it forms part of the tradition of radical theology. At the same time the very fact that I need to defend it in this way reflects the rise to dominance of the cultural populist view. This raises urgent cultural and theological questions about value, discernment and power.

The Question of Values

Perhaps in response to Leavis' arguments (the vocabulary of which it uses) Raymond Williams wrote the essay 'Culture is Ordinary' in 1958. He found, amongst his own working class family, 'as much natural fineness of feeling, as much quick discrimination, as much clear grasp of ideas within the range of experience, as I have found anywhere'.[82] He agreed that much popular culture was 'observably bad' but denied that this was a true guide to the state of mind and feeling of its consumers. On the other hand he remained quite clear on why the things he liked were better than the cultural preferences of the rest of his family.

In the intervening period avowing such clarity has been deemed cultural snobbery. It is of course true that, as Terry Eagleton notes, the boundary between 'high' and 'low' culture has been eroded by such genres as film. This does not mean that it ceases to be worthwhile to talk about high culture nor that the kind of cultural discrimination Leavis championed has ceased to be relevant. The playwright David Hare in a television interview in 1991 rejected the idea that the poetry of Bob Dylan was as good as that of Keats. For him this was an instance of the populist ideology concerning the equivalence of all cultural products. In arguing the contrary he took on 'the current overbearing political correctness of a public opinion which, masquerading as democracy, is in fact only the fear, or at worst the inability, to make critical judgements concerning taste and quality'.[83] This is the aesthetic version of Alasdair MacIntyre's argument about the end of virtue in a culture of emotivism. If we cannot accept a split between ethics and aesthetics, any more than between fact and value, we cannot get away from criteria of value. Hare argued for absolute standards on the ground that good or great art demands 'the greatest effort and engagement on the part of its creator and its audience', and arrived from here at an Arnoldian view of culture as that which extends human potential to its furthest reach.[84]

According to the champions of the cultural populism which has become the new orthodoxy since the 1980s, 'the masses' both discern and discriminate, but they do it in different ways than those imagined by intellectuals like Hare. John

---

82   Williams, *Resources* p.12
83   Jenks, *Culture* p.3
84   Jenks, *Culture* p.3

Fiske, for example, points out that films with major stars and budgets still fail at the box office; that four out of five new prime time TV shows will be axed before the end of the season; that eight or nine out of ten new products, however heavily advertised, fail in their first year. All this shows, he argues, that people are not fooled, and that they discriminate in what they are watching.[85] Critiques of television like Postman's, for Fiske, overlook the complexity and creativity by which the subordinate cope with the commodity system and its ideology in their everyday lives. Television is a cultural resource that people use as they wish, not a cultural tyrant dictating its uses and dominating its users.[86] Jim Collins agrees. Just as in the older folk culture, he believes, people articulate mass media texts in specific ways, and therefore participate actively in the production of any meanings these texts might have as they circulate in society. 'The end result is a fragmentation of a monolithic public into multiple formations that articulate the same texts in quite different ways.'[87]

The difference between high art and popular does not lie in an absence of discrimination in the latter. Rather, people discriminate in different ways. Those who are well off can afford the luxury of aesthetics. People who are subordinate, however, are challenged constantly by the conditions of their social experience. 'They do not need challenge in their art as well. What they need is that art be of use in meeting the challenges of which their daily lives are composed.'[88] The 'what they need' here is arguably as patronizing as anything written by Leavis, which seems to apply as well to Nicholas Abercrombie's argument that viewers appropriate television by paying fitful attention, talking while the set is on, hopping between channels, not following a series episode by episode and using a video recorder to watch favourite episodes over and over again.[89]

The new situation led to a re-evaluation of the work of the Frankfurt school. Their critique, argues John Thompson, was strongly influenced by Weber's idea of rationalization and this resulted in an exaggerated view of the cohesive character of modern societies. It is by no means clear that the culture industry has the consequences they suggest. Echoing Williams' point about the mismatch between the 'observable badness' of popular culture and the fineness of feeling one actually finds, Thompson agrees with the populists that 'the reception and appropriation of cultural products is a complex social process which involves an ongoing activity of interpretation and the assimilation of the meaningful content to the socially structured background characteristics of particular individuals and groups'. Modern societies have a great deal of

85 J.Fiske, 'Popular discrimination' in Naremore and Brantlinger(eds) *Modernity and Mass Culture* p.103
86 Fiske, *Understanding Popular Culture* p.153
87 Collins, *Uncommon Cultures* p.18
88 Fiske, 'Popular discrimination' p.110
89 N.Abercrombie, 'Popular Culture and Ideological Effects' in N.Abercrombie et al(eds) *Dominant Ideologies* London: Unwin Hyman 1990 p.225

diversity, disorganization, dissent and resistance, and individuals are not integrated into the existing social order that easily.[90]

The possibility of resistance in a culture dominated by mass media is one of the key questions at issue. Ben Barber is deeply sceptical of these possibilities. Gangsta rap musicians think they are using rock to take on the official culture, he says:

> But of course the official culture owns them rock, stock and barrel and it is they who are being used ... MTV is about the sound of American hot and American cool, about style and affect where nothing is quite as it seems, where 'bad' is good and lovers are bitches and killing is enlivening and where politics doesn't count but pictures are politics.[91]

Jim McGuigan responds to those who argue for resistance amongst television viewers that they seem not to live in a world where sexism, racism and xenophobia circulate amongst ordinary people. Fiske's conception of popular culture, he argues, 'represents a drastic narrowing of vision: the gap between "popular" and "mass" culture is finally closed with no residual tension ... Fiske's outer limit position represents a kind of neo-Benthamite radicalism, combining utilitarian pleasure-seeking implicitly, and in fact quite consistently, with laissez-faire economics.'[92] There are, he notes, 'questions of critique, quality and explanation to be revisited and developed further if we want to avoid abjectly uncritical complicity with prevailing free market ideology and its hidden powers'.[93] McGuigan dismisses Postman's position as 'essentialist and arrogant', but nevertheless insists that the counter critique seems to imply that there is nothing beyond the unqualified pleasures of consumer sovereignty in the marketplace, and that this signals a loss of the ability to develop a political critique or any vision of a better human future:[94]

> The study of culture is nothing if it is not about values. A disenchanted, anti-moralistic, anti-judgemental stance constructed in opposition to cultural and political zealotry only takes you so far. The posture may be cool, detached and irreverent but it is not value-free. New revisionism is rooted in populist sentiments of an increasingly slippery kind. And it is striking how a pact has been made, overtly or covertly, with economic liberalism, rediscovering the virtues of the market as a cultural provider and incitement to pleasure.[95]

Popular culture is a consumer culture and this is premised on the expansion of capitalist commodity production. To use the term 'consumer culture', argues Mike Featherstone, 'is to emphasize that the world of goods and their principles of structuration are central to the understanding of contemporary society'. A consumer culture puts the emphasis on the cultural dimension of the

---

90 Thompson, *Ideology and Modern Culture* p.107
91 B.Barber, *Jihad vs McWorld* New York: Ballantyne 1995 p.110
92 J.McGuigan, *Cultural Populism* London: Routledge 1992 p.73
93 McGuigan, *Cultural Populism* p.75
94 McGuigan, *Cultural Populism* p.119
95 McGuigan, *Cultural Populism* p.173

economy, and therefore on the subsumption of meaning and value to profit.[96] The effect of this has been seen in programming. One of New York's two classical music channels was closed on the grounds that one channel saturated the market. Ben Barber comments: 'How can the public be represented by markets that privilege individual consumption, taken consumer by consumer, but have no way of representing public goods – what individuals share and thus what makes them more than consumers? Where are the market incentives to protect public interest?'[97] Cultural populism's solidarity with ordinary people, McGuigan notes, has become increasingly sentimental, and the taken for granted schism between micro processes of meaning and the macro processes of political economy means that its explanatory power is increasingly limited.[98] A Church which has opposition to Mammon as part of its credo can only be sceptical of a form of culture which is a function of the market.

In 'Culture is Ordinary' Williams not only argued that culture was found amongst ordinary people but also deplored the fashionable sneer at 'culture vultures'. 'It is plain,' he wrote, 'that what may have started as a feeling about hypocrisy, or about pretentiousness is becoming a guilt ridden tic at the mention of any serious standards whatsoever.'[99] Half a century on, that guilt-ridden tic characterizes a whole culture. Writing in the British newspaper *The Mirror* about an edition of the BBC's 'Top of the Pops' show in which one star sang, 'I love it when you smack my arse', and another used the word 'motherfucker', Tony Parsons commented that he had come to the realization that 'foul-mouthed, dick-grabbing rebellion had gone mainstream. Bad behaviour is as much cliché as spiked hair, discreet tattoos and trousers that look old when they are brand new ... Profanity is the new MOR. Everybody is a foul-mouthed rebel now.'[100] 'Is it all come to this, in the end,' asked Williams in 1961(!), 'that the long history of the press in Britain should reach its consummation in a declining number of newspapers, in ownership by a very few large groups, and in the acceptance (varied between social groups but evident in all) of the worst kind of journalism?'[101]

The working class culture which Williams grew up with, for which education was one of the highest priorities, has, then, evaporated into a populism, of which the UK tabloid the *Sun* is a symbol, which disputes absolutist criteria of quality. Williams agreed with Arnold that 'a desire to know what is best, and to do what is good, is the whole positive nature of man'.[102] By no stretch of the imagination can this be said to characterize the owners or editorial stance of the current mass media, one of whom, in Britain, is currently a pornographer. 'We need to concentrate,' said Williams, presciently, 'not on man's natural goodness or badness but on the nature of the controlling social relations.' It is

96 Featherstone, *Consumer Culture and Postmodernism* p.84
97 Barber, *Jihad vs McWorld* p.86
98 McGuigan, *Cultural Populism* p.171
99 Williams, *Resources* p.12
100 *The Mirror* Monday 25 February 2002
101 Williams, *Long Revolution* p.236
102 Williams, *Resources* p.10

not only intellectuals who have thought in terms of 'the masses'. Those who own the mass media share the same view, perhaps from a more cynical perspective, and seek to profit by it. 'To the degree that we reject this kind of exploitation, we shall reject its ideology, and seek a new definition of communication.' The whole theory of mass communication depends, he said, on a minority in some way exploiting a majority. The easy slogan 'We are all democrats now' is quite untrue, for it ignores relations of power.[103] 'The central problem of our society, in the coming half century,' Williams wrote in 1958, 'is the use of our new resources to make a good common culture.'[104] It is this part of Williams' agenda which has not been addressed, and it raises the question of education. It is in terms of a theology of education that the Church must fundamentally address the issues of cultural populism.

The Role of Education

'L'éducation peut tout': that is Helvétius in 1758. Part of the dialectic of Enlightenment which we cannot challenge is the fundamental question put to such confidence. Since the introduction of universal schooling there has been a tendency to confuse education with school and university, as Ivan Illich famously insisted.[105] It is useful, therefore, to listen to an earlier voice, that of Herder in his *Ideas for a Philosophy of History*:

> All education arises from imitation and exercise, by means of which the model passes into the copy. What better word is there for this transmission than tradition? But the imitator must have powers to retrieve and convert into his own nature what has been transmitted to him, just like the food he eats ... Education, which performs the function of transmitting social traditions, can be said to be genetic, by virtue of the manner in which the transmission takes place, and organic, by virtue of the manner in which that which is being transmitted is assimilated and applied. We may term this second genesis, which permeates man's whole life, *enlightenment*, by the light it affords to his understanding, or *culture*, in so far as it is comparable to the cultivation of the soil. But whichever term we prefer, its connotation is the same in two important respects: it is continuous and it is world wide ... The difference between the so called enlightened and unenlightened, or between the cultured and uncultured peoples, is not one of kind but merely of degree.[106]

Education, then, is not confined to school, but is 'continuous and world wide', co-extensive with culture, and therefore identical with Williams' 'long revolution'. One of the implications of this is that we have to recognize that craft apprenticeships are as important educationally as university training, as Leavis and Thompson insisted.[107]

103   Williams, *Culture and Society* pp.300, 302
104   Williams, *Resources* p.10
105   I.Illich, *Deschooling Society* Harmondsworth: Penguin 1973
106   Herder, 'Ideas for a Philosophy of History' in Barnard(ed) *Herder* p.313
107   Training in craft involved 'a subtle training of hand, eye and body in co-ordination ... Their work trained them aesthetically and morally (consider, for example, their insistence on maintaining

Coleridge shared a similar view. As we saw in the previous chapter, theology occupied a central place in the educational role of the clerisy. Under the name of theology, Coleridge wrote, 'were comprised all the main aids, instruments and materials of NATIONAL EDUCATION, the *nisus formativus* of the body politic, the shaping and informing spirit, which *educing*, i.e.eliciting, the latent *man* in all the natives of the soil, *trains them up* to citizens of the country, free subjects of the realm'.[108] The idea was that 'to every parish throughout the kingdom there is transplanted a germ of civilization; that in the remotest villages there is a nucleus, round which the capabilities of the place may crystallise and brighten; a model sufficiently superior to excite, yet sufficiently near to encourage and facilitate, imitation'.[109]

Some of these ideas, albeit in radically secularized form, filter through to Raymond Williams' account of a common culture. For him education is 'the process of giving to the ordinary members of society its full common meanings, and the skills that will enable them to amend these meanings, in the light of their personal and common experience'.[110] The point of education is to make this transmission common, 'because it must be the case that the whole tradition of what has been thought and valued, a tradition which has been abstracted as a minority possession, is in fact a common human inheritance without which any man's participation would be crippled and disadvantaged'.[111] The point is similar to C.L.R.James' well known assertion that Beethoven belongs to blacks, and not just to Europeans. Arnold, too, of course, shared this view. For Arnold the job of education was, as for Herder, to 'carry from one end of society to the other, the *best* knowledge, the noblest ideas of the time' but, as an Inspector of Schools, his emphasis is naturally on formal training. Educators were the apostles of equality, who sought to make their knowledge efficient outside the clique of the cultivated and learned.[112] Rather than patronizing 'the inferior classes' Arnold wanted to do away with classes. He wanted to meet 'the strong desire of the lower classes to raise themselves' by giving them the means to acquire a full share in cultural life.[113] Out of such convictions sprang the Workers Educational Association in Britain, which contributed enormously to the growth and initial success of the labour movement, and the understanding of education as conscientization we find in Fanon and Freire.[114]

---

a high standard of workmanship). They had a fine code of personal relations with one another and with the master, a dignified notion of their place in the community and an understanding of the necessary part played by their work in the scheme of things.' Leavis and Thompson, *Culture and Environment* p.105 The 'master' here is of course a master craftsman and not a capitalist simply buying their labour.

108   Coleridge, *Constitution* p.48
109   Coleridge, *Constitution* p.75
110   Williams, *Resources* p.14
111   Williams, *Resources* p.37
112   Arnold, *Culture and Anarchy* p.31
113   N.Murray, *A Life of Matthew Arnold* London: Hodder & Stoughton 1996 p.193
114   For Fanon, 'to educate the masses politically ... means to try, relentlessly and passionately, to teach the masses that everything depends on them; that if we stagnate it is their responsibility, and that if we go forward it is due to them too, that there is no such thing as a demiurge, that there

Herder does not make the mistake of confusing education with schooling, nor does he identify it with what happens in the West. Education happens in the course of the transmission of tradition and it embraces skills which go far beyond anything which can be learned in school. This is something which T.S.Eliot understood. Already in *The Idea of a Christian Society* he noted that in what he called 'a negative liberal society' the idea of wisdom disappears, because there is no agreed idea on what every person should know. 'A nation's system of education,' he said, 'is much more important than its system of government; only a proper system of education can unify the active and the contemplative life, action and speculation, politics and the arts.'[115] In the *Notes towards the definition of Culture* Eliot has sport at the expense of liberal theorists like C.E.M.Joad and Herbert Read, who propose a variety of definitions of education in terms of happiness, democracy or earning a living. 'It would be a pity,' he remarks ironically, 'if we overlooked the possibility of education as a means of acquiring wisdom; if we belittled the acquisition of knowledge for the satisfaction of curiosity, without any further motive than the desire to know; and if we lost all our respect for learning.'[116]

His distinctive view of education, however, was bound up with his desire to preserve the class system. This was not so that the ruling class could have helots to do manual work for them, but was born out of an organicist idea that there is a vital unconscious dimension to culture which is represented by the working class. It followed that:

> To treat the 'uneducated' mass of the population as we might treat some innocent tribe of savages to whom we are impelled to deliver the true faith, is to encourage them to neglect or despise that culture which they should possess and *from which the more conscious part of culture draws vitality*; and to aim to make everyone share in the appreciation of the fruits of the more conscious part of culture is to adulterate and cheapen what you give.[117]

It is not, then, that the working class lack culture. On the contrary, the conscious part of culture is dependent on it.

This recognition, that culture is differentiated, that what Arnold calls culture is not the only or even the principal form, is vital to education. The negative view that, if universal education became the rule, standards would be destroyed and the ground prepared 'upon which the barbarian nomads of the future will encamp in their mechanised caravans' was, again, not based upon snobbery. Eliot believed that universal education would disorganize society, by substituting for classes, elites of brains, or perhaps only of sharp wits, and would tend both to restrict education to what will lead to success in the world, and to restrict success in the world to those persons who have been good pupils

---

is no famous man who will take responsibility for everything, but that the demiurge is the people themselves and the magic hands are finally only the hands of the people'. Fanon, *The Wretched of the Earth* p.159

115   Eliot, *Idea* p.41
116   Eliot, *Notes* p.99
117   Eliot, *Notes* p.106 my italics

in the system.[118] Fifty years after he wrote these words we cannot say he was entirely wrong. The denial of universal education is not, of course, something that can be conscionably argued, but what may be drawn from Eliot's observations is a recognition of the equal importance of various *types* of education. The Social Justice Report which constituted the manifesto for the 'New Labour' government urged the extension of higher education on the ground that those with higher qualifications earn more than those without. But this is to adopt the wrong policy from the correct observation. The solution is not to impose one style of education on all, but to seek more equal reward for different vocations. It was this which Eliot, Leavis, and others, were trying to get at.

Eliot's contemporary, Karl Barth, took up the question of education in his 1928 lectures on ethics. At the heart of his argument are three propositions: that education happens in every aspect of life and that every human being is called to be a 'teacher'; that education proceeds through encounter with the Other, the stranger who challenges our complacency and what we take for granted; and that it essentially involves learning something better than what we know at the beginning of the process. It could be said that the last point is analytic to the very idea of education, as Coleridge makes clear, but the polemics of cultural populism call it into question.

Barth took much from Plato, as he cheerfully acknowledged, but not when it came to education. Education, he insisted, is not 'natural' to us. It belongs to the order of reconciliation, the law, and the kingdom of Christ among sinners.[119] At the heart of education, which is both instruction and formation, is the truth that we do not go willingly to school. Education means interference with my autonomy, on the assumption that this is in my best interests and with the implication that I am an impossible creature and that I shall never amount to anything unless I permit this interference. To miss seeing the protest is to miss seeing the other, and this means in turn that education means not sparing an attack, an invasion of the immanence of their being and nature. Barth did not subscribe to what Freire calls the 'banking' concept of education – the idea that education is imparted from on high to those who know nothing. He knew perfectly well that it had to be a vigorous common enterprise between teacher and student. At the same time it involved training, and therefore painful opposition and correction.[120] The teacher, my neighbour as educator, solicits my agreement in the correction of the exercise. All pedagogical method deals with the mode of this invitation.

If the teacher really deals with me in the name and by the commission of God, Barth argued, she or he comes with something 'better' in the expectation and with the demand that I see it and want it as such. If she or he really acts in the name and with the commission of God, what she or he teaches is not just supposedly better but authentically so. *As I learn something truly better divine*

---

118   Eliot, *Notes* p.101
119   K.Barth, *Ethics* Edinburgh: T&T Clark 1981 p.363ff
120   Barth, *Ethics* p.366

authority is to be discerned behind the human teacher. Barth here is re-stating in his own way an insistence found in different forms equally in the Church Fathers, Aquinas and the Reformation, namely that God is active in the education of the human race, and that that activity is not identical simply with the extension of the Church, or conversion. The education of the human race, to use Lessing's phrase, goes on beyond the boundaries of the Church, and shapes culture in all the major senses in which I have defined it. To say this is not, of course, to identify culture with the Spirit in any Hegelian way. The teacher, said Barth (and, he could have said, 'the neighbour') can only teach what is *better*, not 'the best', the truth, or the good – this is a rubric which marks off education from ideology or propaganda. The teacher can stir up a little breeze but cannot make the Spirit blow. It is nevertheless true that the neighbour as teacher can be 'the finger of God' which makes a correction in my exercise and does so in such a way that I see that it is justified.[121]

For Barth, the purpose of education is not primarily to develop a person's talents and interests but to claim them for, and require them to bear, a particular place in human society and history. This sounds rather utilitarian, but we can understand it as insisting that education equips us for our role in the long revolution. It does this only in so far as it is counter cultural, as it involves challenge to what is taken for granted, as it calls me to something 'better'. Here it finds itself at odds with cultural populism and here I return to my distinction between folk and popular culture. The distinction is bound up with the growing control of the market over everyday life. If the purpose of education is humanization, then suspicion must attach to a system for which growth is the ultimate value and which can give no cogent account of the reasons for growth.

If culture is about value, then education, in Barth's sense as that which challenges, corrects and extends me throughout my entire life, is the place where those values are clarified and debated. The reason that the Church has always been involved in education is precisely because it has an account of the values it believes human beings are called to live by, and which it believes are worth sharing. Part of the hostility of cultural populism to the Church is the perception, paradigmatically formulated by William Blake, that the Church sought to bind human desires with briars. Even today, as Norman Lewis' account of the New Tribes Mission depressingly shows, this is not a thing of the past, and there is every reason for the Church to put its house in order.

This is not the same, however, as handing the palm to those who believe that, with the triumph of market capitalism, we have reached the end of history. The passion for education which Freire documents in his peasant communities was earlier shared by working class communities in Britain. It has been sapped by the success of a consumerism which supplies everything necessary for life

---

121   Barth, *Ethics* p.370 The only education I need to refuse is profane education. 'Profane education is that in which an effort is made to make me holy and righteous instead of sinful, to make me forget my limits instead of seeing them more sharply, to deify me instead of putting me in my place on earth. All education is profane which is enthusiastic, which is idealistic ... which aims at mysticism and morals instead of obedience, which tries to teach me not only something better, but openly or secretly a best.'

except a reason for living. In such a situation education is necessarily counter cultural. It cannot do everything, as Helvétius imagined, but it is at the heart of the long revolution, a call to 'fineness of living' not just in the sense of 'high culture' but over the whole range of human activity, from computer programming to cattle rearing, from art to engineering. Such education, 'continuous and world wide', is likewise at the heart of the Church's mission, in its liturgy, its teaching and its praxis.

Worship and Wisdom

Talk of education as liturgy requires further comment. Earlier I mentioned the connection between folk music and Church hymnody. For centuries liturgy was the place where the people of God were educated, the place where faith sought understanding. This remained true even when Protestantism put the Bible into the hands of ordinary people. Liturgy is, however, a peculiar form of education, and in at least three ways. In the first place, worship cannot be understood within the utilitarian calculus. It is 'purpose free rejoicing in God'. Its function is not to 'recharge our batteries', to fit us for work for the rest of the week. It is in essence the response of thanksgiving, praise and adoration. *As such* it puts a question mark against the subsumption of all values by the market, what Marx called commodity fetishism. It is not designed as a protest but it is nevertheless a protest, a counter education in a different set of values, a de-tox from the sickness of consumerism.

Secondly, worship is the place where the story is told and the tradition re-enacted. Here Raymond Williams' 'residual culture' is formed. To be 'residual' in Williams' sense, let us remember, is not to be 'outdated' but to preserve in the present important values from the past. Once again, the *raison d'être* of the Church is not to be a counter culture. That would be a functionalist misunderstanding. Nevertheless, given the nature of the texts, as I shall argue in detail in Chapter 5, this is the actual outcome of regular attendance at liturgy. If it is objected that for centuries nothing like this happened then we can point to the way in which the religion of a Parson Woodforde was so thoroughly colonized by culture to the extent of the complete obscuring of the texts' challenge.

Thirdly, all worship stands under the rubric: 'Be still and know that I am God.' Liturgy provides a space for reflection, where everyday concerns are measured by God's story. It does indeed feed the action–reflection process of Freire's understanding of education, but that is not what it exists for. At a much deeper level it is a vehicle for the cultivation of wisdom. Once again that puts question marks against knowledge as 'know how', as what is designed to extract the maximum benefit from the world. In these ways the worship of the Church is both profoundly educative and profoundly counter cultural. In intention it is 'catholic' – open to the whole world. In this way too it opposes a grotesque parody of catholicity, namely imperialism, and it is to the question of imperialism in its cultural mode that I turn in the following chapter.

Chapter 4

Cultural Imperialism

'Formerly the things which happened in the world had no connection among themselves ... But since then all events are united in a common bundle.' This is Polybius writing two centuries before Christ about what has happened since the founding of Rome. Though in modern terms scarcely global, the Roman empire was certainly one of the most successful ancient empires and for a brief period in the first century, around the birth of Christ, the illusion of the *pax Romana* might be sustained. From Britain to Persia, from the Danube to North Africa, Rome 'ruled the world' and Latin formed a lingua franca over this whole wide area.

The empire was always threatened at its edges, and began to unravel under the pressure of what historians, from a Roman perspective, have called 'the barbarian invasions', beginning in the second century of the Christian era, but becoming irresistible in the fifth. Vikings, Danes, Saxons, Sueves, Franks, Burgundians, Vandals, Lombards, Goths, Huns, Magyars, Avars – amongst others! – undid the Roman ecumene and plunged Europe into what even contemporary commentators thought was a dark age. In the sixth century the spread of Islam formed part of this expansion and movement of peoples, coming to a stop, after one hundred and fifty years, in Spain. This huge movement of peoples, possibly prompted by climate change, petered out in the ninth and tenth centuries. The Norman invasion of England was one of its last throws. What followed, in Europe, the Middle East and North Africa, was a period of consolidation.

It is true, of course, that no culture is 'pure' and that all contain elements from others. A global perspective on cultures is, in Jonathan Friedman's words, of a kind of leaky mosaic in which cultures run over their edges and flow into one another, and therefore what I have called consolidation could never be stasis.[1] At the same time, power struggles amongst regional elites eventually gave rise, at the end of the fifteenth century, to the nation states of Europe, more especially England, France and then, after a century, Holland. These three states were all outside the Holy Roman Empire, which retarded the rise of the nation state wherever it held sway. Italy and Germany remained dense networks of independent city states and small principalities for another two hundred and fifty years.

Despite this, and despite the dynastic and religious wars which plagued Europe more or less continuously from the tenth to the seventeenth centuries, it was in this period that the cultural identities, and the present day European

---

1   J.Friedman, *Cultural Identity and Global Process* London: Sage 1994 p.212

languages, were formed. Without such stability, without long periods of rootedness, regional languages could never have taken shape. Christianity undoubtedly saw that there were family resemblances in the formation of the European states, just as Islam did in the regions where it held sway, and Hinduism amongst the kingdoms of India, but it is at this period that we get the celebration of national difference. What happened in England has its analogies throughout Europe. A Francophone ruling class was, after a period of four hundred years, assimilated into the Anglophone majority. The seven kingdoms of dark-age Britain, in which Dane, Viking, Saxon, Celt and Romano-Briton squared off against one another, melded into a more or less cultural whole, with great variation of dialect and custom to be sure, class divided, and still antagonistically defined by the Celtic fringe, but sufficient to ensure that the ideology of the 'sceptered isle' celebrated by Shakespeare had wide purchase.

On the one hand there was marked regional variation, not just between county and county but between village and village. On the other hand this period saw the rise of nationalism, which Arnason describes as a specifically modern and unprecedentedly close relationship between culture and power. On his account, nationalism defines and justifies power in terms of culture, rather than the opposite.[2] In the next two centuries religion and class would drive people overseas but, by the end of the eighteenth century, a working class figure like the artist J.W.Turner could be intensely patriotic and understand himself through a whole series of myths going back to Hereward the Wake and his struggle against 'the Norman Yoke'. In this, the folk song and popular literature from the period would suggest that he was fairly typical.

To be sure, both Shakespeare's and Turner's moments are snapshots: culture is always process, and even as the moments are caught cultural reality is on the way to something else, as Turner's contemporary Cobbett vividly lamented. What has to be grasped, however, is the relative difference in the pace of change. It is this which quickened so dramatically with the coming of the industrial revolution. Its origins go back to the tenth century, at least, but it is in the eighteenth century that we first get effective steam power, the factory system, the beginning of a huge increase in population and rapid urbanization. These processes, the start of Raymond Williams' 'long revolution', were very often read negatively. Looking back from the 1880s Ferdinand Tönnies saw the period of consolidation as a time characterized by *Gemeinschaft*, close mutual relationships in an organic society in which tradition played a key part. In his view this society had been superseded by *Gesellschaft*, a society where the old regional distinctions were transcended by distinctions between classes or professions. In 1848 Marx and Engels had celebrated with glee the creative destruction the new processes brought:

2   J.P.Arnason, 'Nationalism, Globalization and Modernity' in Featherstone(ed) *Global Culture* pp.213, 217 Held et al rightly insist that all nation states are in part ideological creations which mask gender, race, class and regional divisions. *Global Transformations* Cambridge: Polity 1999 p.369

The bourgeoisie, historically, has played a most revolutionary part ... it has put an end to all feudal, patriarchal, idyllic relations. It has pitilessly torn asunder the motley feudal ties that bound man to his 'natural superiors', and has left remaining no other nexus between man and man than naked self-interest ... The bourgeoisie cannot exist without constantly revolutionising the instruments of production ... uninterrupted disturbance of all social conditions, everlasting uncertainty and agitation distinguish the bourgeois epoch from all earlier ones ... All that is solid melts into air, all that is holy is profaned, and man is at last compelled to face with sober senses, his real condition of life, and his relations with his kind.[3]

What I have called 'consolidation' was followed by a kind of societal big-bang, and the universe following from that explosion is still expanding. Getting on for a century later a reactionary monarchist could give the following gloomy assessment of this process, weighing the relative merits of *Gemeinschaft* and *Gesellschaft*, traditional and modern societies:

For a long enough time we have believed in nothing but the values arising in a mechanised, commercialised, urbanised way of life: it would be as well for us to face the permanent conditions upon which God allows us to live upon this planet. And without sentimentalising the life of the savage, we might practise the humility to observe, in some of the societies upon which we look down as primitive or backward, the operation of a social-religious-artistic complex which we should emulate upon a higher plane. We have been accustomed to regard 'progress' as always integral; and have yet to learn that it is only by an effort and a discipline, greater than society has yet seen the need of imposing upon itself, that material knowledge and power is gained without loss of spiritual knowledge and power ... We need to recover the sense of religious fear, so that it may be overcome by religious hope.[4]

T.S.Eliot puts questions to the process of modernization which continue to resound up to the present. For the great transformation, to use another description of what happened in the wake of the industrial revolution, had momentous cultural consequences.[5] Because humans learn by mimesis memories play a central role in culture, and collective memories constitute tradition. Herder, who believed that languages lay at the heart of culture, pointed out that traditions are handed on, assimilated and constantly reappraised through language. 'The result of this process of transmission at any given time is "culture".'[6] Language, memory and tradition, in turn, are always linked to place. As Geoffrey Hartman puts it, 'The function of individual cultures remains the same throughout history: to convert longing into belonging. Culture is always site specific in this respect.'[7] The changes Marx and Engels celebrate involve the destruction of tradition, a consequent loss of memory, the start of a global movement which has given (what may be a very temporary) dominance to the English language, and the dissolution of place through what David Harvey calls 'space–time compression', which is

3 K.Marx and F.Engels, *The Communist Manifesto* Moscow: Progress 1952[1848] pp.44–46
4 Eliot, *Idea* p.62
5 K.Polanyi, *The Great Transformation* Boston: Harper 1957
6 Barnard, *Herder on Social and Political Culture* p.23
7 Hartman, *Culture* p.180

what happens to our world when we travel by jet and communicate instantly across the globe. The cultural dynamics we considered in the last chapter, between high culture and popular culture, have everywhere been altered in favour of a polarization between cultural populism and the culture of the elite. As we saw there, this development is by no means self-evidently positive.

The great transformation also intensified the problematic which today we know as 'identity politics'. If language is central to culture, then the fact that there are now around one hundred and sixty nations but over three thousand five hundred languages, means that every language offers the possibility of struggle for autonomy, and for the preservation of a distinct view of the world. We know that the process of acquiring national identity in Europe meant the loss of some local languages, like Cornish, and threats to, and sometimes the outright proscription of, languages like Welsh or Gaelic. This process has rightly been described as aiming at 'culture death'. At the same time the possibility of endless balkanization is obvious. Only about twenty of the world's states are ethnically and linguistically homogenous and they cannot get smaller unless they fracture into tribes and clans.[8]

Sensitive to this problem, Herder insisted on celebrating both the universal and the particular, the global and the local. On the one hand he argues that cultures are irreducibly distinct and that their uniqueness is a divine gift which can by no means be compromised. 'Not a man, not a country, not a people, not a natural history, not a state, are like one another. Hence the True, the Good, the Beautiful in them are not similar either.'[9] Each image of humanity is unique and *sui generis*.[10] On the other hand he also recognizes universal human attributes which make a moral demand on us no matter what the culture so that, for example, he can condemn the African slave trade both because it represents the destruction of a local culture, and therefore a God-given mode of life, and also because it is an affront to universal human dignity, what he calls *Humanität*. This necessary dialectic of universal and particular was familiar to him as a theologian, for it forms the leitmotif of the gospel, which, in Matthew's case at any rate, begins in small town Judaea and ends with a command to go to the ends of the earth. In Herder's day it involved him in protests against foreign missions and against colonialism, as we shall see in Chapter 8.

It is this problem which is the theme of the present chapter. It constitutes yet another perspective from which we have to view culture, alongside the questions of elite and popular culture, and of the interrelationship of religion and culture, which we have examined in the previous two chapters. The cultural impact of modernity, I shall argue, and more especially of globalization, threatens to devour all the minute particulars in which Herder, like William Blake, saw the workings of God's Spirit. Resistance to such homogenization, then, follows from the Church's understanding of a world

---

8   Barber, *Jihad vs McWorld* p.9
9   Herder, 'Einzelne Blätter zum "Journal der Reise"' in *Werke* vol IV p.472
10   Herder, 'Ideas for a Philosophy of History' in *Werke* vol XIV pp.210, 217, 230

shaped by God, just as Herder argued. At the same time universality cannot be denied. In the tenth chapter I shall address this problem through the issue of human rights. Here I shall argue that it is the incarnation which helps us to understand how universal and particular are related in a way which respects the integrity of both. I shall examine the arguments for cultural homogenization, by no means universally conceded, before turning to this theological argument.

The Location of Culture

Despite the conventional description of Palestine as 'the Holy land', Christianity never had a geographical centre in the way that Islam has, nor was it identical with the religion of a geographical area, like Hinduism. As the *Epistle to Diognetus* put it at the very beginning of the second century, 'for the Christian every homeland is a foreign land, and every foreign land a home land'. This did not imply, however, a rootless globalism, but rather that the advice of Jeremiah, 'to build houses and dwell in them', or in other words, to commit oneself to the local culture, was followed.

As we have seen, at the end of a long period of consolidation, nationalism, love of and commitment to a particular place and culture – la belle France, Ma Vlást, Mother Russia or India – was the result. In the wake of the great transformation, however, we have a new situation: 'If on arriving at Trude I had not read the city's name written in big letters,' wrote Italo Calvino:

> I would have thought I was landing at the same airport from which I had taken off. This was the first time I had come to Trude, but I already knew the hotel where I happened to be lodged ... Why come to Trude I asked myself. And I already wanted to leave. 'You can resume your flight whenever you like' they said to me, 'but you will arrive at another Trude, absolutely the same, detail by detail. The world is covered by a sole Trude, which does not begin and does not end. Only the name of the airport changes.'[11]

The sense of homogenization is familiar to every traveller. It is part and parcel of the whole process of globalization, of 'space–time compression'. The old sense of place which belonged to the period of consolidation was maintained by the sheer difficulty of travel and communication. The new conditions tend to undo the sense of place. The airport Calvino describes is part of a galaxy of 'non-places' – motorway service stations, shopping malls – remote from the dense marking of a historic community. The non-place of the autoroute, says John Tomlinson, is defined by its routing round real places whilst fixing these in signs commodifying them.[12] The year round availability of imported foods dissolves the particularity of local cuisine, based on the food in season. What it means to be local changes. A few control and initiate 'flows' and 'movements'

---

11   I.Calvino, *Invisible Cities* London: Vintage 1997 p.128
12   J.Tomlinson, *Globalization and Culture* Cambridge: Polity 1999 p.110

but the vast majority have no say in what happens. Old industries disappear and – if you are lucky – new ones take their place. In a globalized world, says Zygmunt Bauman, localities lose their meaning-generating and meaning-negotiating capacity and are increasingly dependent on sense-giving and interpreting actions which they do not control.[13]

The locality no longer belongs to the people who live there but to those who 'invest' in it, people who are not bound by space, and thus constitute a new class of absentee landlords.[14] At the same time, huge movements of peoples, displaced by war, poverty or climate change, mean that there are large cultural groups far from their place of origin – the UN reported that whereas in 1975 there were two million refugees, in 1995 there were twenty-seven million, and the number was growing. And, in an ironic consequence of the creative destruction Marx and Engels celebrated, the character of neighbourhoods is changed as capital finds an opportunity for profit, tearing down environments, or littering sea-coasts with instant hotels.[15]

'We have been party to a massive burst of homogenisation,' argue Sue Clifford and Angela King, 'which is bleaching the richness from our lives.'[16] Their focus is neither the nation nor the region, but the local – the neighbourhood, the locality, the parish, the housing estate, the high street, the village, the suburb, perhaps even the street. It is, they argue, the fineness of grain of our knowledge of neighbourhoods which makes us at home in the world. Playing devil's advocate John Tomlinson asks why we should object if everything looked the same. If we argue that richness, variety and difference are goods in themselves then so are order, uniformity and universality.[17] Clifford and King's answer to this is that human beings respond to mosaic. 'We need the nourishment of detail, in things as ordinary as rumples in a field, detail in doors and windows, dialect, local festival days, seasonal variation in the goods on sale in the market, to subtly stimulate our senses and sensibilities.'[18] Anthony Smith fears that all that will be left of indigenous cultures will be museums for the tourists:

> Beneath a modernist veneer we find a pastiche of cultural motifs, and styles, underpinned by a universal scientific and technical discourse ... Standardized, commercialised mass commodities will draw for their contents upon revivals of traditional, folk or national motifs and styles in fashions, furnishings, music and arts, lifted out of their original context and anaesthetized. A global culture would operate at several levels simultaneously: as a cornucopia of standardized commodities, as a patchwork of denationalised ethnic or folk motifs, as a series of generalized 'human values and interests', as a uniform 'scientific discourse of meaning' and finally as the

---

13   Z.Bauman, *Globalization: The Human Consequences* Cambridge: Polity 1998 p.3
14   Bauman, *Globalization* p.10
15   A.King, 'Architecture, Capital and the Globalization of Culture' in Featherstone(ed) *Global Culture* pp.397–411 Between 1985 and 1987 Japanese banks' investment in British property increased eightfold to £250 million.
16   S.Clifford and A.King, 'Losing Your Place' in *Local Distinctiveness: Place, Particularity and Identity* London: Common Ground 1993 p.8
17   J.Tomlinson, *Cultural Imperialism* London: Continuum 1991 p.98
18   Clifford and King, 'Losing Your Place' p.14

interdependent system of communications which forms the material base for all other components and levels.[19]

Developments such as that in Kenya, where a deal has been struck between a tour operator and the Masai for them to 'act Masai' for the benefit of his customers, can be instanced to support this.[20]

Tomlinson insists, against the pessimism of Calvino, that to test the homogenization thesis you have to venture outside the terminal, and that there remains a great deal of real local difference in the world, but he, too, agrees that the change in our experience of place is particular to global modernity and distinct from the general properties of fluidity, mobility and interactivity that can be attributed to all historical cultures.[21] Travel has been a feature of all cultures and they therefore need to be understood, as James Clifford reminds us, in terms of dwelling *and* travel, of roots *and* routes, and therefore as sites of constant cross fertilization.[22] The point is well taken, but as Stuart Hall remarks, the question is, what stays the same even when you travel, which is the question of the priority of roots to routes, of identity.[23] Even nomad cultures, amongst which I count gypsy cultures, characteristically operated within restricted areas, so that annually traversed routes constituted a kind of home, nourished local and place related roots. The balance between being and becoming varies between periods which I have called those of consolidation and those of rapid change.

Worries about the loss of local distinctiveness ('deterritorialization') are bound up with worries about the loss of tradition ('detraditionalization') for, as nineteenth century sociologists like Tönnies and Durkheim saw, tradition is to some extent bound to place. Thus when McDonald's opened a new 'outlet' in the medieval main square of Krakow one critic protested: 'The activities of this firm are symbolic of mass industrial civilization and a superficial cosmopolitan way of life ... Many historic events happened in this place, and McDonalds would be the beginning of the cultural degradation of this most precious urban area.'[24]

As we have seen, the end of what were understood to be, and indeed often were, oppressive traditions was celebrated by many at the outset of the great transformation. Urbanization and industrialization rescued us from 'the idiocy of rural life' and the narrowness of local culture, battered down the Chinese walls of tradition. Already by the middle of the nineteenth century, argues David Gross, 'the past lay in ruins', and traditions which had provided order and cohesion for societies for hundreds of years were reduced to a mosaic of

---

19 A.Smith, 'Towards a Global Culture?' in Featherstone(ed) *Global Culture* p.176

20 M.Featherstone, *Undoing Culture: Globalization, Postmodernism and Identity* London: Sage 1995 p.121

21 Tomlinson, *Globalization* pp.6, 130

22 J.Clifford, 'Travelling Cultures' in Grossberg et al(eds) *Cultural Studies* London: Routledge 1992 pp.96–116

23 The point was made in discussion. Grossberg et al(eds) *Cultural Studies* p.115

24 G.Ritzer, *The McDonaldization of Society* revised edn Thousand Oaks: Forge 1996 p.180

fragments which the folk-lorists then had to pick up.[25] Others argue, as Dave Harker argues about British folk song, that such 'immemorial' traditions never existed, that tradition is always invented and reinvented and that traditions still retain significance as ways of making sense of the world and creating a sense of belonging.[26] To the extent that any of the major religions still command allegiance this is self-evidently true. Correctly seeing that there is no immutable gold standard of meaning in tradition (which is, however, different from arguing that they have no 'constant core') Timothy Luke even argues that traditions must be seen as dynamic, contemporary and forward looking, because they are actively part of everyone's daily life in the modern world:[27]

> Traditions are manifest, not latent. They are not buried treasures, awaiting excavation like old pirate chests to be forced open and spent as valuable essences of 'old ways' to fix our 'new ways'. Nor are traditions fragmented bits and pieces of a dead past to be cobbled together on the lab-tables of social theory, lifted lifelessly into the thunderstorms of popular protests, struck by lightning bolts of reanimating communal energy, and then awakened to redeem the otherwise lost souls of modernity. Authentic traditions do exist in particular face-to-face relations at a micro level in personal ties, family life, work practices, political groups, religious sects, educational institutions, intellectual discourses and regional culture.[28]

Luke sees this surviving the 'cyber revolution', even though he understands this in a far-reaching way.

Such arguments can only be extrapolations from the evidence as we read it, but it is essential to come to a view about them because, in a globalizing world, they provide a guide to action, and possible resistance. One of the key ways of discussing them is in terms of the discourse of cultural imperialism, which John Tomlinson analyses into claims about media imperialism, cultural invasions of one nation by another, the impact of capitalism and of modernity. It is obvious that all these are mutually implicated in one another, and the distinctions are ultimately difficult to sustain, but they nevertheless form a useful basis for discussion. At stake are the values at the heart of the world's diverse cultures. The amendment of these values, I have argued in the previous three chapters, is the theme of the long revolution, the slow and asymptotic approach to what Jesus speaks of as 'the kingdom'. According to the thesis of cultural imperialism, on the other hand, such amendment is decisively replaced by another narrative, the triumphant narrative of 'modernity'.

25 D.Gross, *The Past in Ruins* Amherst: University of Massachusetts Press 1992

26 J.Thompson, 'Tradition and Self in a Mediated World', in P.Heelas, S.Lash and P.Morris (eds) *Detraditionalization* Oxford: Blackwells 1996 pp.89–108

27 T.W.Luke, 'Identity, Meaning and Globalization: Detraditionalization in Postmodern Space–Time Compression' in Heelas et al(eds) *Detraditionalization* pp.109–133. Here p.116

28 Luke, 'Identity' p.120

Media Imperialism

According to Foucault's famous thesis the eighteenth century is the century of the panopticon, a device for control which allowed one person to supervise a whole prison. In the new world order, however, the many watch the few. Media organizations like the BBC and CNN have a huge global reach and what is broadcast, whether it is news or *Dallas*, conveys the message of a total way of life, that of the consumer culture with its emphasis on youth, fitness, beauty, romance and freedom.[29] Programmes like *Dallas* are, for Serge Latouche, a sign of the West's worldwide domination of the imagination.[30] In their advertising campaigns the great corporations in the same way sell not just their products but American prosperity and imagery and thus its very soul.[31] For Sardar the Disney film *Pocahontas* is an apt expression of neo-colonialism: everything now belongs to a world dominated by America and America is the apogee of all human civilizations and experience, the only perspective through which history is meaningful, which all of history explains.[32] It packages its world view through 'Edutainment' – CD-Roms which have an increasingly global reach combine information with entertainment, and serve as potent educational tools, and as the perfect counterpart to the ideology of the Disney film.

Tomlinson finds a number of problems with these arguments. He objects, first, that they confuse cultural with political and economic domination. This is a weak objection because it presupposes that culture can be separated from economics, a view I have already contested. We cannot separate economics from the realm of values. Every economy presupposes an ethic including the anti-economy of unlimited growth. That the aggressive promotion of Marlborough, Coca-Cola or McDonald's is not only an economic but a cultural phenomenon seems to me beyond doubt. Freire speaks of a cultural invasion which has led to the cultural inauthenticity of those who are invaded, and a conviction of their intrinsic inferiority.[33]

---

29 Bauman, *Globalization* p.53 Johann Baptist Metz argues that 'For a long time non western countries have been under siege from a "second colonization": Through the invasion of the Western culture industry and its mass media, especially that of television which holds people prisoner in an artificial world, a world of make believe. It alienates them more and more from their own cultural images, from their original language and their own history. This colonization of the spirit is so much harder to resist because it appears as a sugar coated poison and because the gentle terror of this Western culture industry operates not as an alienation but as a narcotic drug.' In H.Regan and A.Torrance(eds) *Christ and Context* Edinburgh: T&T Clark 1993 p.212

30 Latouche, *Westernization* p.xii Latouche is what Held et al class a 'hyperglobalist', someone who takes a pessimistic view of the survival of cultural difference. Roland Robertson is a 'sceptic' in their terminology, insisting on the survival of difference; whilst Castells and Giddens are 'transformationalists', insisting on the challenges of globalization whilst noting the possibilities of survival and resistance. *Global Transformations* pp.12, 23ff

31 Barber, *Jihad vs McWorld* p.60 McGrath agrees. The values of a US dominated television are consumerist, repressive, and conservative, he argues. *The Bone Won't Break* p.149

32 Sardar, *Postmodernism* p.116

33 Freire, *Pedagogy* pp.122–123

The argument that allegations of media imperialism are based on hermeneutic naïvety is much stronger. As we shall see in Chapter 6, Disney can be read in many ways, and the same goes for *Dallas*. Interviews with viewers around the world indicate that the popularity of the latter owes more to its melodramatic story line and 'tragic structure of feeling' than to its celebration of affluence.[34] The films of Charlie Chaplin are globally screened and appreciated, but the question is whether the laughter they generate is always the same laughter. Tomlinson is right that this is an extremely difficult claim to verify. He agrees with the popular culture theorists that audiences are more active, complex and critically aware in their readings than the theorists of media imperialism have allowed.[35] He points out that all our experience is mediated by texts or symbolic narratives of one kind or another so that there is a dialectical relationship between lived experience and cultural representation. To put too much emphasis on the power of the media may exaggerate the representational pole and imply a narrow view of culture.

I shall return to the question of the power of the media in Chapter 6, in the context of the exercise of hegemony – obviously one way of construing imperialism. At this stage, however, I turn to Tomlinson's second category, and the allegation that national autonomy is under threat.

The Destruction of National Autonomy

Tomlinson has no difficulty in raising many objections to the claim that Western culture poses a threat to the integrity of national cultures. In the first place, those who make the charge, like Marxists, or members of UNESCO, are internationalists. There is therefore the apparent paradox that the rhetoric of a universal humanism underwrites the defence of cultural difference – though Herder would respond that it is *precisely* universal humanity which respects local differences. More substantially there is the fact that there are scarcely any nations with ethnically homogenous populations. Throughout the world linguistic, ethnic and cultural minorities compete for autonomy. There is also Benedict Anderson's thesis to contend with that nations emerged as 'imagined communities' precisely because the numbers of people involved far exceeded the number one might possibly know.[36] The emergence of nations, Anderson argues, had to await the arrival of the possibility of a mass medium like printing before a widespread sense of belonging could be generated. Further, as already noted, the traditions which differentiate nations are often of very recent provenance, not so much imagined as invented. They can also be curiously

---

34   A Dutch viewer who 'hated capitalism' took it as fantasy and loved it all the same; an Arab group read a scene when a married woman deserted her husband to go to her lover as her flight back to her father's house.

35   Tomlinson, *Imperialism* p.57

36   B.Anderson, *Imagined Communities* 2nd edn. London: Verso 1991 p.6

international.[37] The nation state, then, is a very recent affair, an offshoot of modernity. 'National identities are not cultural belongings rooted in deep quasi natural attachments to a homeland but complex cultural constructions that have arisen in specific historical conditions.'[38]

The discourse of nationality is often couched in terms of the preservation of autonomy, but this is an odd use, since cultures are not agents, and it is rare for anyone to be able to claim to speak for an entire culture with conviction. Cultures are made up of agents who respond to many stimuli. As they change, so cultures change, and why should this be objected to? Cultures are protean entities; their boundaries are shifting and permeable.[39] The survival of a culture is a matter of cultural practices and if, as we saw in the last chapter, folk traditions are exchanged for watching TV, churchgoing for trips to local attractions, then, says Tomlinson, the culture has not survived, but this is not a matter for criticism unless we want to say these choices are mistaken or misguided.[40]

The separation of the discourse of nationality from the impact of capitalism, which Tomlinson proposes, is doubtful. Since states cannot 'buck the market', as has been demonstrated even in the case of relatively big players like France and Germany, they become essentially security devices for the mega companies.[41] This is the essence of neo-colonialism. 'The new masters of the world have no need to govern directly. National governments are charged with the task of administering affairs on their behalf.'[42] The critique of loss of national identity, then, leads directly to the critique of capital.

Cultural Imperialism and Capitalism

A third account of cultural imperialism is, more plausibly, understood in terms of the effects of global capitalism, though it is actually extremely difficult to distinguish this from the following category of the impact of modernity, as the quote from the Communist Manifesto earlier in the chapter indicates. As Marshall Berman puts it epigrammatically in his reflection on that passage, capitalism destroys the human possibilities it creates.[43]

One reason for speaking of capitalism as a form of imperialism is that it has a rhetoric of conquest. Thus the company chairman of McDonald's said in 1994, 'Our goal is to totally dominate the quick service industry worldwide ... I want McDonald's to be more than a leader. I want McDonald's to

---

37 Tomlinson instances a Japanese ritual of singing Beethoven's ninth which one music critic calls 'a Shinto ritual of purification'! *Imperialism* p.93

38 Tomlinson, *Imperialism* p.84

39 Tomlinson, *Imperialism* p.97

40 Tomlinson, *Imperialism* p.165

41 For the German example see J.Petras and H.Veltmeyer, *Globalization Unmasked* London: Zed 2001 p.70

42 Bauman, *Globalization* p.66

43 M.Berman, *All That Is Solid Melts Into Air* London: Verso 1983 p.96

dominate.'[44] At the beginning of 1995 about half of McDonald's profits came from overseas operations, and the firm had opened 'outlets' not only in Krakow and Stratford on Avon, which is quite bad enough, but in Mecca![45] Coca Cola is the same: two thirds of its revenues come from outside the United States, and it has global ambitions. 'As huge as our world of Coca-Cola is today,' says an executive, 'it is just a tiny sliver of the world we can create.'[46] For the corporations to succeed every country has to take on the Western capitalist model. The new transitional democracies, says Ben Barber, have been talked by foreign advisors or bullied by international banks into thinking that laissez faire capitalist economics is a self-sufficient system. In many parts of the world the result has been cultural collapse, 'savage and repulsive forms of behaviour, the plunder of the nation's wealth'.[47]

Contemporary capitalism is multinational, but at present its major centre is the United States. The American philosopher Roy Weatherford is happy to see English displacing all other languages as a result of the dominance of the US as a military, economic and entertainment superpower. In his view it means that we are finally about to become One World, One Government, One Culture.[48] For Thomas Friedman the United States is 'not just a country' but a spiritual value, a role model, a beacon for the whole world. It is 'the ultimate benign hegemon and reluctant enforcer' and needs to recognize that 'The hidden hand of the market will never work without a hidden fist ... And the hidden fist that keeps the world safe for Silicon Valley's technologies to flourish is called the US Army, Air Force, Navy and Marine Corps.'[49]

The North American sociologists James Petras and Henry Veltmeyer understand this process as simple imperialism and, whilst the second Gulf War is clearly not monocausal, many observers have noted the imperialist rhetoric, and the dispensing with the institutions of democratic global governance, that have accompanied it. Whilst the idea of globalization implies the *interdependence* of nations imperialism emphasizes the domination and exploitation by imperial states and multinational corporations of less developed countries and labouring classes. This matches the reality far better than the idea of globalization.[50]

Industrial capitalism began with the factory system and, as Schumpeter argued, does not survive without the creative destruction brought by new inventions. Science and technology have been, and remain, central to its conception, but this, too, has huge cultural effects. When technique enters into every area of life, argues Jacques Ellul, it ceases to be external to human beings but becomes their very substance and absorbs them. In this respect technique is

---

44   Ritzer, *McDonaldization* p.5
45   Ritzer, *McDonaldization* p.2
46   Barber, *Jihad vs McWorld* p.68
47   Alexander Solzhenitsyn cited in Barber, *Jihad vs McWorld* p.238
48   Cited in Tomlinson, *Globalization* p.79
49   T.Friedman, *The Lexus and the Olive Tree* London: HarperCollins 2000 pp.464–475. Friedman's brazen imperialism is the more distasteful for being supported by a 'postmodern theology'.
50   Petras and Veltmeyer, *Globalization Unmasked* pp.29, 30

radically different from the machine.[51] Technique attacks human beings, impairs the sources of their vitality, and takes away their mystery.[52] Aloysius Pieris agrees. Technology, he says, has deprived the human mind of myth and ritual, two things by which humanity enacts its deep yearnings and keeps itself sane in mind and body. Can technology liberate the person? Certainly not in the form in which Christian nations have offered it to us. 'It takes away cosmic religion from the masses, and replaces it with neurosis. It takes away religious poverty only to give us mammon instead.'[53] It is also a key aspect of the balance of power between cultures. When one is capable of building hundred-ton machines which can reach a height of ten kilometres in ten minutes, Latouche remarks, one has rights over those who have not yet invented the wheel. 'The right to dominance ... is a direct attribute of technology deriving from its obvious superiority.' Neo-colonialism is a matter not just of markets but of science, technology, economics and the values of progress which they enshrine. Signing up to development means 'being in communion with the religion of science and revering technology'.[54]

If capitalism began with the factory system, it proceeded through Taylorization. Weber endorsed Marx and Engels' perception that capitalism strips the halo off everything, and predicted that it would disenchant the world by imposing the 'iron cage' of bureaucratic rationality, robbing the world of tradition, magic and charisma.[55] It is fundamentally within this framework that Ritzer understands McDonaldization which, he argues, has increased homogenization both in the United States and throughout the world. Wherever fast food chains are found, in competition with American models, food is rationalized and compromised so that it is acceptable to the tastes of all diners.[56] To those postmodern theorists who argue that diversity is on the increase, Ritzer replies that McDonaldization is here for the foreseeable future and influencing society at an accelerating rate.[57] Rationalization is also introduced through the adoption of cultural forms such as legislature, constitution, bureaucracy, trade unions, national currency and the school system. Once adopted these tend to structure other cultural forms to resemble each other more and more closely.[58]

---

51   J.Ellul, *The Technological Society* revised edn New York: Vintage 1964 p.6

52   Ellul, *Technological Society* p.415

53   A.Pieris, *An Asian Theology of Liberation* p.79

54   Latouche, *Westernization* pp.17, 18 In this respect Aylward Shorter's belief that the 'outermost circle' of a person's culture, the industrial technical, is always relatively superficial and always in flux, instanced by the fact that people of different cultures drive cars, play football and wear trousers without surrendering their commitment to a distinct culture, is extremely superficial. It takes no account of how fundamental an impact these things may have. He does recognize this later in the argument. *Toward A Theology of Inculturation* London: Chapman 1988 pp.35, 51

55   B.Turner, 'The Two Faces of Sociology: Global or National?' in Featherstone(ed) *Global Culture* p.353

56   Ritzer, *McDonaldization* p.136

57   Ritzer, *McDonaldization* p.148

58   I.Wallerstein, 'The National and the Universal: Can there be such a thing as World Culture?' in A.King(ed) *Culture, Globalization and the World System* 2nd edn Minneapolis: University of Minnesota Press 1997 p.93

The adoption of individualism, as opposed to more communitarian ways of understanding society, also follows. A society organized by and around *homo oeconomicus* is geared to 'rational utility maximizing'. 'Through world wide economic integration, through a single world culture, through a thousand different but mutually reinforcing channels, individualism is on the increase everywhere, and is percolating more deeply into non-Western societies.'[59] Latouche puts this down, in part, to Christianity. The Christian message of the gospels has a more universal content than other religions because its recognition of the individual as an absolute value is more pronounced than in the other monotheistic religions. It sets up a privileged relationship between the believer and God, but in so doing detaches people from all cultural roots. It is in theory able to embrace all people – so long as they are detached from their own culture.[60] It is Christianity, therefore, which is radically deculturing. I shall argue the contrary in Chapter 9. Simone Weil's view that it is money which destroys human roots by turning desire for gain into the sole motive seems more plausible.[61]

The growth of a transnational class comprised of intellectuals, bureaucrats, politicians, business people, journalists and diplomats is part of the same process. They share procedures, working practices and organizational cultures. If there is a 'global culture', remarks Antony King, it is that which enables 'an increasing number of scientists, academics, artists and other elites ... of widely different nationalities, languages, ethnicities and races to communicate more easily with each other than with others of their own ethnic or national background'.[62]

All this produces the kind of homogenization Calvino laments, and Tomlinson grants that 'The evidence of a general drift towards cultural convergence at certain levels is undeniable.'[63] Not everyone agrees. Stuart Hall argues that it is precisely in the nature of capital, in its constant state of expansion, penetration and internationalization, to work in and through *difference*, to celebrate, enhance and exaggerate cultural diversity.[64] In a similar way Featherstone argues that there is a strong tendency for the process of globalization to provide a stage for global differences not only to open up a 'world showcase of cultures' but to provide a field for a more discordant clashing of cultures.[65]

The question is whether the difference is more than skin deep, for the impact of the processes just outlined are, just as Marx and Engels said, eliminating the peasantry throughout the world, and with them age old systems of local

---

59   Latouche, *Westernization* p.97
60   Latouche, *Westernization* p.28
61   Weil, *Roots* p.42
62   A.King, 'The Global, the Urban and the World' in King(ed) *Culture, Globalization and the World System* p.153
63   Tomlinson, *Imperialism* p.26
64   S.Hall, 'Globalization and Ethnicity' in King(ed) *Culture, Globalization and the World System* pp.41–68
65   Featherstone, *Undoing Culture* p.13

wisdom and knowledge. Assuming this to be the case, should we worry? Tomlinson, who is expert at putting difficult questions to liberal certitudes, asks whether homogenization is necessarily a bad thing. After all, the universal extension of food hygiene, educational provision, affirmations of honesty, toleration, compassion, and democratic public processes are rarely criticized. The selective nature of the critique of homogenization undermines the case.[66] It may turn out to be the complaint of the Western tourist who wants different places to retreat to, even if he or she wants to come back to their dishwasher, car and colour television. Much liberal critique seems to presuppose a double standard: 'natural' remedies are alright for 'them'. We remain with our pharmaceuticals and our agro chemicals.

The critique often attacks consumerism, but again, Tomlinson asks, what is wrong with it? In attacking materialism and consumerism we have to remember the drudgery, injury and anxiety that are the daily experience of millions and the need to remedy these. There is a danger of a romanticization of poverty which patronizes Third World aspirations for material improvements. It is also not self-evident that affluence makes people more selfish than poverty: Colin Turnbull found that amongst the Ik people of Nigeria it was famine which intensified selfishness. Religious critiques of consumerism may be based on a sense of the superiority of the spiritual to the material with the mistrust of the body that implies. Furthermore, such critiques involve another form of cultural imperialism, judging other cultures in the light of our own norms.

To such moral critiques we might reply, with Raymond Williams, that we are not materialist enough and that the measure of the good of a culture should be related to its ability to satisfy real needs. Here we come to the debate as to the nature of true needs, but who is to decide what these are and for whom? Despite these questions put to those complaining of cultural imperialism, Tomlinson acknowledges that consumer satisfactions, like motor cars, are an extremely mixed blessing exemplifying the 'euphoria in unhappiness' which Marcuse found in capitalist society.[67] That consumerism has an uneasy conscience stems from the fact that it has colonized a moral–cultural space left by other developments in modernity.[68] This point leads to Tomlinson's fourth category, the impact of modernity.

The Impact of Modernity

Assuming, for the sake of argument, that the modernity in which 'all that is solid melts into air' can be separated from capitalism, we come to what Tomlinson believes is the heart of the cultural imperialist case. Toynbee thought that the impact of modernity on all other societies was the great event

66 Tomlinson, *Imperialism* pp.110, 111
67 Tomlinson, *Imperialism* pp.130–133
68 Tomlinson, *Imperialism* p.136

of the twentieth century. He suggested that it generated the same kind of spiritual starvation as led to the rise of Christianity.[69] The success of the modern West has meant the adoption of a whole way of looking at things. Richard Handler writes:

> that most nation states (and many minority groups as well) now seek to objectify unique cultures for themselves; that they import Western (including anthropological) definitions of what culture is; that they import Western technical routines to manage their objectified cultures; that they promote their 'cultural self-image' internationally in an effort to woo the economically crucial tourist trade; that, in short, everyone wants to put (their) own culture in (their) own museums – all this indicates that modernity has not only conquered the world, but has ushered in a 'postmodern' global society of objectified culture, pseudo events and spectacles.[70]

The Cameroonian philosopher Marcien Towa speaks of the way the power of Europe causes African self-doubt, and an imperative to 'become like the Other'.[71]

The man of the 'South', says Latouche, is Westernized in his desires, the framework of his imagination, the importance of the city and of central models of consumption in his daily life. 'He is a tramp in his concrete reality, his profound rootlessness, his miserable shanty-town standard of living.'[72] These effects are caused not just by the masters of capital, but by 'the limitless devotion of empire builders, the self sacrifice of doctors, the fraternal solicitude of benefactors, the altruism of missionaries, the generous competence of technologists, not forgetting the internationalist ardour and self sacrifice of professional revolutionaries'. All these are the real protagonists in the drama of deculturation.[73] Precisely as this happens 'The void created by the insidious and progressive loss of meaning engendered by the existence of the West is filled, in a way, by Western meaning.'[74]

Writing from Canada Gregory Baum distinguishes between primary and secondary cultures.[75] Primary culture refers to the home environment in which the child is born, including language, food, customs and the relations to parents and other members of the family. In traditional cultures the primary culture often stretches out into the street and the village. This, however, does

---

69   A.Toynbee, *Civilization on Trial* Oxford: Oxford University Press 1948 p.214

70   Cited in King, 'The Global, the Urban and the World' p.153

71   Cited in Latouche, *Westernization* p.60

72   Latouche, *Westernization* p.78 S.Sayyid also believes that it is impossible to escape the distinction between 'the West and the rest'. 'It is this distinction that underpins the post-colonial world. Attempts to overcome the West/Rest distinction by pointing to empirical multiculturalism (that is, the existence of many cultures and the impossibility of thinking of one culture) and valorizing hybridity (the normative celebration of multiculturalism) fail because they ignore the way in which the West/Rest distinction is played out as the distinction between the hegemonic and subaltern and between the culturally unmarked and culturally marked.' 'Beyond Westphalia' p.47

73   Latouche, *Westernization* p.58

74   Latouche, *Westernization* p.59

75   G.Baum, 'Two Question Marks: Inculturation and Multiculturalism' in N. Greinacher and N. Mette(eds) *Christianity and Cultures* London: SCM 1994 pp.101–106

not happen in modern society. Alongside primary culture there is a secondary culture, the ideas, values and practices promoted by the capitalist market, technology, the mass media and democratic institutions. This culture has the power to displace primary culture, a process which can be observed in recent immigrants:

> The work ethic, competition, upward mobility and self-promotion are quickly learnt ... Television advertising produces a yearning for more leisure, greater comfort and the enjoyment of more consumer goods. Technology teaches people that they have control over their environment, that their lives can be made easier by mechanical instruments, and even that instrumental rationality is the safest guide in solving personal and social problems.[76]

The result is 'deculturation', the destruction of primary cultures and the creation of a cultural emptiness in the home that is communicated to children and prevents them from acquiring spiritual or non-utilitarian values. It is difficult to resist because the need to survive in a market led society co-opts you, forces you to play by the same rules.[77]

Expounding Marx, Berman reads modernity as essentially ambiguous: on the one side the glory of modern energy and dynamism, on the other the ravages of nihilism, 'a flaring up of radical hopes in the midst of their radical negations'.[78] In virtue of both the concrete goods it brings, and its compelling drive towards self-development, modernity sweeps all before it. Attempts by Third World governments to repress modernity in the name of Western decadence are bound to fail because what they are repressing is their own people's energies, desires and critical spirit. Modernity, then, is in one sense fate, though modernism is the attempt to live within the maelstrom, to use the chaos creatively.

Tomlinson finds Berman's argument hubristic, and wedded to an overly individualistic anthropology. He agrees, however, that modernity has involved a profound form of cultural imperialism which has colonized what Cornelias Castoriadis calls the social imaginary. In the value system of Christianity, Castoriadis argues, God ultimately provides the limits and intrinsic norms of a finite human nature, but at some stage in the European middle ages the infinite was displaced from its position outside this world order and considered part of it. The possibility of infinite development then became the major social imaginary. It is this which provides the orientation of society and answers the basic questions of who we are and what we want.

---

76 Baum, 'Question Marks' pp.104–105

77 Immanuel Wallerstein makes the same point. Cultural resistance utilizes the structures of the system to oppose the system which, however, partially legitimates these structures by appealing to antecedent, broader ideologies and thus accepting in part the terms of the debate as defined by the dominant forces. The powerful of the world co-opt cultural resistance by commodifying it and if one withdraws into small communes in what sense is one sharing a culture with anyone else, even with other individualist resisters? Wallerstein, 'The National and the Universal' p.101

78 Berman, *All That Is Solid* p.121

This imaginary does not provide qualitative goals and visions, any sense of a completion to progress, or any sense of where communities are going. It fails in the pseudo rationality of the actual practices it sets in train and in the vacuity of the concept of development as 'nothing except the capacity to attain new states'.[79] It follows that cultural imperialism is not an invasion of weak cultures by strong ones but almost the opposite – a sort of cultural decay spreading from the West to the rest of the world.[80] The institutions of capitalist modernity colonize the cultural space of less developed societies, stifle cultural creativity and lead to disenchantment with tradition. This is not something to be blamed on 'the West' but is to do with the autonomized institutions of modernity, capitalism as the central dominant positioning of economic practices within the social ordering of existence.[81] Since there seems no retreat from modernity short of nuclear death do we simply have to accept it as fate?

Resistance to Homogenization

Can local distinctiveness survive the acids of modernity? Amongst critics of Westernization, Tomlinson points out, there is a danger of so exaggerating the extent of our helplessness in the face of globalization that possibilities of resistance are discounted. We do not have to accept the case as given. After all, if culture refers fundamentally to world views and beliefs, then there are currently few signs of homogenization.

In making a case against the success of Westernization we can point to the multiple political chauvinisms and counter cultures of the contemporary world. The Tower of Babel trajectory still holds, it is argued. Minorities are on the increase. 'So just as there is a dialectic of creating simultaneously a homogenous world and distinctive national cultures within it, so there is a dialectic of creating simultaneously homogenous national cultures and distinctive ethnic groups or minorities.'[82] New beliefs, cults, messianic movements and small scale alternative economies are also part of this picture.[83] In the last chapter I mentioned the 'singing revolution' of the Baltic states where culture was turned into a political asset. The same happened in East Timor. Alongside globalization, states, 'forms of life' and social movements still structure our lives. All these differ in their centring and de-centring tendencies and in their cultural economies.[84]

The form of life framework involves interpersonal relationships, resulting configurations of self and other, characteristic uses of symbolic modes, providing a core which the market framework cannot reach. It could perhaps

79   Tomlinson, *Imperialism* p.159
80   Tomlinson, *Imperialism* p.164
81   Tomlinson, *Imperialism* p.168
82   Wallerstein, 'Culture as the Ideological Battleground' p.49
83   Latouche, *Westernization* p.xiii
84   U.Hannerz, 'Scenarios for Peripheral Cultures' in King(ed) *Culture, Globalization and the World System* p.116

even colonize the market framework rather than vice versa, for we should not underestimate the creativity of popular culture. Again, it is a common experience to define ourselves in concentric circles, as from Madurai, Tamil Nadu and India, a Highlander, Scots and British, or Yoruba, Nigerian and African. 'The continuing existence of national identities inhibits the emergence of a global, cosmopolitan identity, if only in the way they preoccupy people's cultural imagination to the point of defining its horizons.'[85] The threat of the homogenization of culture can only be deduced, therefore, by ignoring the complexity, reflexivity and sheer recalcitrance of actual, particular cultural responses to modernity.[86]

Arjun Appadurai argues that at least as rapidly as forces from various metropolises are brought into new societies they tend to become indigenized in one way or another.[87] The homogenization thesis is premised on a centre–periphery model which is false in two ways. In the first place, if what we really mean by homogenization is Americanization then we have to point out that this is demonstrably not the case for the people of Irian Jaya, Korea, Sri Lanka, Cambodia, Armenia and the Baltic republics, all of whom are much more worried by the presence of more local neighbours. Secondly, it overlooks the fluidity of the contemporary scene. Technology, finance, media, ideas are all involved in complex flows across the world and there is a growing disjunction between these various flows. The Japanese are hospitable to ideas but not to immigrants, like the Swedes, the Swiss and the Saudis. But the Swedes and the Saudis accept guestworkers thus creating labour diasporas:

> There are nations in search of states: Sikhs, Tamils, Basques, Moros, Quebecois, whilst States seek to monopolize the moral resources of community either by claiming that the state is the nation or by systematically museumizing and representing all the groups within them in a variety of heritage politics that seems remarkably uniform throughout the world.[88]

The globalization of culture is not the same as its homogenization. Globalization involves the use of a variety of instruments of homogenization (armaments, advertising techniques, language hegemonies, clothing styles and the like) which are absorbed into local political and cultural economies, only to be repatriated as heterogeneous dialogues of national sovereignty, free enterprise and fundamentalism.[89] You can even argue, with Antony Giddens, that the universality of Western institutions shows the declining grip of the West over the rest of the world.[90] The fact that India can produce high-tech engineers and the fact that much of southern California was bought up by Japanese investors during the 1980s show the extent of decentralizing

85   Tomlinson, *Globalization* p.102
86   Tomlinson, *Globalization* p.97
87   A.Appadurai, 'Disjuncture and Difference in the Global Cultural Economy' in Featherstone(ed) *Global Culture* pp.295–310
88   Appadurai, 'Disjuncture and Difference' p.304
89   Appadurai, 'Disjuncture and Difference' pp.307–308
90   A.Giddens, *The Consequences of Modernity* Cambridge: Polity 1990 p.92

processes. 'The globalization of fundamentalism and of powerful nationalisms is part of the same process, the violent eruption of cultural identities in the wake of declining modernist identity.'[91]

Any review of the current world situation makes it clear that acceptance of the technological–scientific culture may co-exist with a vigorous rejection of its secular outlook.[92] Many people point to the phenomenon of 'glocalism' and the claim of multinationals such as Coca-Cola that they are in fact multi local. To assume that the sheer global presence of Western goods leads to homogenization, it is argued, is to use an impoverished concept of culture. Symbolic forms are always appropriated in individual ways and homogenizing development is upset by the counter tempo of profound differences and cultural discontinuities.[93]

In the process of the global exchange of cultures it is not all just one way. What we see is not just the Westernization of oriental music but the orientalization of Western music.[94] In this connection we can note what is obviously the growing influence of the Indian film industry, which has successfully maintained its own conventions over against Hollywood. Jonathan Friedman distinguishes between strong and weak globalization. The pre-requisite for strong globalization is the homogenization of local contexts, so that subjects in different positions in the system have a disposition to attribute the same meaning to the same globalized objects, images, representations and so forth. Weak globalization entails that the local assimilates the global into its own realm of practised meaning. On the whole, he believes, there is more evidence for weak rather than strong forms.[95]

It is also true, and a fundamental thesis of liberation theology, that the question of power is not all one way. Marginality, argues Stuart Hall, has become a powerful space. 'You could not describe the movements of colonial nationalism without that moment when the unspoken discovered that they had a history which they could speak; they had languages other than the languages of the master, of the tribe.'[96] Others point out that corporate culture is memoryless and therefore extremely weak and vapid alongside the myths and memories, values and symbols which shaped the culture and boundaries of existing states and nations. These retain their hold because ethnohistory assures collective dignity and answers the question of oblivion. Only these

---

91 Friedman, *Cultural Identity* p.211

92 Tomlinson, *Globalization* p.96. Ulrich Beck is dismissive of claims for cultural homogeniza-tion but his assertion of glocalization, following Roland Robertson, offers no detailed evidence. When firms like McDonald's or Coca-Cola claim to adapt to the local the question is whether it is not an extremely superficial veneer which we are dealing with. The underlying cultural reality is the same. U.Beck, *What is Globalization?* Cambridge: Polity 2000 pp.42–47

93 Tomlinson, *Globalization* pp.83–85

94 Janet Abu-Lughod, 'Going Beyond Global Babble' in King(ed) *Culture, Globalization and the World System* p.133

95 Friedman, *Cultural Identity* p.204

96 S.Hall, 'The Local and the Global: Globalization and Ethnicity' in King(ed) *Culture, Globalization and the World System* p.35

myths and stories tell us who we are, where we come from and where we are going.[97]

Finally, we have to remember that all empires believe themselves to be eternal whereas they do, in fact, all decline. The world system must deal with the problem of its eventual demise and strong states with the problem of relative decline.[98] Wallerstein's view is that hopes for the future have to be based on the inherent lack of long-term equilibria in any phenomena – physical, biological or social – and that this means we shall never have a blandly homogenized world.[99] Since, as many agree, the global balance of power is already shifting away from the West, modernity will not be universalized.[100]

There is a clear analogy between the arguments which dismiss the case for homogenization, and the arguments denying the dominance of mass culture which we saw in the last chapter. Theories of cultural imperialism share with theories of mass culture a strong view of the manipulability of mass audiences and an assumption of the negative cultural effects of the media as self-evident.[101] In any case we must not overplay the alienating character of modern social life at the expense of its emancipatory moments.

Universal and Particular

The case for the homogenization of world culture, and the case against, are both supported by numerous social scientists of the first rank. In view of the complexity of the data under discussion not even the most expert can hazard more than a guess as to which of these two cases is right. Each person will draw on their own experience to make a judgment and take sides. What we can do, however, and need to do, is to make a judgment about the desirability or otherwise of the process. Theologically, as I suggested at the start of the chapter, we do this by reflecting on the relation of universal and particular.

The dialectic of universal and particular has been with us since at least the first century, and perhaps since the very first empire. The great religio-cultural traditions which arose in what Karl Jaspers calls the axial period were, it is argued, developed precisely around the universalism–particularism theme.[102] As this came to be understood and expounded by someone like Herder, there is a claim that universalism and particularism are basically complementary, that each particular culture (*Volk*) makes its contribution to the universal whole. As is obvious from the arguments about Westernization, what we need to do is to

97   Smith, 'Towards a Global Culture?' pp.171–191
98   Wallerstein, 'Culture as the Ideological Battleground' p.49
99   Wallerstein, 'The National and the Universal' p.104
100   Featherstone, *Global Culture* p.10
101   Featherstone, *Undoing Culture* p.115
102   R.Robertson, 'Social Theory, Cultural Relativity and the Problem of Globality' in King(ed) *Culture, Globalization and the World System* pp.77, 78

distinguish between true and false universalism and particularism, and to relate them to the issues of global and local.

Ben Barber's 'Jihad vs McWorld' concept represents precisely such an attempt. By 'McWorld' he means the overweening claim to universality of the market. This is a false universalism because it offers only a contractual relation between persons and cannot ground common identity or a collective membership – something a faith community like Islam does well.[103] Opposition to 'McWorld' – symbolized by the September 11 attacks – is based on hostility not only to its consumption-driven markets and its technocratic imperatives, but to the perceived hollowness of its claim to stand as a foundation for a meaningful moral existence.[104]

Latouche notes how generations were sacrificed to a false universalism in the hope for socialism, which led to Chernobyl and the Gulag, and he asks whether we will have to wait another forty years 'before we realise that development means real, existing development and that the development which really exists means economic war, unlimited pillage of nature, the Westernization of the world and total planetary uniformity, the genocide and ethnocide of all other cultures?':[105]

> The unlimited accumulation of capital is connected with significant social outlooks, meaning values and beliefs which are essentially Western: progress, universalism, the domination of nature, quantifying reason. I believe ... that the peoples who are being oppressed, exploited and strangled want nothing to do either with real, existing development or even with the mirages of development whose consequences they have experienced ... they aspire to survive, first of all, and then if possible to live well ... to live according to their own values, their own cultural choices, and not be crushed by the rat-race for higher per capita GNP.[106]

The false universalism Latouche attacks – and he has said of course that 'the West' is a metaphor, and that it has no geographical centre – is 'the unlimited accumulation of capital'. It is this which ultimately destroys all true particulars. Stuart Hall speaks of globalization as the self-presentation of the dominant particular:

> It is a way in which the dominant particular localizes and naturalizes itself. I don't think we can identify the global with the lowest common denominator stake which we all have in being human ... I do not think we can mobilize people simply through their common humanity ... I think of the global as something having more to do with the hegemonic sweep at which a certain configuration of local particularities tries to dominate the whole scene, to mobilize the technology and to incorporate, in subaltern positions, a variety of more localized identities to construct the next historical project.[107]

---

103   Barber, *Jihad vs McWorld* p.243
104   Barber, *Jihad vs McWorld* p.275
105   Latouche, *Westernization* p.xiv
106   Latouche, *Westernization* p.xv
107   S.Hall, 'Old and New Identities, Old and New Ethnicities' in King(ed) *Culture, Globalization and the World System* p.67

There is, of course, a false particularism – likewise symbolized by the September 11 attacks – which is the mirror image of this bid for dominance, namely 'the retreat into various entrenched nationalist, ethnic, religious, gender, sexual or environmentalist "localist" fundamentalisms'.[108] In this connection we can note that it is a problem with Barber's choice of vocabulary that it might suggest that it is primarily Islam which opposes 'McWorld', and that militant particularism only exists on that side, which is far from the case. On the one hand, as we have seen in Latin America, capitalism is far more violent than what has been dubbed 'terror' in the wake of those attacks (as if the murder of hundreds of thousands by death squads was not terror). On the other hand McWorld is opposed peacefully by a whole spectrum of anti-capitalist movements in the West, and by environmental groups throughout the world. It is not, then, just 'jihad' even if it is 'McWorld' which is opposed.[109]

If false universalism is tied to capital, what would true universalism look like? Identifying the Socratic project of the examined life, Christian commitment to the redemption of all and the Enlightenment project of progress towards a universal human civilization as forms of universalism, John Gray describes such universalism as 'one of the least useful and indeed most dangerous aspects of the western intellectual tradition'.[110] In his view it amounts to a false particularism, a tacit claim that Western values are authoritative for all cultures and peoples. Sardar agrees, adding postmodern-ism to the list of false particularisms.[111] Of course, the first question is whether all these universalisms are really to be lumped together in this way. The first is concerned with self-knowledge, the second has been construed in many different ways, and for many centuries was understood in a rather introverted way, and the third is much more problematic and complex than is often depicted. They are also mutually incompatible. Much Christian polemic, for example, has been devoted to rejecting both the Socratic and the Enlight-enment projects as inadequate – the latter indeed is a cliché of twentieth century discussion as the former is of the Augustinian tradition.

If we do take them together, however, do they amount to false particularism? One could not assert that this was a matter of definition without disallowing any universal claims whatever, which would preclude my protesting at the torture of people from other cultures or belief systems and ultimately even understanding them, as I shall argue in Chapter 10. It might follow from the falsity of what is argued for, as the false universalism of capitalism follows from the hollowness of its account of the human good. It is hard to see how

---

108 Tomlinson, *Globalization* p.182
109 Burbach et al criticize Barber for holding an antiquated, idealistic view of democracy, and failing to understand the new social movements, 'messy and tumultuous' as they are. R.Burbach, O.Nunez, B.Kargarlitsky, *Globalization and its Discontents* London: Pluto 1996 p.147
110 J.Gray, *Endgames: Questions in late modern political thought* Cambridge: Polity 1997 p.158 The inadequacy of Western claims to universality is argued by Paul Gilroy, who maintains that slavery is the premise of modernity, and that this exposes the foundational ethnocentrism of the Enlightenment project with its idea of universality, fixity of meaning and coherence of the subject. Cited in Featherstone, *Undoing Culture* p.11
111 Sardar, *Postmodernism*

this applies to the Socratic '*gnothi seauton*', unless we want to argue, as some theologians have done, that self-knowledge is impossible without grace. The Enlightenment project is another matter, though here again the phrase is used a little too glibly, in the light of counter Enlightenment thinkers like Vico and Herder. The light of the Enlightenment was real light.[112] The problem with the Enlightenment idea of a universal civilization was in measuring what was human by a rationalism born equally from Cartesian doubt, the success of Newtonian physics and the reaction to the religious wars, all of which suggested that 'tradition', which is to say, dialogue with the past, could be dispensed with. What resulted from these initiatives were the utilitarianism and positivism of the nineteenth century, the first of which, if not the second, is the philosophical underpinning of capitalism.

The Christian claim to universal salvation, its account of universalism and particularism, is rooted in the incarnation. The understanding of incarnation hammered out in the fourth to the sixth centuries was not the product of scholastic perversity, but a struggle to know how to be true to the gospel in a milieu foreign to its origin, the milieu of Hellenism. The formulae of Nicaea, Chalcedon, or of Leontius of Byzantium do not, as critics allege, offer us a dated, culture specific and alienating account of what it means for God to become human so much as a set of guidelines for thinking about the engagement of the Wholly Other with human particulars. They are, as it were, the grammar of divine cultural engagement. In the fifth century debates, for example, the Antiochenes fight for particularity and the Alexandrines for universality. As has always been recognized, the formulae which constituted the truce between them do not give an account of *how* the universal and the particular can be combined, but simply set out the rules of engagement. Any failure to respect the claims of either universal or particular, it was claimed, is unworkable.

The doctrine of the incarnation claims that God took flesh at a particular time and place, taught in a particular language, and was tortured to death under particular laws. The purpose of this, however, was the redemption of history, which is to say, the offering of a clue to the meaning of the whole historical process, what we have called the long revolution. Paul characteristically moves from the event of crucifixion (Gal 3.13) to the claim that 'in Christ' the categories of race, class and gender no longer count (Gal 3.28). The 'in Christ' is shorthand for the movement which stems from Christ, the task of which is to live out and witness to the breaking down of all barriers. It is a vision of human history, bound together first 'in Adam' – subject to the law of violence – and then 'in Christ' – subject to the law of peace, or reconciliation – but it is a vision of a *process*. The true universal, claims Slavov Žižek, is an endless struggle and true universalists are not those who preach global tolerance but those who engage in a passionate fight for the Truth which enthuses them.[113] To claim that the process through which alienation is

---

112   As Lesslie Newbigin insists. *Foolishness to the Greeks* London: SPCK 1986 p.43
113   S.Žižek, *The Ticklish Subject* London: Verso 1999 pp.226, 7

addressed is falsely totalizing would require us to deny that race, class and gender are categories which can be used meaningfully about human society in general and that a vision of creation at peace cannot function as a utopian goal. It is emphatically not about establishing a universal culture with one language, and one aesthetic. If we read the story of Pentecost from the standpoint of Herder's claim that language is the heart of culture, then the point of the story is that the gospel comes to all cultures in their own terms, a point I will take up further in Chapter 9.[114]

The doctrine of the incarnation, I wish to claim, does indeed offer a way of affirming both universal and particular in a non-alienating way, in a way that does not involve false particularism, and as such I shall be returning to it repeatedly in the following chapters. To be able to do this is important because, on the one hand, without pluralism there can be no peace, for, as T.S.Eliot argued, diversity affords stability, and, on the other hand, the problem of the environment is too urgent to allow a pluralism where each does what he or she wants – the George Bush solution to global warming. As Herder insisted, in line with the Fathers of Chalcedon, universalism and particularism are equally true, and therefore without either one the long revolution fails. Since every doctrine has political consequences – a fact recognized by Barth in his integration of dogmatics and ethics – this commits us, on the one hand, to a resolute defence of local distinctiveness at every level: languages, cuisines, building styles, customs and so on and so forth. Where these are life giving they represent, in Herder's terms, a response to the Spirit of life. At the same time that very conviction commits us to a universalism, to the cherishing of what Herder called *Humanität* everywhere. No policy informed by incarnation can be universalizing if this means the elimination of difference. Equally, no cultural policy informed by incarnation could be chauvinist. I shall try to explore this double imperative in relation to the contemporary world in the last two chapters of the book. As I shall argue, it is this understanding of incarnation which underlies our approach to mission and multiculturalism and to the so-called 'clash of civilizations'.

Discussion of the incarnation takes us back to the first chapter, and the role of this doctrine in any theology of culture. Before moving on to the next part of the book, and the discussion of culture and power, I will therefore first briefly review where we have got to in terms of a theology of culture. I have rejected Niebuhr's typological approach in favour of greater complexity and what I hope is a more nuanced account. The main lines of this, however, are fourfold. In the first place, whether we come from the doctrine of creation or from the Reformed understanding of the lordship of Christ we have to insist that

---

114 Of course, if ethics and aesthetics are effectively one we have to ask how a common ethic can be indwelt by different cultures in such a way as to allow radically different aesthetics. For St Thomas the answer was in terms of grace and form – grace informs the creature, and the creature's products, without overriding the integrity of the creature: it does not destroy but perfects the creature.

theology is concerned with the whole of human endeavour, and not just with a religious segment. The doctrine of creation teaches us this because all things come from God, and nothing is outwith God's sway, and the lordship of Christ in the same way. Fundamental to the Barmen declaration of 1934 was the proposition that there are no autonomous areas of human activity not subject to theological appraisal. I have read 'culture' as the totality of human creative effort. Of course, it is marked by sin and idolatry, but it is marked by grace as well. To the extent that it represents a life-giving response to the God of life it is part of what I have called 'the long revolution'. In the second chapter I explored the significance of the religious side of culture *vis-à-vis* the non-religious, and *vis-à-vis* faith. Religion, I have argued, is part of culture but not reducible to it. The gospel is, to use Barth's formula, both 100 per cent human and 100 per cent divine, completely part of culture, but a foreign element within as well, an irritant, an immanent critique.

Following on from this, I have taken from Barth the understanding that eschatology is the central category for any theology of culture. Eschatology is not simply about 'last' things but, as Moltmann above all has taught us, about direction and goal, about meaning, about the hope that sustains us in the midst of hopelessness. I began with John Tomlinson's observation that the key failure of modernity was lack of any sense of meaning and value. The eschatological dimension of theology addresses this concern. I have argued that, if we take the priority of the poor seriously, then this points us away from both elite culture and cultural populism. There is space for a popular culture, pre-figured by peasant cultures around the world, which is concerned with fineness of living, and which to that extent leads into and lays the groundwork for 'the best which has been thought and said', all the achievements of high culture which the Church, amongst others, has elicited.

A theology of culture is at the same time a theology of the Spirit, about God active in the historical process, not a God asleep or unconcerned. If God exists then God acts, and that action must call forth results. The life-affirming aspects of culture, I am arguing, are those results. The widespread use of the category of 'inspiration' in relation to the wider sphere of culture is not necessarily a mistake. Why should it not be theologically true? It is a presupposition of my talk of the long revolution that this is the case.

Finally, as I have argued in this chapter, a theology of the Spirit which reflects on Pentecost, will be a theology of diversity in unity. It will be a theology of diversity – of the valuing of real difference. At the same time, if it represents response to the one Spirit it will have an underlying unity – a theme to which I shall return in Chapter 10. I turn now, in the next part of the book, to consider the ideological dimension of culture, and the question of cultural power.

PART II
POWER

How is it that – if *all* meaning were potentially open to conquest, *all* power potentially unfixed – history keeps generating hegemonies that, for long periods, seem able to impose a degree of order and stability on the world?

Jean and John Comaroff

Chapter 5

Opium of the People?

Power, I said in the first chapter, was the great omission from Niebuhr's influential typology of Christianity and culture. Written in a situation when the quantities 'Christ' and 'culture' could be taken for granted, the question seems not to have arisen for him. But if, as I have argued, 'culture' is a way of talking of what human beings make of their world materially, intellectually and spiritually how can we leave power out of this account? Some argue that hunter-gatherer societies are or were democratic and egalitarian but in every other society we know the rich thrive and the poor are sent empty away, and money and influence corrupt the operations of justice. Power is the thread which stitches the seams of the cultural garment. This second part of the book, then, examines power as a cultural matter. I begin with a discussion of ideology, proceed in the next chapter to hegemony, and conclude this second part with a discussion of cultural politics.

No matter how culture is understood – whether as individual habit of mind, as the account of the artistic and intellectual development of society as a whole, or as the whole way of life of a people – ideas, beliefs, philosophies, theologies, in short, what have been called since the late eighteenth century, 'ideologies', are part of it. We cannot consider culture without taking these into account. 'In modern society,' remarks Terry Eagleton, in the sentence I have used as the epigraph for the first part of the book:

> it is not enough to occupy factories or confront the state. What must also be contested is the whole area of culture, defined in its broadest, most everyday sense. The power of the ruling class is spiritual as well as material; and any 'counter-hegemony' must carry its political campaign into this hitherto neglected realm of values and customs, speech habits and ritual practices.[1]

In any society more complex than that of hunter-gatherers, we may add, and not just in modern society – hence the need for an ideological analysis of Scripture. The need for an understanding of ideology applies *a fortiori* to any discussion of theology and culture because the notion of ideology arose, at that moment at the beginning of Williams' 'long revolution', in opposition to theology, and two hundred years later we have to ask how the relation stands.

In the first three sections of this chapter I briefly outline the debate on ideology of the past fifty years before turning to the accusation that the gospel functions as an opiate. I develop a theological reply to that argument in four distinct steps. First, I argue that Scripture functions uniquely as an ideological

---

1 Eagleton, *Ideology* p.114

irritant, critiquing ruling systems of power. We are all familiar with the way in which Hebrew prophecy does that. I argue in addition that the character of Scripture as the record of an ongoing debate enables it to play this role. I develop the account of the function of prophecy in terms of the protocol against idolatry which, following Kosuke Koyama, we must consider as intimately bound up with ideology. In response to an argument that the best defence against ideology is an apophatic theology I argue, to the contrary, that the immensely rich doctrine of God developed by Karl Barth gives us far greater critical resources. Finally, I reply to the kind of worries which prompted Marx's famous phrase by appealing to the materialism of the incarnation. These four strategies, I believe, give us an account of how the gospel functions *critically* within any culture. Taking the notion of ideology seriously develops Niebuhr's idea of 'Christ against culture'. In the next chapter I shall turn to the *constructive* side.

The Meaning of 'Ideology'

In his account of ideology Terry Eagleton notes at least sixteen possible meanings of the term, and concludes by saying that 'It is doubtful that one can ascribe to ideology any invariable characteristics at all. We are dealing less with some essence of ideology than with an overlapping network of "family resemblances" between different styles of signification.'[2] On the whole, however, the twofold classification proposed by Karl Mannheim in 1936, between those meanings which are neutral and those which express bias or interest, often with a pejorative connotation, seems to hold, and this applies to the six major definitions Eagleton himself outlines.[3]

   As is well known, the term was invented by Destutt de Tracy at the end of the eighteenth century, and was from the start polemically opposed to theology. Behind this opposition is a long history, which goes back at least as far as the trial of Galileo, and perhaps even further to popular hostility to the Church in the middle ages.[4] Holbach (1723–1789), for example, argues that man is unhappy:

> because he misunderstands nature. His mind is so infected by prejudices that one may think of him as forever condemned to error ... Reason, guided by experience, must attack at their sources the prejudices of which mankind has been the victim for so long ... Truth is one and necessary for man ... The chains which tyrants and

---

2   Eagleton, *Ideology* p.222
3   K.Mannheim, *Ideology and Utopia* London: Kegan Paul 1936 Eagleton suggests: the general material process of production of ideas, beliefs and values in social life; ideas and beliefs which symbolize the conditions and life experiences of a socially significant group or class; the promotion or legitimation of the interests of such groups; the promotion and legitimation of a dominant social power; those beliefs which legitimate the interests of a ruling group by distortion and dissimulation; and false beliefs which arise from the material structure of society as a whole. *Ideology* pp.28–30
4   Detailed, for example, in K.Thomas, *Religion and the Decline of Magic* Penguin: Harmondsworth 1973

priests forge are due to error ... ignorance and uncertainty are due to errors consecrated by religion.[5]

De Tracy, writing in gaol during the Terror, builds on precisely this sentiment. What he wants is a 'science of ideas' which will set aside metaphysical and religious prejudices and provide the basis for public education. Ideology is a replacement for theology, and all those other obscurantist notions which belong to the *ancien régime*.

De Tracy and his colleagues were at first patronized by Napoleon, but in the wake of his disastrous Russian campaign he turned on them, seeking scapegoats, calling them 'ideologues', which is to say, unrealistic and doctrinaire intellectuals. Marx was familiar both with de Tracy's writing and with Napoleon's attack, and both the neutral and negative senses of ideology can be found in the attack on the 'Left Hegelians' in *The German Ideology*. Marx begins by insisting that 'The production of ideas, of conceptions, of consciousness, is at first directly interwoven with the material activity and the material intercourse of men ... Men are the producers of their conceptions, ideas etc. that is, real active men as they are conditioned by a definite development of their productive forces.'[6] This is to make the simple, though profoundly important, point that ideas can only be understood within their social context, a point later developed in the sociology of knowledge.

Where Marx speaks of ideas and conceptions here Foucault later talks of discourse. Taking up the great theme of Francis Bacon it is one of his central contentions that knowledge and power are inseparable. 'There can be no possible exercise of power without a certain economy of discourses of truth which operates through and on the basis of this association. We are subjected to the production of truth through power and we cannot exercise power except through the production of truth.'[7] All forms of discourse, according to Foucault, involve some exercise of power. 'We should admit ... that power and knowledge directly imply one another; that there is no power relation without the correlative constitution of a field of knowledge, nor any knowledge that does not presuppose and constitute at the same time power relations.'[8]

Marx goes a step further in arguing that it is *forgetting* that ideas are rooted in 'material life process' which constitutes ideology. When we remember this fact we see that morality, religion and so forth:

no longer retain the semblance of independence. They have no history, no development: but men, developing their material production and their material intercourse, alter, along with this their actual world, also their thinking and their modes of thinking. It is not consciousness which determines life, but life which determines consciousness ... Where speculation ends, where real life starts, there

5 Quoted in Jorge Larrain, *The Concept of Ideology* London: Hutchinson 1979 p.24

6 K.Marx and F.Engels, *Collected Works* Moscow: Progress 1975 vol 5 p.36

7 M.Foucault, *Power/Knowledge* Hemel Hempstead: Harvester Wheatsheaf 1980 p.93

8 M.Foucault, *Discipline and Punish* Harmondsworth: Penguin 1991 p.27

consequently begins real, positive science, the expounding of the practical activity, of the practical process of the development of men.[9]

Ideological strategies are, then, as Peter Scott puts it, those which effectively obscure, mis-speak or misrecognize the social history of which they are a part.[10]

The argument is complex. There is a continuation of de Tracy's programme of replacing the existing chaos of the world of ideas with a rigorous 'science', and in this case a science which is empirically verifiable. Marx was born into, and fully acknowledged, the Prometheanism of the Enlightenment: in the preface to his doctoral thesis he described Prometheus as 'the noblest of saints and martyr in the calendar of philosophy'.[11] Secondly there is a polemic against, or better, a desire to invert, Hegelian idealism. For Hegel, acclaimed by the 'Right Hegelians' as the saviour of theology, it is consciousness, Absolute Spirit working itself out in the whole complex of evolution and history, that determines life. Not so, says Marx, but 'life', by which he means material production and intercourse, determines consciousness. This is a stronger claim than the earlier insistence on a necessary dialectic between mind and matter and leads to the whole debate about 'base' and 'superstructure' in which Marx can be read in very different ways. Sometimes he is inclined to speak of ideas as 'reflections' of the society they emanate from, an undialectical idea which caused problems for his passion for Greek tragedy.[12] On the other hand, the third thesis on Feuerbach reminds materialists inclined to read off the human condition simply from circumstances and upbringing that it is 'human beings who change circumstances'. He is, however, insisting on the social determination of all thought and that 'ideology is thought which denies this determination, or thought so socially determined as to deny its own determinants'.[13]

Ideology is often defined as false consciousness, a definition which Marx does not use, and which seems to have originated with a remark of Engels. Jorge Larrain argues that the notion is implicit in Feuerbach's argument that the idea of God is a projection of human consciousness, and not just an arbitrary invention of priests.[14] There are problems with the idea, which Terry Eagleton draws attention to. To suppose that, over extensive historical periods, immense numbers of people have lived and died in the name of ideas which were absolutely vacuous flies in the face of what he calls the 'moderate rationality of people in general'. He appeals to Donald Davidson's argument that most of what people say most of the time must be true for language and communication to be possible. Nevertheless, as he goes on to argue, the idea of false consciousness cannot be abandoned altogether in the sense that people

---

9   Marx and Engels, *Collected Works* vol 5 p.37
10   P.Scott, *Theology, Ideology and Liberation* Cambridge: Cambridge University Press 1994 p.1
11   K.Marx and F.Engels, *On Religion* Moscow: Progress 1955 p.51
12   Marx and Engels, *On Religion* p.135
13   Eagleton, *Ideology* p.89
14   Larrain, *Concept* p.31

may hold beliefs for reasons which one can understand, but which may nevertheless be false and offensively false – such as the view that Jews or Africans are inferior beings, or women less rational than men.[15] The sense in which belief in God might be considered analogous to such beliefs I will consider later.

Larrain distinguishes in Marx's argument between idealistic superstructure and ideology, the former representing the 'neutral' sense of ideology and the latter the pejorative. Ideology in the pejorative sense both conceals social contradictions and does so in the interests of the dominant class. 'Ideology has to be judged by its reference to actual social practice, to the concrete evolution of contradictions. The sharper the contradictions in society become the more ideology "descends to the level of mere idealizing phrases, conscious illusion, deliberate hypocrisy".'[16]

Ideology in this sense is, in John Thompson's phrase, 'meaning in the service of power' or, more fully, a description of the way in which 'the meaning mobilized by symbolic forms serves to establish and sustain relations of domination'. Meaning embraces all symbolic forms, and domination is that situation in which established relations of power are 'systematically asymmetrical.'[17]

Eagleton points out that the idea of ideology as meaning in the service of power overlooks cases of beliefs which are certainly ideological but which never enjoyed power. The Levellers and Diggers are good examples. And on a Foucauldian reading of power, where power is everywhere, it becomes difficult to see what is excluded and how it can be resisted.[18] All the same, the centrality of domination to the pejorative reading of ideology has to be maintained.

The Dominant Ideology Thesis

In *The Communist Manifesto* Marx and Engels famously remarked that the ruling ideas of any age were always the ideas of the ruling class. The link between ideology and domination produced what was dubbed the 'dominant ideology thesis'. The thesis argued that in class divided societies the dominant class subsumes the dominated within a system which is, in fact, operating against their material interests, and this explains the stability of capitalist society.[19] Weber's version of this view argues that each society has a dominant

---

15 Eagleton, *Ideology* pp.14–15
16 Larrain, *Concept* p.61
17 Thompson, *Ideology and Modern Culture* p.59 Ideology plays its role in dominative relations, Thompson argues, by the processes of legitimation, universalization (where the interests of some are represented to be the interests of all), dissimulation (in which relations of domination are concealed), unification (in which a collective identity is constructed irrespective of existing divisions), fragmentation and reification (representing a transitory state of affairs as if it were permanent). Ibid p.61ff
18 Eagleton, *Ideology* pp.6–7
19 N.Abercrombie, S.Hill and B.S.Turner, *The Dominant Ideology Thesis* London: Allen & Unwin 1980 p.2

religious tradition which unites social classes around a common set of religious beliefs and practices and the dominant class has normally been able to contain heterodox, oppositional beliefs by virtue of the fact that it controls the Church.[20]

Abercrombie, Hill and Turner subjected this theory to a well known critique in 1980. If the dominant class really does control the means of mental production, they asked, how do deviant, oppositional and radical views emerge? If the apparatus of ideological control is as strong as some suggest, is there a possibility for change? Examining the medieval period, early capitalism and the twentieth century they came to the conclusion that there was no evidence for a dominant ideology working as Marx and Engels suggest. In the middle ages there was a poorly educated clergy, an indifferent peasantry and periodic heretical uprisings. Widespread illiteracy made a dominant ideology impossible. E.P.Thompson's revival of the thesis that Methodism prevented revolution in the early nineteenth century was contradicted by his own evidence for an autonomous working class culture. In late capitalism managerial and welfarist ideologies were clearly in conflict. Abercrombie and his colleagues conclude that dominant ideologies are in fact fractured and contradictory in most historical periods and have had little effect on the subordinate classes. It is the routines of everyday life which hold society together. Social classes do have different and conflicting ideologies but are, nevertheless, bound together by the network of objective social relations.

When they revisited the question ten years later they concluded that capitalism has no necessary ideological requirements at all. Economic constraints compel people to work and the commitment of subordinates to the system is characterized by pragmatic acquiescence.[21] They argued this on the ground that although the managerial classes did indeed share an ideology endorsing accumulation and property rights, subordinate groups still subscribed widely to a radical–egalitarian and oppositional ideology even after ten years of Thatcherism.

There is no doubt that the dominant ideology critics overstate their case. In the middle ages, for example, the extent to which the Church did in fact influence the hearts and minds of the majority of the population is keenly contested. For the modern period, as Eagleton notes, in claiming that capitalism operates without ideology they certainly went too far. All class divided societies are marred by injustice and this cannot be rectified without putting the ruling class out of business – hence the need for ideology. 'The truth surely is that the diffusion of dominant values and beliefs among oppressed groups in society has some part to play in the reproduction of the system as a whole, but that this factor has been exaggerated in the tradition of Western Marxism.'[22]

---

20 Abercrombie et al, *Thesis* p.39
21 N.Abercrombie, S.Hill and B.S.Turner(eds) *Dominant Ideologies* London: Unwin Hyman 1990 p.3
22 Eagleton, *Ideology* p.36

The End of Ideology?

In the 1990 discussion of dominant ideologies both Scott Lash and Bryan Turner reverted to an even older thesis and suggested that postmodernity might spell the end of ideology. This thesis was originally suggested during the 1950s, as a response to the depression, the war and the camps. Daniel Bell, for example, identified ideology with a way of translating ideas into action, a resumption of the chiliastic ideas of Anabaptism. Calling for the end of ideology meant calling for an end to apocalyptic beliefs that refuse to specify the costs and consequences of the changes they envision.[23] Even at the time many critics felt that the idea of there being an end of ideology was deeply implausible and that what was taken to be growing consensus was symptomatic of the increasing power of ideology over people's lives. Those who argued the case, it was said, underestimated the role of the bulk of the intelligentsia in disseminating the myths of modern democracies and made the mistake of confusing their own fatigue with the idea of ideology with its continued usefulness to the powerful.[24] Alasdair MacIntyre pointed out that the end of ideology thesis, far from marking the end of ideology, was itself a key expression of the ideology of the time and place when it arose and that it was therefore self-refuting.[25] It is certainly ironic that the argument emerged in a society which had the highest per capita spending on advertising anywhere in the world, and this fact suggests that a rather narrow understanding of ideology was under discussion.

Revisiting the topic in 1990 Lash and Turner suggested that the existence of a postmodern culture meant that by definition there cannot be a single, dominant or coherent ideology.[26] We shall have cause to question that in the following chapter. What is certainly the case is that, as Eagleton puts it, the thesis of the end of ideology, taken as a whole, is vastly implausible and fails to account for the vibrancy of debate about political priorities in civil society.[27]

Religion and Ideology

Marx was a materialist in the metaphysical sense that he thought that matter was all there was. It was this philosophical option which prompted the sneer at 'morality, religion, metaphysics, and all the rest of ideology' in *The German Ideology*. If God does not exist, all theology, whether good or bad, must be misleading, and in this sense bound up with false consciousness. Exactly as

---

23 Daniel Bell, 'The End of Ideology in the West' in C.Waxman(ed) *The End of Ideology Debate* New York: Funk and Wagnalls 1968 p.261
24 Donald Hodges, 'The End of "The End of Ideology"' in Waxman(ed) *The End of Ideology Debate* p.388
25 Alasdair MacIntyre, *Against the Self Images of the Age* London: Duckworth 1971 p.5
26 Bryan Turner, 'Concluding Peroration on Ideology' in Abercrombie et al(eds) *Dominant Ideologies* p.250
27 Eagleton, *Ideology* p.42

Holbach and de Tracy thought, it must be done away with. This is one of the points in the famous passage in Marx's *Contribution to Critique of Hegel's Philosophy of Right*:

> Religious distress is at the same time the expression of real distress and the protest against real distress. Religion is the sigh of the oppressed creature, the heart of a heartless world, just as it is the spirit of a spiritless situation. It is the opium of the people.
>
> The abolition of religion as the illusory happiness of the people is required for their real happiness. The demand to give up the illusions about its conditions is the demand to give up a condition which needs illusions. The criticism of religion is therefore in embryo the criticism of the vale of woe the halo of which is religion ... The task of history ... once the world beyond the truth has disappeared, is to establish the truth of this world. The immediate task of philosophy, which is at the service of history, once the saintly form of human self-alienation has been unmasked, is to unmask self-alienation in its unholy forms. Thus the criticism of heaven turns into the criticism of earth, the criticism of religion into the criticism of right and the criticism of theology into the criticism of politics.[28]

Central to this critique is the notion of religion as 'illusion'. To turn from heaven to earth is to turn from fantasy to reality. Religion provides illusory happiness and diverts energy and attention away from the task of revolutionary transformation. The criticism of religion is the beginning of revolutionary action because it strips away the illusion which stops us getting down to action. 'There is a sense,' E.P.Thompson wrote, 'in which any religion which places great emphasis on the after life is the chiliasm of the defeated and the hopeless. The utopian vision aroused a contrary vision. The chiliastic optimism of the revolutionaries ultimately gave birth to the formation of the conservative attitude of resignation.' Freud shared this view arguing, in *The Future of an Illusion*, that religion reconciles men and women to the instinctual renunciations which civilization forces upon them. 'It is thus, one might claim, the very paradigm of ideology, providing an imaginary resolution of real contradictions, and were it not to do so, individuals might well rebel against a form of civilization which exacts so much from them.'[29]

---

28 Marx and Engels, *On Religion* p.42 Max Horkheimer provides his own account of this famous argument: 'The concept of God was for a long time the place where the idea was kept alive that there are other norms besides those to which nature and society give expression in their operation. Dissatisfaction with earthly destiny is the strongest motive for acceptance of a transcendent being. If justice registers with God, then it is not to be found in the same measure in the world. Religion is the record of the wishes, desires and accusations of countless generations.' *Critical Theory* New York: Seabury 1972 p.129

29 Eagleton, *Ideology* p.177 He goes on: 'Freud has little or no conception of human society as nourishing as well as constraining – as a place of reciprocal self-fulfilment as well as a mechanism for keeping us from each other's throats. His view of both individual and society, in short, is classically bourgeois: the individual as an isolated monad powered by its appetites, society as some mere contractual device without which libidinal anarchy would be let loose.' Ibid p.182

Stuart Hall offers an important corrective to this whole way of arguing in his study of religious ideologies in Jamaica.[30] However other-worldly they appear, Hall argues, religious ideologies inform social practices and have a mobilizing 'practical' impact on society:

> They organise men and women into action with 'hearts and minds'. They form the 'common sense' in which everyday practicalities of life are calculated and expressed. Ideologies draw groupings together; they help to constitute and unify congregations, supporters, participants; they cement social alliances. They also serve to divide: for ideological practices have a critical function in marking out and separating – 'drawing the distinctions' – between those who are legitimate, who belong – 'the faithful', brothers and sisters – and those who do not – the enemy, Satan, the demon king, Babylon. Religious ideologies are both the medium in which collective social solidarities are constructed and the means through which ideological conflict and difference is pursued.[31]

Ideologies are not fixed belief systems but express different meanings in different historical circumstances. They have a multi-accentual character. Thus, symbols like 'the promised land' do not carry a single, unilateral meaning. A religious ideology like Rastafarianism may not be 'true' in the literal sense and yet be profoundly true to the real historical experiences of New World blacks, empowering them to make sense of their experience in a way which ordinary language does not. Such ideologies must not be judged on their truth, literally understood, but rather on their capacity to generate meanings around which action and struggle can become socially organized. This argument effectively stands Marx on his head.

For Marx, of course, the critique of religion is only the beginning of the task, as he notes in the fourth thesis on Feuerbach. Feuerbach thinks that once the religious world is resolved into the secular everything is done, whereas 'the fact that the secular basis lifts off from itself and establishes itself in the clouds as an independent realm can only be explained by the inner strife and intrinsic contradictoriness of this secular basis'.[32] The contradiction to which Marx here refers adds another sense to the way in which religion is false consciousness. In its preaching of providence, for example, or, according to E.P.Thompson, in its preaching of the cross, Christianity makes it appear that the present order of things, in which there are a small group who dominate and a large group of those who are dominated, is natural and in the interest of all sections of society. The claim is not that it is *just* religion which does this, but that it is *also* religion which does this, and in a paradigmatic way.

Marx was familiar with the crude propaganda of people like Hannah More and Andrew Ure which did indeed seek to produce a compliant and subservient workforce by resort to Christian doctrine. 'The social principles of

---

30 S.Hall, 'Religious ideologies and social movements in Jamaica' in R.Bocock and K.Thompson(eds) *Religion and Ideology* Manchester: Manchester University Press 1985 pp.269–296

31 Hall, 'Religious ideologies' p.273

32 Marx and Engels, *Collected Works* vol 5 p.7

Christianity,' he wrote in 1847, 'justified the slavery of antiquity, glorified the serfdom of the middle ages and equally know, when necessary, how to defend the oppression of the proletariat, although they make a pitiful face over it':

> The social principles of Christianity preach the necessity of a ruling and an oppressed class, and all they have for the latter is the pious wish the former will be charitable
> . . .
>   The social principles of Christianity declare all vile acts of the oppressors against the oppressed to be ... the just punishment of original sin and other sins or trials that the Lord in his infinite wisdom imposes on those redeemed.

In the footnotes to *Capital* Marx can cite chapter and verse for those who do exactly this. Anticipating Nietzsche he goes on:

> The social principles of Christianity preach cowardice, self-contempt, abasement, submission, dejection, in a word, all the qualities of the canaille; and the proletariat, not wishing to be treated as canaille, needs its courage, its self-feeling, its pride and its sense of independence more than its bread. The social principles of Christianity are sneakish and the proletariat is revolutionary.[33]

In this way, then, Christianity performs an ideological function. It forms 'a condition for the functioning and reproduction of the system of class domination. It plays this role precisely by hiding the true relations between classes, by explaining away the relations of domination and subordination. Thus social relations appear harmonious and individuals carry out their reproductive practices without disruption.'[34] To take a familiar example, the slogan 'liberty, equality, fraternity' seems to propose universal meanings, but in a class divided society it actually means liberty for bourgeoisie and equality of market exchange which together make fraternity an illusion. The doctrine of providence in the early nineteenth century, as urged, for example, by Thomas Chalmers, functioned in the same way.[35]

On the surface it is a strong case but, as Abercrombie, Hill and Turner point out, there are deep inconsistencies in it. Marx argues that, in the first place, religion is consciously manipulated by the dominant class to control the dominated class; secondly, that religion is an aspect of human alienation as a reversed world consciousness; and thirdly, that it is only relevant in certain modes of production and therefore destined to wither away. These various arguments are mutually contradictory, for in the alienation argument Marx suggested that bourgeois Protestant Christianity was particularly well suited to capitalism and therefore as alienation increases, so the dominance of this Christianity increases. In the mode of production argument, on the other hand, Christianity would not be relevant because he identifies Christianity with feudalism.[36] As Nicholas Lash

---

33   Marx and Engels, *On Religion* pp.83–84
34   Larrain, *Concept* p.47
35   As documented, for example, by Boyd Hilton in *The Age of Atonement* Oxford: Oxford University Press 1988
36   Abercrombie et al, *Thesis*

puts it, Marx's treatment of religion and of God is marked by historical superficiality and theoretical insouciance.[37] We can grant both the contradiction and the superficiality but compelling instances of Christianity's implication in oppressive forms of relationship ensure the continuing power of Marx's critique.

Marx's critique of religion can be usefully compared with Daniel Bell's defence of the need for religion in the 1970s. Bell was assuming that Western society in general, and United States society in particular, was highly secularized, a contention that is now widely contested. In this context he pleaded for 'the return in Western society of some conception of religion'.[38] In his view American capitalism had lost its traditional legitimacy, which was based on a moral system of reward rooted in the Protestant sanctification of work, and substituted a hedonism which promises material ease and luxury.[39] This involved the contradiction, to which, as we have seen, T.S.Eliot had already drawn attention, that, in dissolving the bonds of society capitalism saws off the branch on which it sits. Like Eliot, Bell believed that only religion could restore 'the continuity of generations, returning us to the existential predicaments which are the ground of humility and care for others.'[40]

Bell argued that religion in Western society had provided continuity by acting as the guardian of tradition, and had also 'guarded the portals of the demonic' by insisting on limits:

> Once culture began to take over dealing with the demonic, there arose the demand for the 'autonomy of the aesthetic', the idea that experience, in and of itself, is of supreme value. Everything is to be explored, anything is to be permitted ... all authority, all justification [is rooted] in the demands of the imperial self. By turning one's back on the past, one dirempts or shreds the ties which compel continuity; one makes the new and the novel the source of interest, and the curiosity of the self the touchstone of judgement. Thus modernism as a cultural movement trespassed religion and moved the centre of authority from the sacred to the profane.[41]

It is culture sustained by religion which answers our existential questions and religion in particular, awareness of transcendence, which allows us to freely accept the past rather than to allow ourselves simply to be shaped by it, returning us to tradition in order to maintain the continuity of moral meanings.[42]

This instrumental view of religion was shared by Clifford Geertz, writing more or less at the same time.[43] Religion is that system of symbols which establishes pervasive motivations in human beings by formulating conceptions of a general order of existence and clothing these conceptions with such an aura of factuality that the moods and motivations seem uniquely realistic.

---

37   Lash, *A Matter of Hope* p.286
38   Bell, *Contradictions* p.29
39   Bell, *Contradictions* p.84
40   Bell, *Contradictions* p.30
41   Bell, *Contradictions* p.158
42   Bell, *Contradictions* p.170
43   Geertz, *Interpretation* pp.87–125

Above all, in ritual religion shapes the common sense perspective without which we would not survive, going beyond the realities of everyday life to wider perspectives which correct and complete them.[44]

Both Bell and Geertz have a point. There are indeed cultural contradictions within capitalism, and it may well be that common sense needs the correction of religion. On the other hand there is Terry Eagleton's remark that 'the more drearily utilitarian a dominant ideology is, the more refuge will be sought in compensatory rhetorics of a "transcendental" kind'.[45] The reference to 'religion' points us back to Barth's critique. Bell certainly did not have in mind any old religion, but was doubtless thinking of Christianity. As a good liberal he probably did not have in mind the religion of Jerry Falwell and the 'moral majority' which, arguably, is the dominant expression of American Christianity. But both Bell and Geertz understand religion to function precisely as Marx said it did, namely to provide social cement and to prevent the system collapsing. If Christianity is to be defended as non-alienating it will have to be on radically different grounds to this.

Scripture and Ideology

Much of Marx's critique can be granted but I want to ask now whether Christianity is necessarily alienating, whether alienation is bound up in its very nature and title deeds. In considering this question I will begin with some reflections on Scripture because if what Vatican II spoke of as 'the founts of our faith' are irredeemably ideological, in the negative sense, if there is no way of reading them in a non-alienating way, our response cannot even begin. I shall argue that ultimately it is the *content* of Scripture which is decisive, but our *method of reading* is also important, as the liberation theologians have argued.

Terry Eagleton makes a helpful distinction between general ideology, the taken for granted ideology of a class or society, authorial ideology, and the ideology of a text. The ideologies of individual authors in a given society *may* be identical with general ideology but usually stand in relations of partial disjunction or even of severe contradiction to it. Such authorial ideology is different again from the *ideology of the text* which may not be identical with that of the author – the text has its own independence. Authorial and textual ideologies can be understood through the analogy of a dramatic production. Just as a particular production of a play manifests its own ideology, which may be different from that of the author, so a text is not simply an expression of

---

44   Geertz, *Interpretation* p.112 He says of ritual: 'It is in some sort of ceremonial form – even if the form be hardly more than the recitation of a myth, the consultation of an oracle, or the decoration of a grave – that the moods and motivations which sacred symbols invoke in men and the general conceptions of the order of existence which they formulate for men meet and reinforce one another. In a ritual, the world as lived and the world as imagined, fused under the agency of a single set of symbolic forms, turn out to be the same world.'
45   Eagleton, *Ideology* p.155

ideology but a production of it. 'Ideology pre-exists the text; but the *ideology of the text* defines, operates and constitutes that ideology in ways unpremeditated, so to speak, by ideology itself.'[46] But how is ideology present in a text? To answer this question Eagleton turns to the work of Pierre Macherey, who argues that the presence of ideology in a text may be that of significant silence: 'ideology is present in the text in the form of its eloquent silences':

> The text is, as it were, ideologically forbidden to say certain things; in trying to tell the truth in his own way, for example, the author finds himself forced to reveal the limits of the ideology within which he writes. He is forced to reveal its gaps and silences, what it is unable to articulate. Because a text contains these gaps and silences, it is always *incomplete*. Far from constituting a rounded, coherent whole, it displays a conflict and contradiction of meanings; and the significance of the work lies in the difference rather than unity between these meanings.[47]

Edward Said has celebratedly illustrated the way in which this works in novels like Jane Austen's *Mansfield Park* or Conrad's *Nostromo*, where colonialism is the unspoken background of the action.[48] Macherey argues that it is the silence within the text itself which sets up a dissonance. Eagleton, however, argues more plausibly that such silences do not arise from contradictions within ideology, for the whole function of ideology is to eliminate contradictions. They arise rather from the contradiction between ideology and what it occludes – history itself. 'The text *puts* the ideology into contradiction, discloses the limits and absences which mark its relation to history, and in so doing puts itself into question, producing a lack and disorder within itself.'[49]

This discussion clearly has great significance for any doctrine of Scripture. The Bible is part of the 'superstructure' of Western society but it differs from other elements of this superstructure in important ways. In the first place it represents a palimpsest of ideologies in a way which is probably unique. If we think of the five books of the Torah, for example, our texts come to us from pre-monarchical, monarchical and post-monarchical periods, are edited by scribal, priestly and prophetic sources, and reflect equally tribal, settled agricultural and city life. This means that this text is not in a position to tout for any one particular ideology. There is a conflict of ideologies within the text. Scripture differs from other forms of literature also in that it conforms directly to none of the usual categories: it is neither fiction, nor history, nor biography, nor poetry, nor philosophy, though there are aspects of it which resemble *all* these forms of discourse. The emergence in the first century of an entirely new literary form, a 'gospel', is paradigmatic for the way in which Scripture is *sui generis*. If authorial ideology stands athwart general ideology, and the ideology of the text athwart authorial ideology, then the 'cross hatching' which we have in Scripture is exceptionally dense.

---

46 T.Eagleton, *Marxism and Literary Criticism* London: Methuen 1976 p.80
47 Eagleton, *Criticism* p.35
48 E.Said, *Culture and Imperialism* London: Vintage 1994
49 Eagleton, *Criticism* p.95

What would it mean to call this mish-mash of ideologies 'the Word of God'? I rule out the option which simply denies it this ascription, for which Scripture is simply a classic of Western, and therefore and to that extent of world, culture. Barth rejected this option because he began his career from the perception of the extent to which theology was determined by ideology. Scripture he saw as the possibility of dissonance with and resistance to this general ideology. *To call a collection of texts 'the Word of God' is to say that such a possibility of dissonance is permanent and thorough going, that these texts resist every attempt at colonization and all forms of hegemony.* Literature, says Eagleton, 'is a vital instrument for the insertion of individuals into the perceptual and symbolic forms of the dominant ideological formation'.[50] Literature does this in many ways and in varying degrees of consonance with any ideology. To call Scripture 'the Word of God' is to say that its function is to provoke dissonance with respect to every possible ideology.

Barth attempts to answer the question of how Scripture can be both Word of God and a complex of ideologies in the first two volumes of the *Church Dogmatics*. That Scripture is itself embodied in ideologies Barth characterizes as the 'worldliness' of Scripture. The worldliness of the Word is precisely its embodiment in ideology. Barth's strategy in answering the question as to how these ideologies can nevertheless be the Word of God is to refer to the *act* in which God has God's Being, and to the *event* in which, through the Holy Spirit, the biblical writings become the Word of God for us. Properly to do hermeneutics, he says, is to elaborate the doctrine of the Trinity, which is to refer hermeneutics ultimately to the mystery of God's being in the world. This could be an entirely vacuous move of the type Marx satirized in *The German Ideology* if it did not refer to the concrete history of Jesus and to the discipleship movement that history engendered. The doctrine of the Trinity speaks concretely about these two related histories as obedience to God the Father. It is this twofold practice which is what ultimately subverts oppressive ideology (and practice). Scripture may be characterized as 'the Word of God' to the extent that it generates liberative and humanizing practice.

Marx argues that Christianity is the special religion of capital on the grounds that it is uniquely wedded to abstraction. 'In both it is only man in the abstract who counts ... In the one case, all depends on whether or not he has faith, in the other, on whether or not he has credit.'[51] It makes an essential difference, therefore, whether the history of Christianity is presented as an intellectual struggle about dogmas and interpretations of doctrine, or whether these are regarded as the manifestation of the life of Christian communities subject to all manner of historical contingency and to the social conflicts of successive ages.[52]

How is it possible to affirm this when we know very well that Scripture, like any other text, has frequently been harnessed to repression of all kinds? In

---

50   Eagleton, *Criticism* p.56
51   K.Marx, *Theories of Surplus Value* Moscow: Progress 1971 vol 3 p.448
52   Lash, *Hope* p.142

seeking an answer we can learn not only from the subtleties of Barth's hermeneutic method but from the mistakes of his exegetical practice.

In his account of Gen 2.18–25, and of the relations of men and women, in *Church Dogmatics* III/4, Barth takes texts which are themselves influenced by patriarchal ideology, reads them in the context of his own general ideology, which is patriarchal, and concludes to a certain subordination of women in an argument which feminist theologians have characterized as 'irredeemable'. According to Barth's reading of the 'Word of God' patriarchy is divinely guaranteed in much the same way that monarchy and obedience to the state were guaranteed in earlier ages by an appeal to Romans 13. How are we to evaluate this? Barth wrote against the consciousness of a rising feminism and could claim that here too Scripture is opposed to human ideologies, but on the other hand to find the reigning patriarchy of early twentieth century Western society reconfirmed is disconcerting to say the least. In his exegesis of Romans 13 Barth turned politically conservative readings on their head by insisting that the passage be read in the context of the whole letter: the God who makes all things new, he argued, cannot suddenly put the brakes on. But what if, as some feminist theologians have claimed, the biblical writings are so imbued with patriarchal ideology we cannot appeal to the whole context to critique particular patriarchal passages? The easy ploy at this point, corresponding to the liberal dismissal of Scripture as the Word of God, is to appeal to progressive revelation as, for instance, Schleiermacher does. But this simply evades the question of where we derive our criteria for assessing progress from, and ends up with pluralism as the reigning ideology. It is both more difficult and more rewarding to stay with the text and accept the feminist challenge. Do these texts commit us to patriarchy or not? If so are they the 'Word of God', and how would we know?

We have said that to call Scripture 'the Word of God' is to talk of the fact that it creates dissonance with reigning ideologies by giving rise to a distinct kind of praxis. By virtue of *what* does it create this dissonance? It is in attempting to answer this question that I find Macherey's language about silence suggestive.

Although the structure of Barth's answer to the hermeneutical question is the doctrine of the Trinity he also wants to say that a mark of something being the Word of God, is that it tells us something we cannot tell ourselves. It does this because the texts witness ('attest' is Barth's word) to the Wholly Other, the One who is beyond all our ideologies (or as Anselm put it, the Being than which a greater we cannot conceive). That the Wholly Other can find expression in human speech is the problem biblical hermeneutics has to wrestle with. If this is a real possibility, and not just a move made by reactionary ideologies, as Marx thought, it rests on a listening to what Ignatius calls 'the Word of God spoken out of silence'. In David Hare's *Racing Demon* the main protagonist begins:

> God. Where are you? I wish you would talk to me. God. It isn't just me. There's a general feeling. This is what people are saying in the parish. They want to know where you are. The joke wears thin. You must see that. You never say anything. All

right, people expect that, it's understood. But people also think, I didn't realize when
he said *nothing*, he really did mean nothing at all ... There are an awful lot of people
in a very bad way. And they need something beside silence. God.

Is there something besides silence? Yes and no, and Ignatius' 'Word spoken out
of silence' gives expression to both. There is the struggle with silence, and a
struggle to make space for silence amidst the deafening clamours of conflicting
ideologies, and the struggle against being silenced, all of which give rise to the
twofold practice of prophecy and discipleship. This joint practice, essentially a
struggle for the redefinition of power, generates texts (ideologies: the ideology
of 'the Word of God') athwart reigning ideologies. All the different forms of
struggle for and against silence can be found in the gospels. There is the
struggle *for* silence: Jesus' withdrawal into the wilderness, his attempt to create
space for an alternative world view (in his teaching) and therefore an
alternative practice (in founding the new community). The struggle *with*
silence, against the deafness of the disciples and above all in Gethsemane and
on the cross, when no *deus ex machina*, no heavenly Elijah, comes to save Jesus
from death by torture. And the struggle *against being silenced* – against the well
meaning attempts of his family to rescue him from hostility, against the
disciples' refusal to hear his authentic voice and to force him into the
straitjacket of existing triumphalist ideologies, and, above all, against being
sealed in the tomb by a member of the Sanhedrin, so that he would be 'safe at
last'. It is above all from the silence of the cross, and the very different silence
of the tomb, where there is now no body to either accuse or be venerated, that
the Word is spoken which crosses all ideologies.

There is, then, a silence at the heart of the biblical witness which generates
dissonance, in a sense very different from that which Macherey envisages. This
silence is the presence of the Wholly Other in the text. Like Macherey's
ideology, the Wholly Other is present in Scripture in and through the silence. In
particular, to move on to Terry Eagleton's point, the story of the cross, in its
eloquent silence, is the brute historical fact which resists all ideologization.
Recognition of this fact enables us to describe Scripture as the Word of God –
even though it is embedded in patriarchal ideologies – in a way which does not
involve us in implausible exegetical sleight of hand. Barth arrives at a
patriarchal reading of the text partly because his account of Scripture's
'worldliness' is framed in too idealist and generalized a way. Peter Scott draws
on an argument of Raymond Williams to the effect that in order to be
constructive ideologies must not be too close to or too distant from
determining pressures. 'A theoretical practice which is too close to determining
pressures is reactionary; a practice which is too distant is utopian.'[53] Barth is
too close to determining pressures of patriarchal society here and this disables
his argument.

It is clear that, as Nicholas Lash reminds us:

---

53   Scott, *Theology* p.39

Christians do not possess any mechanism or devices that could in principle preserve their forms of discourse, whether religious or theological, from degenerating into 'instruments of class rule'. At this level, the question as to whether the practice of faith and theological reflection are 'ideological' is one that cannot be answered in the abstract, but only by the critical examination of particular instances.[54]

Terry Eagleton makes a similar point in arguing that exactly the same piece of language may be ideological in one context and not in another; and that therefore ideology is a function of an utterance to a social context.[55] Awareness of this fact grounds the practice of the hermeneutic of suspicion. Hermeneutical grounds alone, however, would not allow us to speak of Scripture as the Word of God. Rather, as I have argued, we can do so partly on the grounds of the way in which this text challenges all ideologies. Another, and more traditional, way of coming at this point is to consider the biblical protocol against idolatry.

The Protocol Against Idolatry

Kosuke Koyama writes as a Japanese Christian who grew up during the Second World War. He reads the destruction visited upon Japan as the consequence of idolatry and brings idolatry and ideology into the closest connection.[56] Idolatry, in the first place, is the misuse of centre symbolism. The meaning of the first commandment is that God, and no created thing, is our true centre. When we put nation, race, class, gender, science, technology, the Emperor cult, or whatever it may be in the centre we have idolatry. Koyama adopts a definition of ideology as 'an emotion laden, myth saturated, action laden related system of beliefs and values about man and society, legitimacy and authority, acquired as a matter of routine and habitual enforcement'.[57] Ideologies are the justifications of idolatry. The essential distinction between theology and ideology is that theology, knowing itself to stand under the judgment of God, is essentially broken. Ideology, by contrast, is self-sufficient, and demands the prestige of being at the centre of human thought and life.[58] Theology becomes ideology when it loses the sense of being under judgment and makes a claim that it is at the centre, thus pushing aside the living God. 'That Christian nations should protect themselves by any means at any cost – even a hundred million human lives – because the Christian civilization is the highest value in the world is an ideologized theology.'[59] Ideologized theology is a theology in captivity to our centre complex. 'Ideology is "religious" whether it is capitalism, communism, patriotism, racism or emperor worship in its desire to utter the last word.'[60]

---

54 Lash, *Hope* p.132
55 Eagleton, *Ideology* p.9
56 K.Koyama, *Mount Fuji and Mount Sinai: A Critique of Idols* London: SCM 1984 p.83ff
57 Koyama, *Mount Fuji* p.99
58 Koyama, *Mount Fuji* p.100
59 Koyama, *Mount Fuji* p.100
60 Koyama, *Mount Fuji* p.101

Never has such theology been denounced more vehemently than in the South African Kairos document's denunciation of what it calls 'State theology'. The preamble to the apartheid constitution began, 'In humble submission to Almighty God, who controls the destinies of nations and the history of peoples; who gathered our forebears together from many lands and gave them this their own'. The Kairos document commented:

> This god is an idol. It is as mischievous, sinister and evil as any of the idols that the prophets of Israel had to contend with. Here we have a god who is historically on the side of the white settlers, who dispossesses black people of their land and who gives the major part of the land to his 'chosen people'. It is the god of superior weapons who conquered those who were armed with nothing but spears. It is the god of the casspirs and hippos, the god of teargas, rubber bullets, sjamboks, prison cells and death sentences. Here is a god who exalts the proud and humbles the poor – the very opposite of the God of the Bible who 'scatters the proud of heart, pulls down the mighty from their thrones and exalts the humble'. From a theological point of view the opposite of the God of the Bible is the devil, Satan. The god of the South African State is not merely an idol or false god, it is the devil disguised as Almighty God – the antichrist.[61]

The God of the Bible rejects all centre complexes. Koyama cites Jeremiah:

> O hope of Israel,
> Its saviour in time of trouble,
> Why should you be like a stranger in the land,
> Like a traveller turning aside for the night? (14.8)

This God is not at the centre of community, firm and unmoving, sustaining the direction of life and history. On the contrary, like a stranger, and overnight wayfarer, this God dwells among us. In so doing God challenges all our attempts to claim God for our particular centre, just as the variety of ideologies in Scripture prevent it from being claimed for one particular ideology. All the same, one can ask whether any claim for the revelation of the truth is not implicitly totalitarian. Koyama responds to this with a counter question:

> How can a God who revealed himself in Jesus Christ who is crucified, who walks towards the periphery, and who is passionately concerned about the welfare of people ... be a totalitarian God in the secular parlance? ... There is a delicate distinction between theology and ideology. Theology lives on the basis of the broken circle as it reflects the broken Christ. It is through this brokenness that it exerts its influence upon history. Brokenness is the essential stigmata of theology. Ideology is different. It is not essential for ideology to have a 'broken circle'. Brokenness can be viewed as weakness in ideology. A strong ideology cannot accept the uncertainty of brokenness. Ideology then does not share with theology the 'marks of Christ'.[62]

Of course we are *simul justus et peccata* – the ideological and the theological cannot be neatly separated, and none of us is free from ideology. The question

61   In C.Villa-Vicencio(ed), *Between Christ and Caesar* Michigan: Eerdmans 1986 p.255
62   Koyama, *Mount Fuji* p.258

is then focused upon what kind of ideology it is that is influencing us and one of the hallmarks of the idolatrous is the claim to give us our identity and security more directly and quickly than can the crucified Lord – in effect by magic:

> The theology of the cross is strongly critical of magic. In the light of the theology of the cross, the truth about human salvation is neither 'directly' graspable nor 'instant'. An instant truth, free from the constraints of long suffering love, is not truth. The God of the theology of the cross is a hidden God, who refuses to be grasped by us directly and quickly.[63]

The cross of Christ is then, as Koyama puts it, a critique of idols, and for that very reason a critique of all ideologies, a warning against all false centre symbolism.[64]

Or, as Nicholas Lash argues, in so far as Christianity deploys, in practice and in theory, its iconoclastic resources, it necessarily exercises a subversive rather than a legitimatory role in respect of all absolutizations of particular historical mediations.[65] Ideology critique, then, is not just a hermeneutic rule, but stems from our understanding of God and here, too, we have to go beyond method to the substance of what is witnessed to in Scripture.

The Wholly Otherness of God

In the mid 1960s Alasdair MacIntyre claimed that:

> the attempt to maintain the values and the credibility of Christianity in the intellectual and moral climate of ... contemporary Britain has led to a vacuity that was not present when Christians such as Karl Barth or Dietrich Bonhoeffer or Franz Jaegstatter defined their faith in words and action by contrast with and against Nazi mythology.[66]

He was particularly dismissive of John Robinson's *Honest to God*. The use of Bonhoeffer's vocabulary, outside of its original context, he argued, made it indistinguishable from that of any other sensitive, generous liberals. It amounted to practical atheism, clothing ordinary liberal forms of life with the romantic unreality of a catacombic vocabulary.[67]

This critique is particularly ironic given that Robinson was trying to get away from inadequate conceptions of God. What his attempt revealed, however, was the poverty of theological thought in general, a failure to grapple

---

63 Koyama, *Mount Fuji* p.259
64 Cf Lash: 'If Christian discourse is not to become idolatrous, it must be permanently iconoclastic. The continual "critique of ideology" is as necessary for the truthfulness and "reality" of religious behaviour and language as for all other aspects of social consciousness.' *Hope* p.132
65 Lash, *Hope* p.158
66 MacIntyre, *Images* p.7
67 MacIntyre, *Images* p.19

with the radical otherness of God. MacIntyre adopts a 'base–superstructure' model of ideology, claiming that the poverty of British theology 'reflects' the conditions of British society.[68] But of course Barth might, at any time, have 'reflected' German or Swiss society. That he did not is owing to his rediscovery of the 'wholly Otherness' of God in 'the strange new world of the Bible'. Once again we come back not just to the form of Scripture, but to its content.

In seeking to discern how Christian theology can resist the accusation of being ideological, in the negative sense, Peter Scott opts for an apophatic theology which secures God's openness to the world through the idea of simpleness. This rules out the idea of the suffering God and the idea that human relations can be patterned on God's relationality. God is not present as changing things, but God's presence constitutes the existence of the world. In this strategy 'God-talk resists ideological encoding in its marking of the distinction of God from the world.'[69]

The insistence that God is not a member of this universe or of any universe is certainly key to 'resisting ideological encoding' but it seems to me that Scott pays too high a price for doing so. This God, as Barth said to the young Moltmann, is rather a pauper, and for that reason Barth's alternative route to the same goal offers a far better alternative. The apophatic way does not define the hiddenness of God radically enough, remains too tied to human incapacity. It is premised on a distinction between God in God's revelation and God in Godself and tends to end up with an impersonal God.

Where Scott opts for apophaticism, Barth opts for dialectic, insisting that God is both hidden and revealed. A fully restrained and fully alive doctrine of God's attributes will take as its fundamental point of departure the truth that God is for us fully revealed and fully concealed in God's self-disclosure. At every point we have to be silent but also have to speak. It is a fundamental rule of Barth's theology that reality precedes possibility, the readiness of God the readiness of human beings:

> The type of thinking which wants to begin with the question of the knowability of God and then to pass on from that point to the question of the fulfilment of the knowledge of God is not grateful but grasping, not obedient but self-autonomous ... In view of the fact that the knowledge of God is actually fulfilled we can only ask about its mode.[70]

The revelation of God breaks through the emptiness of what we call our knowledge of God. On the one hand the hiddenness of God is one of God's properties, and the doctrine tells us that 'God does not belong to the objects which we can always subjugate to the process of our viewing, conceiving and expressing and therefore our spiritual oversight and control.'[71] This remains

---

68 'Reassurance is just what Christians should not be looking for at this point in their history ... the fragility of their religion is due not to the theologians but to its role in our social life. This the theologians only reflect.' MacIntyre, *Images* p.25
69 Scott, *Theology* pp.95, 105, 109
70 K.Barth, *Church Dogmatics* II/1 Edinburgh: T&T Clark 1953 p.63
71 Barth, *Dogmatics* II/1 p.187

true even given the fact that God gives Godself to be known. Nevertheless God does do this. God is not invisible and ineffable in the way that the infinite, absolute and indeterminate are but in virtue of God's revelation in Christ and, therefore, is visible only to faith. The knowledge of God is a matter of grace, of faith not sight, in sign not in being. 'Grace is the majesty, the freedom, the undeservedness, the unexpectedness, the newness, the arbitrariness, in which the relationship to God and therefore the possibility of knowing him is opened up to man by God himself.'[72] In revelation God makes Godself apprehensible to those who cannot apprehend God of themselves. Human beings stand before God and conceive God in God's inconceivability. Faith, in fact, consists in being apprehended by, rather than apprehending, the invisible God.

This account of the hiddenness of God seems to me far more satisfactory than the view that 'God is not present as changing things', which smacks of the God who exists but does not want to get involved. The anti-ideology rubric, that God cannot be manipulated, pulled into the service of any programme, is preserved, but at the same time we have an extremely rich understanding of God by which to measure the ideologies which structure human society. Apophatic theology is an attempt to get away from inadequate notions of intervention, but it reduces immanence to being and gives no account of God's continuous creation. God is, on Barth's understanding, the one who loves in freedom, the one who has a real history in and with the world created by God, the one with whom we wrestle 'until the break of day'. There is such a thing as the holy mutability of God and the old rubric of the unchangeableness of God is better expressed by talk of God's constancy, the fact that God is always the same in every change, the constancy of God's knowing, willing and acting. For the apophatic theology, on the other hand, the difference seems to be primarily hermeneutic. Thus Scott says that God makes a difference in the extension of our understanding of ourselves and our world and in the asking of questions about our creatureliness.[73]

The revelation of God, by contrast, says that God turns in righteousness to help the poor and lowly and from this aspect of God's righteousness follows a very definite political task. Where Scott's affirmation of the divine simplicity rules out the divine suffering, for Barth the divine uniqueness and simplicity de-divinizes the world. 'No sentence is more dangerous and revolutionary than that God is One and there is no other like God.' Similarly, God's eternity is not the infinite extension of time backwards and forwards but is God's unique possession of time which means that God precedes time's beginning, accompanies its duration and exists after its end. And God has and is glory, an affirmation of the utmost importance for the theology of culture because art has to be understood as some kind of echo of, perhaps even participation in, the self-communicating joy of God which flows from the beauty of God. I shall return to this in the final chapter. Ultimately it is this richness of the Wholly

---

72 Barth, *Dogmatics* II/1 p.74
73 Scott, *Theology* p.118

Other but revealed God which always tests the inadequacy of our ideologies and cultural constructs.

As Nicholas Lash points out, Marx never seriously investigated the richness of Christian reflection on God, nor the possibility that the autonomy of the creature grows not in inverse but in direct proportion to the degree of the creature's dependence of, and belonging to, God. For him Christianity was necessarily ideological in the negative sense because belief was simply erroneous.[74] In fact, I have argued, understood properly faith in God both leads to and does not distract from practical activity and it critiques idolatry by insisting on the hiddenness of God. We need, says Lash, some principle of discrimination between appropriate and inappropriate objectifications of the mystery of God and God gives us this in the particular event and action of a particular human individual, Jesus Christ.

The Materialism of the Incarnation

The thinkers whom Marx satirizes in *The German Ideology* made the mistake, according to him, of supposing that thought alone could solve social problems. It is by attempting to solve in consciousness contradictions which are not overcome in practice, that ideology necessarily negates and conceals them.[75] When Terry Eagleton says that religion is probably the most purely ideological of the institutions of civil society, this is presumably what he means – that religion talks about peace, reconciliation, and so forth, and imagines that through this Word contradictions will be overcome.[76] Theology, then, is the acme of ideology. But just at that point we remember John's insistence, at the heart of the New Testament, that the Word became flesh. Indeed it seems to me that John's gospel is best summed up by Marx's eleventh thesis on Feuerbach: the philosophers have only interpreted the world; the point, however, is to change it.

Incarnation is not a philosophical first principle. It is a way of reading a particular historical event, the life and death of a first century Jew, as revelatory of the Wholly Other. It is the claim that the hidden God reveals Godself here in this life and death. From this claim, however, follows a particular praxis because, if the flesh taking is true, then bodies and what we do with them, all the issues of housing, food, clothing and so on, are declared issues of decisive importance. Christianity pioneered hospitals and almshouses in the middle ages for precisely this reason. Care for bodies was a sacred command. In the same way culture, in each of its senses, is command, because culture is the record of what we do as ensouled bodies, or bodily souls, from cuisine to Quartets, from poetry to pottery. The incarnation also brings with it a concern for justice because it implies that every human being is a sister or

74   Lash, *Hope* p.166
75   Larrain, *Concept* p.47
76   Eagleton, *Idea* p.113

brother of the Human One, every person is 'family', there are no outsiders. The same can be said on the basis of the crucifixion which, in declaring Christ an outsider, makes all outsiders insiders (Gal 3.13–14). From the incarnation, therefore, follows not just a social but also a political praxis. If Marx's argument is that ideology cannot be dissolved by mental criticism but only by the practical overthrow of the actual social relations which give rise to this idealistic humbug, this, again, seems to be the message of the Johannine corpus, itself a meditation on flesh taking:[77]

> Those who say, 'I love God' and hate their brothers or sisters are liars [that is, ideologues]; for those who do not love a brother or sister whom they have seen, cannot love God whom they have not seen [for the hidden God is mediated only through flesh taking and through encounter with the Other]. The commandment we have from him is this: those who love God must love their brothers and sisters also [be committed to a particular form of praxis].
>
> (1 John 4.20–21)

Far from Christianity being intrinsically ideological, I want to say, it is the very opposite, precisely in view of its commitment to flesh taking, and just for this reason theological criticism that is not, at the same time, socio-economic criticism is inadequately grounded.[78]

If ideology is meaning in the service of power it is hard to see how the doctrine of the incarnation is ideological. It is, of course, paradoxical and there are even theologians who think it nonsensical or a myth, but that claim rests on an inadequate doctrine of God – on the idea of God as another 'thing' within the world, continuous with the whole series of created things. The incarnation would then be impossible.[79] But God is not a member of the universe, and the doctrine of the incarnation is fundamentally about grace, which is to say the gift of God, as that which enables full humanness. As Karl Barth put it:

> The Godhead of the true God is not a prison whose walls have first to be broken through if he is to elect and do what he has elected and done in becoming man. In distinction from that of false gods, and especially the god of Mohammed, his godhead embraces both height and depth, both sovereignty and humility, both lordship and service ... He does not become a stranger to himself when in his son he also goes into a far country ... What is the divine essence? It is the free love, the omnipotent mercy, the holy patience of the father, Son and Holy Spirit. And it is the God of this divine essence who has and maintains the initiative in this event ... This divine essence totally determines Christ's human essence. This is totally determined by the grace of God ... as the recipient of the electing grace of God, Jesus' human essence is proved by its exaltation to be the true essence of all humans. It is genuinely human in the deepest sense to live by the electing grace of God addressed to human beings.[80]

77 Larrain, *Concept* p.47
78 Lash, *Hope* p.177
79 H.McCabe, *God Matters* London: Geoffrey Chapman 1987 p.54ff
80 K.Barth, *Church Dogmatics* IV/2 Edinburgh: T&T Clark 1958 p.84

If meaning in the service of power is what is at issue then, it seems to me, it is Marx's avowed Prometheanism which is ideological, proved to be so by a whole range of practices of domination threatening not simply human cultures but the planet. The incarnation, by contrast, affirms the necessity of gracious living, living as graced, as gift, receiving first and then giving, giving because receiving, and understanding that as the foundation of political praxis.

The idea of incarnation may be paradoxical but it is not absurd, nor is it 'ideological' in Thompson's sense. It is paradoxical both because we cannot say what it means that Jesus was both man and God and because, as Lash puts it, 'this conviction concerns not only past occurrence but also future fulfilment':

> Christological language speaks of one man who died, but it does so in the context of eschatological hope concerning the outcome of the human future for the construction of which we acknowledge, in the employment of such language, our responsibility to work. The hope articulated in christological confession may be unfounded or illusory, but it is a hope that declares not the negation but the affirmation, not the denial but the establishment of authentic humanity.[81]

The incarnation, in other words, commits us to the long revolution, to the ongoing struggle for those things which make and keep human life human.

I have, then, in this chapter, developed an argument that in a number of ways the gospel functions as a form of culture critique. I do not wish to try to make comparisons, to consider ways in which this might be said of the Koran, the Vedas or the teaching of the Buddha. I am concerned with the Christian texts, and their doctrinal development as they relate to those articulations of power in society we call 'ideology'. In four fundamental ways, I have argued, they do not function as an opiate but as a destabilizing force. Reactionaries in eighteenth century England understood this perfectly well, and the government of Korea was not overreacting when, in the mid twentieth century, it banned the Christian scriptures. Of course, we can sanitize these texts by making them holy books, by burying them in deadening exegesis, by establishing them, by subordinating them to class bound doctrines. When the dust is blown off them, however, they have a habit of proving just as uncomfortable as the prophets were to the ruling elites in Israel. This critical function is crucial, Christians believe, in the long revolution of humanization.

---

81 Lash, *Hope* p.144

Chapter 6

Hegemony and the Task of the Church

By a nice irony it was as the idea of a dominant ideology came under attack that the notion of hegemony came to prominence as perhaps the key term of cultural politics – an indication that we cannot do without some framework for thinking of domination. It raises important questions for theology. Does Jesus' teaching on servanthood (Mk 10.42f) or Paul's emphasis on the triumph of weakness (1 Cor 1) mean that Christians should always seek to be on the margins, always eschew hegemony? Is the option for the poor, now fashionably discussed in terms of subalternity, another case of romanticizing the victim and a continuation of what some see as 'the Christian narrative of suffering and redemption that underlies colonial or imperialist domination in the first place'?[1] Christendom obviously aspired to hegemony, and this seems to have been the vision of Coleridge, Arnold, and perhaps of T.S.Eliot.[2] Today this is widely regarded to be a mistake, but in the light of hegemony theory, can we be so sure? Jean and John Comaroff argue that it was the aim of the early Nonconformist missionaries in South Africa to impose hegemony on their would-be subjects.[3] Are they right, and if so, were the missionaries wrong? Chris Rowland and Mark Corner argue that it was the function of the Book of Revelation to overthrow hegemony, and that it has so acted throughout the history of the Church.[4] But is hegemony necessarily negative? If not, how should the Church construe its task in relation to it?

To answer these questions we have to ask about the nature of hegemony. Can there be a stable society without it? If Christianity is 'counter cultural' is it always anti-hegemonic? Can hegemony be fractured otherwise than by the rise of oppressed groups, by the subaltern finding a voice? What role do ideologies play in its fracturing? Or Paulo Freire's conscientization? Is it necessarily replaced by another hegemony, so that history is a lurch from one form of hegemony to the next? What is its relation to domination? As in the previous chapter I begin with an account of the meaning of the term, in two sections, before turning to the way in which hegemony is contested. Developing arguments already outlined in the previous chapter I argue that texts such as the Book of Revelation play a key role in this. However, the principal interest

---

1   So John Beverley in *Subalternity and Representation: Arguments in Cultural Theory* Durham(Ca): Duke University Press 1999 p.73
2   It is Eliot's emphasis on the role of different classes which raises the question.
3   J. and J. Comaroff, *Of Revelation and Revolution* vol 1: *Christianity, Colonialism and Consciousness in South Africa* Chicago: University of Chicago Press 1991 p.17
4   C.Rowland and M.Corner, *Liberating Exegesis: The Challenge of Liberation Theology to Biblical Studies* London: SPCK 1990

of this chapter is not in critique but in construction. Is there a sense in which 'the kingdom' might be a form of hegemony? In the final two sections of the chapter I develop this positive side of the Church's cultural role.

The Nature of Hegemony

Introduced by Russian social democracy at the end of the nineteenth century in order to theorize bourgeois powerlessness, the idea of hegemony was taken up by Gramsci and developed by him whilst in prison. The publication of the *Prison Notebooks* in 1947 brought the term into circulation.[5] In the *Notebooks* Gramsci develops the notion in a number of places but the definition which has become famous is the description of hegemony as 'the spontaneous consent given by the great masses of the population to the general direction imposed on social life by the dominant fundamental group'.[6] The idea of 'spontaneous consent' is what distinguishes hegemony from *rule* of any kind.

Hegemony needs to be distinguished not only from rule but from ideology. For Raymond Williams the difference lies in hegemony's reference to the whole social process by which class inequalities are justified.[7] As the lived system of meanings and values which constitutes our sense of reality hegemony is a 'culture', but a culture which has also to be seen as the lived dominance and subordination of particular classes.[8] Stuart Hall describes hegemony as the process by which dominant ideas accumulate the symbolic power to map the world for others, so that they become the horizon of the taken-for-granted, setting the limit to what will appear as rational, reasonable, credible, indeed sayable or thinkable.[9] In this situation hegemony is not so much a matter of 'spontaneous consent' as of fatalism. When people feel powerless, wrote Richard Hoggart:

> they adopt attitudes toward that situation which allow them to have a liveable life under its shadow, a life without a constant and pressing sense of the large situation. The attitudes remove the main elements in the situation to the realm of natural laws, the given and now, the almost implacable material from which a living has to be carved. Such attitudes, at their least adorned, a fatalism or plain accepting, are generally below the tragic level; they have too much of the conscript's lack of choice about them.[10]

This seems a fair description of the reason for much 'voter apathy' and represents the effective triumph of a given hegemony. What appears to be

5   E.Laclau and C.Mouffe, *Hegemony and Socialist Strategy: Towards a radical democratic politics* London: Verso 1985
6   A.Gramsci, *Selections from the Prison Notebooks* London: Lawrence and Wishart 1971 p.12
7   Williams, *Marxism and Literature* p.108
8   Williams, *Marxism and Literature* p.111
9   S.Hall, 'The Toad in the Garden: Thatcherism among the Theorists' in C.Nelson and L.Grossberg(eds) *Marxism and the Interpretation of Culture* London: Macmillan 1988 p.44
10   R.Hoggart, *The Uses of Literacy* Harmondsworth: Penguin 1954 pp.77–78

'spontaneous consent' may in fact be a feeling that there is no realistic alternative to the government on offer.

Drawing on these discussions the Comaroffs argue that it is through the ideas of hegemony and ideology that the relation between power and culture is to be grasped. If ideology is *an articulated system of meanings, values and beliefs*, hegemony, by contrast, is that taken for granted order of signs and practices whose *power lies in what it silences*, what it prevents people from thinking and saying, and what it puts beyond the limits of the rational and credible.[11] 'Hegemony homogenizes, ideology articulates. Hegemony, at its most effective, is mute; by contrast ... ideology "all the while babbles on".'[12]

Robert Bocock questions the assumption that the Western way of life has achieved hegemony on the grounds that we cannot say that a partial outlook upon the world, such as that of liberal, individualistic hedonism, can be 'hegemonic'. 'Only a coherent world-view, a well-rounded philosophy and related morality could be hegemonic. At any given stage of historical development a particular philosophical world view may provide the major way of grasping what is going on in the world and of living creatively in it.'[13] He has Gramsci's notion of the role of education in producing hegemony in mind. But surely, we can ask, the theory of hegemony is designed precisely to help us to see how control can be exercised in the *absence* of such a clear and cogent ideology. Consumer capitalism is wonderfully placed to exercise hegemony just because it does not have to rely on elaborate theories (though it may rely heavily on advertising and propaganda).

If the Comaroffs are right in linking hegemony to the symbolic realm it follows that hegemony involves control over the superstructure, the modes of symbolic production such as educational and ritual processes, political and legal procedures and, of course, religion. 'It is only by repletion that signs and practices cease to be perceived and remarked; that they are so habituated, so deeply inscribed in everyday routine, that they may no longer be seen as forms of control – or seen at all.'[14] This means that hegemony stands to ideology as form to content. It shapes commodity forms, linguistic forms and epistemological forms in such a way that the world is constructed in terms of them. 'Ideology may take many guises but at root its messages must be communicable. Hegemony represents itself everywhere in its saturating silences or its ritual repetitions.'[15]

Rituals may always be religious but most religions, as Barth insisted, are idolatrous. 'The faith and trust of the heart make both God and idol,' said Luther. There are rituals of consumerism, as there are rituals of the flag, which are obviously idolatrous. The need for ritual, however, naturally suggests a connection between institutional religion and the maintenance of hegemony and it may be broadly granted that every major religion has played such a role.

---

11   J. and J. Comaroff, *Revelation and Revolution* vol 1 p.23

12   J. and J. Comaroff, *Revelation and Revolution* vol 1 p.24 They are citing de Certeau.

13   R.Bocock, *Hegemony* Chichester: Ellis Horwood 1986 p.17

14   J. and J. Comaroff, *Revelation and Revolution* vol 1 p.25

15   J. and J. Comaroff, *Revelation and Revolution* vol 1 p.30

As we have seen, liberal Christianity in nineteenth and early twentieth century Europe certainly played such a role, and perhaps this helps explain Marx's attack on it. At the same time it is clear that such bids for hegemony were always resisted: in Hinduism by Dalit traditions and Bhakti movements, in Christianity by the myriad 'enthusiast' movements charted by Norman Cohn and by the whole series of alternative theologies anthologized by Chris Rowland and Andrew Bradstock.[16] In England the identification of the Church of England with the ruling class meant that any attempt to gain hegemony on its part was bound to fail.

The rituals at the centre of today's hegemony are those of consumerism. Money, through which all relationships are mediated, provides the various forms of liturgy, the altar, and the gifts to be placed there. Symbolic and economic forms come together. Stuart Hall points out that for Gramsci, the question of hegemony was never purely ideological, but was based 'in the decisive nucleus of economic activity':

> All those who therefore gloss Gramsci's concept of hegemony with the qualifying idea that it is ideological are doing a great disservice to his breadth of thought. Gramsci is deeply alive to the ethical, moral, intellectual, ideological, and cultural dimensions of the struggle for hegemony, but hegemony as a concept is not ethical or cultural alone ... On the other hand, for Gramsci, hegemony cannot be economic alone ... since it is by definition something that includes and transcends 'the corporate limits of the purely economic class'.[17]

It is especially important to recognize this in the present state of consumer capitalism. The Bretton Woods Institutions, contrary to the idea of the person who effectively designed them, John Maynard Keynes, have come to take as their brief the construction of a world around the values and vision of corporate capital. The current drive to promote 'liberalization' of trade and services rests on a faith conviction that the narrative of the market is the narrative of the world. It has all the hallmarks of a pseudo religion, with its shrines and altars, its heretics, and its Inquisition. During the Cold War it claimed its martyrs, and today, in a different sense, it claims its victims. This structuring of the current form of hegemony around consumer capitalism means, in turn, that we have to turn to the question of the shaping of desire, for without that the enterprise fails. I turn therefore to the role of the media in maintaining hegemony.

Hegemony and the Media

The dull compulsion of the quotidian is what polices us. Under capitalism production and consumption are supposed to work in a virtuous circle, but in fact consumption has to be maintained by the promotion of desire. William

---

16   C.Rowland and A.Bradstock, *A Radical Reader* Oxford: Blackwell 2001
17   Hall, 'The Toad in the Garden' p.54

Leach has charted the change in North American culture effected by the growth of consumerism which came to dominate American life and functioned as an ersatz religion (hand in glove with a highly individualized Christian pietism).[18] Christopher Lasch argues that today the mass media are centrally structured around consumerism, which is the economic reflection of narcissism. In this situation the categories of truth and falsehood lose all purchase. 'Truth has given way to credibility, facts to statements that sound authoritative without conveying any authoritative information.'[19] James Curran believes the same is true of the British press, whose consumer sections concerned with television, homes, bingo and personal finance 'tacitly promote the seductive view that consumption is a way of expressing individuality and of participating in a "real world" that transcends hierarchies of power'.[20] In these remarks we have already moved beyond consumerism to the political ideology which lies behind it. We return, then, to the question of the exercise of hegemony through the media which we considered in the context of cultural imperialism in Chapter 4.

The dominance of consumerism and the cash nexus, the exercise of hegemony through the colonization of desire, does not mean that more overt strategies of dominance are irrelevant. As the Comaroffs insist, ideology and hegemony have to be taken together. What drives American foreign policy, comments Bill Blum, is a compelling lust for political, economic and military hegemony over the rest of the world, divorced from moral considerations:

> American foreign policy has been fuelled not by devotion to any kind of morality, nor even simple decency but by four imperatives: i. making the world open and hospitable for globalization, particularly American-based transnational corporations ii. enhancing the financial statements of defense contractors at home who have contributed generously to members of Congress iii. preventing the rise of any society that might serve as a successful example of an alternative to the capitalist model iv. extending political, economic and military hegemony over as much of the globe as possible, to prevent the rise of any regional power that might challenge American supremacy, and to create a world order in America's image.[21]

The use of overt power is underpinned by the promotion of the world view of consumer capitalism, the 'American mystique', through the media, as we saw in Chapter 4. The United States is the world's leading producer and distributor of films, TV programmes, books, magazines and music, the U.S. Information Service has libraries in more than 100 countries, the Voice of America has nearly 90 million listeners, and together these have 'flooded the media and the hearts and minds of the earth's multitude with this mystique'.[22] Already in the

---

18   W.Leach, *Land of Desire: Merchants, Power and the Rise of a New American Culture* New York: Vintage 1994 pp.3, 42, 345
19   C.Lasch, *The Culture of Narcissism: American Life in an Age of Diminishing Expectations* New York: Norton 1978 p.75
20   Cited in McGuigan, *Cultural Populism* p.178
21   W.Blum, *Rogue State: A Guide to the World's Only Superpower* London: Zed 2002 pp.13–14. As noted in Chapter 4, this is also the analysis of Petras and Veltmeyer, *Globalization Unmasked*, pp.65–66, 153, 163
22   Blum, *Rogue State* p.246

First World War the U.S. Committee on Public Information had developed strategies for 'regimenting the public mind', which were taken up by advertising men after the war.[23]

The ownership of this media empire is highly concentrated and ideologically uniform. In Britain, although the left wing paper the *Daily Herald* had the largest readership of any newspaper it could not survive because it could not attract advertisers.[24] John Pilger records the story of how the *Daily Mirror*, with a similar political stance, has been 'broken' by ruthless right wing editorial policies.[25] In 1988 three major proprietors owned 73 per cent of British daily and 81 per cent of Sunday newspaper circulation. 'The argument that such concentration restricts the diversity of the press is borne out by the overwhelming preponderance of right wing newspapers.'[26] At the beginning of the decade American films accounted for 94 per cent of foreign films broadcast on British television.[27] In the United States, not a single newspaper opposed the US bombing of Afghanistan, or of Yugoslavia or of Iraq. 'Is this not remarkable,' Blum asks, 'in a supposedly free society, with a supposedly free press, and almost 1,500 daily newspapers?'[28] McGuigan notes that the Murdoch press's habitual transgression of the boundary between entertainment and information implies the fictionality of all news narrative, thereby subverting belief in factual truth. Radicals and dissenters are stigmatized as irrational and unrepresentative. *Sun* readers may read the paper for light relief but in doing so what are addressed are their taken for granted assumptions and expectations. 'The *Sun* is, arguably, symptomatic of and contributory to a political culture in which popular pleasure is routinely articulated through oppressive ideologies that operate in fertile chauvinistic ground. It is populist in the worst sense.'[29]

John Thompson points out that the continuous and reverent portrayal of Ceaucescu did little to win him a secure place in the hearts and minds of the Romanian people, but this is no counter argument to those who believe the Western press exercises profound cultural influence. Such crude dictatorships can dominate but they cannot aspire to hegemony. It is much more difficult to see a propaganda system at work where the media are private and formal censorship is absent. Factors like ownership, advertising, reliance on government information and negative responses to media statements all influence the news. John McGrath records the systematic campaign of disinformation used by the British Government in relation to Northern Ireland, and retailed through the Press.[30] Herman and Chomsky draw

23   Leach, *Land of Desire* p.320
24   E.S.Herman and N.Chomsky, *Manufacturing Consent: The Political Economy of the Mass Media* London: Vintage 1994 p.19
25   J.Pilger, *Hidden Agendas* London: Verso 1998 p.410ff
26   McGuigan, *Cultural Populism* p.176
27   Thompson, *Ideology* p.202
28   Blum, *Rogue State* p.x
29   McGuigan, *Cultural Populism* p.184
30   McGrath, *The Bone Won't Break* pp.1, 2

attention to the huge disparity in the treatment by the United States press of the killing of the Polish priest Jerry Popieluszko on the one hand, and the thousands of Latin American martyrs on the other; of the massacres of the Khmer Rouge and of the Indonesian military in East Timor; the attack on 'meaningless' elections in left wing countries and the description of the election of the Arena government in El Salvador, one of the most murderous governments in the subcontinent, as a 'return to democracy'.[31] Concern over Watergate was not a counter instance because that was only triggered when the interests of the privileged were threatened.

The 'societal purpose' of the media, Herman and Chomsky argue, is to inculcate and defend the economic, social and political agenda of privileged groups that dominate the domestic society and the state.[32] In the United States the sponsorship and support of state terror that cost some 200,000 lives in Central America was not the subject of congressional inquiries or media concern. These actions were conducted in accord with an elite consensus, and they received steady media support.[33] Contrary to the myth, there is no 'adversary press' boldly attacking a pitiful executive giant. Rather, 'the US media encourage spirited debate, criticism and dissent, as long as these remain faithfully within the system of presuppositions and principles that constitute an elite consensus, a system so powerful as to be internalized largely without awareness'.[34] The passionate and widely held belief that the United States is a genuine democracy, contradicted by this analysis, is thus a classic example of the functioning of hegemony.

From a British perspective Stuart Hall seems to be in agreement. The arrival of the popular press, he writes, was instrumental not in the *expression* but in the *containment* of popular democracy. It is organized by capital 'for' the working classes but appeals to the culture and language of the 'underdog':

> The cultural industries don't function on us as if we are blank screens. But they do occupy and rework the interior contradictions of feeling and perception in the dominated classes; they do find or clear a space of recognition in those who respond to them. Cultural domination has real effects – even if these are neither all-powerful nor all-inclusive ... I think there is a continuous and necessarily uneven and unequal struggle, by the dominant culture, constantly to disorganise and reorganise popular culture; to enclose and confine its definitions and forms within a more inclusive range of dominant forms.[35]

The popular press, he argues, offers us a 'canned and neutralised demotic populism' which is a powerful instrument of hegemony. The power it exercises calls into question the optimistic assumption of critical independence by those

---

31   Herman and Chomsky, *Consent* p.38
32   Herman and Chomsky, *Consent* p.298
33   Herman and Chomsky, *Consent* p.300
34   Herman and Chomsky, *Consent* p.302
35   S.Hall, 'Notes on deconstructing "the popular"' in R.Samuel(ed) *People's History* London: Routledge, Kegan & Paul 1981 p.233

hostile to mass culture theory. This means that, as McGuigan notes, some notion of ideological domination, or hegemony, remains indispensable.[36]

Nor is it just a matter of news. Children's literature is also affected. Ariel Dorfman and Armand Mattelart argued that the Disney cosmos was no mere refuge in the area of occasional entertainment but 'our everyday stuff of social oppression'. Their book, *How to Read Donald Duck: Imperialist Ideology in the Disney Comic*, was banned under Pinochet and to be found selling it could incur the death penalty.[37] By 'cleansing' Chile of Marxist art and literature, the Junta sought to protect the cultural envoys of their imperial masters. 'They know what kind of culture best serves their interests, that Mickey and Donald will help keep them in power, hold socialism at bay, restore "virtue and innocence" to a "corrupted" Chile.'[38] David Kunzler suggests that Disney may be the twentieth century's most important figure in bourgeois popular culture. 'He has done more than any single person to disseminate around the world certain myths upon which that culture has thrived, notably that of an "innocence" supposedly universal, beyond place, beyond time – and beyond criticism.'[39] The threat of Disney, for Dorfman and Mattelart, derives not so much from the American way of life as from the American Dream of Life. 'It is the manner in which the US dreams and redeems itself and then imposes that dream upon others for its own salvation, which poses the danger for dependent countries. It forces us Latin Americans to see ourselves as they see us.'[40] To challenge the Disney version of the world is to challenge a whole world view embracing both society and nature.

To many this claim will appear extreme. The Disney message, Tomlinson argues, has many widely differing interpretations. Dorfman and Mattelart read the 'Uncle Scrooge' character as revealing an obsession with money, but others have read it as a mockery of money fetishism, as a critique of capitalism, as a parody of entrepreneurship, whilst others see the overall theme of Disney comics to be 'the ways in which human beings deceive and destroy themselves'.[41] As we saw in Chapter 4, allegations of cultural imperialism have to address questions of reception. That is no doubt true, but equally, the power imbalance between North and South, the prevalence of this kind of literature, is part of that colonization of the social imaginary which Freire, Dorfman and many other Third World critics complain of, and which Tomlinson finally concedes. Since the gospel also addresses the social imaginary this is a matter of profound theological concern. In its own way the contest between Elijah and the prophets of Baal (1 Kings 18) was a contest between two such 'imaginaries' and the call to choose, or to contest, a reigning hegemony which has the support of the ruling elite, remains.

---

36   McGuigan, *Cultural Populism* p.178
37   According to John Tomlinson it was also banned in the United States. *Imperialism* p.41
38   A.Dorfman and A.Mattelart, *How to Read Donald Duck: Imperialist Ideology in the Disney Comic* New York: International General 1975 p.14
39   David Kunzler in Dorfman and Mattelart, *Duck* p.11
40   Dorfman and Mattelart, *Duck* p.95
41   Tomlinson, *Imperialism* p.43 citing the work of Martin Barker

Contesting Hegemony

Hegemony, it is universally agreed, never goes unchallenged, but there is some difference of view as to whether it automatically deconstructs or whether it needs active opposition. Thus Raymond Williams suggests that the theoretical problem is to distinguish between alternative and oppositional initiatives which are made *within* the frame of a specific hegemony 'and other kinds of initiative and contribution which are *irreducible to the terms of the original* or the adaptive hegemony and are in a sense independent'.[42]

On the basis of his studies of peasant societies James Scott feels that the presuppositions of theories of hegemony are false because any hegemonic ideology provides within itself the raw material for contradictions and conflict. 'As far as the realm of ideology is concerned,' he writes:

> no social order seems inevitable to all of its subjects. The fact that serfs, slaves, or untouchables have no direct knowledge or experience of other social orders is ... no obstacle to their creating what would have to qualify as 'revolutionary thought'. The imaginative capacity of subordinate groups to reverse and/or negate dominant ideologies is so widespread that it might be considered part and parcel of their standard cultural and religious equipment.[43]

Abercrombie, Hill and Turner argued that in nineteenth century Britain the labour aristocracy commonly did not agree with the dominant bourgeois society, and if they did it seemed to be the result of the independent evolution of working class culture. The values of self-help, independence, respectability and improvement, were shared by both artisan and bourgeois culture, but had very different meanings in both.[44] In the previous century the peasantry never accepted the enclosure of the commons as justified, and this informed their attitude to poaching.

As instances of ideologies which are internally contradictory Scott cites slavery, communism, or liberal democracy. All these, he says, may turn out to be a provocation and incitement rather than general anaesthesia. This is an odd list. One can see how communism or liberal democracy, or for that matter Christianity or Islam, can be turned against those who seek to harness them to dominant power: in each there are notions of equality or of individual rights which are bound to do this (which is why, in view of the text of the Declaration of Independence, there is a deep inconsistency in the exercise of United States

---

42 Williams, *Marxism and Literature* p.114 my italics

43 J.Scott, *Weapons of the Weak: Everyday forms of peasant resistance* New Haven: Yale University Press 1985 p.331 Chetan Bhatt likewise argues with heavy irony that the poor and oppressed knew about 'scepticism with regard to metanarratives' long before postmodernism. *Liberation* p.3

44 Abercrombie et al(eds), *Dominant Ideology*, pp.111, 117 This is argued in detail by Thomas Laqueur. A model which regards Sunday schools primarily as a weapon of alleged bourgeois assault on working class culture simply will not do. The schools were effective in large measure because they worked from within and because they were not merely organs of middle class propaganda. 'Sunday Schools and social control' in Bocock and Thompson(eds) *Religion and Ideology* pp.184–204

imperialism). But why does slavery provoke dissent? After all, it has seemed morally justifiable to some of the best human minds, and, notoriously, the 'truths held to be self-evident' by the framers of the American constitution did not extend to slaves. John Beverley remarks that it is not an abstract ethical or epistemological principle that drives the 'presumption' of equal worth but 'the specific character of the ... relations of subordination, exploitation, and marginalization.'[45] Similarly, Scott claims that most subordinate classes are able, on the basis of their daily material experience, to penetrate and demystify the prevailing ideology, and this seems to be true.[46]

Underlying such a claim is some notion of natural justice. However unsatisfactory from a philosophical or theological point of view, the claim seems to be that what challenges oppressive ideologies is our shared humanity rather than any articulated counter ideology. Whilst I shall pursue this suggestion both in the next chapter and in Chapter 10 we need to bear in mind studies such as Barrington Moore's account of injustice, which demonstrate the extent to which people can bear with, and internalize, suffering as a coping mechanism for what is felt to be inevitable.[47] The human capacity to ignore and accept suffering is, he argues, necessary for survival. 'Therefore any political movement against oppression has to develop a new diagnosis and remedy for existing forms of suffering, a diagnosis and remedy by this suffering stands morally condemned. *These new moral standards of condemnation constitute the core identity of any oppositional movement.*'[48] The articulation of ideologies, in other words, plays a crucial role in dismantling oppressive hegemonies and, as I argued in the last chapter, and will further illustrate here, Scripture has functioned in this way.

Scott argues that, deprived of the normal weapons of force and the law, the weak develop their own weapons of foot dragging, dissimulation, desertion, false compliance, pilfering, feigned ignorance, slander, arson, sabotage and so on. These tactics may in the end, he believes, make an utter shambles of hegemonic policies. 'Just as millions of anthozoan polyps, create, willy nilly, a coral reef, so do multiple acts of peasant insubordination and evasion create political and economic barrier reefs of their own.'[49] He cites Marc Bloch who feels that the great millennial movements were flashes in the pan compared to the 'patient, silent struggles stubbornly carried on by rural communities' to avoid claims on their surplus and assert their rights to the means of production.[50] In these tactics one can see a spirit and practice that prevents the worst and promises something better.[51] There is clearly much in what Scott says, but at the same time the end result of his story, about resistance to the Green revolution, is that the combine harvesters and the multinationals won,

---

45   Beverley, *Subalternity and Representation* p.146
46   Scott, *Weapons* p.37
47   B.Moore, *Injustice: The Social Bases of Obedience and Revolt* New York: Sharp 1978 chapter 2
48   Moore, *Injustice* p.88 my italics
49   Scott, *Weapons* p.xvii
50   M.Bloch, *French Rural History* Berkeley: University of California Press 1970 p.170
51   Scott, *Weapons* p.350

and the peasantry were gradually eliminated: hegemony restored, more implacable than ever.

Other forms of the claim that hegemony is intrinsically unstable are that, first, since *no dominant culture ever exhausts all human practice and intention* 'all modes of domination select from and consequently exclude the full range of human practice'. We then have to ask of any dominant social order how far it reaches into the whole range of practices and experiences in an attempt at incorporation. However far, its reach will never be total.[52] Relatedly we can say that because *society is always changing*, hegemony must be constantly renewed.[53] Again, a slightly different take to Scott's, it is threatened by 'the *vitality* that remains in the forms of life it thwarts'.

Hegemony is always process, rather than a system or a structure. Because pressures and limits are always changing it can never be singular. 'One way of expressing the necessary distinction between practical and abstract senses within the concept is to speak of "the hegemonic" rather than "hegemony", and of "the dominant" rather than simple "domination".'[54] This is the reason even the most repressive regimes constantly seek to win the consent of subordinate groups to the existing social order. The more successful they are, say the Comaroffs, 'the more of their ideology will disappear into the domain of the hegemonic; the less successful, the more that unremarked truths and unspoken conventions will become remarked, reopened for debate'. At the same time we have to recognize that 'the human capacity to tolerate and rationalize cognitive dissonance is notoriously variable'.[55] The ideologies of the subordinate may give expression to the discordant but hitherto voiceless experience of contradictions that a prevailing hegemony can no longer conceal, though it may be a long road from the dawning of anti-hegemonic consciousness to an ideological struggle won.[56]

Once something leaves the domain of the hegemonic, it frequently becomes a major site of ideological struggle – instances are race and class.[57] Here we have the move from tacit, latent, unarticulated, to articulate forms of resistance based on the moral condemnation Moore speaks of. Whilst he argues that improvement in a society's ability to produce goods is the first essential ingredient for societal change the second is moral outrage. 'Without strong moral feelings and indignation, human beings will not act against the social order.'[58] Wherever Scripture has formed part of the culture, it has engendered such feelings. 'The forms rebellion took,' wrote Marc Bloch of medieval Europe, 'were also traditional: mystical fantasies: a powerful preoccupation with the primitive egalitarianism of the Gospels, which took hold of humble minds well before the Reformation.'[59] In the second chapter we encountered

52   Williams, *Marxism and Literature* p.125
53   Hall, 'The Toad in the Garden' p.54
54   Williams, *Marxism and Literature* p.113
55   J. and J. Comaroff, *Revelation and Revolution* vol 1 p.25
56   J. and J. Comaroff, *Revelation and Revolution* vol 1 pp.25–26
57   J. and J. Comaroff, *Revelation and Revolution* vol 1 p.27
58   Moore, *Injustice* p.469
59   Bloch, *French Rural History* p.169

Raymond Williams' idea of 'residual culture'. The tradition preserved in this aspect of culture is, he remarks, 'the most evident expression of the dominant and hegemonic pressures *and limits* ... Much of the most accessible and influential work of the counter-hegemony is historical: *the recovery of discarded areas, or the redress of selective and reductive interpretations.*'[60]

As Rowland and Corner illustrate, the use of the Book of Revelation within Christian tradition is a perfect example of this. Adorno remarks that the only philosophy which can be responsibly practised in the face of despair:

> is the attempt to contemplate all things as they would present themselves from the standpoint of redemption. Knowledge has no light but that shed on the world by redemption: all else is reconstruction, mere technique. Perspectives must be fashioned that displace and estrange the world, reveal it to be, with its rifts and crevices, as indigent and distorted as it will appear one day in the messianic light.[61]

This is what apocalyptic tries to do. In Wayne Meeks' words: 'The vision of the Apocalypse shreds and rips away that common sense [that is, the taken for granted consensus about the way things are] with as much violence as that with which John sees the sky itself removed.'[62] The Apocalypse unmasks reality, refusing to accept that the dominant powers are the ultimate point of reference for the world. In the Book of Revelation, 'The grandeur of Rome, which seems to be invincible and even divine, is revealed for what it really is. It is a bombastic sham maintained by vicious and diabolical means. This is a stunning critique of the accepted order and received wisdom.' As Rowland and Corner note, the parallels in our own day are striking.[63]

The Mishnah taught that every generation had to live as those which came out of Egypt. In the same way Walter Benjamin said that 'In every era the attempt must be made anew to wrest tradition away from a conformism that is about to overpower it.'[64] Johann Baptist Metz, and the liberation theologians, took this up in the argument that we have to recover the 'dangerous memory' of the biblical texts – dangerous because they motivate for action against prevailing hegemonies. Thus Rigoberta Menchu cited the role the stories of the Exodus and of Judith played in Guatemalan resistance:

> Take exodus for example, that's one we studied and analysed. It talks a lot about the life of Moses who tried to lead his people from oppressions, and did all he could to free his people. We compare the Moses of those days with ourselves, the 'Moses' of today ... We began looking for texts which represented each of us. We tried to relate them to our Indian culture. We took the example of Moses for the men, and we have the example of Judith, who was a very famous woman in her time and appears in the Bible ... She held her victory in her hands, the head of the King. This gave us a vision, a stronger idea of how we Christians must defend ourselves.[65]

---

60   Williams, *Marxism and Literature* pp.115–116 my italics
61   T.Adorno, *Minima Moralia* London: Verso 1974 p.247
62   Cited in Rowland and Corner, *Liberating Exegesis* p.87
63   Rowland and Corner, *Liberating Exegesis* pp.135, 87
64   W.Benjamin, *Illuminations* London: Fontana 1973 pp.257–259
65   R.Menchu, *I Rigoberta Menchu* London: Verso 1984 pp.131–132

Rowland and Corner argue that the Book of Revelation also plays such a role. 'The Apocalypse can remind readers of early Christian literature that the hope for a reign of God on earth, when injustice and oppression will be swept away and the structures of evil society broken down, is an important component of the Christian gospel.'[66] It is counter cultural in resisting compromise and accommodation and advocating a critical distance from dominant ideas of social relations adopted and the language of religious discourse. Laclau and Mouffe argue that without 'utopia', without the possibility of negating an order beyond the point that we are able to threaten it, there is no possibility at all of the constitution of a radical imaginary – whether democratic or of any other type.[67]

Constructing Hegemony

So far we have been discussing hegemony as something which is intrinsically negative, but the question is whether a stable society, a non-anarchic society, does not require some form of hegemony. The concern for order dominant in Western political thought since Augustine often seems oppressive, but we only have to look at Eastern European societies since 1989, or at Angola over the past thirty years, to be reminded of the virtues of stable governments. Gramsci himself seems to have believed that hegemony had to be not only contested but constructed.[68] How does this happen? In the last section we saw the view that all hegemonies are intrinsically unstable and generate their own downfall. The version of this view, often derived from Marx, that the internal contradictions of capitalism will eventually lead to the total breakdown of the system, was dubbed by Gramsci 'economism'. By contrast he believed that a new world view had to be constructed to take the place of the old. To do this, in his view, *education in values* was essential. The alternative society does not grow automatically from the soil of history but must be based on an ideal goal, on a vision of what 'ought to be'. The open and indefinite perspective of the 'ought to be' replaces the closed chain of determinism.[69] Education lies at the heart of the construction of an alternative and progressive hegemony. We shall have to consider this view, measuring Gramsci's ideas with what we saw earlier about education.

Hegemony, we saw, rests on the consent the majority give to the prevailing system. Gramsci set this consent down to 'the prestige (and consequent confidence) which the dominant group enjoys because of its position and function in the world of production'. 'Every relationship of "hegemony",' he wrote, 'is necessarily an educational relationship.'[70] Gramsci wanted ordinary

---

66   Rowland and Corner, *Liberating Exegesis* pp.148–149
67   Laclau and Mouffe, *Hegemony* p.190
68   I failed, in my *Karl Barth: Against Hegemony* Oxford: Oxford University Press 1999, to see that hegemony is a positive as well as a negative reality.
69   Bocock, *Hegemony* p.53
70   Gramsci, *Notebooks* p.350

people to develop critical understanding and thus become capable of determining their own economic–political–cultural relations and practices but believed that 'the masses' were not able to overcome their intellectual and moral subordination on their own. An alternative hegemony, however, cannot be constructed by those who are alien to the masses.

This is where the organic intellectual comes in. For Gramsci classes do not arise automatically. Connections among groups in a society have to be constructed and maintained. Each class tends to create, 'organically', intellectuals who give it homogeneity and create awareness in the economic, social and political fields. They are not just scholars and writers but anyone whose social function it is to serve as a transmitter of ideas within civil society and between government and civil society.[71] Political change is brought about by a process of dialectical interaction between organic intellectuals and ordinary people. 'It is precisely this task of critical education – enabling full and active participation of the masses in all spheres of social life – which distinguishes Gramsci's transformative party and its hegemonic project from the politics of the bourgeoisie.'[72]

We can thus contrast bourgeois hegemony, presupposing the dichotomy of leaders and led, of dominant and subordinate classes, with working class hegemony, which seeks the active participation of all subordinate groups within a unified revolutionary movement. 'The fundamental project of the working class – building a participatory community in which social powers of self-production are commonly and consensually regulated – cannot proceed without them for, were it to do so it would simply reproduce the dichotomy of leaders–led.'[73] This new hegemony or, to use the subalternist phrase, 'politics of the people', has to be built across the whole range of society's functions and institutions. In a similar way Herman and Chomsky believe that the organization and self-education of groups in the community and workplace, and their networking and activism, are the fundamental elements in steps toward the democratization of our social life and any meaningful social change.[74]

There are obvious objections to this view. The working class, as Gramsci and socialist theory in general understood it at that time, has largely disappeared, and Laclau and Mouffe are right that we need to rethink socialist theory in the light of these changes. They point to the role of the 'new social movements', groups organized around ecological, anti-authoritarian, anti-institutional, feminist, anti-racist, ethnic, regional and sexual identities. The common denominator of all of them would be their differentiation from workers' struggles, considered as 'class' struggles.[75] At the same time, the need for these

---

71   W.L.Adamson, *Hegemony and Revolution: A Study of Antonio Gramsci's Political and Cultural Theory* Berkeley: University of California Press 1980 p.143

72   M.Rupert, *Producing Hegemony* Cambridge: Cambridge University Press 1995 p.29

73   Rupert, *Producing Hegemony* p.30

74   Herman and Chomsky, *Consent* p.307

75   Laclau and Mouffe, *Hegemony* p.159 The idea, floated by Marcuse in the 1960s, that art is the positive category of liberation, and that, in Dostoevsky's words, 'beauty will redeem the world', seems by contrast impossibly utopian, in the negative sense of being unrealizable.

groups to win power as parties remains, because a myriad of competing and diverse interest groups are obviously ideal grounds for divide and rule policies. Something is needed to hold such groups together, and here there is an obvious role for an overarching ideology. Earlier I challenged Robert Bocock's idea that hegemony can only be contested by an articulate ideology, but in this respect his point may be granted. He also goes on to draw attention to the anti-intellectualism which modern forms of capitalism encourage, especially in the mass media, and he is surely right that no new hegemony can be produced without challenging this.[76] Anti-intellectualism is convenient to those in power because it precludes rigorous critique.

Again, Gramsci thinks in terms of 'masses' in a way which, as we saw in Chapter 3, has been largely rejected in recent political thought. That the bulk of ordinary people uncritically accept the views of their leaders is rejected by cultural populism, as is the view that intellectual elites are needed to guide them, a view reminiscent, in some ways, of Coleridge's 'clerisy'. On the other hand there is a vital task in making information available, and here campaigning journalism like that of John Pilger, William Blum and George Monbiot, and the oppositional activities of intellectuals like Noam Chomsky, are clearly indispensable. Furthermore, as we saw, again, in the third chapter, the relation of culture and education is indispensable and this has an inevitable political dimension.

John Thompson argues that the best we can hope for, given the complexity of the contemporary world and the limitations of genuinely participatory democracy, is a greater diffusion of information concerning the activities of powerful individuals and organizations, a greater diversity in channels of diffusion and a greater emphasis on the establishment of mechanisms through which these activities can be rendered accountable and controlled.[77] In other words, all we can do is fight for freedom of information and make piecemeal changes by and by. No counter hegemony is realizable. John Beverley is surely right, by contrast, to insist that there has to be a real alternative vision for, 'if to win hegemony the subaltern classes and groups have to become essentially like what is already hegemonic, then in a sense the old ruling classes and the dominant culture win, even in defeat'.[78] Because hegemony has its roots in economic practice, as Hall insists, we need to think in terms not just of cultural change but also of new kinds of transnational political and economic institutions – the kind of demands made at Rio in 1992, articulated in Agenda 21, and still the stuff of dreams.

---

76   Bocock, *Hegemony* p.128
77   Thompson, *Ideology* p.120
78   Beverley, *Subalternity and Representation* p.133

Kingdom, Hegemony, Church

Jesus' teaching, we know, was centred on the idea of the *basileia tou theou*, the reign of God, or God's kingly rule. Contrary to the notorious misinterpretation of John 18.36 (My kingdom is not of this world) this kingdom has real effects in the everyday world: it does not refer only to the eternal world. The context of the interrogation by Pilate makes this perfectly clear: the kingdom Jesus preaches, and which is identified with his person, is not that of the security state, which needs the apparatus of terror for its maintenance. The meaning of the *basileia tou theou* is bound up with the doing of God's will – only this assumption makes sense of Jesus' ethical teaching.[79] Human beings are to seek God's kingdom and God's righteousness (Mt 6.33). The righteousness of God calls forth an answering righteousness of human beings. This involves a history, an ongoing process, something implied in the parables of growth.[80]

When Jesus comes into Nazareth preaching the kingdom he invokes the Jubilee promises of Leviticus – liberty for the captives and a restoration of rights to the poor. In his teaching he tells his disciples that they are privy to the 'secret of the kingdom' but that 'those without' cannot understand it. Why? It is a question of hegemony. Hegemony, we remember, is the realm of taken for granted common sense assumptions. These include the belief that progress can only be made top–down, by the rich on the part of the poor. The disciples shared these assumptions and their corporate education involved unlearning them (Mk 10.26). What takes its place, Jesus goes on to say, is a radically alternative practice.

The preaching of the kingdom was linked with Jesus' calling of twelve, a symbolic act in which 'Israel', the 'chosen people', was reconfigured. Abraham had been called, in the view of the Yahwist, so that 'all the nations of the earth might be blessed'. The Hebrew Bible represents a complex reflection on how that might be the case. Nationalist and imperialist strands stand alongside universalist ones. Most radically, Israel's vocation is rethought in terms of being a servant, and indeed even a suffering servant, to the nations. Jesus takes up this discussion and, if the teaching recorded in Mark 10 is any guide, seems to have learned especially from the school or teacher we call 'Second Isaiah'. The disciples are to constitute a servant community, a community constructed around alternatives: 'it shall not be so amongst you'. Together they are to live for and to be bound by 'the reign of God'. They are to pray that this reign be realized 'on earth as in heaven'. Jesus accepts the designation 'Messiah'. As such he comes preaching good news for the poor and he lives that out in his table fellowship and his day-to-day encounters. His horizons are not bound by the conventional imaginary but shaped by what he believes to be God's possibilities. Matthew records Jesus as speaking of the constitution of an

<hr>

79   I have argued this in detail in *Redeeming Time* London: DLT 1986 chapter 2 Here we can instance the texts Jesus refers to when he uses the phrase. So, Mk 7.1–13 = Is 29.13, Ex 20.12; Mk 10.2f = Gen 1.27, 5.2, 2.24; Mk 11.15 = Is 56.7, Jer 7.11; Mk 12.28 = Dt 6.45, 1 Sam 15.22, Hos 6.6 All refer to the need to act.
80   N.Dahl, 'The Parables of Growth' *Studia Theologica* 5 (1951) pp.132–166

'ecclesia' (Mt 16.18). This word was used in the Septuagint to translate 'quahal'. Both words had inescapable political connotations. The quahal YHWH was the moot of the tribes to consider policy, more especially policy related to defence.[81] The ecclesia was the meeting of the free citizens in Athens to do the same thing. The realization of God's will, then, was not something which referred solely to the next world, but to this, in and through the processes of participation and struggle.

As Paul presents it, the task of the Church is to live out this realization corporately, as a body, forming a contrast society, which will both preach and live out this vision 'to the ends of the earth'. Paul deeply internalizes Jesus' teaching about the nature of the alternative community: God works through the weak and the foolish, he says, and not through the strong and the wise. Just as with the first disciples, the counter intuitive nature of this claim involves a process of re-education, escaping hegemony. So does his account of the implications of living and understanding 'the body'. The image of the body, as is well known, is used in two different ways. The function of the later use, which contrasts the head with the rest of the body (Col 3.9–10), was, says Paul Minnear, 'to attack at its deepest cosmic and psychological roots the perennial human habit of accepting as ultimate the world's way of dividing humankind into competing societies, whether religious, racial, cultural or economic'.

Paul's thought is structured by his reflection on the significance of the cross and the resurrection. The relation between these two events gives him his understanding of God's purposes or, as we might say, his philosophy of history. Freedom stands at the heart of it (Gal 5.1) – freedom from the compulsion of sin, from the idols of power, and from godforsakenness.[82]

Did Paul intend to replace the hegemony of the *pax romana* with that of the *pax Christi*? I think he did. Not, however, through the agency of organic intellectuals, though if there ever was such a person, surely Paul was it, but through the agency of the whole contrast community. This vision, of which the *locus classicus* is 1 Corinthians 12, was lost in the Christendom situation, which, in the distinction between priest and lay, instituted precisely that distinction between expert and everybody else which we have seen to be the mark of an alienating hegemony. At the same time the Church continued to understand itself as a 'school of faith', a tradition in which people were schooled to understand the world and themselves in a certain way. It is no surprise, therefore, that Gramsci recognized, and perhaps learned from, the educational role of the Church, based on popular world views, with a moral value system, a symbolic and ritual system, and an organizational base in Churches, denominations and sects.[83] On the face of it the Catholic parish system, and the Muslim system of mosques, seem better placed to exercise hegemony than almost any other system ever devised. Where they fail, it seems, is in making compacts with dominant groups. The alliance with class systems,

---

81 For example Josh 9.15, 18–27, Josh 22.16–20
82 J.Moltmann, *The Church in the Power of the Spirit* London: SCM 1977 p.85ff
83 Bocock, *Hegemony* p.60

with what, in Scott's terms, are self-evidently repressive forms of governance – in the sense that the rich get the gravy and the poor get the blame – is what generates that suspicion of and resistance to hegemony which undoes it.

The new hegemony which Jesus speaks of as kingdom and Paul as body involves what, these days, is called 'subalternity'. Doubtless with Hegel in mind Freire had argued that the oppressed (the 'weak') must be the agents of liberation because the oppressors dehumanize themselves in the act of oppression.[84] Liberation theology is built on the fundamental biblical insight of the priority of the poor to argue that a new society (hegemony) must be built from the bottom up, not top down. Its notion of the base community was a step towards the recovery of an organic community, and Ernesto Cardenal showed how the priest might function as an organic intellectual within it. The relationship in Solentiname seems to me to evade the dilemmas of subalternity posed by Gayatri Spivak, according to which the desire for representation always ends up speaking for the poor and occluding their voice.[85] As John Beverley remarks, a text like *I, Rigoberta Menchu* forces us to confront the subaltern not as a represented victim of history but rather as the agent of a transformative historical project that aspires to become hegemonic in its own right.[86]

In place of representation liberation theology puts solidarity, 'concrete friendship with the poor'. Solidarity is key in both contesting and constructing hegemony. As we have seen, hegemony is always contested. It is essentially about struggle. That liberation theology has met fierce resistance, therefore, should not surprise us. That it should have failed in some areas, in its inadequate recognition of popular culture for instance, is also scarcely surprising. To think of it as a 'flash in the pan', however, a passing fad like the secular city or death of God theologies of the 1960s, seems to me to be a mistake. These were essentially attempts to theorize the phenomenon of secularization. Liberation theology, on the other hand, has two, related, roots: the rediscovery of Scripture, bound up with Vatican II, and the rediscovery of the priority of the poor. Since the latter leads to the demand for and the attempt to create a radically new order it is inevitably contested. As the liberation theologians have amply demonstrated, however, the witness of Scripture to the priority of the poor, its demand for an alternative which will take concrete shape, is too insistent to be swept aside. The work begun forty years ago marks only beginnings.

Rowland and Corner observe that Christians engaged in reading the signs of the times can hardly be sanguine about the prospects for global peace and

---

84   Freire, *Pedagogy* p.24

85   John Beverley suggests that we can think of subaltern studies as a secular version of the 'preferential option for the poor' of liberation theology, one which shares with liberation theology the essential methodology of what Gutierrez calls 'listening to the poor'. *Subalternity and Representation* pp.38–39

86   Beverley, *Subalternity and Representation* p.83

survival. Their reading of the Bible is aware that the hope for God's Kingdom was often based on a negative rejection of the present order, but such rejection is always a ground for hope:

> We are not condemned by nature to live under the shadow of the beast, and to worry daily about demonic forces outside our control – the arms race, pollution, starvation, runaway levels of inflation and unemployment. We condemn ourselves to live under their shadow. That realization is a condemnation and a judgement, but also an opportunity.[87]

The opportunity is the construction of a new hegemony. Such a hegemony will *not* mean, as Stuart Hall insists, the disappearance or destruction of difference. We might take his words as a gloss on 1 Corinthians 12:

> It is the construction of a collective will through difference ... The notion of a politics which, as it were, increasingly is able to address people through the multiple identities which they have – understanding that those identities do not remain the same, that they are frequently contradictory, that they cross-cut one another, that they tend to locate us differently at different moments, conducting politics in the light of the contingent ... is the only political game that the locals have left at their disposal.[88]

What this means in terms of mission and multicultural society will be the theme of the final four chapters. Here it serves to mark off any understanding of the new hegemony which needs to be constructed from any Christendom model. The Christendom model presupposed force from the very first day: it sought uniformity, and tried to police it by burning those who disagreed. The non-alienating politics of the Corinthian community, on the other hand, was the attempt to achieve unity through respect for difference, but a respect which began with the poor rather than the rich. It is far from clear that this cannot be a matter of practical politics as the 'realists' maintain. On the contrary, the emergence of such a politics might be a precondition of survival.

---

87 Rowland and Corner, *Liberating Exegesis* p.198
88 S.Hall, 'Old and New Identities' in King(ed) *Culture, Globalization and the World System* p.5

Chapter 7

Liberation Theology and Cultural Politics

Ideology and hegemony, we have seen, are the ways in which power is entailed in culture. Power is also articulated, however, in the relation of class, gender and race and this raises the issue of cultural politics. This is the question of what counts in society and what does not, what is at the centre and what at the margins, which voices are heard and which silenced.[1] Cultural institutions like churches, mosques, synagogues, schools, the family and the law play a key part in establishing these priorities. Cultural politics do not necessarily *establish* patterns of inequality – all sorts of other factors like invasion, colonization, immigration and economics play their part here – but once established culture keeps such patterns in place and entrenches them. Think of the dense network of practices which determine caste – dress codes, codes about what is eaten, when and how, codes about living areas and access to water, all giving rise to distinctive forms of music, poetry and religious practice. Similarly, cultural codes are implicit in the distinction between white collar and blue collar workers, which characteristically involves different leisure activities, preferences in music, newspapers, types of literature read, television programmes watched; and between the sexes, as we can see from the paucity of women artists or composers in the Western tradition.

Culture is process: it never stands still. At the same time at any given moment it provides the norms of what it means to be human. Because all societies are class and gender divided, and many are race and caste divided, social inequality is legitimated through culture. These divisions involve profound asymmetries of power. Does that matter? After all, we saw T.S.Eliot's view that the preservation of classes was essential for the health of society, and in other connections we have seen the repeated assertion that monocultures are deadly. *Vive la différence!* The problem with differences which involve inequality, however, is that they affect what are today called life chances. 'I have come that they might have life, and have it in all its fullness' says Jesus (Jn 10.10). Inequality negates that fullness and therefore has to be overcome. This means, in turn, that cultural politics are a task for the Church.

In the first century Paul saw this and understood it. Purity codes insisted on by Jewish Christians made Gentiles second class citizens, and congregations of Jews and Gentiles still treated women as inferior. In the world in which he lived slavery was a fundamental form of unfree labour. No follower of the crucified

---

1 So G.Jordan and C.Weedon, *Cultural Politics: Class, Gender, Race and the Postmodern World* Oxford: Blackwell 1995 p.4

could forget that crucifixion was the punishment for slaves and rebels, and that after Spartacus' rebellion six thousand slaves had been crucified along the Via Appia. In this context Paul was driven by a vision of a different world, a world which he described as being 'in Christ', which for him meant being 'in the new humanity'. 'There is no longer Jew or Greek; there is no longer slave or free; there is no longer male and female; for all of you are one in Christ Jesus' (Gal. 3.25). One of the consequences of ecclesia, for Paul, was the end of asymmetries of power. Ecclesia meant a new kind of cultural politics.

To explore this further I turn first to the question of the nature of power. In order to avoid abstraction I then briefly examine the major forms of unequal power within society, in terms of class, gender and race, before developing a theological response on two lines. First, I argue for the fundamental commitment of the gospel to human equality; indeed, I agree with those authors who argue that the gospel is chiefly responsible for keeping this on the agenda. I then turn to consider the importance of cultural politics for liberation theology.

Defining Power

Power means effective agency, agency which attains its goals. In the Christian Scriptures it is spoken of by two groups of words corresponding, roughly, with power and authority.

The Greek word *dynamis*, power – from where we derive our 'dynamite' and 'dynamic' – comes from a root meaning to be able to, to have strength to.[2] From here there is an easy transition to political power, based on the command of physical force. The Stoics apply it to the Logos, as the all-pervading creative force. In the Septuagint *dynamis* is used to translate *hayil* and *saba*, which apply to God's power, as manifested in the exodus or in creation:

> It is I who by my great power and my outstretched arm have made the earth, with the people and the animals that are on the earth, and I give it to whomever I please.
> (Jer 27.5)

Power, then, involves the right of disposal, ownership. This sense of power was embodied in law and was part of both marriage vows and paternity in Roman and later Western law. Husbands could 'dispose' of their wives and fathers their children as they pleased. 'To you your father should be as a god,' says Theseus to Hermia in Shakespeare's *A Midsummer Night's Dream*:

> One that compos'd your beauties; yea and one
> To whom you are but as a form in wax,
> By him imprinted, and within his power
> To leave the figure, or disfigure it.

---

2   Following Otto Betz in *Dictionary of New Testament Theology* vol 2 Exeter: Paternoster Press 1975 p.601ff

Clearly, Jeremiah's ascription of power to God can work in two ways. It can, on the one hand, critique all such pretensions to earthly power, unmask them as idolatrous. On the other hand, as in Theseus' speech, it was often read as confirming them, in the idea that divine power was delegated to human beings and their institutions. This was why in England until the middle of the eighteenth century the murder of a husband by a wife, or of a master by a slave, was 'petty treason', and involved death by burning. It challenged the whole moral order of things, called all power into question.

In the New Testament Jesus follows the Rabbinic tradition which speaks of God as 'the power'. He himself does *dynameis*, mighty works, and is the 'mightier one' who will subdue the strong man, the devil (Mk 1.8, 3.22–30). For Paul Jesus is 'the power of God' (1 Cor 1.24) and the risen Christ gives power to believers (Phil 4.13).

Alongside this 'dynamic' language, there is the language of authority. *Exousia* is freedom of choice and the related verbs imply the exercise of authority and the right to do so. Jesus has *exousia* which the scribes lack (Mk 1.27). By authority he casts out demons and forgives sins. At the end of Matthew's gospel it is said that he has received from God 'all power in heaven and on earth' (Mt 28.18). Power is gifted to the disciples for the purpose of witness to Christ (Acts 1.8).

So far this profile of power is conventional. In identifying power with God power is viewed as ultimate agency, the accomplishment of creation and redemption, the gifting of life. What puts it in a radically different light is the crucifixion. Paul writes:

> Jews demand signs and Greeks desire wisdom, but we proclaim Christ crucified, a stumbling block to Jews and foolishness to Gentiles, but to those who are called, both Jews and Greeks, Christ the power of God and the wisdom of God. For God's foolishness is wiser than human wisdom, and God's weakness is stronger than human strength.
>
> (1 Cor 1.22–25)

This is perhaps the first time in world literature that anyone speaks of the weakness of God, and ventures a dialectical account of power. Power remains agency, but not that of one who is stronger than anyone else, but a power which overcomes through weakness. This, as Nietzsche rightly saw, is the decisive characteristic of the Christian notion of power. It is a wholly original way of moving beyond the impasse of power and powerlessness. In the conventional model the strong rule the weak. The crucifixion of Jesus, however, reveals the illegitimacy of the power of the strong. Two things now follow. On the one hand, Paul, as a good Jew, has absolute faith in the divine promises. These cannot fail. If the promises are fulfilled in and through crucifixion this must mean that this exercise of agency is stronger than what conventionally passes as power, the exercise of rule. In virtue of the promise there must be a way of understanding the power of the powerless. Second, following Jesus' own teaching, Paul redefines power in terms of forgiveness, of *agape*, love of the enemy. This kind of power is ultimate because it refuses alienation, refuses the last word of violence.

Power is vested in 'the body of Christ' – the Church as composed of all of its members. In this 'body' different parts play different roles, including those of teaching and prophecy (1 Cor 12). Paul does not, in this application of the metaphor, draw the implication that there must be a head amongst the members, which must be obeyed, but follows up his earlier insight about weakness:

> God has so arranged the body, giving the greater honour to the inferior member, that there may be no dissension within the body, but the members may have the same care for one another. If one member suffers, all suffer together with it; if one member is honoured, all rejoice together with it.
>
> (1 Cor 12.24–26)

'Greater honour to the inferior member'. This is a unique cultural politics which teaches us, in the words of a contemporary theorist, that it is from those who have suffered the sentence of history – subjugation, domination, diaspora, displacement – that we learn our most enduring lessons for living and thinking.[3] On it Freire built the edifice of his liberative pedagogy. The problem with liberating the oppressed is that they have internalized the values of their oppressors. The historical task of the oppressed is, therefore, to liberate themselves and their oppressors as well. 'The oppressors, who oppress, exploit, and rape by virtue of their power, cannot find in this power the strength to liberate either the oppressed or themselves. Only power that springs from the weakness of the oppressed will be sufficiently strong to free both.'[4]

Suspicion is cast on this perspective, however, by a number of studies which draw on the most influential recent account of power, deeply indebted to Nietzsche, that of Michel Foucault. Foucault attempts to move beyond the dialectic of power and powerlessness in another way, namely by finding power everywhere. Power circulates or can be understood as a chain. 'It is never localised here or there, never in anybody's hands, never appropriated as a commodity or piece of wealth. Power is employed and exercised through a net like organisation.'[5] Everybody is an actor; everyone both undergoes and exercises power. Instead of beginning our analysis of power with 'the powerful', perhaps with 'that than which a greater cannot be conceived', as Anselm defined God, we must begin from the bottom, with the 'infinitesimal mechanisms' of power, its 'microphysics'. We can then ask how these mechanisms of power have been and are 'invested, colonised, utilised, involuted, transformed, displaced, extended etc, by ever more general mechanisms and by forms of global domination'.

Foucault is interested in the mechanisms of power implicit in prisons, insane asylums, the family, the repression and interdiction of sexuality, and so forth, all of which represent the interests of the bourgeoisie.[6] He draws attention to the shift, in Western society in the thirteenth century, from accusatory

---

3   Bhaba, *Location* p.172
4   Freire, *Pedagogy* p.21
5   Foucault, *Power/Knowledge* p.98
6   Foucault, *Power/Knowledge* p.88ff

procedures to confession. To be sure, the Church was only one of the bodies involved in this move, but it was involved in a paradigmatic way. 'The confession has spread its effects far and wide. It plays a part in justice, medicine, education, family relationships, and love relations, in the most ordinary affairs of everyday life, and in the most solemn rites.'[7] Here is power/ knowledge in action, working by exploring people's minds and innermost secrets, and designed to bring about conformity, 'the quiet game of the well behaved'. A number of commentators have followed up this line of thought and traced it back to Paul. Elizabeth Castelli, for example, draws attention to Paul's many interventions on diet or sexuality and his repeated injunctions that his readers should imitate him. In the second letter to the Corinthian community he highlights his own submission as the basis of an appeal that his readers might submit. This, she argues, is thoroughly manipulative, a form of seeking social control.[8] Stephen Moore instances Paul's threats of divine judgment and likewise agrees that the discipline Paul seeks is intended to produce what Foucault calls 'docile bodies'.[9]

The case is far from proven. Others have argued that Paul demonstrates a keen concern for tolerance; that Paul's models of power were sharply contrasted with those prevailing in Roman society; and that his emphasis on humility and servanthood is not to instil conformity but precisely to protect those who do not fit in.[10] How one reads the evidence depends both on one's experience of the contemporary Church, and on one's understanding of the nature of power. Castelli and Moore are both indebted to Foucault, but his understanding of power, though illuminating, has its own problems. He argues that what replaces the tyranny of the *ancien régime* is normalization, more powerful because less purely repressive:

> What makes power hold good, what makes it accepted, is simply the fact that it doesn't only weigh on us as a force that says no, but that it traverses and produces things, it induces pleasure, forms knowledge, produces discourse. It needs to be considered as a productive network which runs through the whole social body, much more than as a negative instance whose function is repression.[11]

The fact that everyone has power and that it 'saturates all the planes of human existence' means that 'Now everywhere, it is nowhere in particular.'[12] This points to a particular problem with Foucault's analysis. It can be experienced as empowering, in that it insists that there is no person or group which is powerless.[13] In this respect it suggests agency. It also, however, has a non-

---

7 M.Foucault, *The History of Sexuality* vol 1 Harmondsworth: Penguin 1981 p.59

8 E.Castelli, *Imitating Paul: A Discourse of Power* Louisville: Westminster and John Knox 1991

9 S.Moore, *Poststructuralism and the New Testament* Minneapolis: Fortress 1994 pp.83–112

10 A.Thistleton lists the relevant literature in *Interpreting God and the Postmodern Self* Edinburgh: T&T Clark 1995 p.142

11 Foucault, *Power/Knowledge* p.119

12 J. and J. Comaroff, *Revelation and Revolution* vol 1 p.17

13 So, for example, L.McNay, *Foucault and Feminism: power, gender and the self* Cambridge: Polity 1992

agentive side, perhaps ascribed to transcendental or impersonal forces such as gods or ancestors, nature or physics, biological instinct or probability, finding expression, as Foucault suggests, in areas such as ethics, medical knowledge or common sense. Its effects are internalized, 'in their negative guise, as constraints; in their neutral guise, as conventions; and in their positive guise, as values. Yet the silent power of the sign, the unspoken authority of habit, may be as effective as the most violent coercion in shaping, directing, even dominating social thought and action.'[14] Here the suggestion that power is everywhere cancels through and we are left with powerlessness once again.

As noted in the previous two chapters, we need a language for domination, for asymmetries of power. In one of the most powerful recent formulations Homi Bhaba has drawn attention to the 'hybrid moment of political change' in which formations around gender or class contest each other's terms and territories and experience the displacement of their boundaries.[15] I shall try to draw attention to this hybrid experience whilst saying something about the distinct bases of social oppression involved in class, gender and race. The material marshalled here is, to some, tediously familiar. For the post-Reagan–Thatcher generation, however, there is, as the author to the Hebrews found, still a need for milk in the place of solid food (Hebrews 5.12). Those bored with the rehearsal of basic social inequalities can pass on to the next section on the gospel and equality.

Asymmetric Power: Class, Gender and Race

Salvation, in the Hebrew Bible, is understood as *shalom*: 'God will speak peace to his people,' says the psalmist, 'surely his salvation is near at hand.' But peace is not just absence of war, though it is also that, but embraces all the levels of liberation – good health, security, good relations, prosperity, contentedness. It is closely related with righteousness. The psalmist goes on:

> Steadfast love and faithfulness will meet;
> righteousness and peace will kiss each other.

(Ps 85.8–10)

The content of the term is, like salvation, wholeness – the integration of peace, justice and prosperity. The opposite, obviously, is dis-integration, the manifold alienations of human society, structured around class, caste, gender and race. All these forms of alienation are mutually imbricated and can only notionally be disentangled.

---

14   J. and J. Comaroff, *Revelation and Revolution* vol 1 p.22
15   Bhaba, *Location* p.28

Class

'Class' is another of those words which emerges, in the contemporary sense, at the beginning of Williams' 'long revolution'. Its emergence is important because it replaces older words, like estate, degree and order, which imply that social position is simply a given. Behind these older words lies that feudal vision of a hierarchical world the metaphysical justification for which is something like the great chain of being. As is well known, much Christian theology defended such a hierarchical account of society, and the defence became shriller as the case for it became less and less credible. Mrs Alexander's 'God made them high and lowly, and ordered their estate' dates from the middle of the nineteenth century, some years after Marx and Engels had celebrated the gale of modernity tearing apart all feudal bonds in *The Communist Manifesto*. What replaces the feudal and hierarchical idea, at the end of the eighteenth century, is the notion of society as made, and therefore as capable of being remade.[16] The term 'middle class' emerges to mark off the group which stands between the aristocracy and the mob. The working class were defined over against the privileged, 'priests, courtiers, public accountants, commanders of troops, in short, the civil, military or religious agents of government'.[17]

The descriptions of the middle and working classes were further defined through the nineteenth century, not least by legislation, and the general discussion anticipated the different senses of class in Marx and Weber. For Marx class is an *economic* category, referring to where people stand in relation to the means of production. The bourgeoisie own the means of production and the proletariat sell their labour. In this sense class is 'a large scale grouping of people who share common economic resources, which strongly influence the type of life they are able to lead'. Class means objectively structured economic inequalities in society and 'objective conditions which allow some to have greater access to material rewards than others'.[18] For Weber, on the other hand, class is a *social* category, primarily concerned with status. Status expresses the power implicit in a social estimation of honour and status groups are marked by a specific style of life and codes of behaviour.[19] Williams shows how late nineteenth century legislation allowed a distinction between the professional class, dependent on fees, the trading class, dependent on profits, the propertied class, dependent on rents, and the working class, dependent on manual labour. In the discussion around these terms middle class came to express social position, whilst working class reflected economic relationships. Class, as Marx recognized, had a necessary cultural dimension:

---

16 Williams, *Keywords* p.60ff
17 Williams, *Keywords* p.63
18 A.Giddens, *Sociology* Cambridge: Polity 1989 pp.209, 211
19 At the same time Weber recognized that 'class situation is ultimately market situation' and that class is based on economic interest. G and W Mills(eds), *From Max Weber* London: Routledge, Kegan and Paul 1948 p.180f

Insofar as millions of families live under economic conditions of existence that separate their mode of life, their interests and their culture from those of other classes, and put them in hostile opposition to the latter, they form a class. Insofar as there is a merely local interconnection among these small-holding peasants, and the identity of their interests begets no community, no national bond and no political organization among them, they do not form a class.[20]

Eliot's desire to retain classes springs from this recognition, and a hostility to the prospect of social homogeneity. The problem is that classes presuppose a market in which people bid for goods and, allowing for the view that property includes labour, then class is a way of talking about power in relation to the market. Here economic and status definitions come together. The first problem with this, on a theoretical level, is that the philosophical, theological and ethical problems of putting a value on labour are immense. How do we value one person's time against another's? How do we measure the worth of different forms of work? The late eighteenth century discourse I have mentioned implies a basically utilitarian calculus, directed polemically at inherited wealth, at those who do not have to 'work for a living', but live on the labours of others. The survival of the medieval tithe system as a way of paying the clergy did immense damage in a situation where clergy were no longer fellow commoners, like Chaucer's 'poor parson of a toune', but gentry and Justices of the Peace. It identified them with oppression. Nevertheless, the utilitarian calculus will not do, a fact made most clearly and insistently by disabled groups: people cannot be judged by their usefulness or otherwise to society.

No contemporary theologian would any longer defend the class system as such, but many defend the economic system which gives rise to it, convinced that capitalism is the best means for ensuring human progress. In this case what has to be asked is whether these theologians are facing up to the full implications of the views they advocate. Rosemary Ruether argues that, under the patriarchy of Western imperialism, the egalitarianism of early liberalism was soon replaced by a new hierarchialism that made women, workers, peasants and conquered races the images of dominated nature in contrast to the Euro-American male, the true bearer of transcendent consciousness.[21] Having ushered hierarchy out of one door, it returns by another.

The second problem with the equation of class and status is that, as indicated at the start of this chapter, class has effects on life chances. In class societies wealth begets wealth. Equality of opportunity is a myth when wealth buys opportunity in the first place. Inequalities are circular and self-perpetuating. It is true that there are counter examples and, especially in a leisure society, these may involve little more than exceptional physical co-ordination, as may be seen by the list of sportsmen in the ranks of the super rich, but statistically the numbers involved here are tiny. In terms of crime, it remains true that the prisons are full of people from social classes four and five, not because they are

20   K.Marx, 'The Eighteenth Brumaire of Louis Bonaparte' in Marx and Engels *Collected Works* Moscow: Progress vol 11 1975 p.187
21   R.Ruether, *Sexism and Godtalk* London: SCM 1983 p.83

more wicked than others but because the kind of property crime with which they are associated, though small scale compared with insider trading, asset stripping, making fortunes from selling landmines, pornography or illegal logging, is more easily detected and punished. In terms of health 'all the major killer diseases affect the poor more than the rich'.[22] Antony Giddens sums up the evidence when he writes that:

> Working class people have on average lower birth weight and higher rates of infant mortality, are smaller at maturity, less healthy, and die at a younger age, than those in higher class categories. Major types of mental disorder and physical illness including heart disease, cancer, diabetes, pneumonia and bronchitis are all more common at lower levels of class structure than towards the top.[23]

Nick Davies has described the emergence of a widespread subculture of poverty in Britain marked by hopelessness and complete absence of positive goals, lived out in estates which are ruled by drugs barons and pimps, and in which citizens who try to resist are driven out. The major factor in the emergence of such a culture, he believes, is the abandonment of the idea of equality under the market driven regimes of the 1980s and 1990s.[24]

One can set this evidence alongside campaigns for road safety or campaigns to cut down on smoking. In these cases governments campaign to prevent the loss of some thousands of lives each year. The class system, however, is in fact the biggest factor in life chances, in a sense the biggest killer. The effect of poverty on the health of Britain, writes Davies, is the same as a plane crashing and killing 115 passengers every day of the year.[25] Yet, since the abandonment of socialism as a realistic political option, it is unremarked, and accepted as fate, replaced by the fiction of a classless society.

Without wishing to reduce caste to class, the same points may be made about *caste, a fortiori*.[26] The caste system ties people into degrading occupations, the worst housing, inadequate access to water, and the daily receipt of violence from the upper classes by birth, in a system which is theologically and metaphysically justified. Writing in 1816 the Abbé Dubois described the way in which the touch or footprints of the Paraiyar caste was considered defiling, and described the sanctions around their use of water, or cooking vessels. He understood what today we call internalization:

> Notwithstanding the miserable condition of these wretched Paraiahs, they are never heard to murmur of their low estate ... The idea that he was born to be in subjection

---

22   P.Townsend, N.Davidson and M.Whitehead(eds), *Inequalities in Health* Harmondsworth: Penguin 1988 p.254
23   Giddens, *Sociology* p.215
24   N.Davies, *Dark Heart: The Shocking Truth About Hidden Britain* London: Vintage 1998 pp.286, 288
25   Davies, *Dark Heart* p.187
26   It is generally agreed that class must form part at least of the analysis of caste. See P.Damel SJ, 'Dalit Christian Experiences' in X.Irudayaraj(ed) *Emerging Dalit Theology* Madurai: TTS 1990 pp.18–54

to the other castes is so ingrained in his mind that it never occurs to the Pariah to think that his fate is anything but irrevocable.[27]

Made illegal by the Indian Constitution in 1947 caste still persists, and caste violence is a daily fact of life. What has changed is the internalization of oppression. Beginning with Ambedkar conscientization has spawned the variety of social movements which go under the umbrella title of the Dalit movement. 'Dalit' is a Marathi word meaning crushed, or oppressed. We recall that the Kairos theologians pointed out that oppression is a basic theme in Scripture, which has more than twenty words for it. The Bible describes oppression as the experience of being crushed, degraded, humiliated, exploited, impoverished, defrauded, deceived and enslaved, and oppressors are described as cruel, ruthless, arrogant, greedy, violent, tyrannical and as the enemy.[28] Poverty, which is the negative side of the class system, in fact affects the whole of society. As Davies remarks, it inflicts a spiritual damage on society, robbing us of our humanity, turning people into objects because, in such a society, it is actually money which counts.[29] It is for this reason that it is also a theological matter, a matter which the Church has to address if it is true to itself.

Gender

Class cannot be understood apart from the division of labour. The first form of this is the gender division. Thus Engels wrote: 'The first class antagonism that appears in history coincides with the development of the antagonism between man and woman in monogamous marriage, and the first class oppression coincides with that of the female sex by the male.'[30] Engels proposed that the 'great historical defeat of the feminine sex' occurred through changes in technology which followed the discovery of the possibility of smelting metal. Whereas previously the labour of men and women had had equal value now man has recourse to the labour of others, whom he reduces to slavery. Private property appears:

> The same cause which had assured to woman the prime authority in the house – namely her restriction to domestic duties – this same cause now assured the domination there of man; for woman's housework henceforth sank into insignificance in comparison with man's productive labour – the latter was everything, the former a trifling auxiliary.

Maternal authority gives place to paternal authority, property is inherited from father to son, rather than from woman to clan.

---

27   J.Dubois, *Hindu Manners Customs and Ceremonies* Oxford: Clarendon Press 1906 p.55
28   Villa-Vicencio, *Between Christ and Caesar* p.262
29   Davies, *Dark Heart* pp.284, 294
30   F.Engels, *Origins of the family, private property and the state* Peking: Foreign Languages Press 1978 p.75

Simone de Beauvoir seems to have accepted a variant of this story. On her account, it was childbearing which kept women at home, whilst men went out hunting, risking their lives:

> The worst curse that was laid upon woman was that she should be excluded from these warlike forays. For it is not in giving life but in risking life that man is raised above the animal; that is why superiority is accorded in humanity not to the sex that brings forth but to that which kills.[31]

Whatever the truth of the origins of patriarchy, what is indisputable is that myths, philosophies and theologies which legitimize it are found very early on. From the third chapter of Genesis was taken the idea that women, rather than men, were the cause of the Fall. Feminist theologians have familiarized us with the misogyny of the early Fathers, and indeed with those medieval teachers for whom women were 'misbegotten' and not properly made in the image of God.[32] They have established how, through the cult of the Virgin Mary, the myth of female inferiority and dependence was perpetuated. In Marianism, argues Marina Warner, the two arms of the Christian view of woman, the contempt and hatred evident in interpretations of Creation and Fall, and the idealization of her more 'Christian' submissive nature, meet and interlock.[33]

Patriarchy is not exclusive to Western culture, nor is Christianity the only religion which propagated such views of women, but when it comes to the maintenance of patriarchy it clearly has to take its share of responsibility. Its cultural effects are obvious. The fact that no woman reached the heights of Dante or Shakespeare, says Simone de Beauvoir, is explained by the general mediocrity of her situation. Culture was never an attribute of any but the feminine elite.[34] She saw very clearly the connection between Western views of women and Christian fear with regard to sexuality. She also saw that this had implications as regards equality. It was Christianity, she argued, that proclaimed, on a certain plane, the equality of man and woman. In woman, Christianity hates the flesh; if she renounces the flesh, she is God's creature, redeemed by the Saviour, no less than is man. Men and women are both servants of God, almost as asexual as the angels and together through grace, resistant to earthly temptations. If she agrees to deny her animality, woman – from the very fact that she is the incarnation of sin – will also be the most radiant incarnation of the triumph of the elect who have conquered sin.[35]

The impact of these views was manifold: exclusion of women from many forms of work; exclusion from political and cultural rights; double standards in the law and in remuneration; tacit endorsement of widespread patterns of abuse;

---

31   S de Beauvoir, *The Second Sex* London: Pan 1988 p.95
32   Aquinas, *Summa Theologiae* 1.93.4
33   M.Warner, *Alone of all her Sex* London: Pan 1985
34   De Beauvoir, *Second Sex* p.138
35   De Beauvoir, *Second Sex* p.203

femicide.[36] Feminism is a serious issue for the same reason that class is: it bears on the question of fullness of life. In doing so it affects both sexes. Rosalind Miles argues that males are 'the death sex' both in the sense that they are responsible for most forms of violence, but also because they constitute 96 per cent of the prison population, commit suicide three times more often than women, are much more likely to be murdered, die more often in all forms of accidents, have higher alchoholism and drug abuse rates, and live eight years less than women on average.[37] Feminism, therefore, as an attempt to bring about a cultural revolution, is as much a struggle on behalf of men as it is for 'equal rights' for women. On these lines Carole Pateman argues that feminists are trying to develop a theory of a social practice that, for the first time in the Western world, would be a truly general theory – including women and men equally – grounded in the interrelationship of the individual to collective life, or personal to political life, instead of their separation and opposition. She looks towards a new social order resting on a social conception of individuality which includes both women and men as biologically differentiated but not unequal creatures.[38]

Bearing in mind the mutual imbrication of class and gender Maria Mies has argued that capitalist penetration leads to the pauperization and marginalization of large masses of subsistence producers in the Third World, and that women are more affected by these processes than men. She argues that contrary to the common assumptions that second wave feminism means that things are getting better there is, in fact, a growing inequality and polarization between the sexes.[39] The accumulation process of global capitalism destroys the core of the human essence everywhere, because it is based on the destruction of women's autarky over their lives and bodies.[40] In her view the concepts of women's rights and equality need to be discarded as basically bourgeois concepts in the quest for what is essentially human. Since none can be free whilst some are slaves (something Schleiermacher recognized in his views on sin) she argues that only when women attain freedom can humanity as a whole find freedom.

From a North American black perspective bell hooks notes that neither a feminism that focuses on woman as an autonomous human being worthy of personal freedom nor one that focuses on the attainment of equality of opportunity with men can rid society of sexism and male domination. In an argument closely mirrored by Elizabeth Schüssler Fiorenza's work on kyriarchy, she believes that feminism is a struggle to eradicate the ideology

---

36   The aborting, or murder, of female foetuses or babies in India on account of the dowry system is well established. Bhatt finds it also in South Asian communities in the UK resulting from the deployment of ultrasound scans. He links it to fundamentalism. *Liberation* p.57

37   R.Miles, *The Rites of Man: love, sex and death in the making of the male* London: Paladin 1992

38   Carole Pateman, 'Feminist Critiques of the Public/Private Dichotomy' in A.Phillips(ed) *Feminism and Equality* Oxford: Blackwell 1987 p.121 Given the social implications of women's reproductive capacities, however, she believes it is utopian to suppose that tension between the personal and the political, love and justice, and individuality and communality, will disappear with patriarchal liberalism.

39   Maria Mies, 'Capitalist Development and Subsistence Production: Rural Women in India' in M.Mies et al(eds) *Women: The Last Colony* London: Zed 1988 p.41

40   Maria Mies, *Patriarchy and Accumulation on a World Scale* London: Zed 1986 p.2

of domination that permeates Western culture on various levels as well as a commitment to reorganizing society so that the self-development of people can take precedence over imperialism, economic expansion and material desires.[41] Feminism is not an isolated movement:

> Feminism as a movement to end sexist oppression directs our attention to systems of domination and the interrelatedness of sex, race, and class oppression ... The foundation of future feminist struggle must be solidly based on a recognition of the need to eradicate the underlying cultural basis and causes of sexism and other forms of group oppression.[42]

Race

It is often argued that racism and sexism are analogous, but prominent disagreements between feminists from different ethnic backgrounds have called this into question. The black feminist historian Hazel Carby notes that when white feminists write their 'herstory' and call it the story of women, all the while ignoring the story of black women, they are 'acting within the relations of racism'.[43] On reflection it is clear that whilst most women can find some images and modes of femininity with which to identify, some of which will be empowering, positive and valuable, racism does not offer its subjects positive forms of identity.[44] Of course patriarchy rests on a binary logic, but a logic confused, in the first place, by myths of androgyny which express a deep longing for unity, and by the experience noted by Dorothy Sayers that, for all the difference, women are in fact more like men than they are any other creatures in the world. In racism, on the other hand, we have the kind of binary logic of us and them which found expression in Aristotle's view of slaves as 'animated instruments'. For the racist, the other is not properly human. Perhaps she or he may become so at some time in the distant future, but not in such a way as to have any implications for present policy. Caste shares the same structure.

It ought not to be necessary to list the ways in which racism denies fullness of life in the most literal sense: the genocide of Latin American Indians; the slave ships, so foul they could be smelled twenty miles downwind; the two thousand year history of anti-semitism; the continuing persecution of gypsies; the problems of racial minorities in countries throughout the world. Today in the United States black men are six times as likely to be murdered as white, twice as likely to be unemployed and twenty per cent more likely to live below the poverty line. If the male is 'the death sex' then racism is an ideology of death.

---

41 bell hooks, 'Feminism: A Movement to End Sexist Oppression' in Phillips(ed) *Feminism and Equality* p.69
42 bell hooks, 'Feminism' p.75
43 Cited in Jordan and Weedon, *Cultural Politics* p.123 In terms of the mutual imbrication of race, class and gender Benedict Anderson's view that 'dreams of racism ... have their origin in ideologies of class ... above all in claims to divinity among rulers and to "blue" or "white" blood and "breeding"' is worth noting. *Imagined Communities* p.149
44 Jordan and Weedon, *Cultural Politics* pp.208–209

The mention of anti-semitism at once calls to mind theological justifications of racism – the charge, only disavowed by the Catholic Church at Vatican II, that the Jews were responsible for 'deicide'. The way in which this charge arose is only too clear in the light of uncritical readings of John's gospel, unaware of its own Jewish sectarian origins, and in the context of social situations of scapegoating. The theology of apartheid had quite different origins. This was rooted in European nationalism, and in the kind of belief in the destiny of the *Volk* which Herder's teaching could easily, though mistakenly, be seen to endorse. According to this doctrine human beings only realize themselves within a particular national community. The Dutch Reformed Church then went to Genesis 4 and spoke of the existence of a family of nations, each evolving in its own way, each sharing its riches with the other. There were two respects in which this theology was completely specious from the start. First, it was rooted in inequality and oppression – in an existing situation where the black population was forced into townships and Bantustans, to allow white settlers to appropriate the best land and the mineral wealth. Second, the rhetoric of separate development disguised a belief, manifest in the race laws, that the black nations were not only different but inferior – subhuman. It is this belief, for which there is no theological justification, which is at the heart of racism.

Stuart Hall argues that the ways in which black people and their experiences were positioned and subjected in the dominant regimes of representation were the effects of a critical exercise of cultural power and normalization. Just as Foucault argued, regimes of representation (which is to say, knowledge) are regimes of power. Such knowledge was internalized, said Fanon: it was not just bodies but souls which were colonized.[45] bell hooks insists, to the consternation of her white liberal students, on the terror the representation of whiteness causes in the black imagination. The attitude which insists that 'we are all just people', and the eagerness with which contemporary society does away with racism, only serve to mask the reality of its continuance.[46] Recognizing the mutual imbrication of race, class and gender she argues that a culture of domination necessarily promotes addiction to lying and denial:

> That lying takes the presumably innocent form of many white people (and even some black folks) suggesting that racism does not exist any more, and that conditions of social equality are solidly in place that would enable any black person who works hard to achieve economic self-sufficiency. Forget about the fact that capitalism requires the existence of a mass underclass of surplus labour ... Lying takes the form of mass media creating the myth that the feminist movement has completely transformed society, so much so that the politics of patriarchal power have been

---

45　S.Hall, 'Cultural Identity and Diaspora' in J.Rutherford(ed) *Identity* London: Lawrence and Wishart 1990 pp.225–226 Michel Wieviorka insists, rightly in my view, that racism needs to be discussed at the intersection of discourses of both inferiority and difference. 'Is it so difficult to be an anti-racist?' in P.Werbner and T.Modood(eds) *Debating Cultural Hybridity* London: Zed 2000 p.149

46　bell hooks, 'Representing Whiteness in the Black Imagination' in Grossberg et al(eds) *Cultural Studies* p.345

inverted and that men, particularly white men ... have become the victims of dominating women.[47]

Just for this reason Pratibha Parma is right that 'Racial identity, alone, cannot be a basis for collective organising, as black communities are as beset with divisions around culture, sexuality and class as any other community.'[48] *Shalom*, full, authentic human liberation, has to advance on all fronts.

The Gospel and Equality

> Equality is a vital need of the human soul. It consists in a recognition, at once public, general, effective and genuinely expressed in institutions and customs, that the same amount of respect and consideration is due to every human being because this respect is due to the human being as such and is not a matter of degree.[49]

That is Simone Weil, writing in high Platonist and *a priori* style, but expressing a view which the gospels also share. More prosaically, Barrington Moore argues that notions of equality, based on perceived human need, but also notions of inequality, based on a ranking of the value of different tasks and functions, are found in most societies.[50] In hunter–gatherer societies equality is a form of group insurance, in that no member of the group knows when he or she may be likely to be in need, and it is linked to what he calls the 'dog in a manger taboo' which condemns those who keep resources which are in short supply without use. Social equality in 'primitive' societies has often been taken as a datum since Rousseau.[51] Alasdair MacIntyre, on the other hand, arguing that Christianity is the main protagonist of equality in Western discourse, believes that 'the distinctive values of equality and of the criteria of need which Christianity in large part begot could not possibly commend themselves as general values for human life until it began to appear possible for the basic material inequalities of human life to be abolished'.[52] One can agree with this to the extent that the existence of material inequalities must appear as a

---

47   bell hooks, 'A Revolution of Values: The promise of multi cultural change' in S.During(ed) .*The Cultural Studies Reader* London: Routledge 1993 p.237 C.H.Kyung also cites a black woman student in James Cone's seminar who insists that the issue of race and gender cannot be separated. 'We are "Black women" ... We can not give up on one for the other.' *Struggle to be the Sun Again* Maryknoll: Orbis 1990 p.35

48   Jordan and Weedon, *Cultural Politics* pp.212–213

49   Weil, *Roots* p.15

50   Moore, *Injustice* p.37

51   'From the moment one man began to stand in need of the help of another; from the moment it appeared advantageous to any one man to have enough provisions for two, equality disappeared, property was introduced, work became indispensable, and vast forests became smiling fields, which man had to water with the sweat of his brow, and where slavery and misery were soon seen to germinate and grow up with the crops.' J.J.Rousseau, 'Discourse on the Origin of Inequality' in *Social Contract and Discourses* London: Dent 1913 p.215

52   A.MacIntyre, *A Short History of Ethics* London: Routledge 1967 p.115 At the same time, Weil thought Christianity and Stoicism should not be radically distinguished, a view in which she is followed by few theologians.

problem, and not a part of the natural order of the universe, for the attempt to bring about change to start.[53] This is a very different matter from the argument that perceptions about equality arise only with material progress, something the historical record seems to contradict.

As soon as we have class divided, unequal societies, we have 'meaning in the service of power', but we also have counter myths and ideologies, of a primitive golden age where there was no inequality, where humankind was one, or perhaps of androgyny. These myths and ideologies shape society, at the very least by providing it with a goal. This Christianity has done. Despite the fact that medieval theologians accepted a hierarchical world view peasant leaders knew better, and appealed to what were the self-evident implications of the biblical narrative: 'When Adam delved and Eve span, who was then the gentleman?' – the couplet of the 1381 Peasants' Revolt in England, echoed in peasants' revolts across Europe. We saw in the previous chapter James Scott's claim that no alternative ideology was needed to challenge oppression. As if to instantiate that, it is true that the preaching of the egalitarian gospel found fertile soil in Africa. 'The first converts,' remark Jean and John Comaroff, 'would appear to have been made sensitive to the Protestant message by their very marginality':

> the promise of equality before the Lord, of an unfettered moral economy, must have appealed to those who had long been treated as less than human ... Apart from all else, the church presented itself as an alternative, and an altogether new, source of meaning, control and influence ... women of all ranks began to show an interest in the church. This was widely the case throughout Southern Africa: wherever the egalitarian rhetoric of the gospel was heard in communities based on gender inequality, it seems to have had a much greater and quicker impact on females than on males.[54]

What I will call the gospel of equality was, in fact, implicit in each article of the creed. This gospel is challenged from opposite directions. For Lesslie Newbigin, the Bible is informed from first to last by a vision of human nature for which neither freedom nor equality is fundamental, but relatedness. Hostile to the theology of liberation, he insisted that our needs for respect, honour and love call for differentiation rather than for equality.[55] As I hope to have shown, however, proper relatedness presupposes equality, as do respect, honour and love. To talk of these things without equality is to risk an ideological justification of injustice, precisely what the free marketeers, with their proclamation of the arrival of the classless society, have achieved over the past twenty years. What Davies writes about Britain is true for the whole globalized world: 'In a country where values have been commercialised, morals are less than chaff in a breeze. A taint of imbecile rapacity blows through the land, like a whiff from some corpse.'[56]

53   Moore, *Injustice* p.468
54   J. and J. Comaroff, *Revelation and Revolution* vol 1 p.240
55   Newbigin, *Foolishness* pp.118, 121
56   Davies, *Dark Heart* p.304

From the standpoint of liberation theology, on the other hand, Aloysius Pieris considers the language of equality to be rooted in a bourgeois theory of natural law.[57] True liberation theology begins with the oppressed and with the covenant God makes with them. Historically this claim seems to me more than doubtful. I have referred already a number of times to the internalization of oppression. The aim of Freire's conscientization, as we saw earlier, was to undo that internalization in such a way that the oppressed did not become oppressors in turn:

> The central problem is this: How can the oppressed, as divided, unauthentic beings, participate in developing the pedagogy of their liberation? Only as they discover themselves to be 'hosts' of the oppressor can they contribute to the midwifery of their liberating pedagogy. As long as they live in the duality where *to be* is *to be like*, and *to be like* is *to be like the oppressor*, this contribution is impossible. The pedagogy of the oppressed is an instrument for their critical discovery that both they and their oppressors are manifestations of dehumanisation. Liberation is thus a childbirth, and a painful one. The man who emerges is a new man, viable only as the oppressor–oppressed contradiction is superceded by the humanization of all men.[58]

Paul's argument in Romans is visible here just beneath the surface. The new birth at stake does not come from those in positions of power who cannot mediate liberation. It has to be found in the powerless, the oppressed themselves. This, it seems to me, is what we see in the histories of struggle against racial, caste, class and gender discrimination. Of course death, despair and poverty generate these struggles but at the same time there is the perception, vividly expressed by John Ball, by the Tswana in Southern Africa, by black slaves, by women: we share the same humanity. Only on the grounds of this perception can the struggle for the humanization of both oppressor and oppressed be made. The discourse of equality, therefore, is not a purely Western construct, but an essential part of liberationist struggle.[59]

John Ball, broken on the rack at Smithfield for daring to challenge the social consensus of the fourteenth century, appealed to Genesis 3. He could equally have gone to Genesis 1 – the doctrine of the image of God. It follows from the doctrine of the image of God that all human beings are created equal. The Dalit theologian Arvind Nirmal, for instance, writes that the goal of Dalit theology is 'the realization of our full humanness or conversely, our full divinity, the ideal of the imago Dei'.[60] Chung Hyun Kyung illustrates the way this theology has empowered women in Asia.[61] The theologians of the Dutch

---

57   In *Fire and Water*. I consider the argument further in Chapter 9.
58   Freire, *Pedagogy* p.25
59   This is also argued by Jürgen Moltmann who argues that without equality there can be no justice or peace. 'Without equality there is no free world.' *God for a Secular Society* London: SCM 1999 pp.21, 69
60   A.P.Nirmal, 'Towards a Christian Dalit Theology' in A.Nirmal(ed) *A Reader in Dalit Theology* Madras: CMS 1991 p.62
61   Kyung, *Struggle to be the Sun Again* pp.19, 47 The feminist theological journal in Asia was called *In God's Image*.

Reformed Church were in effect forced to deny this, to subscribe to some kind of evolutionary scheme according to which equality might be attained at some stage, but not now. Opponents of social equality sometimes insist that, after all, human beings are not equal – the most obvious truth of experience. We do not all have the same strength, intelligence, musical ability and so on. This has no significance in the light of the doctrine of the image. 'Equality is ascribed by God in the work of creation; it is not a human achievement or an empirical characteristic of human beings.'[62] It is, in other words, grace, pure gift. As Kierkegaard put it, every person is equal simply in virtue of being loved by God.[63] What the Church calls 'sin' is the refusal of gift, the attempt to take one's own human gender or group as the measure of all things.

Equality follows, too, from the second article of the creed. If God takes flesh in Christ, if Christ is 'the human one', the *huios tou anthropou*, then, as the parable in Matthew 25 depicts it, all human beings are his sisters and brothers. He is encountered in all. There is, as Paul says, 'no distinction'. The fourth century Fathers understood this in terms of Christ's assumption of a universal humanity, so that all human beings were saved because all were included in his humanity. If this metaphysic is strange to us we can reinterpret it in terms of solidarity, so that in the incarnation God expresses solidarity with all humans. We can also think of it, as R.G.Collingwood did, in terms of the implication for history. For the Christian, he wrote:

> all men are equal in the sight of God: there is no chosen people, no privileged race or class, no one community whose fortunes are more important than those of another. All persons and all people are involved in the working out of God's purpose, and therefore the historical process is everywhere and always of the same kind, and every part of it is a part of the same whole. The Christian cannot be content with Roman history or Jewish history or any other partial and particularistic history: he demands a history of the world, a universal history whose theme shall be the general development of God's purpose for human life.[64]

Equality follows, too, if we approach Christology as Calvin did and think of Christ as 'prophet, priest and king'. The first 'office' recalls the prophetic denunciations of injustice, of the oppression of the poor by the rich. In this connection we can hardly forget the song with which Mary greets the news of the conception of her son and which is instantiated in his preaching of the kingdom, the reality of the third 'office'. Jesus reveals the kingdom of God to us in a messianic practice, says Gustavo Gutierrez:

> a messianic practice … that turns topsy-turvy not only our values, but historical realities and social status as well. Here the mighty fall weak and the feeble 'gird themselves with strength'. Here the sated hunger, and the hungry are satisfied. Here the humble are lifted on high, and the exalted are cast to the earth.[65]

---

62   D.Forrester, *On Human Worth* London: SCM 2000 p.84
63   Forrester, *Human Worth* p.148
64   R.G.Collingwood, *The Idea of History* London: Oxford University Press 1946 pp.49–50
65   G.Gutierrez, *The Power of the Poor in History* London: SCM 1983 p.96

Christ's 'kingship' is in fact about solidarity. As James Cone put it: 'The finality of Jesus lies in the totality of his existence in complete freedom as the Oppressed One, who reveals through his death and resurrection that God himself is present in all dimensions of human liberation.'[66] Meanwhile, in virtue of the second 'office' it has always been understood that Christ both died and makes intercession, 'for all'.

The centrality of flesh to the doctrine of the incarnation also means that if we try to neuter the doctrine of equality by restricting it to 'equality of opportunity', or 'equality before the law', we make it of none effect. As we saw in looking at race, class and gender, the problem with these realities is that they impact on life chances, and as Duncan Forrester points out, gross social and economic inequalities subvert equality of citizenship, and indeed equality before the law.[67] In the light of the incarnation, equality must mean equality of outcome and this means, in practice, legislation which restricts the possible extent of economic disparities, as Herman Daly has argued.

Equality follows, finally, from the doctrine of the Spirit, which creates the Church as what Fiorenza describes as 'a discipleship of equals'. The earliest Church, she argues, was an egalitarian *koinonia* in which women and other people marginalized by the surrounding culture found a place, dignity, and were widely welcomed into discipleship roles.[68] Even when it sponsors no social or political programme, the Church is to be understood as showing in its life, fellowship and worship an egalitarian alternative to 'the way of the world'.[69] In South Africa opposition to apartheid called forth vehement statements on the implications of Christian *koinonia*. Appealing to Ephesians 2 the South African Council of Churches in 1968 noted that 'God is the conqueror of all forces that threaten to separate and isolate and destroy us' and that 'barriers such as race and nationality have no place in the inclusive brotherhood of Christian disciples':

> We believe that this doctrine of separation is a false faith, a novel gospel; it is inevitably in conflict with the Gospel of Jesus Christ, which offers salvation, both individual and social, through faith in Christ alone ... The Christian gospel requires us to assert the truth proclaimed by the first Christians, who discovered that God was creating a new community in which differences of race, language, nation, culture and tradition no longer had power to separate man from man. The most important features of a man are not the details of his racial group, but the nature which he has in common with all men and also the gifts and abilities which are given to him as a unique individual by the grace of God: to insist that racial characteristics are more important than these is to reject what is most significant about our own humanity as well as the humanity of others.[70]

---

66   J.Cone, *A Black Theology of Liberation* Philadelphia: Lippincott 1970 p.210
67   Forrester, *Human Worth* p.36
68   E.Schüssler Fiorenza, *Discipleship of Equals* London: SCM 1993 p.104ff
69   Forrester, *Human Worth* p.105
70   South African Council of Churches 1968 Message to the People of South Africa in Villa-Vicencio *Between Christ and Caesar* pp.214–215

This account of the demand for equality in the Church might be taken to show precisely the extent to which theology is in fact ideology – not meaning in the service of power, here, but doctrine empty of all practical application. Such demands are high sounding phrases which have no practical application whatsoever. Feminist theology has no problem in showing how human equality has been denied in ecclesiastical practice. Rosemary Ruether argues that the Christological symbols have been used to enforce male dominance, and even if we go back behind masculinist Christology to the praxis of the historical Jesus of the synoptic gospels, it is questionable whether there is a single model of redeemed humanity fully revealed in the past. This does not mean that feminist theology may not be able to affirm the person of Jesus of Nazareth as a positive model of redemptive humanity. But this model must be seen as partial and fragmentary, disclosing from the perspective of one person, circumscribed in time, culture and gender, something of the fullness we seek.[71] Some feminist theologians have renounced Christianity as irredeemably patriarchal and therefore as effectively non-egalitarian. For Ruether, Jesus' ability to speak as liberator does not reside in his maleness but in the fact that he has renounced this system of domination and seeks to embody in his person the new humanity of service and mutual empowerment. Jesus as the Christ, 'the representative of liberated humanity and the liberating Word of God, manifests the kenosis of patriarchy, the announcement of the new humanity through a lifestyle that discards hierarchical caste privilege and speaks on behalf of the lowly'.[72] Duncan Forrester points out that, for all the patriarchy, significant elements of the primitive, more egalitarian tradition remained in the Church. All gathered at the altar; recruitment to the priesthood was to a significant degree open and equal; the monastic movement constituted a counter culture; and the reading of Scripture continued values of equality. For all its failings and hypocrisy, he says, the Church of Jesus Christ in all its various forms is still an extraordinary community which often witnesses to equality in powerful and unusual ways.[73]

We noted Kierkegaard's passionate affirmation of equality. But Kierkegaard is also the prophet of the individual, and it is important to distinguish equality from individualism. For Sardar individualism is the absolute of both liberal democracy and postmodernism. 'The assumption that the individual is prior to society is unique to western culture: it is the defining principle of liberal democracy and shapes its metaphysical, epistemological, methodological, moral, legal, economic and political aspects.'[74] Ultimately it has its roots, for him, in Christianity. This is not a possible derivation, however, because it omits the centrality of thinking about the body in the New Testament. Every person is equal before God, but equally all are bound up in the body. Extrapolating from the Christology of Colossians and Ephesians the fourth century Fathers, as we have seen, argued that all human beings were included in the universal humanity of Christ. Kierkegaard's affirmation of the individual has to be put

71   Ruether, *Sexism* p.114
72   Ruether, *Sexism* p.137
73   Forrester, *Human Worth* p.200
74   Sardar, *Postmodernism* p.61

in its nineteenth century context, where he is protesting against a complacent state Church for which being a Christian is more or less equivalent with being respectable. In attempting to right the boat he is leaning far over to the side. In any understanding based on the New Testament, the fulfilment of our individual vocation is bound up with membership of the body.

Sardar is right that individualism plays a central role in liberal democracy, but its roots do not go back to Christianity but to the struggles for religious freedom of the seventeenth and eighteenth centuries. Corporate thinking was the norm in medieval and Reformation Europe. Individualism was, in fact, heresy – factionalism, following one's own beliefs as opposed to those of the Church. The conclusion of the religious wars established that faith might vary from region to region – *cuius regio, eius religio*. What followed was the struggle for freedom of conscience within nations. This struggle was important and it has given us our individualism. Sardar is right that we have lost some things in the movement which has seen it become hegemonic, but this process is to be understood on the lines of Tönnies and Durkheim, the whole process of urbanization and industrialization.

Equality also has to be distinguished from the belief of liberal humanism that human nature is essentially the same everywhere. What is offered, not always but often, is a false universalism in which actual divisions are glossed over, and the material basis of the oppositions between people left as they are. I shall return to this question in Chapter 10, but here it should be noted that the belief in equality cannot mean a *de facto* privileging of values that are bourgeois, Western, white and male.[75] The distinction between genuine equality and such a view can be retained by remaining concrete. As Duncan Forrester reminds us, the primary issue for theology is not a set of abstract concepts such as 'poverty', 'inequality' or 'justice'. It is rather poor people, and the question why they are poor and what can be done about it.[76] It is this insistence on the concrete which keeps us from a false universalism.

Liberation Theology and Cultural Politics

In the opening paragraph of this chapter I noted the ways in which patterns of domination are rooted in culture. We have looked at some of these, and noted ways in which they are resisted. Cultural politics is not one-way: it is also about resistance, about attempts to see history in a different light, to change educational and Church practices, to re-read Scripture, to conscientize, 'to transform human action and being'.[77] Understood in this way all the varieties of liberation theology which emerged in the 1960s were committed to some form of cultural politics. This was not only because they had no choice –

75 Jordan and Weedon, *Cultural Politics* p.59
76 Forrester, *Human Worth* p.158
77 Jordan and Weedon, *Cultural Politics* p.5

revolutions of the Russian or Chinese kinds were not an option – but as a matter of principle.

In Latin America liberation theology emerged in the context of the failure of the 'development decade', and of dictatorships, of murderous military regimes funded by the United States. Its origins were, from the start, bound up with grass-roots education.[78] Paulo Freire's educational theory, structured around dialogical cultural action, made a decisive contribution. Conscientization leads to the confrontation of the culture of domination and its transformation through praxis. Out of engagement with the poor emerged a new theology, abandoning the Thomistic scholasticism of the seminaries for a more biblical theology informed by social analysis. The base communities, which grew out of literacy classes, were adopted as the fundamental form of the Church, in which social and religious power was restructured. In Freire's vision education as conscientization was both about acquiring concrete goals – a new school, clean water, a new health centre – but also, and through this, about reshaping the understanding of what it meant to be human. It was also a passionately partisan account which began with solidarity with the oppressed. Such solidarity, the political analogy to God's action in Christ, is the fundamental dimension of an ecclesial cultural politics.

Latin American liberation theology was centred on class. For many years some of its most noted theologians dismissed feminist theology as a 'white women's issue'. There was some basis for this charge in the early movement, which likewise began in the late 1960s. Feminist theology, however, was quicker to respond to criticism, and, led by black feminists, quicker to see that liberation cannot be fragmentary. In 1975 Schüssler Fiorenza could say: 'The "maleness" and "sexism" of theology is much more pervasive than the race and class issue.' By 1993 she was writing: 'Rather than posit a structure of binary male–female domination, one must theorize patriarchy as a shifting pyramidal political structure of dominance and subordination, stratified by gender, race, class, sexuality, religion, nation, culture, and other historical formations of domination.'[79] To signify this she began to speak of 'kyriarchy' – rule of the powerful, rather than simply of patriarchy.[80]

The struggle for liberation was recognized from the start to be a matter of cultural politics, because the problem being addressed was exclusion of women from 'the processes by which cultures find meaning, interpret and explain their past and present, and orientate themselves to the future'.[81] Cultural revolution was what was at stake, the reconstituting of the understanding of femininity, and therefore of humanity as a whole. Whilst the goals of feminism are by no means attained it is also true that the feminist movement has unquestionably been the most effective agent for cultural change in the past fifty years.

78　So A.Dawson, *The Birth and Impact of the Base Ecclesial Community and Liberative Theological Discourse in Brazil* New York: International Scholars 1998
79　Fiorenza, *Discipleship* p.341
80　E.Schüssler Fiorenza, *But She Said: Feminist Practices of Biblical Interpretation* Boston(Mass): Beacon Press 1992 p.117
81　A.Loades, *Feminist Theology: A Reader* London: SPCK 1990 p.2

Ironically, the Catholic Church, to which Schüssler Fiorenza belongs, has presented the most determined resistance to change, and other Churches leave much to be desired.

Black theology began in the United States in the mid 1960s and, naturally, addressed the race issue, responding rather slowly to issues of gender and class. The struggle was in the first instance to cleanse the colonized mind, to rid theology of the 'white Jesus'. By 1984 James Cone had taken on board both the necessity of feminism and the need for freedom to include both black and white: 'The Christian faith requires it, and human decency demands it.'[82]

The challenge of apartheid in South Africa is one of the examples where cultural change has been translated into political reality. The Kairos theologians, in 1985, following the example of Barmen, addressed themselves to the Church. They distinguished between a state theology, a Church theology and a prophetic theology. What was meant by state theology has already been seen in Chapter 5. Church theology was described as a theology committed to reconciliation, oblivious of the fact that there are some situations where a distinction between good and evil has to be made:

> To speak of the reconciling of these two is ... a total betrayal of all that Christian faith has ever meant. Nowhere in the Bible or in Christian tradition has it ever been suggested that we ought to try to reconcile good and evil, God and the devil. We are supposed to do away with evil, injustice, oppression and sin – not to come to terms with it.[83]

With the liberation theologians the Kairos divines refused to consider sin as a purely personal issue, but recognized the centrality of structural injustice. Church theology, they said, was characterized by 'a lack of social analysis, of a failure to understand politics and political strategy and an other worldly spirituality and faith'. In its place they put a prophetic theology for which social analysis was the first task. They noted that in the Christian tradition there was a long history of opposition to tyranny, which is that form of rule which opposes the common good. The purpose of all government is the promotion of that good, government in the interest of, and for the benefit of, all people. The task of theology, then, was resistance to tyranny and the proclamation of hope for true peace. Six years later apartheid was overthrown. The Church struggle in South Africa was a classic example of Keith Thompson's contention, against those who argue that religion only serves the status quo, that it can and does provide the language of dissent and resistance for subordinate classes.[84]

Dalit theology, emerging on the scene rather later than the other forms of liberation theology, was quick to see that it could not be sectional. Some Dalit theologians have insisted on rejecting 'salvation theology', based on ideas of sin

82   J.Cone, *For My People: Black Theology and the Black Church* Maryknoll: Orbis 1984 p.203
83   Villa-Vicencio, *Between Christ and Caesar* pp.256–257
84   K.Thompson, 'Religion, Class and Control' in Bocock and Thompson(eds) *Religion and Ideology* pp.126–153

and redemption, as promoting psychological dependence, political passivity and communal exclusiveness.[85] All have read it as a form of cultural struggle in remaking Dalit consciousness.

These examples of the various forms of liberation theology illustrate that from first to last it engages with cultural politics. Cultural politics means changing the attitudes which shape the world, above all changing fatalistic beliefs in the iron laws of economics. To be committed to liberation theology means to be committed to cultural revolution as the Church's task. That the humanity of all is what is at stake, and that the power for change is located decisively in weakness, is what prevents this long revolution from taking the Chinese path.

At the end of this second part of the book I once more review where we have got to in terms of a theology of culture. My overall argument is that culture is the word we use to describe what human beings make of their world. One could take a catastrophic and apocalyptic view of that, or one could take the progressivist view which we know as 'the Whig view of history'. I am attempting to steer between these two extremes. Borrowing the phrase from Herder's great letters of 1793–1797 I take the task of culture to be that of furthering humanity. With him I believe the gospel is at the heart of the very idea of a growth in our true humanity, but that at the same time this is not accomplished by the gospel alone. Culture in the sense of creative achievement plays its part, as do other religions. The other phrase I have used is Raymond Williams' 'long revolution'. If God is active and not absent, and engages with history, then history must go somewhere, and not be aimless. I considered that in three different dimensions in the first part of the book.

In this second part I have addressed the question of power. Foucault has taught us that the question of power is implicit in all human structures and relationships. From one point of view these structures and relationships constitute culture. On the other hand, if we define culture in terms of creative achievement that, too, is bound up with power. Whichever way we look at it, therefore, culture cannot be discussed without taking account of power. Theologically I have attempted to respond to this in three ways. In the first place, religion, or the gospel, is part of the ideological dimension of culture. Is it reducible to this, or does it transcend this in some way? Drawing on Terry Eagleton's account of literature and ideology I have argued that what allows us to speak of 'revelation' with regard to the Christian Scriptures is their continuing capacity to challenge our taken for granted pieties. To some extent that claim is empirical and historical. If, in a given period, Scripture fails to do that, we might argue that the Church of that period had been colonized by its culture. If it consistently failed to do so; if its power to do so had simply died, then we could no longer speak of revelation. To take just one example, Ched

---

85   K.Wilson, *The Twice Alienated: Culture of Dalit Christians* Hyderabad: n.p. 1982 p.26

Myers' 1988 reading of Mark indicates that to date it has lost none of its power.

Calvin spoke of Christ as 'prophet, priest and king'. Protest is part of the prophetic function, but we cannot stop with protest. There is an attempt to build alternative structures, 'concrete utopias', which are not the kingdom but anticipate the kingdom. The enterprise of Christendom was, in my view, mistaken. It misidentified the nature of power according to the gospel. All the same it did in some respects represent this attempt to put in place 'concrete utopias' (in the idea of the 'truce of God' for example, or in the development of hospitals and almshouses). In our day I have spoken of the construction of counter hegemonies, alternatives to the global dominance of the market, which is the true meta narrative of our age. The market as an account of the meaning of life is what is meant in the gospels by Mammon. We cannot accept it: the construction of alternative economic and therefore social and political orders is a gospel imperative, as clearly as it was in the case of German fascism.

Finally there is the cultural reflection of the rule of Christ, the cultural politics of the Church. I have argued that this has been understood most clearly by liberation theology, in its identification with the poor and marginalized. Following the gospel power is redefined as service here. The very idea of the papal triple tiara, the Church ruling over empire, or the incorporation of bishops in the British 'House of Lords' (an unchristian idea in itself), was a profound corruption. The power of the Church is instantiated where it is found alongside the poor. It is counter cultural. We can see here how Niebuhr's typology, with its acme in gradualist 'transformation', fails to address the question of power, effectively makes it impossible to resist co-option. As Paul perceived, power is redefined by the gospel from the base upwards.

In the third and final part of the book I turn to another set of questions about culture. It is widely argued that Christianity shaped the culture of the West. All well and good – but should you export it? Where does the history of Western colonialism leave the Church's mission? 'The church exists by mission as a fire by burning,' said Emil Brunner, famously. But is mission moral? If, as I have argued consistently, all cultures in their life affirming dimensions represent a response to God's Spirit, why bother with mission? These are the questions I wish now to address.

PART III
MISSION

The universal word only speaks dialect.

Pedro Casaldáliga

Chapter 8

Imperialism at Prayer?

Missionaries, Lesslie Newbigin used to say, are those who live on the cultural frontier. His own missionary experience, which began in the 1930s, was rooted in a slower world, before the 'space–time compression' which marks the postmodern world. Today perhaps we are all on the cultural frontier. The idea of the cultural frontier, however, as used by Newbigin, evokes the sense of those cultures which are not fundamentally marked by Christianity. Just as any theology of culture has to address the issue of power, so it has to address the issue of the relation of the Christian faith community to non-Christian cultures.

This is the theme of the third part of the book. I begin with two chapters which consider mission as traditionally understood: as the sending of people from 'Christian' countries into 'non-Christian' countries. In both I am once again concerned with the question of power, but this time in a quite different setting. In the next two chapters I consider the world in which we now live, awash with refugees, with substantial migrant populations in many traditionally Christian countries. How to understand this? Through Samuel Huntington's now notorious thesis of the 'clash of civilizations'? This is the question of the tenth chapter. In chapter eleven I turn to the issue of multiculturalism, and ask whether the acceptance of a multicultural agenda means relativizing our concern for truth. Throughout I am concerned with my central thesis of the furthering of humanity, or the long revolution. If it is true, as Christianity claims, that the gospel is central to that, what does that mean in relation to our non-Christian neighbours? A mere century ago scarcely anyone worried about this question. Today it is at the centre of our agenda.

In this chapter, after a preliminary definition of what we mean by the word 'gospel' I consider first the allegation that mission always involves cultural change, and secondly the charge that it was the ideological wing of Western colonialism.

The Meaning of 'Gospel'

'Euangelion', the word from which we derive our 'gospel', was originally the term for the announcement of victory in the Greek city states. It was 'good news' in a straightforward sense, though necessarily bad news for somebody else. In the course of world history there have been at least five great movements which believed they had a 'gospel', that is, a message promising salvation, for all people: three religious and two secular. I am thinking of Buddhism, Christianity and Islam amongst the religions, and communism and laissez faire capitalism as the secular movements. All of these have involved colonialism in some form or other, and therefore the use of force.

Other candidates for universal gospels might be identified: Hellenism, as a vision of the human good, spread widely and decisively influenced not only Christianity but Islam. When Muslim writers inveigh against 'the West', they need to scrutinize their medieval sources. Some people talk of 'the Enlightenment' as a similar gospel and it is true that Enlightenment values were, to some extent, bound up with Western colonialism. There was, say Jean and John Comaroff, a general post-Enlightenment process of colonization, which went side by side with the nineteenth century Christian mission, in which Europe set out to subdue the forces of savagery, otherness and unreason.[1] The 'gospel of progress' was part of this and it had left wing and right wing forms.[2] Socialism and communism were its left wing forms, assumed to be dead and buried since 1989. 'The destruction of Left ideology,' says Jeremy Seabrook, writing of Bangladesh, 'has repercussions far beyond the end of Communism. The belief of the Left in the people was an *enabling* myth, the certainty that history was on the side of progress.' Without it the task of conscientization is far more difficult, an attempt to make bricks without straw – to make people 'conscious' without faith, to create organization without conviction, to develop people without the empowering psychological support essential for change.[3]

For market capitalism, on the other hand, 'development' was from the 1950s on a grand narrative exported worldwide, a universal gospel. When Jean-François Lyotard announced the death of grand narratives in 1979 he forgot to say that *this* grand narrative was alive and well and, like its Greek predecessor, its announcement has consistently meant bad news for some: first the proletariat of Europe, then the poor of the Third World, and quite probably for all if we do not heed warnings about the need to limit growth. But this gospel is preached and believed in with truly evangelical fervour. It has an eschatology, as evinced in Hayek's image of the moving column in which those at the rear, 'generations yet unborn', finally gain the benefit. In the view of many of its proponents it is the 'free' market alone which will produce '*shalom*', peace and prosperity for all. This is the message relentlessly dinned in by the Bretton Woods Institutions and those states or systems which dare to challenge it are part of the 'empire' or 'axis' of evil – heretics, treated exactly as heretics

---

1 J. and J. Comaroff, *Revelation and Revolution* vol 1 p.11
2 Characteristically Herder challenged the myth of progress. He believed that there was '*Fortgang*' but that it lay in diversity. 'Each age is different, and each has the centre of happiness within itself. The youth is not happier than the innocent, contented child; nor is the peaceful old man less happy than the vigorous man in the prime of life. True *Fortgang* is the development of human beings as integrated wholes and, more particularly, their development as groups, tribes, cultures and communities determined by language and custom, creating out of the "totality of their collective experience" and expressing themselves in works of art that are consequently intelligible to common men, and in sciences and crafts and forms of social and political and cultural life that fulfil the cravings and develop the faculties of a given society, in its interplay with its alterable, but not greatly alterable, natural environment.' I.Berlin, *Vico and Herder* London: Hogarth 1976 p.191
3 Seabrook, *Freedom Unfinished* p.167 my italics

were in the European middle ages, but with more effective technology – napalm, or 'smart' bombs, or economic sanctions.

'The faith and trust of the heart make both God and idol.' We learn what your religion is by seeing what you truly worship. In terms of the discussion in Chapter 5 the religion of the market is a form of idolatry, and a hugely important one with a vast following. Today it claims to be the narrative of the world, a universal gospel. It is a missionary faith: no corner of the globe must be untouched or, indeed, resist conversion. But, though the missionaries are in part well known to us, they are not responsible for what they do. The invisible hand, a secularized providence, works through them, threatening projects for life, whether based on culture or the gospel. In this scenario, asks Paulo Suess, what is the meaning of mission, as a historical quest which brings hope?[4]

Suess is referring to Christian mission as hope giving here, but many critics allege that, at least over the past two centuries, it has involved collusion with colonialism. This involvement, it is said, means that mission represents an assault of Western on non-Western cultures. Mission was the surrogate of Western colonialism and together they aimed to destroy indigenous cultures, and sometimes succeeded.[5] To consider this claim I begin with some reflections on cultural change.

Mission and Cultural Change

The problematic of mission and culture can be viewed from both directions. If mission brings 'a gospel' then it can change a culture, but culture can also radically change the gospel.

I argued in Chapter 4 that cultures know periods of stability and periods of rapid change. If they did not know periods of stability languages, traditions, customs – all the things that go to make up cultures – could not develop. At the same time, as we saw in the first chapter, culture is *process*. Cultures never stand still, though the pace of change may vary. 'To grow is to change, and to be perfect is to change often,' as Newman said, in a remark which he believed applied as much to institutions as to persons. Perhaps, then, it may refer to cultures as well. The impact of mission on culture might be read as part of this necessary ongoing process. Kosuke Koyama observes that as long as people live in a concrete historical world of interactions there can be no such thing as a 'pure, intact self-identity'. 'Self-identity is a concept of historical interaction. It is always "shared identity". We must ask the questions relating to "shared identity" with all the nations of the world. Mission is to relate God's history of shared identity with people's history of shared identity.'[6] If culture is all learned behaviour, socially acquired and passed from one generation to the

4   P.Suess, 'A Confused Mission Scenario: A Critical Analysis of Recent Church Documents and Tendencies' in Greinacher and Mette(eds), *Christianity and Cultures* p.118
5   L.Sanneh, *Translating the Message: The Missionary Impact on Culture* Maryknoll: Orbis 1989 p.4
6   K.Koyama, *Waterbuffalo Theology* London: SCM 1974 p.12

next, 'there are no cultures which are so isolated and restricted by their environment that the people could not do something different from what they are doing'. Culture is transmissible and accumulative, and depends on critical appropriation for its continuing integrity.[7]

If this is the case, Sanneh argues, then denial of mission rests on a denial of the possibility of genuine cultural exchange and seals culture from the possibility of change. 'It is too extreme a position to adopt, recognizing neither the principle of religious autonomy nor that of cultural development stemming from internal and external stimuli.'[8] Cultural inclusiveness is indispensable to the human enterprise as we know it, and we should do all that is necessary to encourage and foster it. To be an agent of structural change is not the same as cultural domination. On the contrary Sanneh claims that, amongst the religions, Christianity is uniquely a force for cultural integration. This is because it alone is peripheral to its place of origin; it alone has abandoned both the religion and the language of its founder; and it alone maintains that God's eternal counsels are compatible with everyday speech, an idea which puts the understanding of ordinary people at the heart of faith, with momentous social and cultural consequences.[9]

Approaching from the other direction there are often worries about what the impact of culture does to the gospel. This is the problem of syncretism, where the essence of the gospel is radically modified, changed into something different from what it was originally. Thus John Paul II, speaking to Zairean bishops in 1983, warned of building a philosophy and theology of 'Africanness' which would be solely indigenous and stripped of any true and deep link with Christ. In such a case, Christianity would be merely a nominal reference, an element that is added on in an artificial way.[10] In a characteristically European way the Pope fails to see that theology in Europe might be purely 'indigenous' and stripped of any true link to Christ there as well. As Sanneh remarks, we need to acknowledge that a successful Western cultural transformation of Christianity indicates a similar possibility for the Third World, and conversely, that the harmful consequences of the cultural adaptation of Christianity in the West will in time extend to the Third World as well.[11]

The question, of course, raised with increasing urgency in the course of the twentieth century, is whether there ever was a 'successful Western cultural transformation of Christianity'. The question can be posed by Robert Schreiter's observation that 'a more autonomous critique of culture' is needed when a culture faces strong challenges and does not seem to have the inner resources to meet those challenges. He instances Eastern European countries 'whose social values were so corroded by forty years of Communism that they find it difficult to marshal the resources for living in a very different kind of

---

7   Sanneh, *Translating* p.201
8   Sanneh, *Translating* p.203
9   Sanneh, *Encountering* pp.118–119
10   Shorter, *Inculturation* p.229
11   Sanneh, *Encountering* p.120

world'.[12] Alongside this we simply need to put Pieris' comment that 'no religious persecution under a Marxist regime can be compared to the subtle undermining of religious values that capitalist technocracy generates in our cultures'.[13]

It can be argued that syncretism is simply another name for cultural change and that it is a general human trait and present in all religions.[14] Wilfred Cantwell Smith claimed that religious traditions exist in a continual process of interpenetration and that adherents of one religion always derive insights and practices from adherents of another.[15] Objections to syncretism, however, are rooted in the prophetic and Deuteronomic protest in the Old Testament. When Israel entered Canaan and exchanged a nomadic life for an agricultural one, many of the names of God, and the shrines and practices, were taken over from Canaan. They even entered the first Temple (1 Kings 7.15ff). Ezekiel was therefore right when he said 'Your origin and your birth are of the land of the Canaanites' (Ez 16.3). He was not, of course, speaking as a cultural anthropologist who would be neutral or even appreciative of these things. From the perspective of the eighth century prophets syncretism was the origin of Israel's downfall, a corrupt playing with power and fertility which should never have been entertained. The prophetic critique has often been a model for later Church reform and had a decisive significance for Protestant missionaries. Steeped in Scripture, when they encountered temples with erotic statuary, sacred lingams, ritual dance, drumming which stirred the blood, shamans or witch doctors, they felt they were with Elijah on Mount Carmel, or the Deuteronomists condemning the asherah. To read these phenomena differently they needed a profounder understanding both of idolatry and of culture.

Change can obviously be both positive and negative. John Taylor agrees with the accusation, made in Africa, that Europeans eat people. This is a reference, he says, to the change we make in children and grown-ups when we have converted them to the Western interpretation of Christianity. 'We are modern cannibals who eat a man's personality and leave him an unattractive, rude specimen of humanity, out of harmony with himself and those with whom he has to live.'[16] On the other hand Kosuke Koyama experienced his conversion to Christianity, in Japan, as primarily positive. He is clear about what he gained, but it did not lead him to despise what he came from. 'When I became a Christian,' he writes:

> I moved from a polytheistic, cosmological world (fertile nature orientation) to a monotheistic, eschatological world (critical time orientation), from cyclical culture to linear culture, and from a relaxed culture to a tense culture. Yet there are elements of

---

12   R.Schreiter, 'Inculturation of Faith or Identification with Culture?' in Greinacher and Mette(eds) *Christianity and Cultures* p.21
13   Pieris, *Asian Theology* p.76
14   A.Droogers, 'Syncretism: The Problem of Definition, the Definition of the Problem' citing J.H.Kamstra in Gort et al(eds) *Dialogue and Syncretism* Grand Rapids: Eerdmans 1989 p.10
15   Cited by H.Vroom, 'Syncretism and Dialogue: A Philosophical Analysis' in Gort et al(eds) *Dialogue and Syncretism* p.27
16   J.V.Taylor, *The Primal Vision* London: SCM 1963 p.115

the polytheistic cosmological world, the cyclical, relaxed culture, which are too rich and precious to be lightly discarded, and which can make very significant and positive contribution to the Christian faith, such as loyalty, filial piety to lord and community, and self-negation.

The relationship of Buddhism and Christianity is not that of 'true religion' and 'false religion'. It is to do with two different yet intertwined understandings of the history of human greed.[17] C.H.Kyung calls for a 'survival–liberation centred syncretism' which emerges from 'diving deep into our Eastern traditions' and complains, justifiably, that Western theologians seem to think they have a copyright on Christianity.[18]

The problematic of change has been central to theological discussion since at least 1780, when Lessing first raised the question of the 'foul wide gap' between his century and the first. How is it possible to be sure that meanings remain the same? What connection is there between a first century peasant culture and the Europe of the Enlightenment? The question of change is raised in another way by heresy. To call a development a heresy is to say that it proposes changes which are incompatible with what the Church as a whole agrees to be the faith. In the middle of the fifth century Vincent of Lerins proposed the famous test that what was orthodox was *quod ubique, quod semper, quod ab omnibus creditum est* – what has been believed everywhere, always and by all. Lesslie Newbigin, longtime missionary in India, invokes this canon in speaking of the gospel as 'universal truth, truth for all peoples and for all times, the truth which creates the possibility of freedom'. But is there any such thing? Is what is claimed to be truth not just the truth of one moment of European theology dressed up as being perennial? Is a so-called universal theology not simply the translation into many languages of a theology evolved wholly within a particular cultural tradition?[19]

Nicholas Lash puts the problem like this: if the message proclaimed in the life, death and resurrection of Jesus of Nazareth is God's definitive word to humankind it must in some significant sense be the same word in every generation. But it is clear that what Christians do, think and say today is very different from what they did yesterday or the day before. How are we to reconcile these?[20] We need to ask what has changed, what stayed the same and what the criteria for evaluating the changes are. In answer to the first question, virtually everything has changed: language, rituals, philosophical presuppositions, Church order. There is, in fact, 'no aspect of Christian life, structure and language that is immune to the process of history'.[21] In that case, what has remained unchanged? First, the story: historical facts concerning people, places and events, in particular the story of the life, death and resurrection of Christ. With regard to rituals, intention remains the same. So, with the eucharist: the

17   Koyama, *Mount Fuji* pp.7, 128
18   Kyung, *Struggle* p.113
19   Shorter, *Inculturation* p.149
20   N.Lash, *Change in Focus* London: Sheed & Ward 1973
21   Lash, *Change* p.67

Church has always assembled to hear the Word of God; its rites have been public and communal; and it has sought to respond to the Word. There are no guarantees of continuity of meaning and we have to accept this in faith that the Spirit continues to assist us, in different cultural contexts, to 'hear' the events of Jesus' life, teaching and death as the one Word of God to humankind.[22] Kathryn Tanner glosses the account of continuity of intention by speaking of the shared concern for true discipleship to the God who always remains the same. The diversity of Christian practices and meanings are united around a common task.[23]

When it comes to evaluating change, Lash rejects both the Protestant idea of *sola scriptura*, because it denies all authority to subsequent Christian history, and the Tridentine emphasis on tradition, as representing an idolatry of the historical process. Equally unsatisfactory is the liberal option of ascribing normative significance to present belief and understanding. He proposes, therefore, that the liturgy provides the model because it is the place where Christian memory and hope achieve their paradigmatic expression. 'It is the church's task in every age so to relate to its past as to enable the past, interpreted in the present, effectively to function as a challenge.'[24] The historical problem has an obvious relevance to mission:

> If doctrines, rites or institutions which, in one cultural context, appropriately expressed or protected the central affirmations of Christian belief are simply carried over, 'untranslated' into a different context, then they become not merely useless but harmful. In the new context they do not and cannot express the same meanings as they originally did.[25]

Equally, we cannot solve the problems of the present without reference to the problems of yesterday. 'Our language, our symbols, our institutions, ourselves, are products of our past. To neglect that past, or to suppress it, leads not to liberation but to a form of "false consciousness" on the part of society.'[26]

Change in a culture and change in a religion, though related, are not on all fours. It was part of Herder's reading of culture that every culture had its essential essence, the gift it had to make to the whole. In this case there is something absolutely distinctive, which makes Tswana culture Tswana, English English and Serbian Serbian. The final example shows where that logic can lead. On the one hand I have insisted all along that the real cultural differences that exist are a good, and need to be preserved against homogenization. On the other hand, as Homi Bhaba argues, all cultures are hybrids – necessarily so since people travel, migrate, trade, flee for refuge, and the impact of encounter is always mutual. Religions also change, but their framework of identity is tighter, even in a non-creedal religion like Hinduism.

---

22   Lash, *Change* p.69
23   K.Tanner, *Theories of Culture* Minneapolis: Fortress 1997 pp.136, 153 She goes on to suggest that the search for identity *is* the task of the Church.
24   Lash, *Change* p.72
25   Lash, *Change* p.147
26   Lash, *Change* p.149

In a culture, for there to be 'change beyond recognition' there has to be loss of language. In a religion, especially in a religion like Christianity which 'goes native', change beyond recognition is what is at stake in syncretism and heresy, which is why these are so hotly contested. It raises the question of the 'essence' of the gospel, those things which might be genuinely cross-culturally unchanging. I shall take up this question in the final section of this chapter.

The cause of change is often misidentified. Theologians are familiar with the idea of 'double-agency', the concept that God works through what appear to be purely human actions. But was this what was at work when, according to the Comaroffs, the Tswana identified the power of the whites, not with the Word, but with their goods, their knowledge and their technical skills?[27] This example raises the critical ambivalence attending missionary work over the past two centuries. The World Missionary Conference in Mexico in 1963 described the Christian approach to people of other faiths as one of love, respect and patience – rather an irony given the setting. This kind of dialogical encounter includes a concern both for the gospel and for the other man. 'Without the first,' the Conference went on, 'dialogue becomes a pleasant conversation. Without the second it becomes irrelevant, unconvincing and arrogant'.[28]

This is surely true, but, as we have already noted, much of the objection to Christian mission lies in its collusion with, or even identity with, Western colonialism. To this charge I now turn.

Mission and Colonialism

Lamin Sanneh remarks that historians who are instinctively critical of received tradition in other spheres are more credulous in perpetuating the notion of mission as 'imperialism at prayer':

> Modern political nationalism has capitalized on this by strengthening the prejudice against mission as a discredited relic of colonialism. The forces pitted against a fair understanding of mission in the late twentieth century are formidable. To start with, many people are committed to the ideological position that mission is oppressive, and anachronistic to boot, and Christians have been afflicted by the consequences. For the other part, many third-world writers have added their voice of criticism, encouraged in part by the vogue enjoyed by liberation theology. Most mainline Western Christian bodies have, as a consequence, retreated from the subject afflicted by a heavy sense of guilt. It is not, therefore, easy to inveigh against such a strong and deep obstruction.[29]

Lurking in the background, Sanneh thinks, is a Hobbesian assumption that violence and alienation are the only forms culture contact can take, or at least, that domination and submission is the only language Christianity knows as the

---

27   J. and J. Comaroff, *Revelation and Revolution* vol 2 p.77
28   Cited in S.Neill, *Colonialism and Christian Missions* London: Lutterworth 1966 p.43
29   Sanneh, *Translating* p.88

price of its European captivity.[30] This is a fair protest, but it has to be said that the record, though not all in one direction, is at least as much darkness as light.

On the one hand the Christian missions of the first three centuries clearly did not involve abusive power, nor did the Nestorian or Celtic missions, nor the Jesuit missions of Matteo Ricci or Roberto di Nobili. Thomas Aquinas stated unequivocally that 'Unbelievers who have never accepted the faith, Jews and pagans, should under no circumstances be coerced into becoming believers.'[31] Luther agreed with him. The Franciscan Raymond Lull denounced the practice of crusades. During the Latin American *conquista* some priests, like Antonio de Montesinos and Bartolemeo de las Casas, protested the violence visited on the indigenous population. Preaching on 'a voice crying in the wilderness' Montesinos told his Spanish congregation: 'This voice says that you are in mortal sin, that you live and die in it, for the cruelty and tyranny you use in dealing with these innocent people. Tell me, by what right or justice do you keep these Indians in such cruel and horrible servitude?'[32] Under pressure from these priests a papal bull in 1537 established that the Indians were not 'by nature slaves', that they were capable of understanding the Catholic faith, and not to be deprived of their liberty and goods.[33]

At a later stage of the colonial process companies like the East India Company were deeply hostile to missions. When the question of allowing missionaries access was mooted on the occasion of the renewal of the Company charter in 1793 one representative objected:

> He was fully convinced that suffering clergymen, under the name of missionaries, or any other name, to overrun India, and penetrate the interior parts of it, would in the first instance be dangerous and prove utterly destructive of the Company's interests, if not wholly annihilate their power in Hindustan; that so far from wishing that they might make converts of ten, fifty, or a hundred thousand natives of any degree of character, he should lament such a circumstance as the most serious and fatal disaster that could happen ... The moment that event took place in India, there was an end of British supremacy.[34]

British colonists at the end of the eighteenth century, concerned to preserve British power, paid 'a tribute of almost exaggerated respect to the manners, customs and morals of India in all particulars, and an almost subservient concern to do nothing which could in any way offend the susceptibilities of Hindus or Muslims'.[35]

A more principled protest can be found in Herder, who inveighed against the very idea of European superiority as a 'blatant insult to the majesty of

30   Sanneh, *Encountering* p.16
31   Summa Theologiae II-2 q.10 a.8
32   Neill, *Colonialism* p.47
33   Neill, *Colonialism* p.54
34   Neill, *Colonialism* p.85
35   Neill, *Colonialism* p.86 In a footnote he tells us: 'The anti-missionary party were almost to a man "Orientalists", supporters of the ancient languages and learning, and opposed to the introduction of the English language, a dangerous medium through which Indians might be introduced to the thinking of dangerous thoughts!'

Nature'.[36] He denied the idea of a '*Favoritvolk*', and thought the idea that this might be Europe grotesque:

> 'European culture' is a mere abstraction, an empty concept. Where does, or did, it actually exist in its entirety? In which nation? In which period? Besides, it can scarcely pose as the most perfect manifestation of man's culture, having – who can deny? – far too many deficiencies, weaknesses, perversions and abominations associated with it. Only a real misanthrope could regard European culture as the universal condition of our species. The culture of man is not the culture of Europeans; it manifests itself according to place and time in every people.[37]

It could almost be Fanon speaking. He excoriated merchant capitalism:

> System of trade! The magnitude and uniqueness of the enterprise is manifest! Three continents are devastated, yet policed by us; we in turn are depopulated, emasculated and debauched as a result. Such is the happy nature of the exchange. Who does not have a hand in this grand European sponging enterprise? Who does not compete as a trader, even of his own children? The old name 'shepherd' has been changed into 'monopolist': Mammon is the god we all serve.[38]

In the 'Letters on the furthering of Humanity', published between 1793 and 1797, Herder linked colonialism to mission:

> Can you name a land where Europeans have entered without defiling themselves forever before defenceless, trusting mankind, by the unjust word, greedy deceit, crushing oppression, diseases, fatal gifts they have brought? Our part of the earth should be called not the wisest, but the most arrogant, aggressive, money-minded: what it has given these people is not civilization but the destruction of the rudiments of their own cultures wherever they could achieve this. Tell me, have you still not lost the habit of trying to convert to your faith peoples whose property you steal, whom you rob, enslave, murder, deprive of their land, their state, to whom your customs seem revolting? Supposing that one of them came to your country, and with an insolent air pronounced absurd all that is most sacred to you – your laws, your religion, your wisdom, your institutions and so on, what would you do to such a man? 'Oh, but that is quite a different matter' replied the European, 'we have power, ships, money, cannon, culture.'[39]

Herder, of course, was unusual, but it is true that colonial regimes did not actively encourage missions. The historian of the early British mission to India, J.C.Marshman, believed that the Government never at any time identified itself with the missionary cause, and Neill, himself bishop of Tiruneveli in the 1940s, felt that an attitude of unfriendliness towards missions never entirely ceased to exist as long as British rule was maintained in India.[40] This was in part because missionaries were often in favour of independence.[41] In China, in the 1860s, the

---

36 Herder, 'Ideas for a Philosophy of History' in *Werke* vol 13 p.342
37 Herder, 'Letters on the advancement of Humanity (*Humanität*)' in *Werke* vol 18 pp.247–249
38 Herder, 'Yet Another Philosophy of History' in Barnard, *Herder* p.209
39 Cited in Berlin, *Vico and Herder* p.160
40 Neill, *Colonialism* pp.93, 99
41 Two hundred British missionaries urged the Round Table conference in 1930 to accept the wishes of the people of India with respect to independence. Neill, *Colonialism* p.111

British representative informed the government that 'It would be decidedly for the peace of China if Christianity and its emissaries were, for the present at least, excluded altogether.'[42] This opposition calls in question Latouche's rhetorical insistence that 'Merchants, missionaries and the military were the three Ms of triumphant imperialism.'[43]

This, then, is one side of the picture. On the other hand the 'conversion' of the North German tribes under Charlemagne was backed up by the threat of violence. When one tribe was offered the gospel and, after a period of reflection, refused, Charlemagne executed 40,000 of them. Christendom was born, says Latouche, through the enslavement of the Saxon and the reconquest of Spain. The move to Westernize the world started as a crusade.[44] The violence of the Latin American *conquista* is one of the great crimes of history, in which, as an Indian delegation to Pope John Paul II put it in 1985, the sword was used by day, and the cross by night. The later Jesuit missions in Paraguay tried the paternalist experiment of the reductions. These abjured violence, but no Guarani man became a priest nor Guarani woman a nun, even though some expressed a sense of vocation.[45] The Portuguese mission to Goa involved, in Stephen Neill's judgement, an 'almost absolute' identity between mission and colonialism.[46] The same is true of the Catholic endorsement of the conquest of Ethiopia four centuries later when the bishop of Cremona told departing troops that they would 'on African soil ... conquer new and fertile lands for the Italian genius, thereby bringing to them Roman and Christian culture'.[47] Jomo Kenyatta claimed that missionaries imposed their religion of individualism on Africa and thus wrought havoc with indigenous culture and that they could only assume in African culture a satanic enemy.[48] Fanon wrote:

> It is not enough for the settler to delimit physically ... the place of the native ... The customs of the colonized people, their traditions, their myths – above all, their myths – are the very sign of that poverty of spirit and of their constitutional depravity. That is why we must put the DDT which destroys parasites, the bearers of disease, on the same level as the Christian religion which wages war on embryonic heresies and instincts, and on evil as yet unborn. The recession of yellow fever and the advance of evangelization form part of the same balance sheet ... The Church in the colonies is the white people's Church. She does not call the native to God's ways but to the ways of the white man, of the master, of the oppressor.[49]

---

42 Neill, *Colonialism* p.147
43 Latouche, *Westernization* p.8
44 Latouche, *Westernization* pp.7–8 At the same time let us note, since it is currently fashionable to invoke the Crusades as the root of all evil, that they were a highly complex phenomenon and in part a response to Muslim military expansion – ultimately more successful than the 'Christian' counter attack. This historical note of course does not detract from the fact that the very idea of crusade is absolutely sub-Christian and forbidden by the gospel.
45 Neill, *Colonialism* p.66
46 Neill, *Colonialism* p.73
47 Sanneh, *Encountering* p.48
48 J.Kenyatta, *Facing Mount Kenya* London: Heinemann 1974
49 Fanon, *Wretched of the Earth* pp.31–32

Norman Lewis has documented the destruction of indigenous Latin American cultures by the New Tribes Mission, driven by a belief that only those who share their particular brand of Christianity will be 'saved' from hell. These missionaries banned Indian ceremonies of all kinds, Indian dances, the playing of native instruments, the self-treatment by Indians by their own medicinal remedies, self-decoration in any form, or the wearing of apparel other than of the plainest and inevitably drabbest kind.[50] The result was 'ethnocide' and the reduction of a vibrant culture to dereliction. 'These Indians had suffered to the full the processes of what is now spoken of as acculturation. They had walked with the Lord, and come to the end of the road.'[51] In case we protest that this is a mission undertaken by an extreme Protestant sect, he couples it with what London Missionary Society (LMS) missionaries did in Oceania in the nineteenth century.

For Latouche the effort to translate the gospels into all languages is a continuation of colonialism. Noting that most infrastructure development projects in the Third World are directly or indirectly Christian he regards this, again, as aimed at a kind of world domination.[52] Sardar agrees, believing that non-governmental organizations (NGOs) are exercising their power and prestige cynically. 'Humanitarian work', 'charitable work', 'development assistance' and 'disaster relief' are all smokescreens for the real motives behind the NGO presence in the South: promotion of Western values and culture, including conversion to Christianity, inducing dependency, demonstrating the helplessness of those they are supposedly helping.[53]

Jean and John Comaroff's brilliant study of the Nonconformist mission to the Southern Tswana, of which we so far have the first two volumes, presents a highly nuanced account of the interaction of mission and colonialism. They too, however, argue that the final objective of generations of colonizers was to colonize the consciousness of the indigenous inhabitants with the axioms and aesthetics of an alien culture.[54] In their story the missionaries were 'the footsoldiers of imperialism', the most active cultural agents, driven by the explicit aim of reconstructing the native world in the name of God and

---

50   N.Lewis, *The Missionaries* London: Arena 1989 p.96

51   Lewis, *Missionaries* p.196

52   Latouche, *Westernization* p.31

53   Sardar, *Postmodernism* p.78 He instances Bangladesh. Jeremy Seabrook, on the other hand, in his report on Bangladesh, has a very different view. He cites a Bangladeshi informant who argues that the rise of Islamic parties is, in part, a response to the growing power of NGOs in civil society – human rights groups, women, the rural and urban poor, cultural groups. These now form a *de facto* opposition, filling spaces deserted by mainstream politics. This is why NGOs are the objects of the wrath of fundamentalists. Women, above all, are both the site of struggle and the agents of resistance to a politicized version of Islam, which 'has little to do with religion, and everything to do with power'. *Freedom Unfinished* p.30. Petras and Veltmeyer, from a socialist standpoint, share the view of NGOs as agents of imperialism. *Globalization Unmasked* p.129ff

54   To support that case they could have cited T.B.Macaulay's notorious recommendation for English education in India: 'We must at present do our best to form a class who may be interpreters between us and the millions whom we govern; a class of persons, Indian in blood and colour, but English in taste, in opinions, in morals, and in intellect. To that class we may leave it to refine the vernacular dialects with terms of science borrowed from the Western nomenclature, and to render

European civilization. The settler and mining magnate 'merely wanted Africans' land and labour. Missionaries wanted their souls.'[55]

We encountered the Comaroffs' understanding of hegemony in Chapter 6, and they elaborate it precisely to understand the nineteenth century missions. For them colonization inheres less in political overrule than in 'seizing and transforming "others" by the very act of conceptualising, inscribing and interacting with them on terms not of their choosing'.[56] Missions were involved in this willy nilly because the goods and techniques the missionaries brought with them, from medicine to Gatling guns, from the design of schoolbuildings to new agricultural techniques, presupposed the messages and meanings they proclaimed in the pulpit and vice versa.[57]

The missionaries often opposed colonialists like Rhodes but, despite their best intentions, could not but further the colonial enterprise. Brilliantly situating the missionaries in their home context, the Comaroffs show how missionaries like Moffat and Livingstone sought to re-create in Africa the Eden that had been despoiled in Britain by the industrial revolution. The African peasant would be modelled on the sturdy yeoman of Cobbett's dreams. The 'timeless gospel' of the missionaries was of sin and redemption but this was expressed through that ethos of Victorian Nonconformity which both Arnold and Dickens so loathed: 'commerce and manufacture, methodical self-construction and the practical arts of life, reason and good works'.[58] They brought with them the ambivalent European understanding of nature, part Rousseauesque innocence and part savagery, the consequence of the Fall. The civilizing mission therefore sought to remake the African both as modernist citizen and as ethnic subject.[59]

In their understanding of what was really 'good news' the missionaries naturally drew on their own experience. They had been poor, and made good through education, thrift and hard work. The African should do the same. Moffat wanted Africans to learn to read and reflect, as he had done, 'to master the practical arts of civilization, to cultivate and sell his labour, and to see the value of industry and charity. In this way he too might better himself.'[60] Stephen Neill points out that hostility to the slave trade was one of the principal factors driving both missions and, in some cases, imperial

---

them by degrees, fit vehicles for conveying knowledge to the great mass of the population.' T.B.Macaulay, *Speeches by Lord Macaulay: With his Minute on Indian Education* ed G.Young Oxford: Oxford University Press 1979 p.359

55   J. and J. Comaroff, *Revelation and Revolution* vol 1 pp.4, 6

56   J. and J. Comaroff, *Revelation and Revolution* vol 1 p.15 They comment on the design of a mission school that 'it had done more than express a cogent vision of subject and society. It had actually created it. In the sturdiness of its structures and the refined ornamental finish of its public buildings, in its Spartan student accommodation and its overall plan, it had made real and natural the forms of a would-be hegemony.' Ibid p.33

57   J. and J. Comaroff, *Revelation and Revolution* vol 1 p.9

58   J. and J. Comaroff, *Revelation and Revolution* vol 1 p.79

59   J. and J. Comaroff, *Revelation and Revolution* vol 1 p.368 It shows, as they argue, the inherent contradictions of colonialism.

60   J. and J. Comaroff, *Revelation and Revolution* vol 1 p.83

expansion.[61] However, as the Comaroffs respond, the chains of slavery were unwittingly replaced with the bonds of an imperialism based on the free market.[62] 3Accepting Weber's thesis of the elective affinity between Protestantism and capitalism they argue that the colonial enterprise in general was the product of this affinity.[63] The biographer of the Evangelical colonizer, Evan Lugard, responsible for appropriating Uganda as part of the British empire (in order to prevent it from being taken either by Muslims or the French), notes that men like him 'had no doubt that the greatest conceivable good for this unhappy continent was for it to come under the rule of civilised powers, and their faith and their interest, fused beyond distinction in their minds, made them seek to bring as much of it as possible under the rule of their own country'.[64]

Lamin Sanneh comments that the Comaroffs offer a sophisticated presentation of the classical theory of Christianity as a tool of colonial subjugation, and of Africans as victims. 'As such, the book represents the European metropolitan viewpoint, the viewpoint of the transmitters over against the recipients of the message.'[65] This is to do their work far less than justice. Though Sanneh and the Comaroffs may be polar opposites in their view of the intrinsic desirability of missions, they both agree that missions sparked an independent response. From the start, the Comaroffs point out, 'would-be subjects of the church turned its own rhetoric against it, calling on the fertile potential of the Bible to ally themselves with righteous sufferers elsewhere'.[66] The missionary encounter, they stress over and over again, was a two sided process and had consequences for the missionaries no less than for the Africans, and the colonizing process cannot be captured in some neat dialectic of domination and resistance.[67]

---

61   The British Government was for a long time hesitant about involvement in Africa. When a proposal came before parliament to withdraw from the Gold Coast it was a member of the Basle mission, Schrenk, who persuaded them to stay. Schrenk argued that the withdrawal of the British would leave the whole territory to be overrun by the Ashanti, or colonized by the French, which would mean the introduction of Jesuits, slave trade and penal colonies for malefactors from Europe(!). He laid the greatest stress on the responsibility of Britain as a Christian country to spread abroad in Africa the blessings of knowledge and to make reparation for the grave injuries Europe had inflicted on Africa. Neill, *Colonialism* p.303

62   J. and J. Comaroff, *Revelation and Revolution* vol 1 p.119 They show that missionaries took up Adam Smith's argument that slave labour was costlier than free. This does not, of course, have to be taken cynically.

63   J. and J. Comaroff, *Revelation and Revolution* vol 2 p.409

64   Cited in Neill, *Colonialism* p.281 Such views were not uncontested. In an early attack on Kipling as 'the voice of the hooligan' Robert Buchanan wrote: 'There is a universal scramble for plunder, for excitement, for amusement, for speculation and, above it all, the flag of a Hooligan Imperialism is raised, with the proclamation that it is the sole mission of Anglo Saxon England, forgetful of the task of keeping its own drains in order, to expand and extend its boundaries indefinitely, and, again in the name of the Christianity it has practically abandoned, to conquer and inherit the earth.' Brantlinger, *Bread and Circuses* p.137

65   Sanneh, *Encountering* p.91

66   J. and J. Comaroff, *Revelation and Revolution* vol 1 p.192

67   J. and J. Comaroff, *Revelation and Revolution* vol 1 pp.53, 32, 5

Another study of the missionary encounter in Southern Africa, Paul Landau's *The Realm of the Word*, shows how missionary preaching was harnessed by an African kingdom to underwrite its power.[68] Far from representing an alien imposition African Christians used it to construct a new polity. 'By providing a transcendent appeal, Christianity offered a way to oppose the patriarchal or ethnic domination within villages and homesteads, and often benefited the direct authority of the king, but Christians occasionally fought the kingdom itself.'[69] Women in particular gained from this development. 'Women and the state shared the mutual interest of substituting a new form of status and association for that of the *kgotla*, the male public forum and court ... By participating in the making of the power of the king, Christian women remade themselves.'[70] Women's citizenship changed the understanding of gender and the whole nature of Ngwato society. To be sure, what was actually going on was very different from the understanding expressed in the reports back to London of the LMS missionaries. They read events in terms of a narrative of the triumphant spread and conquest of 'the Word'. In fact 'Christianity grew through dynastic quarrels, the manner in which the soil was tilled, and the clinical practices of pulling teeth.'[71] Nevertheless an authentic and indigenous Church did materialize from missionary labours, one in which Africans were at the centre and had real power. 'The historical framework in which the Protectorate government is said to have held the "real" power in GammaNgwato,' Landau concludes, 'and in which mission Churches were "controlled" by missionaries, should be discarded.'[72]

Summing up his account of mission and colonialism from the fifteenth to the twentieth centuries Neill acknowledges that racist attitudes characterized many missionaries, especially from the late nineteenth century on.[73] 'There have been Western Christians who have deplored colonialism in all its forms, and have condemned it without measure as being nothing but exploitation and robbery,' he writes. 'But these have been in a small minority, and often heard against much louder voices raised in support of a very different point of view.'[74] The primary concern of almost all missionaries was the well-being of the people whom they had come to serve but all too often the missionary held that he could judge better of the real interests of his people than they could themselves.

68 P.Landau, *The Realm of the Word: Language, Gender, and Christianity in a Southern African Kingdom* London: Currey 1995
69 Landau, *Realm* p.xvii
70 Landau, *Realm* p.214
71 Landau, *Realm* p.xviii
72 Landau, *Realm* p.210
73 He writes that there is reason to think that the 'imperialistic spirit', a belief in the innate superiority of the white man, became stronger in the second half of the nineteenth century than it had previously been. *Colonialism* p.417
74 Neill, *Colonialism* p.412 Towards the end of World War I, the Catholic Crusade used to hawk a pamphlet on the London streets called 'Sins and their cure'. Anyone who paid 6d for it found, on turning to the first page, that 'sin' was above all British imperialism and that the 'cure' was 'to smash it to bits'. Conrad Noel was the leading light, combining his political militancy with a passion for morris dancing and high Anglican ceremonial.

'His objectivity was blurred by a certain patronizing, and sometimes even contemptuous attitude towards men whom he could never quite persuade himself to regard as grown up.'[75] Missionaries were often timid and calculating although, from the days of Las Casas onwards, there were those who opposed their own governments for the sake of what they understood to be justice.[76]

In the light of all this Paulo Suess rightly demands that there is need to reflect on the potential of Christianity as a whole for violence. There is, he says, an inability to put a comprehensive request for forgiveness to Indios and Afro Americans. The demand put to other peoples in missionary praxis to forget their culture and history always also corrupts the Church's own memory and promises of solidarity in the present are credible only when they also take responsibility for the past.[77]

For Sardar, belief in the incarnation itself is the root of the problem. The attribution of divinity to Jesus, he writes, has had serious consequences for non-Western cultures. The idea that God allows himself to be edged out of the world and on to the cross and helps us through his weakness and suffering, has led Christians to impose a submissive love on the members of non-Western cultures they converted, thus paving the way for their colonization or sustaining the unjust status quo. The allusion to Bonhoeffer here is clearly anachronistic and the idea that the cross was used in this way probably derives from Marx's observations on the likes of Andrew Ure, which we considered in Chapter 5. As an overt mission strategy it can certainly be discounted in most cases, although here again Lewis' documentation of the New Tribes Mission is cause for shame.

Sardar goes on to observe that, if there is salvation in 'no other name', then 'any and all means' are justified to see that others are saved. 'Christianity's universal mission amounted to little more than the total subjugation of all Others in the name of God and salvation through Jesus.'[78] There is a will to power in Christianity expressed in the divinity of Jesus, replaced in modernity with the divinity of European man.[79] Again this seems too undiscriminating a polemic, this time reading mission through Feuerbach, which does no justice to the complexity of the historical case. Studies like those of the Comaroffs tell a rather different story. It is also true that, despite the famous verses about other 'peoples of the Book', the claim to a uniquely salvific gospel is shared by Islam, another imperial and colonial religion. Any absolute claim has a potential for violence, especially if that absolute is 'God', the author of all truth, and both Christianity and Islam have to face their violent past as an essential hermeneutic for any contemporary mission.[80]

---

75   Neill, *Colonialism* p.413
76   Neill, *Colonialism* p.415
77   Suess, 'A Confused Mission Scenario' pp.114, 115
78   Sardar, *Postmodernism* p.235
79   Sardar, *Postmodernism* p.244
80   Sardar concludes his book in this way. *Postmodernism* p.290 A recent article in *New Internationalist* (No 345 May 2002) was more irenic than this highly polemical book, much of which is directed at Christianity.

There would not be a problem of evil if we did not believe in a good God, and similarly, there would be no problem of Christianity and culture if we were not committed to mission, and the belief that the gospel has something to offer which is of unique value to all people. I am arguing that the gospel may be understood as part of the 'long revolution' through which God makes and keeps human beings human. To make such a claim we cannot deal with abstractions: we must face the reality of the Christian past, and hear the voice of our critics. Violent, imperialist, a form of cultural acid? Whilst acknowledging the criticisms I have tried to argue that these by no means constitute the heart of the historical record. In the following chapter I develop this argument, outlining ways in which Christian missions sought to eschew both colonialism and violence.

Chapter 9

Translation and Inculturation

Continuing the theme of the previous chapter I resume my exploration of what happens when the gospel encounters a 'non-Christian' culture. In the second part of the book I argued that the gospel lays on the Church a *sui generis* approach to power, which privileges the weaker sections of society. In the last chapter, however, I conceded that, in the context of mission, the Church had to face up to the violence of its past. Was that violence more subtle than the crudities of colonialism? Is it, as some critics allege, part of the very implication of incarnation? I pursue this question by reflecting on two models of mission.

As a subdiscipline within theology, mission is of relatively recent origin, though, as we know, the command to mission belongs to the gospels.[1] David Bosch follows Hans Küng in attempting to apply paradigm theory to the history of mission, and argues that the patristic period, the middle ages, the Reformation and the Enlightenment period all had distinctive paradigms of mission, which he attempts to organize around key texts. If the replacement of the Galenic by the Copernican world view is our model for paradigm change, however, then it is very doubtful if we can use this to map Church or mission history, as there is much more continuity and overlap than in this transition. We also lack adequate sources for understanding what seems to have been the most vigorous mission of the patristic period, the Nestorian mission. It is not until the eighteenth century and the 'Awakening' which accompanied the Enlightenment as its affective side that a theology of mission began to be properly articulated, and this very quickly developed into two main emphases, driven by the desire on the one hand to 'save' people from sin and damnation, and on the other to extend the Christian duty of care as spelled out in Matthew 25. The emphasis was sometimes on one side and sometimes on the other, but they were rarely completely separated.

In this chapter, however, I do not want to follow Bosch's paradigms but instead to consider another, and slightly different, twofold emphasis, between translation and inculturation, which correspond, roughly, to Protestant and Catholic approaches, though of course both approaches have a foot in the other camp.

---

1 The Jesuits first used 'mission' to refer to spreading the gospel to non-Christians in the sixteenth century. Though there were some seventeenth century experiments 'mission' first became a separate subject in theology in the mid nineteenth century. D.Bosch, *Transforming Mission* Maryknoll: Orbis 1991 p.490f

Mission as Translation

R.S.Sugirtharajah argues that the translation of Scripture into the vernacular, a key imperative of Protestant missions, involved multiple acts of violence, what he calls 'Scriptural imperialism'. Missionaries commended it, he argues, as a vehicle for inculcating European manners.[2] Translation introduced alien values; it displaced native customs and manners which were seen as undermining the viability of Christian virtues and the colonial project; it promoted the assumption that oral cultures were empty and were waiting to be filled with written texts; whilst the heightened notion of historicization meant that non-biblical religions were seen as the pagan 'other' needing deliverance.[3] On this understanding almost any translation must do violence to another culture.

The contrary view is argued by Lamin Sanneh. Commenting on the thesis that Christian mission was covert colonialism he remarks that 'unless we were to accept the victim view of non-Western populations it would seem remarkable that missionary contact should always and everywhere lead to the same unvarying result of leaving the Western initiative triumphant and unchallenged while Africans grovelled in unmitigated defeat'.[4] He is concerned that claims about missionary oppression have magnified Africa's victim image and promoted an idyllic picture of traditional societies. It is important, he writes, 'not to view non-Western cultures as prelapsarian specimens of primordial purity and innocence which a herpetoid West proceeded to despoil with projects of exploitation, subterfuge and subjugation, though we must oppose Western exploitation'.[5]

He distinguishes two basic ways of mission, which he calls diffusion and translation. The first is to make the missionary culture the inseparable carrier of the message, so that the new religion is implanted in other societies primarily as a matter of cultural identity. In his view Islam works in this way. The second is to make the recipient culture the true and final locus of the proclamation, so

---

2   He cites a missionary in Uganda who wrote: 'Uganda today is no savage wilderness. It has its railways, its harnessed water-power, its post office and roads, its cultivated farms and neat homes. The Bible is the sole and sufficient cause of this transformation. There are other African tribes whose trade has gone without the Bible and degraded the people even as it has purchased their goods.' R.S.Sugirtharajah, *The Bible and the Third World* Cambridge: Cambridge University Press 2001 p.63

3   Sugirtharajah, *Bible* pp.64–70

4   Sanneh, *Encountering* p.72 Cf the view of Robert Stam and Ella Shohat who argue that the outlook which posits Europe as the source of all social evils in the world 'remains Eurocentric ... while exempting Third World patriarchal elites from all responsibility. Such "victimology" reduces non-European life to a pathological response to western penetration; it merely turns colonialist claims upside down. Rather than saying that "we" (that is, the First World) have brought "them" civilization, it claims instead that everywhere "we" have brought Diabolical Evil, and everywhere "their" enfeebled societies have succumbed to "our" insidious influence. The vision remains Promethean, but here Prometheus has brought not fire but the Holocaust, reproducing what Barbara Christian calls the "West's outlandish claim to have invented everything, including evil".' 'Contested Histories' in D.Goldberg(ed) *Multiculturalism* Oxford: Blackwell 1994 p.298

5   Sanneh, *Encountering* p.232

that the religion arrives without the presumption of cultural rejection. This is mission by translation.[6] Translation, he notes, entails a distinction between the essence of the message, and its cultural presuppositions, with the assumption that such a separation enables us to affirm the primacy of the message over its cultural underpinnings. In his view this was characteristic of both the Judaic and Hellenic phases of Christian mission, and characterized mission in Africa in the nineteenth century. What Sanneh calls 'the essence of the message' here is the core proclamation of the gospel, and I shall return to this at the end of the chapter. The *sola scriptura* principle, in his view, decoupled the Bible from Western interpretation and helped to suppress the transmission of Western cultural presuppositions to indigenous societies.[7]

The translation process had at least five consequences, which represent more or less opposite arguments to those of Sugirtharajah. First, it represents an endorsement of the host culture. 'The "many tongues" of Pentecost affirmed God's acceptance of all cultures within the scheme of salvation, reinforcing the position that Jews and Gentiles were equal before God. The gentile breakthrough became the paradigm of the church's missionary experience.'[8] As Peter's experience in the house of Cornelius shows, Pentecost was an endorsement of a pluralism in which no culture is unclean, all can provide access to God, and no culture is the exclusive norm of truth. Mission as translation rests on the assumption that the recipient culture is the destination of God's promise of salvation. The One gospel becomes meaningfully mediated through the 'Many' refractions of culture and historical contingency.[9]

The reverse side of this was that the culture of the message bearer became peripheral. When missionaries put the gospel into the vernacular Africans had the first and last advantage. Sanneh compares this with Paul's self-critical stance toward his own culture. Translation involves some degree of cultural alienation on the part of the translator. The work of translating the Scriptures involved being out of step with Western cultural suppositions and proceeding on the terms of indigenous societies and at their pace.[10] Furthermore, the missionary movement meant the end of Christendom, because it meant that religion could be separated from its Western territorial identity.[11]

The endorsement of different cultures implicit in vernacular translation, again, fosters accountability and guards against cultural idolatry. It has produced, Sanneh argues, a worldwide pluralist movement distinguished by the forces of radical pluralism and social destigmatization.[12] Not only did the idea of cultural relativism not demolish the case for missions, it was promoted by it. Nothing so promoted cultural particularity as the huge plethora of vernacular translations:

---

6   Sanneh, *Translating* p.29
7   Sanneh, *Translating* p.203
8   Sanneh, *Translating* p.46
9   Sanneh, *Encountering* p.149
10   Sanneh, *Encountering* p.101
11   Sanneh, *Encountering* p.191
12   Sanneh, *Translating* p.234

> The problem for cultural relativists is that in their concern to reject the unhealthy consequences of western cultural and religious imperialism they reverted to a form of ethnocentrism in which other cultures are given a licence to be a law unto themselves and thus to be ethnocentric ... the relativists have thus replaced the progressive ethnocentrism of the Enlightenment with their own serial ethnocentrism.[13]

Translation led to a renaissance of the host culture. The correlation between Christian mission and the revitalization of indigenous culture 'remains one of the most undervalued themes in the study of Christian expansion, although in Africa and elsewhere it stares us in the face at almost every turn of the road'.[14] If, as Herder argued, language lies at the heart of culture, then vernacular translations touch the springs of life – a fact indicated, for example, by the honour in which Roberto di Nobili is held in Tamil Nadu. Work on the vernacular enabled many peoples to acquire pride and dignity about themselves in the modern world.

The self-confidence engendered by this renaissance led, in turn, to a critique of the colonial cultures. Africans learned from the gospel that mission as European cultural hegemony was a catastrophic departure from the Bible. Translation led African Christians to question, and sometimes to renounce, the Western presuppositions of the Church.[15] The success of indigenizing mission can be established by the many examples where missionaries failed in the attempt to impose Western cultural norms on non-Western people.[16] It had, in other words, an anti-colonial force. In encouraging pride and confidence in the people, it prepared the ground for the rejection of colonialism. In this sense it is the logical opposite of colonialism. Sugirtharajah also gives a number of instances where colonized subjects appealed to Scripture against the colonizer. In South Africa in particular the black population discovered 'a revolutionary potential in the Bible. They recovered episodes from the Hebrew Scriptures which identified with nationalistic anti foreign and revolutionary causes.'[17]

In the last chapter we saw Sanneh's critique of the Comaroffs. They return the compliment by describing Sanneh's thesis as a form of neo-revisionism. 'The reduction of the story of African Christianity to one of "native" appropriation alone is at once a mystification and a compression; one which, no less than the alternative that reads the story as a tale of unremitting

---

13   Sanneh, *Encountering* p.62

14   Sanneh, *Translating* p.185

15   Sanneh, *Translating* p.4 The Comaroffs argue, on the other hand, that 'Those who chose to peruse the Tswana Bible learned more than the sacred story, more even than how to read. They were subjected to a form of cultural translation in which vernacular poetics were re-presented to them as a thin *sekgoa* (Western) narrative – and their language itself reduced to an instrument of empirical knowledge, Christian prayer and just-so stories. It is little wonder that the Tlhaping and Rolong became ever more self-conscious about their own culture as a distinct system of signs and practices; that *tswana* came to stand in opposition to *sekgoa* as, among other things, tradition to modernity.' J. and J. Comaroff, *Revelation and Revolution* vol 1 p.311

16   Sanneh, *Translating* p.90 The Comaroffs ascribe this to African determination not to be colonized.

17   Sugirtharajah, *Bible* p.106 Cf pp.83, 89

domination, denudes history of its dialectics.'[18] This, too, seems to under-estimate the extent to which Sanneh recognizes the negative effects of colonialism. It is true that Sanneh is a Christian apologist, and not an ethnographer, but the determination not to see the African as victim is one that the Comaroffs share.

The Comaroffs also allege that 'the Word' was not the primary factor in the success of Christian mission. 'In the long conversation with the colonial evangelists,' they write:

> [the Southern Tswana] listened to the Word professed, but were moved by the word-made-flesh: by the promissory power of the Protestant God, as manifest in His emissaries, to heal and promote communal well-being. Thus did divinity 'show' itself, and proclaim its ineffable presence, both as an ontological reality and as a force in the world.[19]

Perhaps it is so, but such claims are hard to prove and their own emphasis on dialectic, and on the complexity of dialogue and resistance, forecloses any simple reading of the history. Homi Bhaba problematizes the whole issue of the reception of the Word in somewhat the way the Comaroffs do, and forces us to ask what actually is understood in the process of translation.[20] At the same time to doubt the possibility of cross cultural translation at all, at the deepest level, is both historically infeasible and implies an impossibly monadic view of culture. We can argue the possibility of translation from the hybridity of all cultures even whilst acknowledging the complexity of the process which is always involved. In terms of the argument between Sanneh and the Comaroffs, probably both accounts are true. At the very least, it is far too simple to reject Sanneh's argument as 'neo-revisionism'.

Mission as Inculturation

Used for the first time in 1962, according to Aylward Shorter, and then officially by the Pope in 1979, the idea of inculturation has become a favoured way of describing the method of Christian mission. The idea, however, is much older than the term.[21] It is implicit in the practice of seventeenth century Jesuits like Matteo Ricci and Roberto de Nobili, who learned Chinese or Tamil, and became Mandarins or Brahmins in an effort to commend the gospel. It is a conscious attempt, corporate and systematic, to hasten the process of human mimetic learning, the process by which we unconsciously adopt the culture in which we live, and which any parent who has brought up children in a culture radically different to their own will have seen at work. There is no 'kit' for inculturation. As Aloysius Pieris puts it:

---

18   J. and J. Comaroff, *Revelation and Revolution* vol 2 p.49
19   J. and J. Comaroff, *Revelation and Revolution* vol 2 p.109
20   See Chapter 7 of *The Location of Culture*, 'Signs taken for Wonders'
21   Prior to this term it was common to speak of 'indigenization'.

Inculturation is something that happens naturally. It can never be induced artificially ... inculturation is the by-product of an involvement with a people rather than the conscious target of a programme of action. For it is a people that creates a culture. It is, therefore, from the people with whom one becomes involved that one understands and acquires a culture ... The questions that are foremost in the minds of inculturationists are, therefore, totally irrelevant – namely, whether a particular church is inculturated or not, or why it is not inculturated, and how it could be inculturated.[22]

These questions arise because the ministerial Church is elitist, and the clergy represent the dominant sector in society.[23] In the same way the Bishops of Eastern Africa in 1973 felt that the best way of safeguarding human values and of rooting the Church in the life and culture of the people was by building small Christian communities.[24] Since culture is a way of life, inculturation refers to the renewal of culture as lived out by the community, especially the basic communities at the hub of social and cultural life.[25]

The idea of inculturation draws partly on the theology of the second century Apologists, but chiefly on the logic of incarnation.[26] The Apologists discerned a 'seed of the Word' in all human cultures. On this understanding the gospel not only converts other cultures but needs to be opened up to other cultures to attain fullness of meaning. Because the Logos is the ground of all creation whatever is true, good and beautiful derives from it. There is, as it were, a taking form of the divine Logos wherever these things are found.

This idea was an early form of Christology, but inculturation characteristically appeals to the more fully developed ideas of the fourth and fifth centuries. If God takes flesh in Christ, is culturally formed as a first century Jew, speaks Aramaic and Hebrew, then, it is argued, wherever the gospel goes it must follow the same method. The Word becomes incarnate in every culture, finding its own appropriate form in each.[27] As Donovan puts it:

---

22   Pieris, *Asian Theology* p.38
23   Pieris, *Asian Theology* p.38
24   Shorter, *Inculturation* p.265
25   Shorter, *Inculturation* p.268 Kathryn Tanner likewise argues that one does not first determine what the Christian message is and then bring it into relation with culture. Rather, cultural practices are the materials from which the message is constructed. *Theories* p.116 Perhaps 'through which they are refracted' would be a better way of putting it.
26   Justin Upkong distinguishes five models for inculturation. In addition to the three I consider he also outlines a functional analogy approach, in which Christ's redemptive work is described in terms of the thought categories of another culture, describing Christ as proto ancestor, or as Guru. Another approach is biblical and, on the basis of Christ's identity with the Father as proclaimed in John, argues that Christ was present in non-Christian cultures before the coming of missionaries. His own view is based on the pattern of evangelization in the gospels. Jesus challenged his own culture from within it. He preached a universal kingdom which eventually inspired the disciples to undertake a universal mission to evangelize all peoples, but adopting as a method change from within. J.Upkong, 'Christology and Inculturation: A New Testament Perspective' in R.Gibellini(ed) *Paths of African Theology* London: SCM 1994 pp.40–61
27   Robert Schreiter points out that our understanding of inculturation depends on both how we understand the gospel and how we understand culture. Is the gospel to be inculturated a matter of getting the words right, of symbolic enhancement, of the replication of certain values or of the representation of the Christian story? Similarly, is culture a worldwide system of rules governing

God enables a people, any people, to reach salvation through their culture and tribal, racial customs and traditions … An evangelist, a missionary must respect the culture of a people, not destroy it. The incarnation of the gospel, the flesh and blood which must grow on the gospel is up to the people of a culture.[28]

It is a very powerful model, but it is not without problems. If, for example, it is equated with the cultural education of Jesus it overlooks the ongoing dialogue between gospel and culture. If, on the other hand, the emphasis is on the flesh taking, it may encourage a view of inculturation from above, rather than from below. It also encourages the temptation of what Shorter calls 'culturalism', namely the process of absorption of the gospel into culture. In concentrating upon the inculturation of Jesus we may forget how he challenges the culture of his adoption.[29] As Collett correctly insists, inculturation cannot succeed without repentance.[30] The gospel is, in a fundamental way, about metanoia and if the gospel enters culture and nothing changes then there is no effective inculturation. Cultures cannot pick and choose which parts of the gospel they want to hear and which parts they do not.

For these reasons Aylward Shorter commends what he calls the Paschal mystery approach. After the resurrection Christ belongs to all cultures and can identify with them through the proclamation of the Good News. Cultures are to be evangelized and challenged to metanoia, to die to all that is not worthy of humanity in their traditions, but then to rise in greater splendour. As there was continuity between the crucified and risen body so there is a real continuity with the pre-Christian culture. After evangelization the culture is changed, but also identifiably the same culture that it always was.[31]

To attempt to discuss inculturation in the abstract is an obvious paradox and I turn, therefore, to a brief consideration of the way it has been understood in Africa and Asia.

---

behaviour, a set of values that offer guidelines for making decisions, a conversation, or a tool kit into which we reach when we have a problem? Each of these variables will affect our understanding of inculturation. Schreiter, 'Inculturation of Faith or Identification with Culture?' p.18

28 V.Donovan, *Christianity Rediscovered* London: SCM 1978 p.30 Cf James Johnson in 1900: 'Christianity is a Religion intended for, and suitable for, every race and Tribe of people on the face of the Globe. Acceptance of it was never intended by its Founder to denationalise any people and it is indeed its glory that every race of people may profess and practise it and imprint upon it its own native characteristics, giving it a peculiar type among themselves without its losing anything of its virtue.' Cited in Sanneh, *Encountering* p.144

29 Shorter, *Inculturation* p.82

30 G.Collet, 'From Theological Vandalism to Theological Romanticism? Questions about a Multicultural Identity of Christianity' in Greinacher and Mette(eds) *Christianity and Cultures* pp.25–38 'Inculturation cannot succeed without repentance in the sense of a radical renunciation of knowing better and asserting oneself, with the sole aim of reproducing one's own previous identity … If it is not itself to compromise the concern for inculturation, a community of faith which wants to take multiculturalism in its own ranks seriously cannot leave out or suppress fundamental conflicts like the North–South conflict, racial conflict or the conflict between the sexes.' Ibid pp.34–35

31 Shorter, *Inculturation* p.84

Inculturation: The African Experience

'After a century of missionary work,' writes Jean-Marc Éla, 'few Africans feel really at home in the Church.' Christianity remains a religion of the cities whilst in the villages, the people practise fetishism.[32] Part of the reason for this is that the Church has not inculturated, but remains tied to Western ways of thinking and expression. Its theology is still tied to scholasticism; its liturgical year is organized around four seasons which are not relevant to Africa; the eucharist is still celebrated with bread and wine. This reveals the domination at the heart of the faith as lived in Africa, says Éla. 'The symbolism of the Eucharist escapes the savanna people or the forest people because the meaning of wheat bread and grape wine in European culture escapes them. This is a serious matter when we consider what it means for a sacrament to belong to the universe of signs.'[33] In many African countries Christians are defined as people who had to abandon their traditional customs, such as the use of dance or drumming. Faith has to be totally reformulated through the mediation of African culture. 'We should not say anything, think anything, or do anything in the church unless it springs from daily reality, from the living traditions of the African peoples, or from the concrete tasks of villages and slums.'[34]

Éla and other African theologians have many examples of what incultura-tion might involve. Discussion of whether the gospel really requires monogamy, for example, has gone on since the mid nineteenth century. Polygamy, it is insisted, is not about male lust, but about the peasant economy. The man took a second wife if the first was infertile. It provided a peasant family with labour and made divorce superfluous. There was also hardly any prostitution in traditional Africa. Polygamy also promoted peace within the clan by the network of relationships.[35] Éla argues that the logic of African symbolism has to replace that of Logos and ratio. Bujo suggests that the title of proto Ancestor for Christ will have much more meaning for Africans than titles such as Word and Lord, and that theology of the ancestors should also provide the starting point for ecclesiology.[36] African understandings can provide new readings of the gospel story. For example, the positive African attitude to death suggests a re-reading of the Passion narratives in which the relationship of humanity to the universe is integrated into the drama of life and death.[37]

At the same time Éla puts sharp questions to romantic understandings of Africa. It is often said (as it is said of India) that Africa is incurably religious. Is belief in God as widespread as people think, he asks. Is there not a sort of atheism in traditional milieus? (Exactly the same questions may be put to India.) Does not popular religion imply a providentialism that will ultimately alienate human beings and force them into a mentality of resignation in the

---

32 Jean-Marc Éla, *My Faith as an African* Maryknoll: Orbis 1989 p.33
33 Jean-Marc Éla, *African Cry* Maryknoll: Orbis 1986 p.5
34 Éla, *African Cry* p.143
35 B.Bujo, *African Theology in its Social Context* Maryknoll: Orbis 1992 p.48
36 Bujo, *African Theology* pp.83, 92
37 Éla, *African Cry* p.168

face of misery and injustice? In its continual appeal to supernatural forces in the phenomena of nature, does ancestral religion not threaten to keep human beings in a state of dependency that will preclude any human intervention in the difficulties of life?[38] Donovan remarks that paganism is a closed and fatalistic system. 'In prayer we ask them to believe that creation is open-ended and continuing ... it is a Christian idea to believe in God being constantly present and continually creating.'[39]

Éla's questions point up the nature of inculturation as a two way process. It is true that African traditions may obstruct the perverse profit-oriented developmentalism of capitalism but at the same time Christianity, in challenging the religion of nature, points to the everyday, to the political, as the sphere where God's will is revealed and lived. 'What animates a Christian's faith is the perception of an unfinished world placed in our hands by God. In a sense, the world is not to be saved, but reinvented – or, if one prefers, made over by the power of the gospel.'[40] Ultimately, to believe is to respond to the call to be horrified at and intolerant of the sufferings of this life, of injustice and torture, of institutionalized violence, of mystifying ideologies and fear, of fatalism and resignation.

Éla insists that human rights are a key issue in Africa. Torture is a matter of fact in many African countries. Why, he asks, does the West not speak out about it? He suspects that the twofold European construction of the African subject, part innocent and childlike and part savage, may have something to do with this.[41] Traditional culture, therefore, is not simply taken for granted but must be the object of a radical revolution, which will enable it to discover its creative thrust.[42] From a feminist perspective Mercy Oduyoye notes that African culture has guaranteed the patriarchal takeover of even the most mother-centred structures. It is too easy, she says, to lay the blame solely at the feet of Westernization. We know that within the African religio-cultural heritage are to be found the seeds of the objectification and marginalization of women.[43]

Other challenges to traditional thought are represented by the lordship of Christ, the idea of forgiveness, and, surprisingly in view of the anti-individualist rhetoric of most Third World thinkers, individualism. John Taylor believes that the traditional African community, for all its solidarity and the truth of its human vision, is corrupted by a twofold mistrust – mistrust of the stranger because he or she is outside the kinship bond, and mistrust of the unknown witch because she or he is outside of humanity. The 'Good

---

38 Éla, *African Cry* p.40
39 Donovan, *Christianity* p.136
40 Éla, *African Cry* p.93
41 Éla, *African Cry* pp.74–76 To be fair, Amnesty International campaigns regularly feature African countries. If we consider caste atrocities and bonded labour, human rights are a key issue in India as well.
42 Éla, *African Cry* p.129
43 Mercy Oduyoye, 'Feminist Theology in an African Perspective' in Gibellini(ed) *Paths of African Theology* p.173 Vincent Donovan reports the challenge the eucharist posed to Masai men, who did not eat with women because women would pollute food.

News', in that case, consists in the fact that there are no strangers and no realms of terror that lie beyond Christ's sovereignty.[44] For Bujo Jesus corrects and completes the traditional morality of Africa. The moral perspective is no longer limited to my clan, my elders, my friends but extends to the whole human race, in loving service of the Father.[45]

Vincent Donovan finds the content of good news in the possibility of forgiveness. He instances a man who had committed a great sin against the taboos of the Masai tribe and who was destined to live the rest of his life as an outcast. For such a person the promise of forgiveness was certainly good news.[46] Like the first disciples the Masai believed God loves rich people and hates poor people. Donovan responded: 'There is no God like that. There is only the God who loves us no matter how good or how evil we are, the God you have worshipped without really knowing him, the truly unknown God – the High God.'[47]

Many African theologians, and theologians writing out of Africa, insist that Western individualism has to be dropped. The Masai cannot be converted as individuals, writes Donovan, but only as groups. Western missionaries have to drop the idols of their tribe – individualism and love of organization. At the same time Bénézet Bujo believes that there is a danger that the individual will be treated as of little account in the African system. Too much emphasis on the interests of the clan can obscure individual freedom and individual rights, and Christianity has a corrective role to play here.[48]

Amidst all this debate there is remarkable unanimity amongst African theologians that this kind of process is no substitute for justice. For disciples of Nkrumah, for readers of Césaire, Fanon, Sembene Ousmane, or Mongo Beti, it will no longer be enough to hear that Jesus has come not to destroy traditional values but to perfect them, writes Éla.[49] 'Let us be realistic. It is not enough to replace the gothic chasuble with an indigo loincloth. The essential thing is to take up the gospel in everyday life, reminding ourselves that it should be believed as a message of human liberation.'[50] The situation of Africa, 'overwhelmed with debt, strangled by the claws of structural readjustment, prostrate before the International Monetary Fund, on its knees to the captains of cooperation and technological assistance, the black African state is today the most humiliating and shocking incarnation of the debasement of and contempt for black people'.[51]

---

44   Taylor, *Primal Vision* pp.165, 193
45   Bujo, *African Theology* p.88
46   Donovan, *Christianity* p.59
47   Donovan, *Christianity* p.44
48   Bujo, *African Theology* p.105
49   Éla, *African Cry* p.101
50   Éla, *African Cry* p.119 Cf Bujo, who writes: 'if your God is talking to us more by means of our ancestral traditions and customs rather than in the drama of four million refugees in Africa, I should like to return my baptismal certificate'. *African Theology* p.71
51   E.Mveng, 'Impoverishment and Liberation' in Gibellini(ed) *Paths of African Theology* p.157 The chapter contains an electrifying condemnation of the effect of IMF policies on Africa (p.162). If this is not the voice of the prophet Amos in our day I do not know what is.

Preoccupation with inculturation can lead to a neglect of economics and politics. African culture cannot be reduced to music and dance. A species of orientalism is involved in the claim that Africa has the sense of the sacred, as opposed to the materialism of the West. As this claim is celebrated, the process of stripping Africa of its riches continues:

> The rhetoric of Africa's contribution to universal civilization is a disguise for a system in which the spirits are condemned to recite on command, to mouth empty slogans. It is convenient, to say the least, to be able to offer the new generations a mystifying theory that will doom them to the reproduction of the elements of tradition without affording them the wherewithal for a critical examination of the situation that actually calls for radical transformation of structures and institutions.[52]

For this reason it is liberation from oppression which must become the locus of the rediscovery of the gospel nature of the Church. Cultural autonomy cannot be had without economic autonomy. Africa is a region of the world where the powers of Mammon have decided that this portion of humanity shall be slaves:

> Our villages and popular neighbourhoods today are steeped to the skin in situations of domination and new forms of dependency. They are caught in the grip of multinational companies, which are scarcely philanthropic societies. Here base communities can enable people to discover who it is that is really responsible for poverty. A fact is a fact: the word of God is heard through questions that commit us to build a society in which nutrition, employment and health, education and a share of happiness are no longer luxuries for a small elite group. We must return to the grassroots. We must open our ears to Africa, take account of the mute voice of a people – in the street, in the village, in the neighbourhood, in places where ordinary folk gather to talk – a voice not necessarily heard in official discourse, or in the media, often part of the machinery of the parties in power.[53]

In this situation the question posed by the gospel is whether the Church will help write the history of the real liberation of the oppressed.[54]

Inculturation: The Asian Experience

The situation in Asia is very different from that of Africa, though it is far from homogenous. There are very poor countries, like Bangladesh, but there are also the 'Asian Tigers'. The Indian economy is booming and China is undoubtedly the economic giant of the future. In terms of culture, the nineteenth century missionaries encountered philosophical systems as old as those of Greece if not older. Despite this, there are many important similarities between the African and Asian experiences, as we shall see.

---

52 Éla, *African Cry* p.125
53 Jean-Marc Éla, 'Christianity and Liberation in Africa' in Gibellini(ed) *Paths of African Theology* p.139
54 Éla, *African Cry* p.139

Aloysius Pieris is quite clear that Asia will never be 'Christian' in the sense that Europe was 'Christian'. The reason for this is bound up with his account of the relation of cosmic and metacosmic religions. Cosmic religions represent the basic psychological posture of each of us towards the mysteries of life – the basic forces, heat, fire, winds and cyclones, earth and its quakes, oceans, rains and floods. Recalling the discussion of syncretism, the religion of Canaan was obviously 'cosmic'. Metacosmic religions, on the other hand, postulate the existence of a transcendent Reality which makes salvation available either through redeeming love or redeeming knowledge. Pieris sketches what he calls a 'helicopter landing pad' theory of the relation of these two. Metacosmic religions need to be rooted in a cosmic religion. Once a metacosmic religion has taken root, history shows that one metacosmic religion cannot be dislodged by another one except by force.

The example of Korea provides a partial exception to this argument. The arrival of American missionaries at the end of the nineteenth century, followed speedily by a vernacular translation, led to a rapid growth of the Korean Church based around the promise of liberation – a striking confirmation of some of Sanneh's theses about translation.[55] There the Church has developed a 'Minjung theology' or theology of the oppressed people.[56] In Korea the biblical language, especially the language of the book of Exodus, the book of Revelation, and the gospels – became the historical language of the Korean Christian fellowship. The Japanese government were so worried by the effects of this that they even banned the book of Exodus! Christian involvement in the struggle for freedom, and later in protests against President Park, forged an identity with the suffering of the people as a whole. Whilst the Minjung theologians appreciated positive elements in Shamanism and Buddhism they found that, in contrast to the meta psychology of Confucianism and the Confucian form of self-cultivation (which had been the religion of the upper class), a form of transformation which dealt with the basic structure of the human person was potentially revolutionary. The incursion of a prophetic religion conscientized people to dehumanizing aspects of their situation and awakened their passion for justice.

With this partial exception, Pieris must be right that Christianity can expect always to be a minority religion in Asia. What, then, is the force of the discussion about inculturation? Pieris offers a highly original and extremely challenging thesis: instead of the Church baptizing Asia, it has, in the first place, to be 'baptised in the Jordan of Asian religiousness' and to pass through passion and death on the cross of Asian poverty. He is profoundly hostile to much of what passes as inculturation – the use of Hindu rites in worship, for

---

55   Pieris notes that monks in Korea were oppressive. He argues that we can draw this conclusion: 'the Bible, when made accessible to the oppressed in Asia, easily becomes the seed of an authentically Asian Christianity, as it allows the best of Asia's (non-Christian) liberative traditions to be absorbed into the church's conscience'. A.Pieris, 'Does Christ Have a Place in Asia? A Panoramic View' in L.Boff and V.Elizondo(eds) *Any Room for Christ in Asia?* London: SCM 1993 pp.33–48

56   Kim Yong Bock(ed), *Minjung Theology* Maryknoll: Orbis 1983

example, or of Hindu or Buddhist categories in theology.[57] In his view this is a form of theological vandalism, implies an irreverent disregard for the soteriological matrix of non-Christian religious symbolism, and lends itself to the charge of being a disguised form of imperialism.[58] It uses the language of baptism, as we speak of Boniface 'baptizing' the north German festival we now celebrate as Christmas, but, says Pieris, in Scripture baptism expressed the most self-effacing act of Christ. 'Now it comes to mean Christian triumphalism which turns everything it touches to its own advantage.'

This kind of inculturation is attempted by Churches which are in, but not of, Asia, esoteric communities ranting in the occult language of colonial founders, understood only by the initiated. True inculturation, on the other hand, consists in forming Churches of Asia, 'theological communities of Christians and non-Christians who form basic human communes with the poor ... It is they who will interpret sacred texts in the light of their religious aspiration for freedom.'[59] The first meaningful Christological formula would be, not theologies based on Advaita, but such an authentically Asian Church. 'Inculturation is the ecclesiological revolution already initiated by basic human communities, with Christian and non-Christian membership, wherein mysticism and militancy meet and merge – mysticism based on voluntary poverty and militancy pitched against forced poverty.'[60] The vast majority of God's poor (in India something like 98 per cent) perceive their ultimate concern and symbolize their struggle for liberation in the idiom of non-Christian religions and cultures. In this situation a theology that does not speak to or through this non-Christian peoplehood is 'an esoteric luxury of a Christian minority'.[61]

Despite the phenomenon of the 'Asian Tigers', Pieris still regards poverty as a major problem in Asia. It is, however, not only a problem but also a resource. Asian religion profoundly understood the freedom that comes from poverty. As we see with crystal clarity in the West, the 'freedom from poverty' delivered by capitalism can be an enslaving pursuit ending up in hedonism if not

---

57   Commenting on Dalit theology, he notes that Christologies which drew on the categories of Brahmanical Hinduism were, of course, profoundly alienating. Casteism is, unfortunately, experienced within the Church as well. Therefore, 'Since it is not only in civil society but also in Christian communities that the Dalit Christ is refused a place, the struggle is both against the Euro ecclesiastical Christ of the official church and against the Hindu Christ of the Ashramites, both of whom fear the consequences of abdicating their place in favour of the Broken Christ. So the Indian Christ has a broken body. Since Dalitness is the constitutive dimension of their theology, the broken Christ whom they can identify themselves with, follow behind and minister to is for the most part non Christian!' Pieris, 'Does Christ Have a Place in Asia?', p.38
58   Pieris, *Asian Theology* p.53. Cf this, however, with Aylward Shorter's contention that acculturation is not cultural alienation and that the borrowing of images and conceptions from other cultures is necessary when it is a question of expressing new and unfamiliar experiences and meanings. *Inculturation* p.57 Pieris himself seems to suspend the rule in commenting on paintings of Christ by a Buddhist monk which depict Christ in Buddhist poses. *Fire and Water* p.133
59   Pieris, *Asian Theology* p.125
60   Pieris, *Asian Theology* p.57
61   Pieris, *Asian Theology* p.87 C.S.Song argues that missiology needs to be dropped from the theological syllabus because it fails to respect the experience of the majority of the world's people. *Theology from the Womb of Asia* London: SCM 1988 p.126

tempered by freedom from Mammon. One source of the Church's failure in Asia was its association with Mammon and its refusal to enter into the monastic spirit of non-Christian soteriologies. To evangelize Asia is 'to evoke in the poor the liberative dimension of Asian religiousness, Christian and non-Christian'. This is a task of evangelization because the unevangelized poor tend to reduce religion to an opiate, to struggle without hope. How to do this? 'The first and last word about the church's mission to the poor of Asia is total identification with monks and peasants who have conserved for us in their religious socialism, the seeds of liberation that religion and poverty have combined to produce.'[62]

Pieris recognizes that the Church has a twofold ministry, roughly corresponding to the division between salvation and service. On the one hand there is a healing ministry, represented by Mother Teresa's Missionaries of Charity, and on the other a prophetic ministry, represented by the basic human communities. The separation of these two ministries is an obstacle to the coming of God's Reign. Both are necessary:

> The healing ministry can only serve to perpetuate the sinful order if the Asian Christ is not prophetically announced in word and deed as God's judgement over the nations ... But the prophetic activity of basic human communities can lead to ideological grooves through despair, unless healing miracles illuminate their word of liberation with a spark of hope, i.e. with glimpses into eschatological wholeness.[63]

Asian theology, says Pieris, in a brilliantly suggestive phrase, is 'a christic apocalypse of the non-Christian struggle for liberation'. Baptism is not a convenient mechanism to expand the Church but consists of 'making disciples of nations' along the *via crucis* of greedless sharing so that the life of each nation will be radically reordered in terms of the demands made by the Asian Christ.[64]

Pieris' positive appreciation of the great Asian religions is not without its problems, as the Dalit issue shows. In Chapter 2 I argued that he does not pay sufficient attention to the dehumanizing aspect of religion. It could also be argued that he understates the difference between the Christian vision of reality and that of the Asian religions. Kosuke Koyama, a Japanese Christian who worked as a missionary in Thailand, found that the gospel of the passionate God had something new to offer in the framework of a belief in Buddhist detachment. 'Where the gospel of Christ is encircled by the spirit of tranquillity of soul, the openly contradictory force of God's perturbation of soul, the wrath of God, is needed in order to break through the front line of the anti-historical theological construction.'[65] He describes Christianity as 'a noisy religion'

---

62   Pieris, *Asian Theology* p.45 C.H.Kyung agrees. *Struggle* p.110
63   Pieris, 'Does Christ Have a Place in Asia?' p.45
64   We can compare this with John Taylor's view that Christian mission consists in accompanying Christ as he stands in the midst of Islam, of Hinduism, of the primal world view, and watch with him 'as he becomes – dare we say it? – Muslim, or Hindu or Animist, as once he became a Man and a Jew'. Taylor, *Primal Vision* p.113
65   Koyama, *Waterbuffalo Theology* p.102

because it lives in believing in God's decisive and irreversible attachment to human beings in Christ.[66]

Pieris' account of the gospel's unique contribution is that there is one axiom in Scripture which is totally absent in all non-Semitic religions – that God has made a defence pact – a covenant – with the poor against the agents of Mammon, so that the struggle of the poor for their liberation coincides with God's own salvific action. 'No liberation theology can claim to be rooted in the word of God if it does not hold together the two biblical axioms of the irreconcilable antagonism between God and mammon and the irrevocable covenant between God and the poor.'[67] Elsewhere he glosses this in arguing that the incarnation is the scandalous agreement (covenant) between God and slaves, embodied in Jesus who sided with the non-persons as a sign and proof of his divine nature. 'This is unique to Christianity in that it proclaims a God who lives and dies a slave on a cross reserved for the humiliores that create social conflicts.'[68]

Pieris, as we see, uses the language of liberation, but he warns that Christian use of this term can also be a form of Christian megalomania. The Church cannot claim to offer 'liberation' to Asia without first being liberated by Asia. Before it can be truly liberative it itself must be liberated of its Latinity.[69] This need raises once again the question of whether there is any such thing as a universal gospel, and if so, what it might look like.

A Gospel to Proclaim?

The five missionary movements I identified in the previous chapter all believe they have a gospel to proclaim. Today, now that the socialist gospel has few leading champions, the two most confident (and opposed) gospels are those of the market and of Islam. Christianity's loss of confidence has much to do with the guilt complex identified by Sanneh. Some will follow Sugirtharajah in arguing, with postcolonialist writers, that the idea of liberation and its praxis must come from the collective unconscious of the people.[70] Postcolonialism, he believes, is sceptical about the monopolistic and prescriptive nature of Christianity, and wants to say that no one scripture conveys the full divine human experience.[71] But of course this critique does not begin with postcolonialism, but has been a staple of theological liberalism for nearly

---

66 Koyama, *Waterbuffalo Theology* p.226
67 Pieris, *Asian Theology* p.120
68 Pieris, *Fire and Water* p.134
69 Pieris, *Asian Theology* p.50
70 Sugirtharajah, *Bible* p.262
71 Sugirtharajah, *Bible* pp.265, 282 Gayatri Chakravorty Spivak in turn critiques postcolonialism. She proposes what is in effect a form of intellectual ascesis, permanently on guard against self-deception, wary of all pretension, especially pretensions to having the answer, or having a gospel. There is a sort of gospel of humility here, of the necessary modesty of human reason, which is deeply attractive. Is it all we have, however? *A Critique of Postcolonial Reason* Cambridge(Mass): Harvard University Press 1999

two centuries.[72] In the light of the violence attached to the proclamation of the gospel which I highlighted in the previous chapter, is there something which can credibly be regarded as 'gospel' which is not falsely totalizing, and which might, as Lesslie Newbigin believed, be true for all people and for all times? In the discussion of inculturation I have identified some things which Africans or Asians have regarded as constituting such a gospel. I now want to pursue this question more systematically. If we could not identify a coherent cross cultural gospel then the claim that Christianity stood at the heart of the long revolution of humanization would fall to the ground. What, then, is this gospel?

In his work with the Masai Vincent Donovan rejected the approach through mission hospitals, schools and aid and wanted, instead, to go with 'the bare message of Christianity, untied to any outside influence'.[73] This 'bare message' perhaps resembles Lash's assertion that in the first instance it is the story which remains the same across the ages and in all cultures. But of course, all stories are interpreted, and all translation is interpretation. Part of the 'scandal of particularity' is that there is no escape from culture. If Christianity is true then revelation is inescapably attached to a semitic story, just as it is if Islam is true. This returns us at once to the question whether the particular can be universal, and if so how. However global denotation may appear to be, remark the Comaroffs, however universal its pretensions, 'connotation, meaning-as-lived, is always finally local. And culturally constituted.'[74]

Nevertheless, if there is a God, and if God has revealed Godself, then there must be a meaning which is not only universal, but in some sense transcendent to all human culture, and able to critique it. If it cannot do that, it is not clear that we have a revelation. The claim to revelation marks a limit to cultural relativism because ultimate truth relativizes all cultures, and because the destiny of all cultures is in God.[75] If God exists then the truth of God has to be capable of being conceived beyond and through all cultural systems if it is to amount to anything more than ethnocentrism.[76]

A 'gospel' promises or announces salvation, and we have seen that this includes fundamental aspects of justice between races, classes and between men and women, and also the fulfilment of fundamental human needs. It is the latter which capitalism claims to fulfil, and does in fact for some people. In Chapter 4, however, we saw John Tomlinson's concern that capitalism ultimately gave people nothing to live by, and this has been a persistent critique from the mid nineteenth century. Lesslie Newbigin, who had two missionary lives, one in India and one in Britain, sometimes describes the gospel as 'the clue to history' so that the Church is 'the hermeneutic of the world's continuing history'. It was an account of meaning and purpose which he ultimately had in mind. However, Christianity has conventionally talked about salvation from

72 Thinking of Schleiermacher's Fifth Speech, 1799.
73 Donovan, *Christianity* p.24
74 J. and J. Comaroff, *Revelation and Revolution* vol 2 p.115
75 Shorter, *Inculturation* pp.25, 27
76 Sanneh, *Encountering* p.133

sin, evil, suffering and death. What do these mean, and can the claim that we are 'saved' from them be applied universally?

In the first place we have to note that both 'sin' and 'evil' are signifiers which need concrete instantiation. 'Sin', as it is used in Scripture, refers to forms of behaviour which destroy or diminish life. It is an offence against God, to be sure, but not against some Freudian projection but against the God of life. A useful illustration of what is at stake here is the debate about the blasphemy laws which followed the furore over the *Satanic Verses*. At present, in England, the blasphemy laws, which are scarcely ever invoked, only serve to protect Christianity. Some Labour MPs, in the name of parity, called for them to be extended to all religions. What was at issue was a call for the murder of Salman Rushdie on the grounds that he had committed blasphemy.

In this regard we should be absolutely clear that God can be wounded by human beings, but God's honour, or, in the Christian tradition, God's glory, cannot be affected by what human beings do or say. The blasphemy laws actually relate to the wounded feelings of the faith community. The community's wounded feelings are projected on to God, and in the name of God punishment of the offender is called for. But, as Irenaeus put it in the second century, learning from the incarnation, 'the glory of God is a living human being'. It follows that to blaspheme God, to treat God with contempt, is to attack or kill such a living human being.

Far from extending the blasphemy laws, they should be taken off the statute books altogether, as an instance of community deification. To argue like this is not a matter of liberal carelessness about God's honour but follows from the logic of the incarnation. One can understand distaste and even hurt at blasphemy. As a Christian I wince every time someone uses the name of Christ as an expletive, possibly all that many people know it as. At the same time some reactions to blasphemy certainly exemplify that centre complex of which Koyama speaks, and which I discussed in Chapter 5. In that case, the fault is promptly turned back on to the believer. Communities which put their honour before human life are worshipping not God, but themselves.

Whatever we think of in terms of 'sin' we will find that it wounds the God of life by alienating, estranging and destroying God's creation, whether people or planet. Thus, the exclusion of the person who had broken taboo by the Masai, without possibility of forgiveness, was 'sin'. As the stories in the gospels illustrate, much which the religious call 'sin' is dwarfed by their own exclusionary and life-diminishing behaviour. One thinks, for example, of attitudes to various forms of sexuality. How does 'the gospel' help us in this regard? In what sense does it offer salvation? It functions exactly as Donovan said it did amongst the Masai: it calls us to the discipline of forgiveness, to learn it as a craft in which we are apprenticed for a lifetime. Only as such a practice, and not simply as an 'announcement', is it 'good news'. It becomes gospel and not law as it is practised together within a community of forgiveness which knows that moralism, as well as sin, can destroy us – another fundamental aspect of the gospel stories which Protestant Churches in particular have been astonishingly blind to.

In giving the example of the exclusion from community I have already tacitly moved from discussion of sin to evil, or, to use the language of Colossians and Ephesians, of the 'principalities and powers'. As Walter Wink has demonstrated so convincingly, this language refers to the structural sediment of human wrong choices, the way in which whole cultural systems and practices become systematically life denying. The forces we were examining in Chapter 7 – racism, class and patriarchy – are principalities and powers in this sense. We are born into them, they structure our choices for us, in such a way that it needs extraordinary courage to resist anti-semitism, or racism, or to break out of patriarchal ways of thinking. More difficult still, capitalism, which comes disguised as an angel of light, is also one of these principalities and, as Pieris insists, we need to resist it. But who can resist the allure of the commodity? In face of the principalities, how does the gospel help us? It helps us, Wink argues, by revealing the hollowness of their pretensions, by calling us, not simply to lives of individual righteousness, but to the construction of an alternative *culture*. Of the early Fathers it was Tertullian, for all his faults, who perhaps saw this most clearly, who saw the call of the gospels to a new world, in which military conflict and service to Caesar had no part. In Chapter 6 we looked at the way in which Scripture functioned to challenge hegemony. Just so, in relation to the principalities and powers, does it constitute gospel.

I have repeatedly referred to the incarnation as the heart of the gospel. Again we saw the significance of this in Chapter 7 but its positive significance as gospel can be illustrated by Sebastian Kappen's claim that with Jesus a new humanism entered into the mainstream of Indian history, a humanism that proclaimed the equality of all men and women irrespective of race, caste or colour.[77] Although the Christ of dogma has had very little impact on India, the Jesus of history has had an impact far beyond the confines of the Christian community. Whilst the West has developed a culture of craving for pleasure, profit and power, Kappen argued, India perfected a culture of fear, the fear of being defiled by things, events, gestures, persons. Of this culture of fear Jesus' message is the antithesis. He repudiated the distinction between the pure and the impure. His message is an antidote for the spirituality of self-castration propagated by the Brahminic tradition. This is not to say that Christianity has nothing to learn from Hinduism: it does. But, in the framework of the caste system, it also has this distinct gospel to contribute.

Then there is suffering. It is very striking, in reading Asian theology, how marked is the emphasis on God's sharing of human suffering, as revealed in Christ. Thirty years before Moltmann Kazoh Kitamori reflected on the pain of God, from the perspective of Hiroshima; Minjung theology reflects on the suffering and humiliation of the Korean people, through the cross; C.H.Kyung shows how poor Filipino women understand their lives in the light of the cross; and C.S.Song likewise understands the suffering of the poor of Asia in this

---

77   S.Kappen, *Jesus and Freedom* Maryknoll: Orbis 1977

way.[78] What does 'gospel' mean here? It means solidarity, *hesed* – the steadfast love, the sharing of creation's pain by the Creator. Solidarity, we have grown increasingly to realize, is not just sentiment. It is a tool kit for survival.

Finally, there is death. The gospel of the resurrection is not 'pie in the sky', even if Hannah More may have preached it that way. It is, as Moltmann has insisted, following Horkheimer, the promise that the torturer will not triumph over his victim. It is also the promise that our lives are not just 'sound and fury, signifying nothing', but have a place in God's eternal meaningfulness. The resurrection is the promise of meaning and purpose, as well as of reconciliation, for all people no matter how insignificant they may seem in the whole historical process.

Traditionally Christianity has not always used the language of liberation but, as Paul insisted, freedom is at the heart of the gospel (Gal 5.1). Pieris is right to insist that inasmuch as any movement claims to be liberative, it is only the poor who decide who is competent to liberate them. 'Neither textual proofs ... nor the appeal to tradition ... are adequate today. Authority is the spontaneous manifestation of a church's competence to mediate total liberation for the peoples of Asia.'[79] 'Total liberation', I am arguing, is *shalom*, release from injustice, oppression and poverty, but also, and only through, release from inner compulsions, patterns of violence, patterns of domination, and ultimately death. Whether the promises contained in the gospel are genuinely promises, or whether they are delusory, is only known 'in the proof of spirit and of power', which is to say, on the historical record of what changes the gospel actually brings about. In that respect, the case is still before the court of history.

As we have seen in the past two chapters there is an energetic debate about whether the Church 'furthers humanity' or not, and those who deny that it does have a strong case. Equally I have tried to argue that the weight of evidence is in the other direction and that precisely in view of the incarnation, and the methods it lays upon us, the claim that the Christian gospel lies at the heart of the long revolution can be cogently argued. In the following chapter I argue this in a somewhat different context, that of the 'clash of civilizations'.

---

78 E.g. Kazoh Kitamori, *Theology of the Pain of God* London: SCM 1966 (orig 1946) – reflecting on Hiroshima; Song, *Theology from the Womb of Asia* pp.76, 187; Kyung, *Struggle* p.56, speaking of Filipino women.
79 Pieris, *Asian Theology* p.37

Chapter 10

Universal Humanity and the Clash of Civilizations

The Church, I argued in Chapter 7, is committed to a doctrine of human equality on account of its universal gospel, a gospel which privileges all people without distinction. Universal claims in ethics have been disparaged by postmodernists, in the name of the collapse of grand narratives, and postcolonialists, in the name of resisting Western cultural imperialism. Examples of the oppression of minorities, or the devaluation of cultures, in the name of specious universals are easy to find and the objections therefore have cogency. They are similarly disparaged, however, by every variety of religious fundamentalism, which all have their own hotline to God and therefore their own unique account of the categorical imperative. Implicitly they are also denied by the latest attempt to divide humankind up and argue for paths of 'separate development' in the by now notorious thesis of the North American political analyst and foreign affairs advisor, Samuel Huntington, about the 'clash of civilizations'.

After outlining his case I am going to follow the unfashionable course of arguing for a universal ethic. In such an attempt, Barrington Moore remarked, there is a great risk of being either wrong or banal or both.[1] The risk is worth taking, however, given the stakes in the contemporary world. The prioritization of difference, sometimes elaborated on the best possible grounds, allows people to get away with murder, as we saw throughout the twentieth century. We cannot be silent in the face of any form of cultural apartheid. In making a case for universality I appeal partly to arguments which might be considered part of natural theology – sociological or anthropological versions of older arguments from the structure of creation. Such arguments can, of course, be turned on their head, as in the case of Social Darwinism, but cumulatively they seem to me to be strong. From here I turn to a theological defence of the language of rights, appealing to the implications of the incarnation. After briefly considering the way in which cultures can be compared and evaluated I conclude with some reflections on grace, ethics and freedom in the light of the accusation that Christianity is the pre-eminent form of moral monism.

The 'clash of civilizations' is essentially a crusading version, or perhaps a 'pull up the drawbridge' version, of the idea of the long revolution. It denies the possibility of genuine catholicity. A genuinely ecumenical theology of culture must therefore address it, and I begin this task here.

---

1   Moore, *Injustice* p.5

The 'Clash of Civilizations'

Following the collapse of the Soviet Union Huntington argued that ideology had ceased to be the primary marker of conflict. Accepting the description of the Gulf War by a Moroccan scholar as 'the first civilizational war' he argued that with the economic advance of Asian societies, and the demographic advance of Muslim societies, a civilization based order is emerging.[2] Human history has thrown up seven major civilizations – Sinic, Japanese, Hindu, Islamic, Orthodox, Western, and Latin American – and we can expect these to be the leading foci of conflict. Analysing conflicts around the world, Huntington argues that we can see that most conflicts happen around civilizational fault lines, especially between Muslim and non-Muslim countries, and solidarity can be expected primarily from 'civilizational kin'. The West will rally to the West, Muslims will help Muslims, and Confucian countries will rally to Confucian countries. Countries which share major civilizations are 'cleft countries' and many are involved in conflict.[3]

Civilizations, in Huntington's view, are the ultimate human tribes, and the clash of civilizations is tribal conflict on a global scale. At present the dominant division is between 'the West and the rest'. Dangerous clashes of the future are likely to arise from the interaction of Western arrogance, Islamic intolerance and Sinic assertiveness.[4] The Gulf War showed the futility of taking on the United States without nuclear capacity. Since, with the exception of China, other countries cannot mobilize similar conventional forces, the way to mount a challenge to the West is to acquire weapons of mass destruction. Terrorism and nuclear weapons are the weapons of the non-Western weak.

For some time now, Huntington argues, the West (Europe and the United States) has lost its dominance and, on most models of the growth and decline of civilizations, can be expected to decline. The survival of the West depends on Americans reaffirming their Western identity and Westerners accepting their civilization as unique rather than universal and uniting to renew and preserve it against challenges from non-Western societies. Although it is China which will be the next great power, at present it is Islam which generates most conflicts. Islam and Christianity have each been the other's Other since the first Muslim conquests, and memories of the last siege of Vienna in 1683 still haunt Europe. On the other side, the Dean of the Islamic College in Mecca, Safar al-Hawali, wrote during the Gulf War, 'Those Ba'athists of Iraq are our enemies for a few hours, but Rome is our enemy until doomsday.'[5] Nineteen of twenty-eight fault line conflicts in the mid 1990s between Muslim and non-Muslim were between Muslim and Christians. Muslims resent Western power and see Western

---

2   First in an article in 1993, and then in a book *The Clash of Civilizations and the Remaking of World Order* New York: Touchstone 1996

3   Examples are Cyprus, Sudan, Nigeria, Tanzania, Kenya, Ethiopia/Eritrea, Sri Lanka, Malaysia and Singapore, China, the Philippines, and Indonesia. In his view, immigration could lead both Europe and the United States to become cleft countries.

4   Huntington, *Clash* p.183

5   Huntington, *Clash* p.250

culture as materialistic, corrupt, decadent and immoral. 'They also see it as seductive, and hence stress all the more the need to resist its impact on their way of life ... In Muslim eyes Western secularism, irreligiosity, and hence immorality are worse evils than the Western Christianity that produced them.'[6] It is not, as the Press suggest, fundamentalism which is the problem but Islam, 'a different civilization whose people are convinced of the superiority of their culture and are obsessed with the inferiority of their power'.[7] Influential from the moment it appeared, Huntington's analysis took on the character of prophecy after the September 11 attacks.

Whatever one thinks of this analysis one can see how accurate a guide it is to contemporary United States' foreign policy, in all but one respect. Huntington's solution to the problem he outlines is, first, that the West must maintain technological and military superiority over other civilizations but equally that Western intervention in the affairs of other civilizations is the single most dangerous source of instability and potential global conflict in a multicivilizational world. The West, therefore, must not intervene. He calls this the abstention rule. This is the part of his analysis which has not been followed. Avoidance of a global war of civilizations depends on world leaders accepting and co-operating to maintain the multicivilizational character of global politics. Civilizations must renounce universalism, accept diversity and seek commonalities.[8] He also believes that the various post Second World War institutions, largely designed by Europe, the United States and Russia, who are civilizational kin, will have to be reshaped to accommodate the interests of other civilizations.

Religion plays a key part in Huntington's analysis. The crucial distinctions amongst groups, he argues, are their values, beliefs, institutions and social structures, and it is religions above all which are generators of value. Most of the great civilizations are grouped around one or other great religion. The tide of modernity which Marx and Engels saw sweeping superstition aside has in fact led to a regeneration of religion around the world, in response to the failure of modernity. This is not a traditionalist peasant movement but urban and middle class, perfectly at home with technology. The religious revival is an urban phenomenon and appeals to people who are modern-oriented, well educated, and pursue careers in the professions, government and commerce. It is not just a Muslim phenomenon, but is true in India, in South Korea, in Russia and Latin America.[9] Hinduism, Islam, but also Christianity are once again major political facts.

How are we to evaluate this thesis? In the first place the omission of economics from the argument is deeply disingenuous. According to many analysts, as we saw in Chapter 4, the dominance of Western corporations, trade and media means that the whole world is being Westernized. We saw that there were strong arguments against that view but that in many areas the

6   Huntington, *Clash* p.213
7   Huntington, *Clash* p.217
8   Huntington, *Clash* p.318
9   Huntington, *Clash* p.101

evidence for homogenization is irresistible. Fundamentalisms are only partially to be understood as reactions to modernity. In some respects, in their positivism and their eager use of technology, for example, they are forms of it.[10] The idea of a 'clash of civilizations' therefore flies in the face of the impact of modernity on every world culture, aggressively exported by US based transnational corporations.

Edward Said believes the thesis is preposterous because all cultures are hybrid and heterogeneous, 'so interrelated and interdependent as to beggar any unitary or simply delineated description of their individuality'.[11] It is a typical piece of orientalism, and the question is whether one can divide human reality into clearly different cultures, histories, traditions and societies in this way and survive the consequences humanly. The notion of distinct cultures seems always to get involved either in self-congratulation or in hostility and aggression. Hans Küng agrees, pointing out that the civilizations overlap and interpenetrate, not least in the great cities of 'the West'.[12] One can apply to Huntington the words Said applies to another American analyst:

> No merely asserted generality is denied the dignity of truth; no theoretical list of Oriental attributes is without application to the behaviour of Orientals in the real world. On the one hand there are Westerners, and on the other hand there are Arab-Orientals; the former are ... rational, peaceful, liberal, logical, capable of holding real values, without natural suspicion; the latter are none of these things.[13]

This applies particularly to the description of 'Islam's bloody borders', invoked not thirty years after the end of the Vietnam war, and within living memory of the two most destructive conflicts in history, both originating in Europe. The rhetoric of 'weapons of mass destruction' belies the fact that the possessor of most of these is the United States, and that only the West has so far used them. Bloody borders indeed.

Even if we grant civilizational difference we can arrive at a very different view of the likely outcome. One analyst concludes, for example, that 'The partial mixing of cultures, the rise of lingua franca and of wider "Pan" nationalisms, though working sometimes in opposed directions, have created the possibilities of "families of culture" which portend wider regional patchwork culture areas.'[14] Not conflict, then, but co-operation. Alternatively one can point out, with Chomsky, that the United States has supported Muslim dictators whom it favours, and persecuted the Catholic Church in Latin America.[15]

---

10 Burbach et al comment that Huntington obscures the reality that it is the onslaught of capitalism which is provoking violent reactions all over the world. *Globalization* p.147
11 E.Said, *Orientalism* 2nd edn Harmondsworth: Penguin 1995 p.351
12 H.Küng, *A Global Ethic for Global Politics and Economics* London: SCM 1997 p.116
13 Said, *Orientalism* p.49
14 Anthony Smith argues that there are overlapping cultures based on Arabic, Swahili, English, French, Chinese, and in Europe there is a family of cultures which shares certain traditions. 'Towards a Global Culture?' p.188
15 N.Chomsky, *9–11* New York: Seven Stories 2001 p.78

The thesis is inherently essentialist, although in this the compliment is returned. Both Huntington and Sardar identify 'the West' with Christianity.[16] But, the theologian at once responds, Christianity is no monolith, but, rather, an ongoing debate in which complete consensus is unlikely to be found. We can remind ourselves, for example, that there were Christians, like Billy Graham, who thought the 'crusade against communism' was of God, and those, like Daniel Berrigan, who thought it was of the devil. Arguments about insiders and outsiders are amongst the earliest disputes in the community (Galatians), alongside arguments about power and hierarchy (Mark 10). Christianity lived with monarchy – in fact what today we would call tyranny – far longer than it has lived with democracy. Karl Barth thought that Christianity had a 'nisus' towards democracy but he, and virtually every other major theologian, has insisted that it is identified with no one form of government. As we saw in the last chapter, there is a respectable argument to the effect that Christianity gave rise to concern for the individual, but in every manifestation except perhaps American Protestantism it has always insisted on the priority of the community. As for private property, this is something the Church has always had, and continues to have, the severest reservations about. Of course Christianity has shaped the history of the West, but often in oppositional ways, and the two cannot be identified.

Huntington eschews such nuances. He defines 'the West' not by modernity but by Christianity, language, separation of Church and state, centrality of the rule of law, social pluralism, representative bodies, and individualism. The United States is culturally defined by 'the heritage of Western civilization' and politically by the principles of the American creed on which Americans overwhelmingly agree: liberty, democracy, individualism, equality before the law, constitutionalism, and private property. Since he sees the United States as the champion of 'the West' these factors also come to be defining characteristics of that entity. But some of these things, like democracy, are exceptionally late on the scene – it is not yet a century since women acquired the vote, and scarcely a century since this was extended to all men. The separation of Church and state had to be struggled for over a thousand years and is not everywhere complete, for example in Britain. The rule of law is also central to Islam, though it is a different law in view. In general Huntington's definition of the West owes a great deal to Locke. But Marx and Lenin are also products of 'the West', Bernard of Clairvaux, Francis, Luther and Karl Barth as well as Voltaire, Rousseau, Darwin and Nietzsche. In general, Huntington simply overlooks the extent of dissent to the capitalist vision he represents both in North America and in Europe.

The same anti-essentialist point may be made about all the other civilizations, and of course it ignores the point that there are many conflicts which are intra civilizational and which are basically struggles for autonomy, around language or smaller cultural units. This was the view Hedley Bull took

---

16 It is surely clear that if there is, as Said has convincingly demonstrated, an 'Orientalism', there is also an 'Occidentalism' of which we do not yet have an extensive account in Western languages.

in his thesis that the most likely future for the world was increased balkanization – smaller states grouped in larger federations.[17] These might of course be civilizational, but it suggests that local cultures come first. As Benedict Anderson puts it, an analysis of our contemporary world might also suggest that 'the end of the era of nationalism is not remotely in sight'.[18] If Huntington's thesis is an argument premised on cultural apartheid, what are the arguments which, allowing for cultural difference, nevertheless affirm human unity?[19] I consider four before concluding with some reflections on the issue of intercultural evaluation.

Hath not a Jew eyes?

The claim to a shared humanity is famously expressed by Shylock in his retort to Salerio in *The Merchant of Venice*:

> I am a Jew. Hath not a Jew eyes? Hath not a Jew hands, organs, dimensions, senses, affections, passions, fed with the same food, hurt with the same weapons, subject to the same diseases, healed by the same means, warmed and cooled by the same winter and summer, as a Christian is? If you prick us, do we not bleed? If you tickle us, do we not laugh? If you poison us, do we not die? And if you wrong us, shall we not revenge?
> (Act 3 sc.1)

In the last question Shakespeare moves from biological commonalities to cultural construction. We are all social constructionists now, and scepticism concerning the grounds for universal judgements is widespread, but, as Shakespeare indicates, there is also a strong, and widely spread, case for accepting them based on the physical and psychological makeup all human beings share.[20] Melford Spiro, for example, argues that the helplessness of the human infant means that children are everywhere raised in family or family-like groups:

> As a result children everywhere have the following characteristics: the need to receive love from, and the motivation to express love for, the loving and loved objects; feelings of rivalry toward those who seek love from the same (scarce) love objects; hostility toward those who would deprive them of these objects, and so on. In short, everywhere (due to Oedipal struggles and conflicts with siblings) children's love is necessarily thwarted, as well as gratified, to some extent.

17   H.Bull, *The Anarchical Society* Basingstoke: Macmillan 1947
18   Anderson, *Imagined Communities* p.3
19   Thomas Meyer describes it as 'cultural racism'. *Identity* p.8
20   Amongst the sceptics Latouche believes that the idea of the universality of transhistorical and ontological values is an illusion. 'Our dislike of other people's barbarous customs is not founded on a respect for truly universal values, but for our own Western reasons – that is all.' Latouche, *Westernization* p.125 Tomlinson argues that different cultural perspectives are a simple given, and 'we possess neither any superordinate moral criteria which would allow us to hierarchize such interests, nor any effective political–institutional mechanisms that could institute such a hierarchy in practical policies'. *Globalization* p.193

Life in social groups is another biological requirement and the demand that children learn to behave in compliance with cultural norms, means that everywhere their needs, desires and wishes are necessarily frustrated, as well as gratified to some extent.[21] It follows from the fact that all cultures must cope with common biological features that human beings have a nature as well as a history. 'The adaptively viable means for coping with the latter condition exhibit common social and cultural features across a narrow range of social and cultural variability; these common biological, social and cultural features are a set of constants which, in their interaction, produce a universal human nature.'[22]

A wide range of sociologists and philosophers concur with this basic standpoint. In his study of reactions to injustice Barrington Moore wants to talk of 'innate human nature' in terms of physical and psychic needs. 'To the extent that such a conception is valid it implies the existence of a "natural morality" in the sense that some moral preferences, particularly negative ones, are not merely the consequence of social training and conditioning.' Moral codes, moral anger, and hence the sense of social injustice have, he argues, some, though not all, important roots in human biology.[23] Bhikhu Parekh argues, similarly, that the term 'human nature' refers to those permanent and universal capacities, desires and dispositions that all human beings share by virtue of belonging to a common species. Human beings have a common physical and mental structure, possess identical sense organs, share a common mental structure and possess capacities such as rationality, ability to form concepts and to learn language and they all share the capacity to will, judge, fantasize, dream, build theories, construct myths, feel nostalgic about the past, anticipate future events, make plans and so forth.[24] These facts constitute grounds for talking of a universal human nature. Martha Nussbaum agrees, arguing on the basis of the existential dilemmas all humans have to face. All humans have to negotiate death, they have to regulate bodily appetites and make judgements in the areas of food, drink and sex, and they have to take a stand about property and the distribution of scarce resources and planning their own lives.[25] These shared dilemmas enable us to talk of shared humanity.

A very different claim to universal human experience is based on the peasant cultures most of humankind shared until less than a century ago. Richard Critchfield argues that peasant cultures 'share something of a universal culture', though he acknowledges they differ on religion. As a journalist who spent years in villages in Poland, Egypt, India and China he noted that 'much of the "foreignness" of a society dropped away once you entered a village'. This sprang, he suggested, from the fact that all peasants face common tasks.[26]

---

21 M.Spiro, *Culture and human nature; theoretical papers of Melford S. Spiro* ed B.Kilbane and L.Langness Chicago: Chicago University Press 1987 p.25
22 Spiro, *Culture* p.27
23 Moore, *Injustice* p.7
24 B.Parekh, *Rethinking Multiculturalism* Basingstoke: Palgrave 2000 p.116
25 M.Nussbaum, *Cultivating Humanity* Cambridge(Mass): Harvard University Press 1997 p.138
26 R.Critchfield, *The Villagers* New York: Doubleday 1994 pp.7, 19

The anthropologist Robert Redfield compared the peasant societies of the Mayan Indians of Yucatan, nineteenth century Britain and Hesiod's Greece. He wrote:

> If a peasant from any one of these three widely separated communities could have been transported by some convenient genie to any one of the others and equipped with a knowledge of the language in the village to which he had been moved, he would very quickly come to feel at home. And this would be because the fundamental orientations of life would be unchanged.[27]

Rather similarly Moore argues that if a given type of social relationship or human behaviour arouses moral outrage in the very different civilizations of Europe, Asia and a scattering of non-literate societies, 'we are probably on the track of some pan-human or universal characteristic'.[28]

These facts may, then, be the basis of the remarkable level of agreement in terms of culture as creative achievement to which Terry Eagleton draws attention. There are, as he says, few cherished works of art which advocate torture and mutilation as a form of human flourishing, or celebrate rape and famine as precious forms of human experiences:

> This fact is so baldly obvious that we are tempted to pass over its curiousness. For why, from a culturalist or historicist standpoint, should this be so? Why this imposing consensus? If we really are nothing but our local, ephemeral cultural conditions, of which there have been countless millions in the history of the species, how come that artistic culture over the ages does not affirm almost as many different moral values? Why is it that, with some egregious exceptions and in countless different cultural modes, culture in this sense has not on the whole elevated rapacious egoism over loving kindness, or material acquisitiveness over generosity?[29]

The universality this attests grounds a universal ethic of compassion which we cannot disavow.[30]

It is true that traditional accounts of human nature did not allow enough space for cultural construction and that gender, sexuality, death, reason, emotion, value, conscience, and so forth are differently understood in different cultures.[31] We can be human in very different ways. At the same time, Shylock's point remains. Cultural *difference* is not the same as cultural *untranslatability* and it is not clear that, if it was, notions of the human *species*

---

27   R.Redfield, *Peasant Society and Culture* Chicago: University of Chicago Press 1956 p.62
28   Moore, *Injustice* p.14
29   Eagleton, *Idea* p.105
30   Cf Raymond Williams' argument that meanings and values, discovered in particular societies and by particular individuals, have proved to be universal in the sense that when they are learned, in any particular situation, they can contribute radically to the growth of man's powers to enrich his life, to regulate his society, and to control his environment. 'It seems reasonable to speak of this tradition as a general human culture, while adding that it can only become active within particular societies, being shaped, as it does so, by more local and temporary systems.' Williams, *Revolution* p.59
31   Parekh, *Multiculturalism* p.121

could have arisen. It seems to amount to positing a private language argument on a global scale.

The Women's Movement

I have noted a number of times that the women's movement is culturally the most important force for change in the contemporary world. A second ground for arguing for human universality is the cross cultural challenge of feminism. All major religions and all of Huntington's civilizations are structured by patriarchy. The interviews gathered by Miranda Davies from all over the Third World, and from most major civilizational areas, show that much that is claimed to be culturally specific is in fact patriarchy at work.[32]

C.H.Kyung records many protests by African and Asian Christian men, and some women, that feminism is a Western import, a form of cultural imperialism. In our societies, such men claimed, 'women know their place and play their role ungrudgingly'. Not so, objected Mercy Oduyoye, from Africa. 'The fact is that sexism is part of the intricate web of oppression in which most of us live, and that having attuned ourselves to it does not make it any less a fact of oppression.'[33] A Filipino peasant woman attending a Bible study group shared how her reading of Scripture had changed her marriage, based on her perception of the need for freedom and equal rights.[34] A Burmese woman makes the same discovery as Simone de Beauvoir, out of her experience of marriage. In Burmese culture the woman bows to the man twice a day, when he goes out to work and before going to bed. Today, says this speaker, women must be 'involved in the making of history'.[35] In sum, 'Asian women are determined to recover their full humanity and ripened "womanity". They are also renaming their own God who gives birth to their dignity and nourishes and empowers them in their life struggle.'[36]

Gita Sahgal cites the case of the Sikh woman Kiranjit Ahluwalia, who murdered her husband after ten years of abuse. She explained how the notion of *izzat*, honour, was used to control women and prevented them from complaining or exercising any independence. Sahgal comments: 'She was not a victim of fundamentalist control, merely of patriarchal oppression buttressed by popularly understood, codified religion. It was not the exercise of religion according to a text which she challenged, but custom and practice which

---

32 M.Davies(ed), *Third World, Second Sex* London: Zed 1983, 1987 She has interviews from Mexico, Peru, Guatemala, Nicaragua, Dominican Republic, Jamaica, Uruguay, Brazil, South Africa, Namibia, Kenya, Ethiopia, Nigeria, New Caledonia (South Pacific), New Guinea, Kurdistan, Iran, Pakistan, India, Sri Lanka, Vietnam, Thailand and the Philippines.
33 Kyung, *Struggle* p.17
34 Kyung, *Struggle* p.45
35 Kyung, *Struggle* p.88
36 Kyung, *Struggle* p.23

determine and sanction behaviour.'[37] Ahluwalia was supported by a women's collective which included Jews, Christians and Muslims.[38]

Marie Aimée Hélie-Lucas, a Muslim Algerian, appeals to an internationalist humanism against anti-Western chauvinism. When offers to take abandoned Algerian children in Sweden were refused on the grounds that it was better for them to die in Algeria than live in Sweden she responded:

> We will not support injustice and discrimination in the name of national identity. It is in our own interest that internationalism should prevail over nationalism, and that we should link our struggles from one country to another for reasons of ethics, as well as solidarity, in the hope that more such struggles will begin and receive national, regional and international support.[39]

Chetan Bhatt documents the reactionary nature of political movements in Pakistan, and their essentially patriarchal agenda.[40] In this context Pakistani feminists have protested. 'Today,' wrote one Muslim feminist:

> women in Pakistan are speaking out in the face of continued social, religious and political repression. Male dominated society resents any expression of the woman's self-realisation as an equal, and continues to disregard her contribution to economic development; religious fanatics obsessed by woman's sexuality would confine her to the four walls of the house or to the anonymity of a shroud.[41]

A Palestinian delegation at a women's conference in Nairobi insisted that feminist issues related to the wider political picture, and were not just about wife-beating or polygamy. The context in which such abuses occur, they said, the structural political violence or economic violence, is even more important than the abuses themselves, and until this framework is removed, the particular manifestations of women's oppression cannot be overcome. 'The attempt to impose a Western, non-political concept of "women's issues" is a kind of cultural imperialism … It aims at forcing Third World women to accept the status quo and acquiesce in their national subordination.'[42]

In Iran one feminist commented: 'all laws today are in favour of men and their dominance over women'.[43] A woman from Mali, campaigning against

---

37   Kiranjit said, in a taped message from prison: 'My culture is like my blood – coursing through every vein in my body. It is the culture into which I was born and where I grew up, which sees the woman as the honour of the house. In order to uphold this false "honour" and "glory" she is taught to endure many kinds of oppression and pain in silence. In addition, religion also teaches that her husband is her god and fulfilling his every desire is her religious duty. A woman who does not follow this path in our society has no respect or place in it.' Gita Sahgal, 'Secular Spaces: The Experience of Asian Women Organizing' in G.Sahgal and N.Yuval-Davis(eds) *Refusing Holy Orders* London: Virago 1992 p.188
38   Bhatt points out that in Britain only black and multiracial feminism has consistently opposed fundamentalism. *Liberation* p.265
39   Davies, *Third World* vol 2 p.15
40   Bhatt, *Liberation* p.115ff
41   Davies, *Third World* vol 2 p.19
42   Davies, *Third World* vol 2 p.59
43   Davies, *Third World* vol 2 p.193

female circumcision, was asked what she thought about Westerners getting
involved in the struggle. She replied:

> Life is complex. We have been colonised by this Western world and we have …
> something against them. That means we don't want them to overwhelm our lives any
> more. For my part, I want their help. I want to collaborate with them. But I don't
> think I can be in the same group with them to fight something in my own country,
> because I will feel, 'Here they go again, colonisation'.[44]

What is clear from the interviews is that whilst there is a deep resistance to neo-
colonialism, at the same time there is a wide agreement across all cultures that
patriarchy oppresses women. There is, in other words, an aspect of the human
condition, experienced as oppression and suffered by half the world's
population, which makes nonsense of Huntington's analysis, and which
articulates what is in effect a universal demand.

Globalization and the Global Ethic

A third argument for human universality seeks cross cultural agreement
between the world's religions and ethical systems. Hans Küng has attempted to
address the kind of issues raised by Huntington for some twenty years in his
proposals for a global ethic. He draws on the work of Michael Walzer arguing
that whilst all ethics are culturally situated, and in that sense need 'thick
description', there is also a 'thin ethic' which is common to all human cultures.
The various United Nations Declarations appeal to a shared human
understanding but in so far as law has no permanent existence without ethics,
so there will be no new world order without a world ethic. Resources for a
global ethic are to be found partly in the great cultural traditions.
Formulations of what is involved in it were drawn up at the Parliament of
Religions held in Assisi in 1993, and then in the 'Universal Declaration of
Human Responsibilities' drawn up by an international gathering of retired
statespersons in 1997 addressing concerns that the United Nations Declaration
was focused on rights to the exclusion of responsibilities.[45]
  The global ethic project differs from the Western human rights movement in
so far as it does not attempt simply to disseminate human rights deriving from
Western natural-law thinking but rather the values, criteria and attitudes of the
ethnic and religious traditions peculiar to each people in order to make fruitful
use of them. It also appeals to the idea of human vulnerability, and the
attendant ethical impulse to alleviate suffering where this is possible and to
provide security to each individual. The two basic principles for a global ethic
are that every human being should be treated humanely, and the golden rule.
These are augmented by what Küng calls four irrevocable directives: a culture

---

44 Davies, *Third World* vol 2 p.247
45 Küng also garners opinions from both political and religious leaders around the world in *Yes
To A Global Ethic* London: SCM 1995

of non-violence and respect for life; a culture of solidarity and just economic order; a culture of tolerance and a life of truthfulness; and a culture of equal rights and partnership between women and men.

Küng is seeking agreement across all cultures, and does not claim that religion is the only way in which agreement can be achieved. On the other hand, as a theologian, he does give it an important place and here he agrees with Huntington's analysis. The modern liberal social order has relied on 'habits of the heart', on pre-modern systems of meaning and obligation which are now beginning to look threadbare. Furthermore, in response to Huntington he argues that there can be no peace between civilizations without a peace between religions and no peace there without dialogue. The Parliament of Religions was clear that they did not mean by a global ethic a global ideology or a single unified religion beyond all existing religions, and certainly not the domination of one religion over all others. 'By a global ethic we mean a fundamental consensus on binding values, irrevocable standards and personal attitudes.'[46] The slogan should not be 'ethics instead of religion', which would be an Enlightenment form of moralism. There is a distinction between a purely human ethic on the one hand and what can ultimately be communicated only by religion, as something rooted in trust in God.[47] Religion has an ultimacy which philosophy alone lacks. For example, Küng doubts that the proposition that humankind has no right to suicide can be underpinned other than by religion.[48]

The growth of the global economy is one of the things which has stimulated the global ethic initiative. Global problems demand global solutions which can only be achieved through ideas, values and norms respected by all cultures and societies. Küng recognizes the tendency of 'the market' to drive law, politics and science. 'Culture deteriorates into being a contributor to the market and art declines into commerce. Ethics is sacrificed to power and profit and replaced by what brings success.'[49] We need, he says, the primacy of politics over the economy and of ethics over the economy and politics. Moral norms in economic life change, and have to change, but their aim remains the same, namely to 'preserve life'.

Huntington also argues that in a multicivilizational world the constructive course is to renounce universalism, accept diversity and seek commonalities.[50] Even on his account of the clash of civilizations he agrees that the major civilizations do share key values in common. People in all civilizations should search for and attempt to expand the values, institutions and practices they have in common with peoples of other civilizations.[51]

For Bhikhu Parekh the problem with universal moral values of this kind is that they are too thin and too few to cover all important areas of life. Similarly,

---

46   H.Küng and H.Schmidt, *A Global Ethic and Global Responsibilities* London: SCM 1997 p.13
47   Küng, *Global Ethic* p.142
48   Küng, *Global Ethic* p.249
49   Küng, *Global Ethic* p.212
50   Huntington, *Clash* p.318
51   Huntington, *Clash* p.320

the argument about core values is shaky because it is doubtful if any but the most traditional society has core values in this sense. S.Sayyid observes that the values and beliefs that arise from our common humanity tend to correspond also with boundaries of the Enlightenment project. 'This conflation of what is essentially western with what is essentially human is what excavates the heterogeneity from the globalization of McWorld.'[52]

On the other hand the German sociologist Thomas Meyer undertook research into core cross cultural values in response to Huntington's thesis. He surveyed IBM employees across sixty-five countries on attitudes to equality and inequality, individualism and collectivism, masculinity and femininity, uncertainty avoidance and long term/short term orientation. He examined Western Christian, Islamic, Confucian and Latin American groups of cultures. His result was that there are just as many congruent value profiles between countries of varying cultural affiliations as there are between countries of corresponding affiliations. Some countries whose basic-value profiles resemble each other the most belong to entirely different cultural groups, though the socio-economic level of development is comparable.[53]

His conclusion is that the thesis depicting the political polarization of whole civilizations has no basis in reality. Rather, it is within each culture and society that the most interesting and politically significant differences develop. If you can divide cultures between traditionalist, modernist and fundamentalist tendencies, then no cultures are necessarily fundamentalist. Under certain conditions every culture generates currents of fundamentalism alongside the modernizing and the traditionalist ones.[54] The term fundamentalist, in fact, which emerged in the United States in the first decade of the twentieth century amongst Christian groups suspicious of theological liberalism, applies to the refusal to respect cultural differences in a fair, peaceful and open minded way. It treats culture as a tool to gain power over others and this, as we have seen, is more characteristic of the modern West than of those cultures we usually deem fundamentalist. Far from a clash of civilizations what we are seeing is, in a variant of Clifford Geertz's image, the 'weaving of transcultural nets'.

Meyer argues that political conflicts supposedly culturally generated in fact stem from an exclusionary dynamic that marginalizes growing numbers of people. The conflict between Hutus and Tutsi, for example, emerged from a colonial history in which membership of the two groups was 'firmed up, instrumentalized and substantiated by a racialistically tinged ethnohistory'. Prior to that there had been no objective criteria for belonging to one of the groups.[55] The way to prevent such conflicts, it follows, is to seek economic structures which do not exclude or make people insecure.

---

52 Sayyid, 'Beyond Westphalia' p.45 As I have noted at several places, the question is what is 'essentially Western'. Aung San Suu Kyi, for example, makes a resolute demand for democracy as essential to any kind of social progress. Küng, *Yes To A Global Ethic* p.223ff As with patriarchy, objections to Western cultural imperialism can be a cover for some pretty repressive policies.
53 Meyer, *Identity* p.78
54 Meyer, *Identity* pp.85, 67
55 Meyer, *Identity* p.35

Human Rights

The proposal for a global ethic looks back to, and seeks to learn from, the 1948 Declaration of Human Rights. That was framed principally by Western Christian nations, but endorsed at the time by the distinguished Pakistani lawyer, Zafrulla Khan.[56] Within three years Egypt had challenged the freedom of religion clause, and dissatisfaction with the Declaration has grown. Non-Western societies want to prioritize values such as social harmony, respect for authority, orderly society, a united and extended family and a sense of filial piety.[57] Liberal society, it is argued, cannot nurture the spirit of community and social responsibility. The Declaration seems to presuppose liberal democracy, but many point out that not all freedoms are a good thing: some societies wish to ban pornography, protect religious beliefs and censure films that incite intercommunal hatred. Some argue that the discourse of rights is irretrievably individualist. Sardar, for example, thinks that the Declaration as it stands presupposes a view of human beings as 'simply packages of material and psychological needs, wrapped in an atomised microcosm', something with which 'non-western cultures' disagree.[58]

After Tianamen Square a Japanese Government spokesman said: we will not let 'abstract notions of human rights' affect our relations with China. Non-Western governments talk of 'human rights imperialism'. At the UN World Conference on human rights in Vienna in June 1993 Western countries were largely defeated.[59] Meeting in Bangkok prior to the conference the Asian countries emphasized that human rights must be considered 'in the context ... of national and regional particularities and various historical religious and cultural backgrounds', that human rights monitoring violated state sovereignty and that conditioning economic assistance on human rights performance was contrary to the right of development.[60] The Vienna declaration contained no explicit endorsement of the rights to freedom of speech, the press, assembly and religion and was thus in many respects weaker than the Universal Declaration of Human Rights adopted in 1948.

---

56 Frederick Nolde, who participated in the 1948 discussions, thinks that 'an international Christian influence played a determining part in achieving the more extensive provisions for human rights and fundamental freedoms which ultimately found their way into the Charter'. *Free and Equal* Geneva: World Council of Churches 1968 p.25 Zafrulla Khan of Pakistan endorsed the freedom of religion clause: 'Islam is a missionary religion. It claims the right and the freedom to persuade any man to change his faith and accept Islam. Surely and obviously, it must equally yield to other faiths the free right of conversion. There cannot be any doubt on that point ... We therefore have the greatest pleasure in declaring from the rostrum that we shall support this article as it stands, without any kind of limitation upon its operation whatsoever.' Ibid p.46
57 On the family, it should be noted that the Catholic Church prided itself on strengthening the clause on the family in the Declaration.
58 Sardar, *Postmodernism* p.69 This is a bizarre piece of polemic which overlooks the resolute opposition to individualism by most aspects of the Western tradition.
59 The issues on which the countries divided included universality vs cultural relativism with respect to human rights; relative priority of economic vs political and civil rights; and the creation of a UN commissioner for human rights.
60 Huntington, *Clash* p.196

There has been an extensive discussion within Islam about human rights, and in 1981 the Islamic Council of Europe issued the Universal Islamic Declaration of Human Rights. It follows the provisions of the United Nations Declaration but envisages the shariah becoming normative for all societies. The provision on religious freedom guarantees the rights of non-Muslims 'within the limits prescribed by the Law' (that is, shariah law) and the issues of apostasy and blasphemy are not openly confronted.[61] Chetan Bhatt cites a pamphlet circulated by Young Muslims UK objecting to Amnesty International's criticism of the use of flogging. This punishment was endorsed, they argue, by 'the Words of God in the Qu'ran and the blessed Prophet Muhammed'.[62] I have encountered similar arguments on the part of young Christians in response to the question whether God could really have commanded genocide, as seems to be the case in the story of the Amalekites in 1 Samuel 15. Time and again I have been told, 'God's ways are mysterious.' If they include genocide (or flogging or amputation for that matter) that is certainly true – though not so mysterious on a Feuerbachian understanding of God.[63]

Opposition to the discourse of rights is by no means limited to non-Westerners. Bentham famously dismissed it as 'nonsense on stilts'. Alasdair MacIntyre finds it on the same level as belief in witches or unicorns, on the grounds that no good reasons have ever been advanced for proving that there are such rights, and theologians attack them from several different directions.[64] Stanley Hauerwas thinks that rights are necessary when it is assumed that citizens fundamentally relate to one another as strangers, if not outright enemies. From such a perspective society appears as a collection of individuals who of necessity must enter into a bargain to insure their individual survival through providing for the survival of the society.[65] Rights language carries with

---

61 Katerina Dalacoura points out that other Muslim commentaries on human rights are still more problematical. Sultanhussein Tabandeh's Muslim Commentary on the Universal Declaration of Human Rights recognizes distinctions based on religion, faith and conviction and awards different punishments for Muslims and non-Muslims. Only Muslims can hold public office and apostasy is unacceptable. It accepts freedom in political but not in religious thought. The Koran states unequivocally that unbelievers or idolaters must be slain (2.190). The shariah, she points out, did not contemplate the permanent residence of non-Muslims within Islamic society and in theory they could feel secure there only when they were under temporary safe conduct. Being a non-Muslim in an Islamic state entails the status of a second-class citizen. Dalacoura comments that 'The frequent assertion by Muslims ... that their religion has best safeguarded human rights since its inception is similar to governmental declarations to the same effect.' *Islam, Liberalism and Human Rights* London: Tauris 1998 pp.53, 54
62 Bhatt, *Liberation* p.19 Bhatt points out that much Muslim critique of rights uses the idea of rights to do so, thus involving an internal contradiction and a tacit endorsement of the principles. Ibid p.20 The very same groups appeal to their 'rights' to have Muslim schools in the UK.
63 Moltmann insists that all religions have to subordinate their legal codes to the minimum demands of human rights and the rights of nature. 'To cling to the divergencies and contradictions between the religious groups would make them enemies of the human race.' *God for a Secular Society* p.133
64 MacIntyre, *After Virtue* p.69
65 S.Hauerwas, *Suffering Presence* Edinburgh: T & T Clark 1988 p.128

it the implication that anyone who does not respect them is morally obtuse and should be 'forced' to recognize the error of their ways. In this respect they contain a powerful justification for violence.[66] Slavov Žižek contrasts the enthusiasm for human rights with the Decalogue. The former, he argues, are ultimately rights to violate the latter. They represent the soggy postmodern ethic of self-realization, for which the Other is really my mirror image. The logic of the Decalogue, on the other hand, is the truly Christian logic which does not appeal to some abstract subject but confronts us with the demand to love the Other in all their inhumanity.[67] Aloysius Pieris grants their usefulness for Western liberal theologians but argues that Third World liberation theologians have a different logic, based on the foundational election of the oppressed class as God's equal partners in the common mission of creating a new order of love. The call for liberation theologians to use the language of rights he sees as a form of theological imperialism.[68]

Should we then abandon the language of rights as a way of building bridges across cultures or civilizations? Pieris acknowledges that there are several roots to rights discourse, one of which may have been from the underside of history, but in my view he does not do this sufficient justice. The language of the United Nations Declaration has, in fact, complex origins. There are ancient appeals to rights and duties expressed in Greek tragedy and the Stoics.[69] In seventeenth century Europe, and especially England, a quite different origin is in the demand for religious freedom. The language of rights entered the United States bloodstream precisely because Dissenters left Britain in the search for freedom to worship. These groups were usually artisan in origin. From this pressure came a more general language of rights which found expression in the emancipatory discourse of the eighteenth century, and especially in political radicals like Tom Paine. Some contemporary multiculturalist discourse, which demands respect for group autonomy, is very close to this older language.

The United Nations Declaration partly appeals to these ideas, but even more importantly it was formulated in reaction to the Holocaust and the other atrocities of the Second World War. When the Declaration starts 'All human beings are born free and equal in dignity and rights' this is not, as Pieris thinks, the abstract language of the philosophers, but the concrete language of those who have seen Belsen, and who sought ways to prevent such atrocities happening again.[70] As Moltmann puts it, starkly, 'There is only one alternative to the humanitarian ideas of human dignity and the universality of human

66 S.Hauerwas, *The Peaceable Kingdom* London: SCM 1984 p.61
67 S.Žižek, *The Fragile Absolute* London: Verso 2000 p.107ff
68 A.Pieris, 'Human Rights Language and Liberation Theology' in M.Ellis and O.Maduro(eds) *The Future of Liberation Theology* Maryknoll: Orbis 1989 pp.299–310
69 Sophocles' *Antigone* turns on the perception that there are human duties which transcend positive law. The Stoics generalized this perception, and argued that human beings are worthy of rights and duties as all possessing seeds of the Logos. You did not have to belong to a particular city state to qualify for fully human treatment.
70 The psychiatrist Walter Reich, reviewing a study of the executioners in Nazi concentration camps, wrote: 'What stands between civilization and genocide is the respect for the rights and lives of all human beings that societies must struggle to protect.' Cited in Critchfield, *Villagers* p.445

rights, and that alternative is barbarism.'[71] Žižek's challenge is correct in the need to go beyond human rights but not in its call to abandon this form of discourse. To insist that the discourse of human rights is inadequate is one thing; to say that we should dispense with it quite another.

It is true that, as rights language has developed, it has come to represent the idea of individual claim, the antagonistic use disliked by Hauerwas. One can object to rights that they promote egoism. 'Since a right involves a claim that a person makes for the support of his or her own interests,' writes Alan Gewirth:

> it evinces a preoccupation with fulfilment of one's own desires or needs regardless of broader social goals; hence it operates to submerge the values of community and to obscure or annul the responsibilities that one ought to have to other persons or to society at large. The insistence on one's rights may also, in certain circumstances, violate duties of generosity and charity, as when a landowner evicts a needy family in the depths of winter for non-payment of rent.[72]

The fact that a society may recognize rights but still allow people to exist in extreme want again explains suspicion of them.

I wish to argue nevertheless that rights are more than just 'the West's own indigenous way of communicating the gospel of justice to the rich and powerful'. Stuart Hall argues that the discourse of rights may have developed within the Western liberal tradition but has now become cosmopolitan and is 'as pertinent to Third World workers struggling at the periphery of the global system, women in the developing world up against patriarchal conceptions of a woman's role, or political dissenters subject to the threat of torture, as it is to western consumers in the weightless economy'.[73] The work of Amnesty International, which has found it necessary to put every civilization, and virtually every country, in the dock for the use of 'cruel and unusual punishments', which is to say, for torture, is essentially a continuation of the protest evoked by Belsen. The claim that it is a form of Western cultural imperialism seems to me special pleading on the grounds that, were that the case, it would endorse different standards for treatment of humans across cultures and hand Huntington the palm (torture is alright for Arabs but not for Westerners, for blacks but not for whites, for Jews but not for Aryans, and so on).[74] In the light of the Holocaust the Declaration wanted to assert that there are some things you simply cannot do to people just in view of their humanity. As Simone Weil put it, in an insight very close to Levinas, 'The object of any obligation in the realm of human affairs, is always the human being as such. There exists an obligation towards every human being for the sole reason that he or she is a human being, without any other condition requiring to be fulfilled.'[75]

---

71   Moltmann, *God for a Secular Society* p.17

72   A.Gewirth, 'Why Rights are Indispensable' *Mind* 95 (1986) pp.329–44 here p.332

73   S.Hall, 'The Multi-Cultural Question' in Hesse(ed) *Un/settled Multiculturalisms* p.233

74   Muslim feminists in Britain have appealed to universal rights, as Bhatt notes. *Liberation* p.264

75   Weil, *Roots* p.4 Weil herself objected to rights language, but as Michael Ignatieff has objected, 'The language of rights represents the extent of our agreement about human ends.' 'The Limits of Sainthood', *The New Republic* 18 June 1990 p.44

Pieris is right that there are specific theological justifications for this, which I shall come to in a moment, and the difficulties philosophers have with the idea perhaps indicates that this is an area where theological justification is needed, but it seems to me to go beyond what Pieris calls 'the spiritual nucleus of Western culture'. In liberation theology, he writes:

> the transcendental and universal principle of 'the dignity of the human person' fades away into the larger picture: God's election of the oppressed as God's co-creators of the kingdom and God's co-redeemers of the world; it is not an ontological status conferred by grace through creation and atonement, as in human rights theology, but an elevation of the oppressed, insofar as they are a class, to the status of God's covenantal partners engaged in God's project of liberation.[76]

But is it an either–or? Thinking of the hundreds of thousands of victims of the death squads in Latin America over the past forty years, not just the killed, but those who survived torture, is it not essential to insist that such treatment is unconscionable? Jean-Marc Éla asks why the West is silent about torture in Africa. He is right to ask. In the same way we have to ask about the rights of Palestinians, of Dalits, of Tibetans, of Kurds. This is not *in place* of the struggle for liberation but is part of Freire's understanding that liberation only comes when the oppressed do not mimic the oppressor. There are no persons about whom I need not give a damn. The foundation of human rights is the inalienable dignity of the human person.[77]

The theological justification for the language of rights has nothing to do with individualism as such. It has everything to do with the acceptance of a fundamental human dignity in the name of which we protest the treatment of some groups, or individuals, as effectively subhuman. In the light, not just of creation and atonement, but, for Paul, of incarnation, all humans are 'no longer slaves but sons and heirs' (Gal 4.7). To the extent that the language of liberation is a proper way of construing the witness of Scripture, and I believe that it is, then 'rights' are implicit in the election of the oppressed as well. *Why* has God elected them? Because God hates injustice, seeks liberation and loves the oppressed. Kieran Cronin argues that rights are required by humans because they are weak, and that the disturbing presence of God can be found through the claims of the weak.[78] Donal Murray roots the discourse of rights in the doctrine of the Trinity. 'I respect another person,' he writes, 'not just because he or she is like me. I respect every other person because Jesus Christ, the Son of God, has united himself to that person to set him or her free (Gal 5.1); the Spirit, whose presence gives freedom (2 Cor 3.17) is within them; the Father, the source and goal of freedom, has loved them first.' The freedom which we respect is not only an 'exceptional sign of the image of God in the human being', it is a sign of God's presence; its deepest meaning lies in God's

---

76   Pieris, 'Human Rights' p.308
77   Moltmann, *God for a Secular Society* p.119ff. He also insists, rightly, that if human dignity is identified with market value that dignity is enduringly destroyed. Ibid p.223
78   K.Cronin, *Rights and Christian Ethics* Cambridge: Cambridge University Press 1992 p.247

friendship. This is the ultimate reason why human rights are unconditional and inalienable. To respect them is to respond not just to one's equals but to God.[79]

This is not to argue that liberation theologians, or anyone else, must promptly adopt the language of rights. It *is* to contest the idea that doing so is a form of cultural imperialism. For what do we want to deny in denying the priority of rights? That torture, after all, is an appropriate way to treat people? Or that race, caste, class or gender discrimination is, after all, of no account? Of course not. We need a language to express our hatred of such things, wherever they are found, and the language of the United Nations Declaration sought to articulate such a language.

Sardar, from a Muslim standpoint, remarks that even if human rights were desirable and universal, their introduction in other cultures, by force or tying it to foreign aid if necessary, amounts to the continuation of the colonial belief that the perceptions of a particular culture contain superior values giving them a moral right to spread them all over the planet.[80] Like Pieris, he reproaches the United Nations Declaration with cultural imperialism. To such allegations Parekh replies that the Declaration was born out of cross cultural dialogue and has a genuinely universal feel about it. In his view it does have a liberal bias and thinks some rights are universal which are not: the rights to more or less unlimited freedom of expression, to marriage based on free and full consent and to relatively unlimited property. It takes a statist view of human rights, and does not primarily address all persons, but he nevertheless wants to defend it as a genuinely universal declaration. To the objection that it takes a statist view of human rights we have to respond that, with the Nuremberg trials in the background, it precisely did address all persons. The affirmation of universal dignity is one of the reasons immoral orders given by a state must be disobeyed.

Clearly the discourse of rights is not going to command universal assent. There are, however, from both secular and Christian points of view, strong reasons for arguing that it should do and that what is expressed in the discourse counters any kind of cultural apartheid.

Intercultural Evaluation

In earlier chapters in this book I have defended cultural diversity. At the same time in this chapter I have argued that Huntington's thesis of mutually antagonistic civilizations founders on those things which human beings have in common. It follows from these common experiences and realities that

---

79 Donal Murray, 'The Theological Basis for Human Rights' *Irish Theological Quarterly* 56/2 (1990) pp.81–101 here p.92

80 Sardar, *Postmodernism* p.68 Sanneh, however, argues that Herskovits, who drafted the Declaration, was an extreme cultural relativist. Such relativists, reacting to perceived cultural and religious imperialism, 'reverted to a form of ethnocentrism in which other cultures are given licence to be a law unto themselves and thus to be ethnocentric, with the stage set for proliferating plural cultural ethnocentrisms'. *Encountering* p.62

intercultural evaluation is possible. The view that cultures should only be judged internally or in their own terms, Parekh argues, rests on a positivist view of culture and assumes that the latter has a fixed body of values carrying a fixed set of meanings. 'No culture is like that. Its beliefs and values are of different levels of generality and need to be interpreted to suit new unexpected situations.'[81]

It ought to be obvious that we do not automatically have to respect cultures: Nazi culture, or Afrikaner culture or caste culture, are obvious examples. It may be true that different ways of life cannot be measured in terms of a single master value or principle, but some norms of evaluation are nevertheless essential. Martha Nussbaum believes that the refusal to judge which characterizes Western liberal society is in fact a patronizing form of behaviour. It amounts to saying that a form of life is so alien and bizarre that it cannot be expected to be measured by the standards we hold. She cites the anthropologist Dan Sperber: 'In pre relativist anthropology, Westerners thought of themselves as superior to all other people. Relativism replaced this despicable hierarchical gap by a kind of cognitive apartheid. If we cannot be superior in the same world, let each people live in its own world.'[82] Melford Spiro argues that it is because the emotionally driven irrational has no limits or, because its limiting case is Auschwitz, that there are standards 'worthy of universal respect' by which cultural frames can be evaluated. These standards are based, in Freudian terms, on the self-reflective ego:

> If it turned out that in some headhunting societies ... even the philosophers judged headhunting to be preferable to feeding, say, the starving Ifugao, I would then argue that the contrary judgement of the Buddha and Christ, of Isaiah and Laotzu, of Socrates and Gandhi is worthy of greater respect. For, I would argue, the Ilongot philosophers are unable because of emotional constraints to apply the standards of the self-reflective ego to this question.[83]

As indicated in the list of moral authorities Spiro cites, cross cultural comparison seems to be the route to such necessary evaluation. Parekh, for example, believes that there is no single principle in terms of which disputed practices can be evaluated. A society's operative public values are questioned in the light of other values which yields 'an inherently tentative consensus that helps us to decide on a generally acceptable response to disputed practices'.[84] He takes polygamy as an example.[85]

What is at stake is equality which, he argues, is not just a Western or liberal but a rationally defensible universal moral value. Men and women share distinctly human capacities and needs in common, have a broadly equal

---

81 Parekh, *Multiculturalism* p.174
82 Nussbaum, *Cultivating* pp.138–139
83 Spiro, *Culture* p.56
84 Parekh, *Multiculturalism* p.267
85 The Comaroffs point out that the Setswana word for polygyny, *lefufa*, was also the generic term for 'jealousy'; the vernacular for co-wife derived from *go gadika*, to rival, to annoy, or, even more vividly, 'to cause a pain in the stomach'. *Revelation and Revolution* vol 1 p.133

potential, are equally capable of choice and self-determination and so on and are therefore entitled to equal dignity and rights. The opposite assertion is extremely difficult to substantiate, as opponents of the ordination of women have found to their embarrassment. A ban on polygyny follows from the equality of the sexes. If Muslims respond that they do not accept the principle of equality of the sexes, and that imposing it on them amounts to cultural imperialism, Parekh replies that he has offered a reasonably persuasive defence of it, that they have advanced no convincing arguments against it, and that he is therefore entitled to insist on it.[86]

There is no view from nowhere, but there are 'mini-Archimedean standpoints' in the form of other cultures that enable them to view their own from the outside, tease out its strengths and weaknesses, and deepen their self-consciousness.[87] Cross cultural dialogue 'subjects our reasons for holding them to a cross-cultural test and requires us to ensure that they are accessible and acceptable to members of very different cultures'.[88] Sanneh likewise believes that we should grasp the ethical challenge implied in cross cultural relationships, approach human difference and diversity as a resource for truth seeking and accept the possibility of mutual correction and instruction as profoundly consistent with the enterprise of being human.[89]

Grace, Ethics and Freedom

Parekh describes the view that only one way of life is fully human, true, or the best, and that all others are defective to the extent that they fall short of it, as 'moral monism'.[90] The monist assumes the uniformity of human nature, argues that similarities are ontologically far more important than differences and that human nature inheres in human beings as their natural endowment.[91] Plato and Aristotle were moral monists, as are modern liberals, but for Christianity moral monism is a matter of faith.[92] The problem with monism is that human beings are culturally embedded, and a culture not only gives a distinct tone and

---

86 Parekh, *Multiculturalism* p.285
87 Parekh, *Multiculturalism* p.167
88 Parekh, *Multiculturalism* p.128
89 Sanneh, *Encountering* p.235
90 Parekh, *Multiculturalism* p.16
91 Parekh, *Multiculturalism* p.128
92 Christianity, says Parekh, introduced the idea of moral universalism, missionary work and religious intolerance. It cannot abandon its claim to uniqueness, which would deny its historical and doctrinal identity, but it is wrong to claim that it exhausts all possible forms of religious goodness, that there is no salvation outside of it, and that all other religions are misguided or inferior. *Multiculturalism* pp.25, 32 Islam too is a form of moral monism on this account. At the inauguration of the King Fahd Chair in Islamic Studies at London University in 1996 Seyyed Hossein Nasr spoke of Western civilization as a cup drained of religious faith. The global village paradigm, which replaced Christianity, was foisted on the Islamic world and cannot be global. 'There is another reality out there that wants to claim for itself the pre-eminence of religion, because it challenges the predominance of secularism.' Newbigin et al, *Faith and Power* London: SCM 1998 p.78

structure to shared human capacities but also develops new ones of its own. Since cultures mediate and reconstitute human nature in their own different ways, and moral life is necessarily embedded in culture, no vision of the good life can be based on an abstract conception of human nature alone.[93]

In Parekh's view the idea that one way of life is the highest or truly human is logically incoherent, first, because it assumes that human capacities, desires, virtues and dispositions form a harmonious whole and can be combined without loss, which is incorrect; second, because human energies, motivations and resources are necessarily limited and one can cultivate only some of the valuable human capacities; and third, because every social order has a specific structure with its inescapable tendency to develop some capacities rather than others. Since human capacities conflict, the good they aspire to also conflicts. From Greek tragedy onwards human beings have reflected on the clash of opposing 'goods'. Every way of life, however good it may be, entails a loss.[94] Moral monism also runs the danger of misunderstanding other ways of life and tends to view differences as deviations, as expressions of moral pathology. 'The ease with which [Greeks, Christians, liberals and Marxists] have justified or condoned egregious violence against alternative ways of life, often in the name of human equality and universal love, should alert us to the danger of all forms of monism.'[95]

Parekh's charge here takes us to the heart of the theology of culture I am trying to elaborate. I have argued that the gospel is necessarily involved in the whole of life, and not just in its religious dimension. 'Culture', as the totality of what human beings make of their world, is its sphere of operation. In the light of the incarnation I have argued that its role within all human cultures is furthering humanity. But is that not a form of moral monism, with all the implicit violence that that implies? Some caution against accepting the charge is indicated by the two millennia long argument about faith and works, grace and freedom. We cannot deny the violence, and we cannot deny that many theologians, and forms of the Church at various times, have identified one way of life as fully human, to the exclusion of others. Continuing arguments about sexuality and gender show that this tradition is far from dead, and it goes back to the very beginning. In the Apostolic period, wrote Kenneth Kirk, 'writer after writer seems to have little other interest than to express the genius of Christianity wholly in terms of law and obedience, reward and punishment'.[96] There has, however, equally always been the insistence, from the earliest documents we have, that Christianity is fundamentally a religion of grace. Grace means gift and, as Paul insists, 'there is a diversity of gifts'. Gift and freedom are the gospel's central categories, emphasizing the infinite scope for creativity. 'Love God and do what you like,' wrote Augustine. Christian life is

---

93   Parekh, *Multiculturalism* p.47
94   Parekh, *Multiculturalism* p.48
95   Parekh, *Multiculturalism* p.49
96   K.Kirk, *The Vision of God: the Christian Doctrine of the Summum Bonum* London: Longmans 1931 p.111

the relation of the free person to the free God, wrote Barth. To this extent it may be that Christianity is not a form of moral monism in Parekh's sense.

At the same time there surely is, in the New Testament, a claim that a particular kind of life is most deeply fulfilling of humanity. Paul speaks of the fruit of the Spirit as 'love, joy, peace, patience, kindness, generosity, faithfulness, gentleness and self-control' (Gal 5.22). It is true that Mandeville, in his *Fable of the Bees*, suggested that were such virtues universal the world would stagnate and that therefore the Pauline virtues could not be combined with the virtues of entrepreneurship without loss. The loss in question is the developments of Williams' 'long revolution' and we cannot lightly dismiss the cultural attitudes which have led to these. On the other hand such attitudes are also responsible for threatening humanity with nuclear destruction and with ecocide. Is it really certain that we cannot have technological, economic and social progress alongside the Pauline virtues? Are they necessarily castrating? In the same way we can ask whether it is true that only some of these virtues can be developed. Let us say that 'moral monism' involves a particular construal of what constitutes the mature human person, and that this construal is set out by Paul. True, we do not live up to it, but is that grounds for questioning it? Does taking this as our image of such maturity involve developing some capacities rather than others? Are not these attributes a framework within which human behaviour may be differently culturally constructed?

I have argued that similarities between persons are ontologically far more important than differences. As implied in Chapter 7, I do not see how we can avoid such a view if we are to avoid racism or sexism of one form or another. The idea of the image of God, one of the most important Christian grounds of equality, is not abstract because it is always concretely, which is to say, culturally, instantiated. Despite this cultural differentiation it insists that all persons are of equal worth, all equally redeemable. There are indeed often moral quandaries, but these do not entail that we cannot discern models of what it is to be human which evoke admiration and the desire for imitation across cultures, which can properly be advanced as a universal human aspiration.

Grace and freedom, in the Christian understanding, are universal parameters of human behaviour. It is freedom which grounds cultural diversity, and response to grace which accounts for human unity (Romans 1). Once again we turn up the dialectic of universal and particular, a dialectic which rules out any monism. The fact that there is only an ethics of freedom means that there cannot be Christian cultures, though there may be cultures which exemplify important aspects of the Christian virtues (such as compassion for the sick and outcast). This also means, of course, that Huntington's identification of 'the West' with Christianity is very wide of the mark, especially as, on his account, it involves arming yourself to the teeth. The fact that to be human means to be called to respond to grace, on the other hand, means that we cannot think of the world in apartheid terms, as carved up between competing cultures. What they share is more important, finally, than what divides them. That is rather an optimistic, and perhaps it will be said idealist, conclusion to the dismal claims with which I began the chapter. I turn, now, to see whether such claims can be substantiated in the idea of a multicultural society.

Chapter 11

The Gospel in a Multicultural Society

Some argue that any response to Huntington's thesis will have to be rooted in multiculturalism.[1] Multiculturalism, however, is not a self-evident value and has to be defended. To some extent it rides on a tide of political correctness in which the Red Cross has to disavow all Christian symbolism and where it is now regarded as inappropriate by some public bodies in traditionally Christian countries to celebrate Christmas. Is multiculturalism simply the triumph of secular humanism? Does it imply abandoning the quest for truth? To what extent may the Church still pursue evangelism in a multicultural society?

Multiculturalism and its Discontents

'Ancient Rome,' wrote Schleiermacher, 'truly pious, and in a high style religious, was hospitable to every god.'[2] The Rome of the first to the third centuries has a good claim to being the first truly multicultural society and this possibility rested on the fact that Rome had a civic religion and then cults: it was not organized around one major missionary religion.[3] According to Gibbon, the adoption of such a religion was a major factor in its decline and fall.

Medieval and early modern Europe, and perhaps most other societies as well, have dealt with difference by assimilation, by ghettoization and by repression. Behind these strategies, as we saw in the last chapter, was the view that there was one normative way to be human – the moral monism Parekh criticizes. Nevertheless it is not true to say that these societies were monocultural. Groups like the Jews and the Gypsies resisted all attempts at assimilation. Regional cultures varied, and still vary, very significantly as do class and occupational cultures.[4] There were a great many cultures, in this sense, and, as Parekh points out, cultures are always shaped by others, which provide their context and remain their points of reference, so that almost all cultures are, and always have been, multiculturally constituted.[5]

---

1   Burbach et al, *Globalization* p.145
2   Schleiermacher, *Speeches* p.55
3   Stuart Hall remarks that all the major empires from the Greek to the European were multi-ethnic and multicultural. 'The Multi-Cultural Question' p.212
4   John McGrath speaks of his upbringing in Wales and Liverpool, and his courtship in the Highlands and his awareness of the multiplicity of British culture: 'each one of these cultures ... has to me a totally distinct landscape, an emotional and linguistic and interpersonal specificity, a distinctness from every one of the others which is complete, yet with a variety of contiguities'. *The Bone Won't Break* p.54 We can replicate this the world over.
5   Parekh, *Multiculturalism* p.163

A new model of assimilation, the 'melting pot', was attempted in the United States in the second half of the nineteenth century. Having displaced the indigenous Indians, however, the dream of the European and Scandinavian settlers in the United States was to meld together a new society which would not be class based in the way the old European societies were, and which would overcome centuries of hostility between Protestant and Catholic, Christian and Jew. Assimilation was not into an ancient and established culture but into what was understood as a 'new' world, representing the possibility of a fresh start. On the level of religious integration it largely succeeded. On the level of class and of race it failed. This failure, especially in the area of race, is one of the major factors in the emergence of multiculturalism, the realization first in the USA, and then in Britain, 'that the melting pot doesn't melt, and that ethnic and racial divisions get reproduced from generation to generation'.[6]

It is worth pausing over this observation. From generation to generation? By and large shared tasks produce shared histories, especially if that task involves facing a common enemy. In England four hundred years of conflict between Dane, Jute and Saxon eventually melded, under Norman domination, into 'Englishness'. Without doubt the acceptance of Christianity as the common religion facilitated this process. In contemporary Britain intermarriage between different races, ethnicities and religions is increasingly common. What happens when these couples become 'one flesh' in their children? Zimitri Erasmus, in South Africa, writes of the difficulty of responding to the demand to take sides on the race issue when your grandparents are *both* Dutch *and* Khoisan.[7] How many generations are we talking in the preservation of difference?

Religion, of course, is more stubbornly resistant of assimilation than race. I mentioned the survival of the Jewish diaspora in the first chapter; one can also think of Coptic Christians in Egypt, Maronite Christians in Syria, and the divisions in Northern Ireland or Bosnia. A shared struggle against imperialism failed to hold the Indian subcontinent together at Independence. These are sobering examples to contemplate. All the same, the assumption of a difference which will continue, like the sins of the fathers, 'from generation to generation' and which will resist the emergence of a common story seems improbable. To recall Raymond Williams' account of the making of society, cited in the second chapter: it is, he said, 'the finding of common meanings and directions, and its growth is an active debate and amendment under the pressures of experience, contact, and discovery'.[8]

Perhaps this does not happen in caste or apartheid societies, but even that is arguable. Yasmin Ali notes the difference in the experience of the Asian community in Britain between those in the South of the country and those in the North. 'Northern English Muslim communities are as they are *in part*

6   F.Anthias and N.Yuval-Davis, *Racialized Boundaries* London: Routledge 1992 p.158
7   Z.Erasmus, 'Some Kind of White, Some Kind of Black: Living the Moments of Entanglement in South Africa and its Academy' in Hesse(ed) *Un/settled Multiculturalisms* pp.185–208
8   Williams, *Resources* p.4

because of their specifically English regional qualities, not their "alienness".[9]
On the historical record this is exactly what would be expected: think of the
difference between the cultures of Sephardic, Ashkenazi and German Jewry.
Since humans learn by mimesis, osmosis is a fundamental part of their cultural
experience. To recall Herder's insistence on language as lying at the heart of
culture once more: what the eye is to the lover, says Benedict Anderson,
language is to the patriot. Through shared languages pasts are restored,
fellowships imagined and futures dreamed.[10] But as two generations of
experience have shown us in Britain, to live together is to acquire a common
language. What then follows from that?

The issue of multiculturalism has provoked intense debate over the past
thirty years and there are manifold definitions and accounts of what is meant
by it. Issues of race, organized around visible bodily signifiers, and of ethnicity,
organized around cultural and religious difference, are central to much of the
discussion but the discourse has spread wider to include sexual preference,
political convictions, and gender.[11] In Britain and other Western societies,
alongside immigration there has also been 'a massive internal diversification of
social life' such that 'it would be difficult to find a significant national
consensus around any of the critical social issues about which there are deep
differences of opinion and lived experience'.[12] This diversification has fed the
demand for multiculturalism. As the term implies, 'culture', those things which
I share with my group, which I inherit, which give me identity, has become a
crucial political signifier, in both progressive and reactionary ways.[13]

The presuppositions behind multicultural discourse are those of Enlightenment ideas of liberty and equality, applied now not to the individual but to
the group. The aim of the good society is not just equality of opportunity for
individuals but equality amongst socially and culturally differentiated groups
which mutually respect one another.[14] The rationale for the new multiculturalism is ethical and involves a change in the understanding of justice. In
the Western understanding of justice, inherited from Rome, justice is
blindfolded. Blindness to difference, however, can involve a tacit setting of
standards by the dominant group which makes their norms universal and

9   Y.Ali, 'Muslim Women and the Politics of Ethnicity and Culture in Northern England' in
Sahgal and Yuval-Davis(eds) *Refusing Holy Orders* p.108 my italics
10   Anderson, *Imagined Communities* p.154
11   Hall points out that race is not a scientific category but a political and social construct. Visible
signifiers are appealed to such as skin, colour, hair, body type etc. Ethnicity is a discourse where
difference is grounded in cultural and religious features. Biological racism and cultural
differentialism are, he argues, racism's two registers. 'The Multi-Cultural Question' p.235
12   Hall, 'The Multi-Cultural Question' p.230 Hall himself gives priority to the questions of race
and ethnicity.
13   T.Turner, 'Anthropology and Multiculturalism' in Goldberg(ed) *Multiculturalism* p.421
14   I.M.Young, *Justice and the Politics of Difference* Princeton: Princeton University Press 1990
p.163 At the same time Araeen argues that all the discussion of the need for difference has taken us
away from the basic question of equality for all peoples within a modern society – from issues of
ensuring basic human rights and equality of opportunity for all; from issues of jobs, education,
housing, health care and policing; from legitimate demands of the underprivileged and exploited.
Jordan and Weedon, *Cultural Politics* p.478

produces an internalized devaluation by members of minority groups. In such circumstances justice needs to stand not just for equality but for the right to difference, though multiculturalism then faces the classic liberal dilemma of what to do about groups in society which are illiberal, or committed to imposing their own religion or polity.[15]

The way in which this could be defended from Herder's position is obvious, and Parekh does so. Different cultures represent different talents, skills, forms of imagination, ways of looking at things, forms of social organization, senses of humour and psychological and moral energies. All need radical changes because of their deep-seated sexist, racist and other biases.[16] In this situation different cultures correct and complement, educate and civilize each other. Homogenous cultures, to the extent that they exist, are narrowly based and lack the conditions necessary for the development of intellectual and moral virtues such as openness, humility, tolerance of differences, critical self-consciousness, powers of intellectual and moral imagination and extensive sympathy.[17] To the charge that such an advocacy is a form of moral monism Parekh replies there is 'more to be said' for a culturally open and diverse than for a culturally self-contained way of life. He wants to recognize that such self-contained societies (the Amish are an example) also have their virtues, suit some communities 'and represents their autonomous choices'. In this respect the kind of multiculturalism he advocates does not set up a universal human model to which all should conform. However, a multiculturalism driven by a spirit of critical self-understanding opens up a theoretical and moral space for a dialogue with other ways of life in a common search for a deeper understanding of the human project.[18]

In a typically energetic challenge to such liberal pieties, Slavov Žižek argues that multiculturalism functions as a screen for global capital. It adopts the empty global position of the corporation and, just as the postmodern dismissal of meta narratives conceals the meta narrative of the market, so multiculturalist respect for the other's specificity is in fact a way of asserting one's superiority.[19] The way to fight ethnic hatred effectively, he argues, is not through the negotiation of difference but proper political hatred, hatred directed at the common enemy, by which he means capitalism.[20] Rather similarly it is argued that the multicultural agenda papers over the problem of racism. Like those forms of Christianity which make reconciliation prior to justice, it cultivates the illusion that dominant and subordinate can somehow

15   Bhatt shows how Shabir Akhtar, for instance, uses multiculturalism to articulate a discourse of minority rights which denies such rights to others. *Liberation* p.243 Khurram Murad, Director of the Islamic Foundation, describes the Islamic Movement as 'an organised struggle to change the existing society into an Islamic Society based on the Quran and the Suna and make Islam, which is a code for entire life, supreme and dominant, especially in the socio-political sphere'. Cited in Newbigin et al, *Faith and Power* p.110
16   Parekh, *Multiculturalism* pp.168–169
17   Parekh, *Multiculturalism* p.170
18   Parekh, *Multiculturalism* p.111
19   Žižek, *Ticklish Subject* p.216
20   Žižek, *Fragile Absolute* p.11

swap places and learn how the other half lives, whilst leaving the structures of power intact.[21] Under the terms of the multiculturalist consensus, write Gita Sahgal and Nira Yuval-Davis, fighting against racism is reduced to preserving the 'traditions and cultures' of different ethnic minorities. 'Cultural differences between various groups in society become of paramount importance, rather than tackling the central problem of racism itself: unequal power relations which bring about "modes of exclusion", inferiorisation, subordination and exploitation.'[22]

Other critics allege that multiculturalism has functioned as a weak form of ghettoization. Yasmin Ali considers that this discourse provided the ideological justification of a range of policies designed to contain communities and isolate them from the local political arena. 'Ethnic' communities were viewed primarily as targets of social policy rather than as actors in the democratic system. She argues that the impact of multiculturalist policies was to work through self-appointed mediators of the community, always men, 'who could represent the community to the state (usually the local state) and interpret the state to the community, without recourse to the ballot box or the *slower processes of political socialization* which accountability would have required'.[23] Ethnic communities are represented, with the connivance of community 'leaders', in a two dimensional way so that 'all families are extended, children respect their elders, religious faith is total and unquestioning, and women are veiled creatures living in the shadows'. Male community leaders mediate between this community and the authorities, like local elites under a colonial administration!

The Women against Fundamentalism alliance raise the question, which we have already encountered numerous times before, of who speaks for the community. When someone like Kalim Siddiqui says that 'the option of assimilation should be firmly resisted' or when we are told that, if faith is the primary identity of any community, then that minority cannot fully identify with and participate in a polity that privileges a 'rival faith', one needs to ask whether this is the whole community speaking.[24] Yasmin Ali concludes that there is a symbiotic relationship between the state and the dominant culture in Britain on the one hand, and sections of the leadership in South Asian Muslim communities on the other, which has had damaging effects for the development of the community as a whole, and particularly for women. 'Its consequence has

21 Cited by Hesse in *Un/settled Multiculturalisms* p.8
22 Sahgal and Yuval-Davis, 'Introduction' in *Refusing Holy Orders* p.15 Cf Bhatt, *Liberation* p.134 arguing that the demands of any 'black community' are not equivalent to 'black political' demands. John Hutnyk agrees. 'Adorno at Womad' in Werbner and Modood(eds) *Debating Cultural Hybridity* p.122
23 Ali, 'Muslim Women' pp.103–104 my italics. The 'slower processes of political socialization' again put a question mark against the idea of permanently separated communities.
24 Cited in Newbigin et al, *Faith and Power* p.125 It is in general a failure of this book to put this question. Spokesmen (always) for Islam are always cited from what Sahgal and Yuval-Davis would regard as a fundamentalist position, but as they insist, the community is not homogenous. Gerd Baumann shares this view. 'Dominant and Demotic Discourses of Culture' in Werbner and Modood(eds) *Debating Cultural Hybridity* p.221

been a collusion between (unequal) partners to maintain a narrow and static definition of community which severely circumscribes the stage upon which women are permitted to perform as political and social actors.'[25]

By the same token, liberal fear of treading on 'ethnic' toes has led, in Britain at least, to double standards in social policy, such as the refusal to intervene in child marriages, or ignoring domestic abuse or violence within the Asian community. This in its own way is a form of racism because it is tantamount to saying that under-age sex has a different effect on Muslim girls than secular girls.[26] In this way, critics argue, multiculturalism can disguise confusion, cowardice and indifference and lead to an uncritical solidarity.[27]

A fourth objection is that multiculturalism fails to do justice to the complexity of minority situations. Cultural differences, Homi Bhaba insists, are not simply given but are constantly contested, performed and re-formed. Minority discourse 'acknowledges the status of national culture – and the people – as a contentious, performative space'.[28] The model suggests that it is a question of fully formed cultures somehow living together, and this is how many spokespersons of groups within such societies represent it. The reality is of a much more complex interweaving of identities.

Though communities are not homogenous, the question of identity remains close to the heart of the difficulties of constructing a multicultural society. In so far as multiculturalism arose to do justice to the claims of different groups within society then groups can only be defined in terms of what they stand for or who they are. These identities are by nature exclusive. When people speak of identities which are 'multiple, unstable, historically situated products of ongoing differentiation' this is not only oxymoronic, but tacitly privileges a fairly extreme individualism.[29] In a situation where identities are completely unstable there cannot be groups for which claims are made.

The problems of identity politics are familiar: a set of possibly acrimonious contests for scarce resources and educational and political space which often enough end up in out and out violence. At worst identity politics is what is identified on the Indian subcontinent as communalism, in which community solidarity is turned against other communities. The assumption that knowledge of other cultures will lead to tolerance is belied by the widespread experience that it often fosters chauvinism.[30] Religion is often enough at the heart of such communalism. T.S.Eliot felt that there was no option but to seek a common world culture, but very little chance of ever attaining one. 'Here of course, we

25   Ali, 'Muslim Women' p.119

26   Jenny Taylor in Newbigin et al, *Faith and Power* p.89

27   Taylor in Newbigin et al, *Faith and Power* p.98 She cites an Asian woman who found the failure of the white community to condemn Asian hooliganism both stupid and patronizing. Cf Nira Yuval-Davis, 'Ethnicity, Gender Relations and Multiculturalism' in Werbner and Modood(eds) *Debating Cultural Hybridity* p.205

28   Bhaba, *Location* pp.3, 157 For a critique of his views see Bhatt, *Liberation*, chapter 1 and A.Ahmad, *In Theory* London: Verso pp.67–69

29   Stam and Shohat, 'Contested Histories' p.301 The same goes for Bhaba's emphasis on the contingent and liminal. *Location* p.179

30   Hartman, *Culture* p.181

are finally up against religion ... Ultimately, antagonistic religions must mean antagonistic cultures; and, ultimately, religions cannot be reconciled.'[31] Of course, people of one race may include diverse cultures and religions, and people of one religion can embrace a vast variety of races and cultures. That fact led Lesslie Newbigin to wonder whether the idea of multiculturalism has any meaning.[32]

The religious prioritization of difference constitutes an ironic parallel to postmodernism, which likewise valorizes difference. In fact, we have to distinguish two trends within postmodernism with sharply differing origins. The first form, with its famous rejection of meta narratives, can be understood as a development of the critique of Enlightenment. It is hostile to universalizing and totalizing claims because it sees how these have been used to oppress people. The other side of postmodernism is its sense as 'the cultural logic of late capitalism', as representing a valorization of choice as the human project.

Jordan and Weedon represent the first form. In the postmodern world, they argue, there is no single truth. Truths are discursive constructs which differ across histories and cultures, as well as between different interest groups within the same culture. Whoever has the power to define Truth in any society has also the power to define Others. Universals are discursive constructs with which particular groups seek to legitimate their own particular interests.[33] It may be tactically useful to claim universal moral standards but we must recognize that such standards are in fact always historically and socially specific and subject to change.

To this form of postmodernism feminists, Muslims and Christian theologians alike have reacted with profound scepticism. Why is it, asks Nancy Hartsock, that at the precise moment when so many groups have been engaged in nationalisms which involve redefinitions of the marginalized Others suspicions emerge about the nature of the 'subject', about the possibilities for a generalized theory which can describe the world, about historical 'progress'?:

> Why is it that just at the moment when so many of us who have been silenced begin to demand the right to name ourselves, to act as subjects rather than objects of history, that just then the concept of subjecthood becomes problematic? Just when we are forming our own theories about the world, uncertainty emerges about whether the world can be theorized. Just when we are talking about the changes we want, ideas of progress and the possibility of systematically and rationally organizing human society become dubious and suspect?[34]

In effect she is saying: give us back our meta narrative!

For Sardar postmodernism is simply a new wave of domination riding on the crest of colonialism and modernity. It avoids, by glossing over, the politics of non-Western marginalization in history by suddenly discovering Otherness everywhere. 'Colonialism was about the physical occupation of non-western

31 Eliot, *Notes* p.62
32 In Newbigin et al, *Faith and Power* p.5
33 Jordan and Weedon, *Cultural Politics* p.547
34 Jordan and Weedon, *Cultural Politics* pp.203–204

cultures. Modernity was about displacing the present and occupying the minds of non-western cultures. Postmodernism is about appropriating the history and identity of non-western cultures as an integral facet of itself, colonising their future and occupying their being.'[35] The surface pluralism of postmodern pluralism masks a monolithic matrix at its core. Its language, logic, analytical grammar, are intrinsically Eurocentric and shamelessly cannibalistic of Others.[36] The West now doubts the validity of its own reality and truth and in consequence calls in question all criteria of reality and truth. 'When it looks out from the dark enclosure of its soul, western civilisation now perceives nothing but the echo of its inner emptiness. Unless it is consciously resisted, this dismal emptiness will envelop all that is distinctive about the Other cultures and makes them genuinely Other: alternatives to the West.'[37] The postmodern liberalism of Jordan and Weedon is construed as the latest ploy to keep the West in power.[38]

The second form of postmodernism can be illustrated by Peter Caws. He extends Parekh's argument about the value of other cultures to the individual. Each person has to construct their identity. To confine the development of one's identity within the variables of any single culture is a wanton neglect of the vast riches that are available in the world:[39]

> Any native culture is an imposed one: we do not choose to be born when, where, and to whom we are born … it is an obligation upon parents to help free their children of their culture of origin if that is what the children decide they want … The idea of a culture – Jewish culture comes to mind – once born into which a child, by the common consent of members and non-members alike, simply is not permitted to disavow his or her identification with, seems to me incompatible with human freedom.[40]

The immediate response to this is that it represents an impossible version of cultural formation. The end result of the process envisaged by Caws, it is argued, would be an individual adrift in a sea with no horizon in any direction, a landscape with no landmarks, and no fixed points to plot a route.[41] If human identity is socially constructed we cannot simply pick the culture we prefer off the cultural supermarket shelf. Geoffrey Hartman notes that cultural pluralism poses a problem to the extent that we take local attachment seriously. Is it really possible to participate fully in several cultures? Is not that as improbable as the older ideal of becoming a citizen of the world? Multiculturalism, he

---

35   Sardar, *Postmodernism* p.13
36   Sardar, *Postmodernism* p.20
37   Sardar, *Postmodernism* p.16
38   This point is also made by Said. The interest of Western academics in subjects such as multiculturalism and 'post-coloniality', he writes, can be a cultural and intellectual retreat from the new realities of global power. *Orientalism* p.351
39   P.Caws, 'Identity: Cultural, Transcultural, Multicultural' in Goldberg(ed) *Multiculturalism* p.381
40   Caws, 'Identity' p.384
41   Cited by Newbigin in Newbigin et al, *Faith and Power* p.5

remarks, remains undertheorized and seems as unrealistic or abstract as the cosmopolitanism it intends to replace.[42]

In the United States multiculturalism provoked vehement struggles over the content of the curriculum which reflected, so it was said, the hegemony of 'dead white males'. Huntington, who belongs to that group who believe that multiculturalists are 'the enemy within', argues that no society can survive without a cultural core. Recognizing the force of cultural politics he argues that political creeds are insufficient to sustain a lasting community. In this situation 'The clash between multiculturalists and the defenders of Western civilization and the American Creed is the real clash within the American segment of Western civilization.' The futures of the United States and of the West, in his view, depend upon Americans reaffirming their commitment to Western civilization (which, as we have seen, turns out to be capitalism).[43] Norman Tebbit argued similarly that multiculturalism is a divisive force because one cannot uphold two sets of ethics or be loyal to two nations, any more than a man can have two masters. 'It perpetuates ethnic divisions because nationality is in the long term more about culture than ethnics [*sic*]. Youngsters of all races born here should be taught that British history is their history, or they will forever be foreigners holding British passports and this kingdom will become a Yugoslavia.'[44] As I have noted earlier, this is actually a reprise of an older British argument, deriving from the Elizabethan settlement and the struggle with Spain, that no state survives if its citizens have dual loyalties.[45]

I have great sympathy for these challenges to the multiculturalist consensus. The problem is understanding how they work out in the actual situations in which we all find ourselves. Solidarity in a common struggle is fine, but its presupposition is respect for my comrade (which includes the preparedness to argue, challenge and be challenged and so forth). In terms of practical politics it seems we cannot avoid the footslogging Parekh calls for. As Michele Wallace puts it, multiculturalism is not the promised land but it stands for something worth pursuing, namely the recognition of the significance of cultural diversity and of integrating the contributions of minority groups into the fabric of society.[46]

In disavowing the traditional strategies of assimilation, repression and ghettoization multicultural societies, says Parekh, throw up problems that have no parallel in history:

> They need to find ways of reconciling the legitimate demands of unity and diversity, achieving political unity without cultural uniformity, being inclusive without being assimilationist, cultivating among their citizens a common sense of belonging while

---

42   Hartman, *Culture* p.181
43   Huntington, *Clash* p.307
44   Cited by Hesse in *Un/settled Multiculturalisms* p.3
45   Cf also this sentiment of King Sapor II in Mesopotamia, speaking of Christians: 'They live in our territory but they share the sentiments of Caesar.' Bosch, *Transforming Mission* p.203
46   Cited by Hall in 'The Multi-Cultural Question' p.211

respecting their legitimate cultural differences, and cherishing plural cultural identities without weakening the shared and precious identity of shared citizenship.[47]

Religion, as we have seen, is one of the most stubborn of divisive forces. Can proselytization really be condoned in a multicultural society?

Evangelism in a Multicultural Society

Martin Buber went to a predominantly Christian school in the palmy days of the Austro-Hungarian empire. He was never aware of anti-semitism and none of his teachers made any attempt to convert him. Nevertheless, he and his small group of fellow Jews had to sit in silence each day for eight years whilst the creed was said. This experience, he said, stamped itself on his soul as nothing else could have done and gave him a lifelong antipathy to all missionary effort.[48] Anyone who has been at the receiving end of perhaps well-meaning but nevertheless deeply offensive attempts to 'convert' them will sympathize. At the same time, none of the missionary religions can abandon mission without abandoning their self-understanding. Is there a way in which it can be morally pursued in a multicultural society?

Maurice Friedman offers Buber's model of dialogue, which involves going out to meet the other and holding your ground while you meet them. 'We do not have to liberate the world from those who have different witnesses from us. The converse of this also holds, namely that each must hold his ground and witness for his truth even while at the same time affirming the ground and the truth of the other.'[49] In place of absolutism or relativism he wants to put what he calls 'the mutual confirmation of dialogue of touchstones of reality'. The true fellowship of the committed is made up of those who can meet and talk with one another because they really care about one another and the common goal they are serving, however differently that goal may be stated. The partnership of Gandhi and C.F.Andrews would be a classic example. This fellowship is found as much across as within organizational, institutional and denominational lines:

> A true dialogue presupposes that one does not fall into the idolatry of objectifying one's touchstones into universal truths that one wishes to impose upon others and force everyone to subscribe to. If this is so then the answer to the dilemma of cultural relativism is ... a mutually confirming dialogue of touchstones.[50]

It could be argued that Friedman presents a classical Jewish view, for Judaism has never been a missionary religion. Adherents of missionary religions, on the other hand, have to grant Peter Caws' argument to the extent that they defend

---

47 Parekh, *Multiculturalism* p.343
48 M.Friedman, 'The Dialogue of Touchstones as an Approach to Interreligious Dialogue' in Gort et al(eds) *Dialogue and Syncretism* pp.76–84
49 Friedman, 'Dialogue' p.78
50 Friedman, 'Dialogue' p.81

the possibility of conversion. Since religion shapes culture, a change of religion involves some change in culture and ways of life, which is why conversion is such a live issue in India, where the question whether one can be a true Indian and a Christian has been debated for more than a century. From the standpoint of the inescapability of cultural traditions Newbigin argues that these must be understood as analogous to contact lenses in our eyes, through which we achieve clarity and coherence in understanding the world. 'We abandon them only when they fail to give us clarity and coherence in our efforts to understand and cope with the world around us, and when someone is able to offer us a better set of lenses.' He argues that there is an implicitly racist distinction between 'evangelism' and 'dialogue', the former reserved for our unbelieving English neighbours, the latter for our Asian and West Indian neighbours. 'The gospel is, like South African parks, for whites only.'[51] The response to this, however, is that all evangelism, to the extent that it is moral, must take the form of dialogue. Newbigin presumably dislikes the term because of its use by pluralist theologians for whom all religions are equal routes to the same goal, but, when understood from Buber's perspective, this is not the case.

Michael Barnes has recently developed a theology of dialogue drawing, significantly, on the work of another Jew, Emmanuel Levinas.[52] The heart of his proposal is to understand God as involved in the experience of otherness. God is the primary Other, whom we encounter in human others. This means that openness to the Other is the *sine qua non* of any theology, creating the context or atmosphere in which theology is to be done.[53] Encounter is not a matter of attaining a smooth consensus. On the contrary, power and the possibility of violence are always latent in it. Given this fact can there ever be genuine encounter, without crushing passivity or assimilation? The question is especially pertinent in interfaith encounter where exhortations to tolerance risk doing violence to the wider fabric of story, ritual, devotion and custom on which faith depends to give it real energy and motivation.[54] The answer he gives is that encounter always happens in what Gillian Rose calls the 'broken middle', a relationship which is always under negotiation. This is true of all meeting, including the encounter of religions. The Church's Jewish 'primary otherness', as set out in Paul's argument in Romans, makes clear that Christianity cannot claim finality for itself, for there is no end to negotiation. Understood thus we can envisage a relationship where we can be passive in the face of the other without being crushed by them – a reality Barnes finds in the

---

51 L.Newbigin, *The Gospel in a Pluralist Society* London: SPCK 1986 p.4

52 M.Barnes, *Theology and the Dialogue of Religions* Cambridge: Cambridge University Press 2002 Hans Küng agrees with the emphasis on dialogue. In answer to the question whether mission is still possible he responds that we need to replace the word 'mission' by 'witness' and that this should be done by actions rather than by word; that it is possible only from within indigenous communities; that it can only be done by understanding inculturation; that it must be given by the whole people of God; that it must be given through dialogue rather than confrontation; that it must be given through shared ecumenical testimony; and that it must be given through a strengthened solidarity with others and an orientation on a common future. *Global Ethic* p.156

53 Barnes, *Dialogue* p.55

54 Barnes, *Dialogue* p.248

kenosis of Philippians 2. Christian theology is rooted in the story of the God who is Emmanuel, the Word spoken in the 'broken middle' of the world, who still goes on speaking through the spirit which leads the disciples into all the truth. What they share is what God can do in and through human weakness.

A second presupposition, that there are 'seeds of the Word' in all cultures, is taken, as we saw in Chapter 9, from the second century Apologists. God's salvific action is not coterminous with the Church. Christians in a multi-faith society are called to be mediators and bridge builders, border crossers constantly departing for 'elsewhere' in imitation of the homeless Christ.[55] If Christians mediate the Word spoken in Christ they do so motivated by the Spirit of love, 'in imitation of God's own action of welcome and hospitality toward all people. The God whom Christians celebrate is the source of the gift which they presume to communicate to others and the means by which the gift is shared.'[56] This means, in a rather curious mixed metaphor, that we have to listen for seeds of the Word and that witness is impossible without such listening. Barnes wants to replace Enlightenment tolerance with humility – a love for the particular in a way that does not negate the stranger or hide from itself its own temptations to coercion, its own lust for power, its own proclivities to sin.[57] This humility can only be learned in the school of faith which religions are. They are not complete systems of meaning but learn and grow by responding to the others who confront them. In the Christian life it is liturgy which is our school of attention, for discerning seeds of the Word is a practice which has to be learned. In this school we can learn how to narrate a story which neither totalizes nor relativizes but, in Gerald Loughlin's words, 'imagines the possibility of harmonious difference and peace as the inner dynamic of the Triune God'.[58] In imitation of that conversation which is revealed within the Trinity, Christian life is intrinsically dialogical.[59] Engagement with people of other faiths is informed by a vision of the Trinitarian God who acts as both host and guest.

Barnes' fellow Jesuit, Aloysius Pieris, takes us further by raising the political dimension of dialogue. In Chapter 9 we encountered his idea that in Jesus the irreconcilable antinomy between God and Mammon and the irrevocable covenant between God and the poor is made flesh. True evangelism is to live this out in fellowship with the authentic spirituality and liberative dimensions of other religions. Each of these religions has its own version of the Sermon on the Mount, the Truth that sets us free from being tied to things that cannot give us freedom. The Asian Churches (but why just the Asian Churches?) have to experience solidarity with non-Christians, by witnessing to the spirituality common to all religions (by practising the beatitudes) and reveal their Christian uniqueness in proclaiming Jesus as the new covenant by joining the poor against Mammon's principalities and powers that create poverty and

---

55   Barnes, *Dialogue* p.249
56   Barnes, *Dialogue* p.192
57   Barnes, *Dialogue* p.129
58   Barnes, *Dialogue* p.28
59   Barnes, *Dialogue* p.228

oppression. It follows that much of what passes for evangelization in the mainline Churches is the total negation of true evangelism:

> I shudder to think that any church that claims to be the spouse-body-servant of Christ would launch a mission campaign in Asia on the strength of massive quantities of money ... the advocates of this new evangelization are hell-bent on liquidating the two things we consider absolutely essential for integral evangelization, namely, interreligious dialogue and liberation theology.[60]

What it means to make disciples of nations is to baptize them into a spirituality of non-acquisitiveness and non-accumulativeness which guarantees a healthy, ecologically balanced sharing of our resources. The cross is not, as it is for much Protestant preaching, 'the price for sinners paid' but the price fixed by the rich who refuse to be evangelized by the poor:

> If one day we truly take up this cross as a body and go underground and pay that price for the sake of our intimidated masses, that day the world will see the miracle it is yearning to see, a church which has been evangelised by the poor, and therefore, a church that has become Good News to the poor, as Jesus was.[61]

What happens in the Base Human Communities is a symbiosis of religions. 'Each religion, challenged by the other religion's unique approach to the liberation aspiration of the poor, discovers and renames itself in its specificity in response to other approaches.'[62]

Pieris warns that the liberating spirituality of the religions is gradually being extinguished by the wave of capitalistic techniculture that has begun to shake the religious foundation of all cultures. 'The market economy (which thrives on the quest for profit) and consumerism (which plays to our accumulative instinct) have enthroned Mammon where, once, the human person and the human community as well as the earth on which we live, were the sole beneficiary.' Lesslie Newbigin agrees with him. The eighteenth century, he remarks, found in covetousness not only a law of nature but the engine of progress by which the purpose of nature and nature's God was to be carried out.[63] This represented an inversion of the entire Christian witness up to then. 'Growth' became the watchword. But growth for the sake of growth is a form of cancer. 'In the long perspective of history, it would be difficult to deny that the exuberant capitalism of the past two hundred and fifty years will be diagnosed in the future as a desperately dangerous case of cancer in the body of human society.'[64]

---

60   Pieris, *Fire and Water* p.151
61   Pieris, *Fire and Water* p.153
62   Pieris, *Fire and Water* p.161
63   Newbigin, *Foolishness* p.109
64   Newbigin, *Foolishness* p.114

Truth, Power and Secularity

One of the objections to a multicultural society is that, if it means equal respect
for all its groups, and if these groups have incompatible ideas about what
constitutes truth, this seems to imply indifference to the truth. But, critics point
out, no society can survive in such conditions. This was the burden of much of
Lesslie Newbigin's polemic in the last twenty-five years of his life. Given that
the impact of modernity is not confined to the West but constitutes a world
culture, the divorce between facts and values which it brings with it and its
abandonment of teleology are being exported everywhere.

In the first case it is commonplace that whereas in science and economics we
talk about 'facts', in the realm of values we talk about subjective opinions. The
belief that the truth is much greater than any one person or any one religious
tradition can grasp is used to neutralize any affirmation of truth. As in the
parable of the blind men and the elephant it actually privileges the relativist
standpoint, enshrining relativism as ultimately true. Religious pluralism,
Newbigin argued, is the belief that the differences between the religions are not
a matter of truth and falsehood, but of different perceptions of the one truth;
that to speak of religious beliefs as true or false is inadmissible because
religious belief is a private matter. The effect of this is that values have no
purchase in the realm of public truth, but are simply an expression of 'what is
true for me', something which Newbigin believed was indicative of cultural
collapse. A supermarket approach to religions is adopted, the result of which is
that there is no objective reality which calls our sovereignty into question, no
power 'out there' to challenge us.[65]

The abandonment of teleology, on the other hand, meant that people were
left without values to orientate themselves. Values have traditionally been
rooted in religion but the modern scientific view does not provide a basis for
them. It excludes purpose as a factor in the ultimate constitution of things. To
eliminate from the public life of a nation any accepted vision of a shared goal,
leaving each individual to pursue self-chosen goals and making covetousness
the prime mover of human affairs, is to invite destruction from within.[66]

Newbigin's response to these two difficulties was to draw on the
epistemological work of Michael Polanyi and to claim that all forms of
rationality are part of socially embodied traditions. This does not abandon us
to relativism because we recognize, with Alasdair MacIntyre, that there can be
a contest between traditions. Christians must welcome plurality, therefore, but
reject the ideology of pluralism. They argue for the public truth of their beliefs,
but in a way that is prepared to meet, and be convinced by, the truth of others'
positions.

Commitment to public truth means a commitment to politics, and therefore
raises the question of power. This has two aspects. In the first place it means a

---

65 L.Newbigin, 'Religion for the Marketplace' in G.D'Costa(ed) *Christian Uniqueness
Reconsidered* Maryknoll: Orbis 1990 pp.135–148
66 Newbigin, *Foolishness* p.122

disavowal of coercion. Johann Baptist Metz argues that if Western Christianity is to mature into a culturally polycentric World Christianity, then it must realize its biblical heritage as the ferment of a hermeneutical culture, a culture of the acknowledgement of others in their otherness, which in its heart is freed from the will to power.[67] For Newbigin one of the major points of difference between Christianity and Islam is that for the latter it is impossible that the cause of God should be defeated and for this reason the crucifixion must be denied. What is unique about the Christian gospel is that those who are called to be its witnesses are committed to the public affirmation that it is true and are at the same time forbidden to use coercion to enforce it – an ironic point given Christianity's history.[68] Constantinianism, the identity of Church and state, has to be disavowed. 'The sacralizing of politics, the total identification of a political goal with the will of God, always unleashes demonic powers.'[69] For Newbigin it is only the gospel which enables us to affirm both that God has made God's will and purpose known, and that God has ordained a space in which disbelief can have the freedom to flourish.[70]

Disavowing coercion does not mean that we believe that the gospel has no implications for practical politics. On the contrary, the lordship of Christ over all life means the very opposite. For that reason, 'any preaching that does not make it clear that discipleship means commitment to a vision of a society radically different from that which controls society today must be condemned as false'.[71] How are Christians to effect political change in a democracy? To answer that question Newbigin went back to the tradition of argument I outlined in the second chapter. Drawing on Eliot's *Idea of a Christian Society* he wanted to see a renewed lay understanding of the Church, so that 'through the presence and activity of committed and competent Christian men and women in the various areas of the common life of society ... the Christian vision of society could become effective in practice'.[72] Christian actions need to be understood as acted prayers to God that God may give us the kingdom – a view of political praxis which brings him uncomfortably near to the liberation theology with which he so disagreed.

Newbigin's response to the liberal dilemma I outlined earlier was that the development and persistence of democracy in Western Europe was made possible by the continuing persistence of a residual Christianity among its people, and that as this faded into the pure individualism of the consumer society the future of democracy would become increasingly problematical.[73] Only religious grounds, he argued, guaranteed that the human individual has

---

67   Metz, 'The One world' p.219
68   Newbigin et al, *Faith and Power* p.148
69   He contrasted this with Islam, where the laws of the state are the law of God and Church and state are one. *Foolishness* p.116
70   Newbigin et al, *Faith and Power* p.159
71   Newbigin et al, *Faith and Power* p.132
72   Newbigin et al, *Faith and Power* p.157
73   Newbigin et al, *Faith and Power* p.145

rights against the collective.[74] This is by no means evident. It might follow from the utilitarianism which underpins capitalism, but not from many other political philosophies. He followed Eliot, too, in arguing that capitalism undid the system it created. This, too, is contested by those who argue that the shift to aesthetic criteria for the sacred may not lead to nihilism and social disintegration but to mutual self-restraint and respect for the other.[75] To that we have to reply that there are no signs of it yet.

As the American discussion about multiculturalism recognized, education is a key issue and in relation to religion there is another conundrum. According to MacIntyre, learning takes place within traditions and, as Newbigin puts it, no seeking can be called serious which is without any clue. If this is the case how can it be recognized in a multicultural state? Do we, as is currently proposed in Britain, have schools for the different faiths? If so, does that not perpetuate differences, prejudices and misunderstandings as separate schooling did in Northern Ireland for generations? Where is the boundary between being inculturated within a given faith tradition and indoctrination? Parekh argues, in essentially liberal terms, that the aim of education is to develop intellectual curiosity, self-criticism, the ability to weigh up arguments and evidence and form an independent judgement, to cultivate such attitudes as intellectual and moral humility, respect for others and sensitivity to different ways of thought and life, and to open students' minds to the great achievements of humankind. To achieve this end, he urges, the educational system should be as free of Eurocentrism and all other varieties of ethnocentrism as is humanly possible.[76] One of the central aims of education should be to equip the student to participate in the conversation between traditions and enable students to appreciate the complexity of truth and the irreducible diversity of interpretations without nervously seeking for a final answer.[77]

But how is this to be done given that there is no neutral standpoint? No satisfactory way has been found of 'teaching religion':

> Themes such as festivals and rites of passage, grasped eagerly by schools desperate to include multi-faith work in a way which might be interesting and make sense to their pupils without upsetting religious believers or offending secular consciences, normally receive predominantly sociological treatment, or consist of largely factual information with little discussion of the fundamental beliefs behind the ritual.[78]

Omitting religion from the syllabus altogether is equally unsatisfactory because it suggests that, alongside serious subjects like mathematics, languages and the

---

74   Newbigin et al, *Faith and Power* p.148
75   Featherstone, *Consumer Culture and Postmodernism* p.126
76   Parekh, *Multiculturalism* p.227
77   Parekh, *Multiculturalism* p.229 Newbigin believed, similarly, that Christians have a duty to share with those who hold other beliefs, whether religious or secular, to create a public educational system which will train future citizens to live in mutual respect and mutual responsibility while acknowledging their differences in fundamental belief. *Foolishness* p.159
78   B.Watson, 'Education and the Gospel' in H.Montefiore(ed) *The Gospel and Contemporary Culture* London: Mowbray 1992 p.138

sciences, it is of little importance.[79] On the other hand, the fact that religions can only finally be learned from the inside, by indwelling traditions, means that the ultimate responsibility for this side of education has to be with the faith communities, whilst state education makes sure that at least a minimum, though non-caricatured, knowledge of other communities is made available.

The whole discussion so far has presupposed the existence of the nation state but Sayyid asks whether we may not be moving 'beyond Westphalia'. He points to phenomena such as the emergence of a global civil society, as instanced, for example, by the work of NGOs across state boundaries; the emergence of supra-national state-like formations such as the European Union; the rise of cosmopolitan centres like London, New York or Tokyo; the generalization of the experience of distant travel; and the development and increasing integration of the global economy.[80] In this context he seeks to understand the Muslim Umma. What he calls fissures within the nation state allow different kinds of political formations that are neither in nor out of the nation state, but that have an undecidable relationship to it.[81] The response to this must be, whatever the status of the Umma (and he may be right to understand it in terms of diaspora), that such formations can only exist parasitically in relation to the nation state if education, health care, transport and all the other services taken for granted in the contemporary world are to be available. 'Nation states' are those bodies which raise taxes to provide services for citizens. Up to the present we have not found any realistic alternative to this arrangement.[82] Tax evasion by some bodies which go 'beyond Westphalia' in Sayyid's sense, and which, as is well known, have economies greater than many nations, is a major problem. Such practices effectively deny democracy. 'Nation states' refers to those boundaries which make democratic decision making possible.[83]

This returns us, then, to the secular, liberal, democratic state which is needed to hold the ring between different groups in a multicultural society. This was, of course, the vision of the Indian state in 1947, currently under enormous strain from a communalism structured around religion. The difficulties of this model may seem to call it into question, but we need to ask what other credible options there are for a multicultural society. Stuart Hall sounds cautions against enthroning liberalism as the 'culture that is beyond cultures'. It is, instead, he says, the culture that won: that particularism which successfully universalized and hegemonized itself across the globe.[84] But if it has done that,

---

79 Parekh argues that there is a strong educational and political case for teaching religion in schools since one of the principal aims of education is to enable pupils to appreciate the great achievements of the human spirit, religion being one of these. *Multiculturalism* p.331
80 Sayyid, 'Beyond Westphalia' p.35
81 Sayyid, 'Beyond Westphalia' p.49
82 Held et al note that there are no guarantees that nation states as we understand them can be protected and nurtured. Urgent changes are needed if the functions fulfilled by this entity are to be met in the millennium ahead. *Global Transformations* p.452
83 Leach (*Land of Desire* p.383) and Petras and Veltmeyer (*Globalization Unmasked* pp.53–54) insist on the continued importance of nation states. So too does Beck (*What is Globalization?* p.108) despite his enthusiasm for a vaguely conceived 'transnational state'.
84 Hall, 'The Multi-Cultural Question' p.228

perhaps it has done so for good reasons. The achievements of religious toleration, free speech, the rule of law, formal equality and procedural legality, a universal franchise, are, as he says, not to be lightly discarded. Could they be discarded at all and allow multiculturalism, as currently understood, to continue?

That every liberal state is also an imagined community with particular histories, social codes and so forth does not mean that we can put a question mark alongside liberal achievements but that we need to find ways to make them more solid and more inclusive. As Hall argues, we need to recognize that democracy is an ongoing struggle, and that the goal is to produce a genuinely heterogeneous space.[85] Democracy of some sort has to be involved if all parts of the society are to have a voice. As long as ghettoization is avoided a shared culture should grow out of the interaction of the constituent parts and provide that common culture which Eliot and Raymond Williams wrote of. Such a shared culture can only grow out of the interaction of society's constituent parts, respecting and nurturing their diversity.[86]

This process is part of Williams' long revolution. We cannot pretend, of course, that Christianity, let alone religion in general, is key to its emergence. At the same time the past thirty years have emphasized that any stable multicultural society has to take account of religion, and cannot simply hope that it will fade away. The best hope for this is, as Parekh argues, an inclusive and religiously sensitive secularism. To make a positive contribution to this the discipleship community requires not just generosity of spirit and humility, but a deepening and continuation of that hermeneutic debate which has been such an important part of its life since the sixteenth century. Only thus can it be counter cultural without being divisive and sectarian – a stone throwing Church. More than enough evidence of that Church remains. Equally, however, there is ample evidence of grace and solidarity in the struggle for a more human future.

At the end of this third part of the book I return for the last time to the question of where the discussion leaves us in terms of a theology of culture. I conclude with three points. First, 'mission' originated in the resurrection and Pentecost: it was about spreading the good news of the death of death, of the overcoming of alienation, of the possibility of a new type of human community not marked by class, race and gender divides. To use Paul's shorthand, it was about the overcoming of 'sin'. The new community, 'Church', was at the heart of this mission. Not that the new community was itself the sum of the gospel – that was about God and God's act. But without the new community the gospel could be neither preached nor seen in action.

Three specific failures made this mission impossible. The first was the adoption of non-evangelical structures of power, first through Christendom,

85 Hall, 'The Multi-Cultural Question' p.235
86 Parekh, *Multiculturalism* p.219

and then through colonialism. Such structures stand outside the Church as a minus sign, which negates all it says and does. For the gospel to ride on the back of crusade or colonialism meant death to the Church. In order to survive it had to free itself from this, as its best representatives always saw. Crusade is the opposite of mission. Literally or metaphorically (we can argue in which sense) it is diabolical. The second failure was the reduction of the gospel to a message about individual salvation from 'sin' no longer understood as a portmanteau word referring, in the New Testament, to the complex ways in which human beings destroy themselves and God's good creation, but to a narrow and pre-defined understanding of what human beings do wrong. This theological move unwittingly rode on the back of the increasing individualization of the market society, and had nothing with which to challenge it. Only too often, as in the case of Thomas Chalmers, a gospel of 'sin and salvation' and an enthusiasm for capitalism were comfortable bedfellows. This understanding has to be renounced root and branch for the capitalism it is comfortable with is destroying us all. The third failure was the creation of 'boards of mission', which led to the loss of the perception that the Church itself was missionary, that the living, and therefore the spreading, of the good news of the divine flesh taking was simply the nature of the Church. This was again part of a movement of cultural retreat in which the Church became introverted and, in the postcolonial era, preoccupied with apology. But the Church has always known it lives by forgiveness; this fact is part of the secret of its carefree joy. Authentic mission is the sharing of this joy.

The second of my three concluding points is that I began this book with the logic of incarnation, and I return to it once more. The missionary theologians of the past century have insisted that mission involves both translation and inculturation. The Word takes flesh, becomes culture: this is at the heart of any theology of culture. The Word takes flesh as dialect, and it takes flesh in liturgy and therefore in doctrine. As in the early Church the rule that *lex orandi lex credendi est* is fundamental. Of course, as we saw in the fourth chapter, and we explored further in the tenth, universal and particular are not opposites, but exist in dialectical relationship. There are not, as some cultural relativists have argued, many mutually unintelligible Churches. There is one gospel and therefore one Church. Again, the idea that this unity was dependent on Latin (or indeed on a male priesthood) was an imperial corruption. Rather, what gives unity is the pattern of the action, the details of the story. These, as the artists above all have seen, are infinitely varied. The one gospel is culturally differentiated. In so far as the life affirming aspects of culture represent, as I have argued throughout, a response to the Spirit, we have in this cultural differentiation a response to the divine economy.

Lastly, I have tried to address questions about cultural apartheid, and its opposite, the attempt to live multiculturally. Does Christianity square off, in crusading mode, against the other great religions? Is the negotiation of multicultural difference a failure of nerve with regard to claims to truth? I have argued the negative in both cases. In the fury of the first reaction to the *Satanic Verses* Shabir Akhtar argued that 'any religion which has lost its temper of militant wrath is destined for the dustbin of history'. I argue, to the contrary, that on the Christian understanding all cultures, and therefore all religions, in what is life affirming, represent a response to God's Spirit. Because there is one Spirit these cultures and religions are united by far more than they are divided. The reality is not a clash of civilizations. The reality is strife between brethren. The biblical story of the meeting of Jacob and Esau instructs us about this strife. In their final meeting, after many years, the biblical narrative constantly takes us back to the 'face'. Esau tells his brother that to see his face is to see the face of God. Church, at the very least, is called to learn and live by that lesson in its meeting with alienated brethren.

With regard to multiculturalism, I have argued in this chapter that it does not commit us to a relativist neglect of the truth. Slavov Žižek may be right that the common struggle for a new society not dominated by the market is the priority, rather than multiculturalism in itself, but such a common struggle is fatally compromised by ethnic and religious hatreds. Against the politically correct multiculturalism of liberal society we have to insist that we can only live multiculturally if we struggle for the truth. Conversely, if we fail to live multiculturally then the truth, as it is enfleshed in our neighbour, certainly suffers. The constant and painful negotiation of difference does not commit us to a soggy liberalism. On the contrary, it involves the living of Torah, living life respectful of the Word become flesh. In its concern for the other it is, as Michael Barnes argues, profoundly theologically grounded. A theology of culture, in this sense, is a theology which understands the full implications of the gospel claim that I meet God in my neighbour.

Conclusion

The Gospel and the Long Revolution

It was in 1910 that the excited delegates at the International Missionary Conference in Edinburgh spoke of 'the evangelization of the world in this generation'. From the perspective of less than a century it is clear that this optimism was bound up with what, at that time, seemed to be the unstoppable success of Western colonialism. A mere thirty-five years later it lay in ruins. Effectively, after the Second World War, evangelical enthusiasm passed to laissez faire capitalism. Though the number of true believers seems to grow the probability of ecological collapse if the present model is not radically adjusted calls this particular gospel into question. This is part of the situation which humankind as a whole has to face. The other major factor is what we examined in Chapter 4, the continuing fall out of modernity.

When Muslim critics castigate the 'corrupt bog land' of Western culture it is really this which they are attacking. What is called 'postmodernity' is in fact just part of this continuing fall out, as Lyotard understood.[1] It is a way of talking about the fact that modernity necessarily stumbles over itself, because you can only be modern in relation to something which precedes you. Some cultural analysts have been insisting that we have been post-postmodern for some time. In 1990, only four years after publishing one of the most incisive analyses of postmodernity, David Harvey joined those suggesting that postmodernism was finished. It looks more and more, he wrote, like an epiphenomenon of the 1980s, 'a product of the profligate, credit fuelled entrepreneurialism of the Reagan–Thatcher years'.[2] But of course, those credit fuelled years have gone on and on. The Enron stage of capitalism is still with us.[3]

On the positive side, as we have seen, the postmodern condition valorizes difference – attention to the voice of the other, whether of the Third World, of women, of ecologists, or of regional autonomists. The voice of modernity, we are told, was the voice of the white colonizing male. In the postcolonial era the rest talk back to the West, women to men, and black to white. On the other hand this latest stage of modernity is characterized by 'widespread aversion to

---

1 'A work can become modern only if it is first postmodern. Postmodernism thus understood is not modernism at its end but in the nascent state, and this state is constant.' J.F.Lyotard, *The Postmodern Condition* Manchester: Manchester University Press 1984 p.79 I follow the standard distinction between 'postmodernism' as an intellectual stance, and 'postmodernity' as referring to the wider cultural impact which postmodernism theorizes.

2 D.Harvey, 'Looking Backwards on Postmodernism' in A.Papadakis(ed) *Postmodernism on Trial* London: Academy 1990 p.10

3 See V.Prashad, *Fat Cats and Running Dogs: The Enron Stage of Capitalism* London: Zed 2002

grand social designs, the loss of interest in absolute truths, privatization of redemptive urges, reconciliation with the relative ... value of all life techniques, acceptance of the irredeemable plurality of the world'.[4] Frederic Jameson, for whom postmodernism is 'the cultural logic of late capitalism', finds postmodern culture to be characterized by a new depthlessness.[5] Modernism constructed models of depth: the dialectic of essence and appearance; the Freudian model of latent and repressed; the existential model of authentic and inauthentic. What replaces these is the conception of practices, discourses and textual play. In this world ethics become aesthetics. Key words are euphoria, play, *jouissance*. The moral idealism of modernity, which packed its bags to go and fight Franco, is now ironized, for the end of all these struggles is the free play of the market and the pleasure of the commodity. Both the novel and the film *Trainspotting* are typical postmodern products: people have completely the wrong idea about heroin addicts, says the central character. We take it because we enjoy it, because the experience goes beyond any possible orgasm. The alternative, as the film suggests more clearly than the book, is the humdrum life of the accumulation of consumer goods, with holidays and consumer sprees taking the place of shooting up. In both, of course, it is consumption which is the ultimate value.

A key aspect to the new depthlessness is, for some, cynicism with regard to the truth. Nietzsche saw that all history involves interpretation. Postmodernism draws the radical conclusion from this premise that we cannot distinguish fact from fiction. In the world of Jean Baudrillard we cannot tell the difference between a TV soap and reality, and it is pointless to ask the difference:

> We live in hyperreality. Reality is 'more real than real', in that it no longer sets itself against something else, which unlike itself is phoney, illusionary or imaginary ... What is real politics, for instance? Smiling faces on the TV screen emitting headline catching one-liners, or the profound visions and world shattering deeds they simulate? ... In hyperreality, truth has not been destroyed. It has been made irrelevant.[6]

Our sense of history is the victim of this movement: history becomes heritage, packaged and sanitized, an exercise in nostalgia.

Some theologians have welcomed the postmodern turn as an opportunity. Where modernity was secular and atheistic, postmodernity, it is argued, enables thinking about other, alternative worlds. Modernism was obsessed with finding grounds for things, and endorsing various modes of legislation. Postmodernism follows the fall of the legislators and reminds us we can never exhaustively account for the conditions which make the world, time, knowledge, the human animal, language, possible. Once again it becomes possible to think seriously about God.[7] Reading postmodernism more

4   Z.Bauman, *Intimations of Post Modernity* London: Routledge 1992 p.97
5   Bauman, *Intimations* p.9
6   Bauman, *Intimations* p.151
7   So G.Ward, *The Postmodern God* Oxford: Blackwell 1997

comprehensively in terms of the logic of the market I am more sceptical about this position.

Throughout the book I have, following Herder, celebrated difference as a gift of the Spirit. This theological understanding grounds my approach to the variety of cultures. When this is theorized as multiculturalism the problem is that it actually marks the hegemony of the market, a culture based on consumption, in which faiths and values likewise appear on the supermarket shelves. 'Choice' is held up as the key ethical value, but it is simply the absolutization of individualism. When Matthew Arnold satirized the English principle of 'doing what one likes' he could never have imagined the way in which modernity would make this a fundamental societal principle. 'Post-modernity' is simply this principle become absolute. The car triumphs over public transport because it allows you to go where you like, when you like, and to hell with the environmental damage. On the World Wide Web, along with much that is worthwhile, the possibilities of limitless voyeurism have been exploited. As the boundaries of hierarchy and patriarchy slowly crumble unlimited hedonism takes their place. The lid is really off centuries of cultural restraint and pleasure is the gospel.

Certainly the situation is not ecologically sustainable and if, as I argued in the first chapter, the material and the spiritual are inextricable, this means it is not spiritually survivable either. Of course Christians should not rush to join the Malvolios. William Blake was right that the Church, and other religions as well, bound human pleasures with briars. Doubtless we are in a new situation, still more radically than Parekh considers in regard to multiculturalism. If it is true that human beings are *homo orans*, creatures which pray and contemplate, at least as deeply as they are *homo sapiens*, and if, therefore, the idea that the great religions would all disappear was a rationalist pipe dream, then these religions will have to build on the new situation and not repress it. At the same time, if there is anything to be learned from the sum of human experience so far it is that no society can be structured around the principle that 'anything goes'. Limits are vital not just to ecological but to cultural and spiritual life. They represent guidelines for the long revolution, the process by which we become and remain truly human.

What might the Church contribute to the coming negotiation of both ecological and spiritual problems – problems of a magnitude we probably cannot begin to guess? I have tried to reflect on this question around the headings of culture, power and mission. In terms of culture, I have argued, Church is committed to difference; in terms of power, to equality and a hermeneutic of suspicion; in terms of mission, to dialogue. None of these commitments are simple or self-evident. We saw with regard to culture that T.S.Eliot regarded it as a logical extension of that view that class differences, maintained by education, should continue. I have argued, by contrast, that what is needed is social equality grounded in an appreciation of the value of different kinds of education, and the political will to address the age old thinking which values some skilled work so much more highly than others, failing in this respect to understand what Paul has to say about our mutual dependence. Eliot was right that the equation of education with what goes on in universities is an intolerable narrowing. He was wrong in wanting to keep the system of deference in place.

With regard to power, we saw that conventionally Christianity has been regarded as a prime cause, rather than a solvent, of class, race and gender differentiation. Understood properly, I have argued, it is committed to an equality in difference which follows from both incarnation and Pentecost, our understanding of the work of the Son and the Spirit. The former is about local distinctiveness, engagement with the minute particulars of human history, the latter with God's work beyond the bounds of the Church. In virtue of both the Church is politically committed, not as the opiate of the people, but as constructing a counter hegemony to all imperialisms which rule by repression and violence.

To speak of imperialism is to call the Church's nineteenth century expansion to mind. Is the Church committed to some kind of religious imperialism, the reduction of every other to the same? The answer, I have argued in the third part of this book, is emphatically 'no'. Rather than the crusading mentality of the clash of civilizations it is committed to the ongoing negotiation of difference of which multiculturalism is currently the practical outcome. This does not involve for a moment surrendering belief in the truths of the creed, of replacing faith with benevolent relativism. It does mean, as I argued in the last chapter, rethinking mission and evangelism.

In this new situation, characterized by the imperialism of the market and the – postmodern – disintegration which follows from that, I want to ask where the Church stands, and what it contributes to the continuance of the long revolution. Alasdair MacIntyre famously ends *After Virtue* by invoking 'new Benedictine communities'. Newman had anticipated him. St Benedict, he wrote, found the world in physical and social ruins and his mission was to restore it. He did this by beginning a process of organic growth:

> It was a restoration, rather than a visitation, correction or conversion. The new world he helped to create was a growth rather than a structure. Silent men were observed about the country, or discovered in the forest, digging, clearing, and building; and other silent men, not seen, were sitting in the cold cloister, tiring their eyes, and keeping their attention on stretch, while they painfully deciphered and copied and re-copied the manuscripts which they had saved. There was no one that 'contended, or cried out', or drew attention to what was going on; but by degrees the wooded swamp became a hermitage, a religious house, a farm, an abbey, a village, a seminary, a school of learning, and a city. Roads and bridges connected it with other abbeys and cities, which had similarly grown up; and what the haughty Alaric or the fierce Attila had broken to pieces, these patient meditative men had brought together and made to live again.[8]

Newman's account is beautiful, though romanticized – as true to what actually happened as his contemporary William Morris' understanding of the middle ages. There was darkness as well as light, and merchants and trade played at least as big a part as monks and scholarship. That fact reminds us that, given

---

8   J.H.Newman, *Historical Sketches* vol 2 Maryland: Christian Classics 1970 p.410

the dialectical relationship between economy and culture noted in the first chapter, constructive changes in the latter will need constructive changes in the former. We have to insist on the dialectic. It is true that the Benedictine commitment to work and to agriculture did make a huge difference to European culture, whilst changes in the economy profoundly altered the Church and understandings of spirituality. What is the contemporary equivalent to that Benedictine initiative, an initiative which could contribute constructively to a more just and culturally rich human future? It will certainly not be one movement, but a multiplicity of them, and it will certainly not be wholly or even primarily 'religious'. At the same time the religions will make their contribution and, as far as Christianity goes, Newman and MacIntyre's evocation of the Benedictine movement does hold some important clues for our thinking about the future.

Let me return once more to Raymond Williams' notion of the values of a 'residual' form of culture, remembering that what is residual is not out of date, but can represent a challenge to the present which effectively shapes the future. Just so, I have tried to argue, the Church engages with 'the cultural logic of late capitalism'. It does so not by a regress to a pre-modern fantasy world. On the contrary, it represents, as I argued in the third chapter, an appeal to the wisdom of the past. It is a serious reckoning with means of survival in a world committed, by the insane imperative of 'economic growth' and the logic of the market, to ecological suicide. A theology of culture, in this situation, represents, as it always has done, a call to metanoia, repentance and a new way of doing things. The Church offers critique, and in a situation of 'new depthlessness' it does so by insisting on the need for reflection. Reflection does not mean passivity. It means the profound reflection out of which constructive action springs. Theology contributes, alongside philosophy, literature and the rest, by providing space for that reflection, by testing our dreams. The dialectic between religion and culture explored in the second chapter remains crucial. In this sense those who argue that 'the age of systematic theologies is over' are surely wrong. The moment of reflection is vital to our survival. It contributes to that 'fineness of living' which we saw was the aspiration of a truly common culture. At the same time it is at the heart both of any challenge to hegemony as well as of mission conceived outside of the framework of cultural imperialism.

Second, I have argued, in the spirit of Chalcedon, that Word and flesh cannot be divided. The constructive action which issues from reflection will be, as the Isaianic school insisted over and over again, action for justice, action for liberation and action for peace for both people and planet. But this means the restructuring of the global economy. It means a refusal to accept capitalism as the narrative of the world. What Isaiah envisages in this passage is not the next world but this world structured around use values rather than exchange values. Culture, we saw in the first chapter, is concerned with values, and values lie at the heart of economics. The conceit that economics might be purely 'scientific' and independent of moral questions, a conceit fostered from the 1860s on, is now finally being exposed. Rather, as Keynes recognized in the Preface to his *General Theory*, economics is a form of moral reasoning. It follows, therefore, not only that we cannot have a thriving culture without a new kind of economy, an economy for life, but also that *a change in cultural attitudes is essential to attaining that*. The dialectic is inescapable. In this sense culture is most vitally part of the Church's task. The politics this leads to is, in Žižek's splendid phrase, the art of the impossible – the attempt to change what is considered 'possible' – precisely the political significance of the resurrection.[9] Politics driven by an understanding of incarnation is not the 'Christian realism' which was urged by Reinhold Niebuhr, which amounts to little more than the view that there is no alternative to capitalism. On the contrary, it insists that history under God both can be and is full of surprises because it exists within the field of force of God's kingdom.

Third, in the discussion of high and low culture I addressed the question of memory loss – another part of the new depthlessness of our culture. In this respect, as I argued, we have to learn from the liturgy. The Benedictine rule structured time around the *lectio divina*, or in our terms around the telling and the re-telling of the story, that aspect of what we believe which remains constant through change. The story concerns sin, evil, failure, wickedness, grace, forgiveness, violence and the overcoming of violence, greed and the overcoming of greed, death – physical, spiritual and cultural – and the overcoming of death. We have seen the charge, from social scientists as well as from theologians, that modernity is marked by lack of purpose.[10] C.S.Song takes the name 'Immanuel' as a code word for the destination of the human project:

> Life without Immanuel is an illusion. It comes from nowhere and goes nowhere. It drifts like an abandoned ship in a vast ocean. It has no home. It has no destination. History is a terror without God-is-with-us. It is an eternal darkness devouring all truth, goodness, and beauty. But life is God-is-with-us. History is Immanuel.[11]

Song finds the reality of the claim that God-is-with-us in other religions besides Christianity, but the point is that it does also have a profoundly elaborated Christian version centred, as we saw in Chapters 7 and 9, on issues of freedom and equality, suffering and hope.

The *lectio divina*, the telling of the story, is ordered around praise of the Triune God, the God who is relationship, movement, history in Godself and to whom we correspond in just relationships, purposeful action and the struggle for community. Liturgy exists for life, not life for liturgy, but, as theologians have always argued, it is praise which is most genuinely ec-centric, which redeems us from our preoccupation with our own narratives, dreams and aspirations, from the idolatry of our own communities, and which puts all human affairs in a larger context.[12] Barth stimulated a huge train of theological

9   Žižek, *Ticklish Subject* p.199 For the political significance of the resurrection, see J.Moltmann, *Theology of Hope* London: SCM 1966
10   Cf Tomlinson, *Imperialism* p.169
11   Song, *Theology from the Womb of Asia* p.26
12   At the same time, as noted in Chapter 2, de-centring has its dangers. As Bhatt puts it: 'the coupling of human self-importance and a denial of responsibility for human agency' is a dangerous self- ... deception found in all forms of religious fundamentalism. *Liberation* pp.106, 73 All the more necessary is the discipline of the *lectio divina* around the story of human liberation.

reflection in speaking of the Trinity as 'the secret of God's beauty'. Simone Weil believed that 'contact with the beauty of Christianity, presented simply as a beautiful thing to be savoured' was far more important than dogmatic teaching.[13] It is this beauty which the liturgy celebrates. The medieval theology which wanted to speak of sacraments as 'instruments of grace' may have been mistaken in the way in which this was elaborated, but beneath it lay a profound insight into the connection between praise and liberation. There is, as it were, a Benedictine version of Rosa Luxemburg's insight that there is no democracy without socialism: there is no true revolution without the divine office.

Having said that, and bearing in mind T.S.Eliot's comment that Simone Weil was 'absolutely devoid of a sense of humour', it is important to recall the hostility to laughter in the Christian tradition and the way in which the repressed returned in carnival, and in the feast of fools. John McGrath notes that this was not purely negative mockery of the Christian ritual. 'The negative derisive element was deeply immersed in the triumphant theme of bodily regeneration and renewal. It was "man's second nature" that was laughing, the lower bodily stratum which could not express itself in official cult and ideology.'[14] The celebration of popular culture, in the true sense, and of high culture – and these two are not necessarily alternatives – is not part of the *lectio divina*, but the *lectio divina* is starved and wasted without it. There is a sense in which the Rabelaisian dimension of culture is also a part of 'liturgy' which is life – that emphatic celebration of 'the joy of living' which is, with a complete absence of pretension, and with tremendous gusto, response to grace. Culture without the *lectio divina* is blind, we can say; the *lectio divina* without culture is empty.

I began with the observation that the failure of modernity is specifically cultural. I end by concluding that, as I hope to have demonstrated, the Church's task is also 'specifically cultural' and for that very reason 'specifically political'. In the insistence on the values by which culture lives, known in the goodness and mercy of God; in the cultivation of 'fineness of living' – 'whatever is honourable, just, pure, lovely of good report' (Phil 4.8); in its commitment to education; in its challenge to power as violence; in the work of translation and inculturation; in the celebration of difference rooted in the knowledge of God in the face of the Other; in its telling of the story; and in its reflection – in all these ways the Church acts on and within culture and contributes to the long revolution. This revolution is the working out of the faith, hope and love of which Paul speaks: faith in the God who raised Jesus from the dead; hope in the possibilities for creation living under the God of hope; and arduous and patient work for a society which echoes or corresponds more closely to God's kingdom, which is the work of love.[15]

---

13   Weil, *Roots* p.89
14   McGrath, *The Bone Won't Break* p.153 The passage is a citation, but McGrath does not name his source.
15   Cf Žižek on Badiou, *Ticklish Subject* p.135

The obsequies of both Church and gospel have been read for some centuries, and they are pronounced now by secularists, feminists and members of other faith communities. But as Lessing said, in *Nathan the Wise*, such obsequies are of no account: we learn what is truly redemptive in the proof of spirit and of power. Christians should not be desperate in the face of these critiques. They should learn from them, of course, but they also need to follow Paul's advice and 'Rejoice in the Lord always'. They need to tell the story, trust in God, pray in the darkness, act for justice as the prophets commanded, and cheerfully wait to see what happens. What transpires will be the redemption of modernity, or postmodernity, as what happened from the fifth century on was the redemption of what we call the 'dark ages'. It depends on our cultural imagination, on our creativity, on the search for the best which both has been and will be thought and known. But it depends even more on hope in the God who calls the dead to life.

Select Bibliography

Abercrombie, Nicholas (1990) 'Popular Culture and Ideological Effects' in Abercrombie et al(eds) *Dominant Ideologies* pp.199–228

Abercrombie, N., Hill, S. and Turner, B.S. (1980) *The Dominant Ideology Thesis* London: Allen & Unwin

Abercrombie, N., Hill, S. and Turner, B.S.(eds) (1990) *Dominant Ideologies* London: Unwin Hyman

Abu-Lughod, Janet (1997) 'Going Beyond Global Babble' in King(ed) *Culture, Globalization and the World System* 2nd edn pp.131–138

Adamson, W.L. (1980) *Hegemony and Revolution: A Study of Antonio Gramsci's Political and Cultural Theory* Berkeley: University of California Press

Adorno, Theodore (1974) *Minima Moralia* London: Verso

Adorno, T. and Horkheimer, M. (1979) *Dialectic of Enlightenment* London: Verso

Ahmad, Aijaz (1992) *In Theory* London: Verso

Anderson, Benedict (1991) *Imagined Communities* 2nd edn London: Verso

Appadurai, Arjun (1990) 'Disjuncture and Difference in the Global Cultural Economy' in Featherstone(ed) *Global Culture* pp.295–310

Appavoo, Theophilus (1986) *Folk Lore for Change* Madurai: TTS

Arendt, Hannah (1961) 'Society and Culture' in *Culture for the Millions?* ed N.Jacobs Princeton: Van Nostrand

Arnason, J.P. (1990) 'Nationalism, Globalization and Modernity' in Featherstone(ed) *Global Culture* pp.207–236

Arnold, Matthew (1877) *Last Essays on Church and Religion* London: Smith and Elder

Arnold, Matthew (1884) *God and the Bible* London: Smith and Elder

Arnold, Matthew (1900) *Literature and Dogma* London: Smith and Elder

Arnold, Matthew (1920) *Culture and Anarchy* London: John Murray

Asher, K. (1998) *T.S.Eliot and Ideology* Cambridge: Cambridge University Press

Barber, Benjamin (1995) *Jihad vs McWorld* New York: Ballantyne

Barnard, F.M. (1969) *Herder on Social and Political Culture* Cambridge: Cambridge University Press

Barnes, Michael (2002) *Theology and the Dialogue of Religions* Cambridge: Cambridge University Press

Barth, Karl (1933) *The Epistle to the Romans* 2nd edn tr Hoskyns Oxford: Oxford University Press

Barth, Karl (1953) *Church Dogmatics* II/1 Edinburgh: T&T Clark

Barth, Karl (1956) *Church Dogmatics* I/2 Edinburgh: T&T Clark

Barth, Karl (1958) *Church Dogmatics* IV/2 Edinburgh: T&T Clark

Barth, Karl (1962) *Theology and Church* London: SCM

Barth, Karl (1981) *Ethics* Edinburgh: T&T Clark

Baum, Gregory (1994) 'Two Question Marks: Inculturation and Multi-culturalism' in Greinacher and Mette(eds) *Christianity and Cultures* pp.101–106

Bauman, Zygmunt (1998) *Globalization: The Human Consequences* Cambridge: Polity

Baumann, Gerd (2000) 'Dominant and Demotic Discourses of Culture: Their Relevance to Multi-Ethnic Alliances' in Werbner and Modood(eds) *Debating Cultural Hybridity* pp.209–225

Beauvoir, Simone de (1988) *The Second Sex* London: Pan

Beck, Ulrich (2000) *What is Globalization?* Cambridge: Polity

Bell, Daniel (1965) 'The End of Ideology in the West' in Waxman(ed) *The End of Ideology Debate* pp.87–105

Bell, Daniel (1976) *The Cultural Contradictions of Capitalism* London: Heinemann

Benjamin, Walter (1973) *Illuminations* London: Fontana

Bergonzi, B.(ed) (1969) *Four Quartets: A Selection of Critical Essays* London: Macmillan

Berlin, Isaiah (1976) *Vico and Herder* London: Hogarth

Berman, Marshall (1983) *All That Is Solid Melts Into Air* London: Verso

Beverley, John (1999) *Subalternity and Representation: Arguments in Cultural Theory* Durham(Ca): Duke University Press

Bhaba, Homi (1994) *The Location of Culture* London: Routledge

Bhatt, Chetan (1997) *Liberation and Purity: Race, New Religious Movements and the Ethics of Postmodernity* London: UCL

Bloch, Marc (1970) *French Rural History* Berkeley: University of California Press

Blum, William (2002) *Rogue State: A Guide to the World's Only Superpower* London: Zed

Bock, Kim Yong(ed) (1983) *Minjung Theology: People as the Subjects of History* Maryknoll: Orbis

Bocock, Robert (1986) *Hegemony* Chichester: Ellis Horwood

Bocock, R. and Thompson, K. (1985) *Religion and Ideology* Manchester: Manchester University Press

Boff, L. and Elizondo, V.(eds) (1993) *Any Room for Christ in Asia?* London: SCM

Bosch, David (1991) *Transforming Mission* Maryknoll: Orbis

Bové, José (2001) *The World Is not for Sale* London: Verso

Boyes, Georgina (1993) *The Imagined Village: Culture, Ideology and the English Folk Revival* Manchester: Manchester University Press

Brantlinger, Patrick (1983) *Bread and Circuses: Theories of Mass Culture as Social Decay* Ithaca: Cornell University Press

Bujo, Bénézet (1992) *African Theology in its Social Context* Maryknoll: Orbis

Burbach, R., Nunez, O. and Kargarlitsky, B. (1996) *Globalization and its Discontents* London: Pluto

Castelli, Elizabeth (1991) *Imitating Paul: A Discourse of Power* Louisville: Westminster and John Knox

Chomsky, Noam (2001) *9–11* New York: Seven Stories

Clifford, J. (1992) 'Travelling Cultures' in Grossberg et al(eds) *Cultural Studies* pp.96–116

Clifford, S. and King, A. (1993) 'Losing Your Place' in *Local Distinctiveness: Place, Particularity and Identity* London: Common Ground

Cobb, John (1990) 'Beyond "Pluralism"' in D'Costa(ed) *Christian Uniqueness Reconsidered* pp.81–95

Coleridge, S.T. (1976) *On the Constitution of Church and State* ed T.Colmer London: Routledge

Coleridge, S.T. (1990) *Table Talk vol 1* ed C.Woodring London: Routledge

Collet, Giancarlo (1994) 'From Theological Vandalism to Theological Romanticism? Questions about a Multicultural Identity of Christianity' in Greinacher and Mette(eds) *Christianity and Cultures* pp.25–38

Collingwood, R.G. (1946) *The Idea of History* London: Oxford University Press

Collins, Jim (1989) *Uncommon Cultures: Popular Culture and Postmodernism* London: Routledge

Comaroff, Jean and John (1991) *Of Revelation and Revolution* vol 1 Chicago: Chicago University Press

Comaroff, Jean and John (1997) *Of Revelation and Revolution* vol 2: *The Dialectics of Modernity on a South African Frontier* Chicago: Chicago University Press

Cone, James (1970) *A Black Theology of Liberation* Philadelphia: Lippincott

Cone, James (1984) *For My People: Black Theology and the Black Church* Maryknoll: Orbis

Critchfield, Richard (1994) *The Villagers: Changed Values, Altered Lives The Closing of the Urban Rural Gap* New York: Doubleday

Cronin, Kieran (1992) *Rights and Christian Ethics* Cambridge: Cambridge University Press

Dalacoura, Katerina (1998) *Islam, Liberalism and Human Rights* London: Tauris

Damel, P. SJ (1990) 'Dalit Christian Experiences' in Irudayaraj(ed) *Emerging Dalit Theology* Madurai: TTS pp.18–54

Davies, Miranda(ed) (1983) *Third World, Second Sex* vol 1 London: Zed

Davies, Miranda(ed) (1987) *Third World, Second Sex* vol 2 London: Zed

Davies, Nick (1998) *Dark Heart: The Shocking Truth About Hidden Britain* London: Vintage

Dawson, Andrew (1998) *The Birth and Impact of the Base Ecclesial Community and Liberative Theological Discourse in Brazil* New York: International Scholars

Dawson, Christopher (1933) *Enquiries into Religion and Culture* London: Sheed & Ward

D'Costa, Gavin(ed) (1990) *Christian Uniqueness Reconsidered* Maryknoll: Orbis

Denning, M. (1991) 'The End of Mass Culture' in Naremore and Brantlinger(eds) *Modernity and Mass Culture* pp.253–268

Donoghue, D. (1969) 'T.S.Eliot's "Quartets": A New Reading' in Bergonzi(ed) *Four Quartets: A Selection of Critical Essays* pp.212–238

Donovan, Vincent (1978) *Christianity Rediscovered* London: SCM

Dorfman, A. and Mattelart, A. (1975) *How to Read Donald Duck: Imperialist Ideology in the Disney Comic* New York: International General

Droogers, André (1989) 'Syncretism: The Problem of Definition, the Definition of the Problem' in Gort et al(eds) *Dialogue and Syncretism* pp.7–26

Dubois, J. (1906) *Hindu Manners, Customs and Ceremonies* Oxford: Clarendon Press

During, Simon(ed) (1993) *The Cultural Studies Reader* Routledge: London

Eagleton, Terry (1976) *Marxism and Literary Criticism* London: Methuen

Eagleton, Terry (1991) *Ideology* London: Verso

Eagleton, Terry (1996) *The Illusions of Postmodernism* Oxford: Blackwell

Eagleton, Terry (2000) *The Idea of Culture* Oxford: Blackwell

Éla, Jean-Marc (1986) *African Cry* Maryknoll: Orbis

Éla, Jean-Marc (1989) *My Faith as an African* Maryknoll: Orbis

Éla, Jean-Marc (1994) 'Christianity and Liberation in Africa' in Gibellini(ed) *Paths of African Theology* pp.136–153

Elias, Norbert (1994) *The Civilising Process* Oxford: Blackwell

Eliot, T.S. (1932) *Selected Essays* New York: Harcourt Brace

Eliot, T.S. (1939) *The Idea of a Christian Society* London: Faber and Faber

Eliot, T.S. (1948) *Notes towards the definition of Culture* London: Faber and Faber

Ellis, Marc (1997) *Unholy Alliance: Religion and Atrocity in our Time* London: SCM

Ellul, Jacques (1964) *The Technological Society* revised edn New York: Vintage

Engels, Friedrich (1978) *Origins of the family, private property and the state* Peking: Foreign Languages Press

Fanon, Franz (1967) *The Wretched of the Earth* Harmondsworth: Penguin

Farrell, Frank (1996) *Subjectivity, Realism and Postmodernism* Cambridge: Cambridge University Press

Featherstone, Mike(ed) (1990) *Global Culture* London: Sage

Featherstone, Mike (1991) *Consumer Culture and Postmodernism* London: Sage

Featherstone, Mike (1995) *Undoing Culture: Globalization, Postmodernism and Identity* London: Sage

Feuerbach, Ludwig (1957) *The Essence of Christianity* New York: Harper

Fiske, John (1989) *Understanding Popular Culture* London: Routledge

Fiske, John (1991) 'Popular discrimination' in Naremore and Brantlinger(eds) *Modernity and Mass Culture* pp.103–116

Forrester, Duncan (2000) *On Human Worth* London: SCM

Foucault, Michel (1980) *Power/Knowledge* Hemel Hempstead: Harvester Wheatsheaf

Foucault, Michel (1981) *The History of Sexuality* vol 1 Harmondsworth: Penguin

Foucault, Michel (1991) *Discipline and Punish* Harmondsworth: Penguin

Freire, Paulo (1972) *The Pedagogy of the Oppressed* Harmondsworth: Penguin

Friedman, Jonathan (1994) *Cultural Identity and Global Process* London: Sage

Friedman, Maurice (1989) 'The Dialogue of Touchstones as an Approach to Interreligious Dialogue' in Gort et al(eds) *Dialogue and Syncretism* pp.76–84

Friedman, Thomas (2000) *The Lexus and the Olive Tree* London: Harper Collins

Gasset, J. Ortega y (1957) *The Revolt of the Masses* New York: Norton

Geertz, Clifford (1993) *The Interpretation of Cultures* London: Fontana

Gibellini, Rosino(ed) (1994) *Paths of African Theology* London: SCM

Giddens, Antony (1989) *Sociology* Cambridge: Polity

Giddens, Antony (1990) *The Consequences of Modernity* Cambridge: Polity

Goldberg, David(ed) (1994) *Multiculturalism: A Critical Reader* Oxford: Blackwell

Gort, Jerald (1989) 'Syncretism and Dialogue: Christian Historical and Earlier Ecumenical Perceptions' in Gort et al(eds) *Dialogue and Syncretism* pp.36–51

Gort, Jerald et al(eds) (1989) *Dialogue and Syncretism: An Interdisciplinary Approach* Grand Rapids: Eerdmans

Gramsci, Antonio (1971) *Selections from the Prison Notebooks* London: Lawrence and Wishart

Gray, John (1997) *Endgames: Questions in late modern political thought* Cambridge: Polity

Greinacher, N. and Mette, N.(eds) (1994) *Christianity and Cultures* London: SCM

Gross, D. (1992) *The Past in Ruins* Amherst: University of Massachusetts Press

Grossberg, L., Nelson, C. and Treicher, P.(eds) (1992) *Cultural Studies* London: Routledge

Gutierrez, Gustavo (1983) *The Power of the Poor in History* London: SCM

Hall, Stuart (1981) 'Notes on deconstructing "the popular"' in Samuel(ed) *People's History* pp.227–241

Hall, Stuart (1985) 'Religious ideologies and social movements in Jamaica' in Bocock and Thompson(eds) *Religion and Ideology* pp.269–296

Hall, Stuart (1988) 'The Toad in the Garden: Thatcherism among the Theorists' in Nelson and Grossberg(eds) *Marxism and the Interpretation of Culture* pp.35–57

Hall, Stuart (1990) 'Cultural Identity and Diaspora' in Rutherford(ed) *Identity* pp.225–226

Hall, Stuart (1997a) 'The Local and the Global: Globalization and Ethnicity' in King(ed) *Culture, Globalization and the World System* pp.19–40

Hall, Stuart (1997b) 'Old and New Identities, Old and New Ethnicities' in King(ed) *Culture, Globalization and the World System* pp.41–68

Hall, Stuart (2000) 'The Multi-Cultural Question' in Hesse(ed) *Un/settled Multiculturalisms* pp.209–240

Hall, S. and Whannel, P. (1964) *The Popular Arts* London: Hutchinson

Hannerz, Ulf 'Scenarios for Peripheral Cultures' in King(ed) *Culture, Globalization and the World System* 2nd edn pp.107–128

Harker, Dave (1985) *Fakesong: The manufacture of British 'folksong' 1700 to the present day* Milton Keynes: Open University Press

Hartman, G. (1997) *The Fateful Question of Culture* New York: Columbia University Press

Heelas, P., Lash, S. and Morris, P. (1996) *Detraditionalization* Oxford: Blackwells

Held, D., McGrew, A., Goldblatt, D. and Perraton, J. (1999) *Global Transformations: Politics, Economics and Culture* Cambridge: Polity

Herder, J.G. (1877–1913) *Sämtliche Werke* 33 vols ed B.Suphan Hildesheim: Olms

Herman, E.S. and Chomsky, N. (1994) *Manufacturing Consent: The Political Economy of the Mass Media* London: Vintage

Hesse, Barnor(ed) (2000) *Un/settled Multiculturalisms* London: Zed

Hodges, Donald (1965) 'The End of "The End of Ideology"' in Waxman(ed) *The End of Ideology Debate* pp.373–388

Hoggart, Richard (1954) *The Uses of Literacy* Harmondsworth: Penguin

hooks, bell (1987) 'Feminism: A Movement to End Sexist Oppression' in Phillips(ed) *Feminism and Equality* pp.62–76

hooks, bell (1992) 'Representing Whiteness in the Black Imagination' in Grossberg et al(eds) *Cultural Studies* pp.338–346

hooks, bell (1993) 'A Revolution of Values: The promise of multi cultural change' in During(ed) *The Cultural Studies Reader* pp.233–240

Huntington, Samuel (1996) *The Clash of Civilizations and the Remaking of World Order* New York: Touchstone

Hussain, Shaikh Shaukat (1990) *Human Rights in Islam* New Delhi: Kitab Bhavan

Hutnyk, John (2000) 'Adorno at Womad: South Asian Crossovers and the Limits of Hybridity Talk' in Werbner and Modood(eds) *Debating Cultural Hybridity* pp.106–136

Illich, Ivan (1973) *Deschooling Society* Harmondsworth: Penguin

Irudayaraj, Xavier(ed) (1990) *Emerging Dalit Theology* Madurai: TTS

Jenks, C. (1993) *Culture* London: Routledge

Jordan, G. and Weedon, C. (1995) *Cultural Politics: Class, Gender, Race and the Postmodern World* Oxford: Blackwell

Kappen, Sebastian (1977) *Jesus and Freedom* Maryknoll: Orbis

Khan, Muhammad Zafrulla (1967) *Islam and Human Rights* Tilford: Islam International Publications

King, Antony (1990) 'Architecture, Capital and the Globalization of Culture' in Featherstone(ed) *Global Culture* pp.397–411

King, Antony(ed) (1997) *Culture, Globalization and the World System* 2nd edn Minneapolis: University of Minnesota Press

King, Antony (1997) 'The Global, the Urban and the World' in King(ed) *Culture, Globalization and the World System* pp.149–154

Kovel, Joel (2002) *The Enemy of Nature* London: Zed

Koyama, Kosuke (1974) *Waterbuffalo Theology* London: SCM

Koyama, Kosuke (1984) *Mount Fuji and Mount Sinai: A Critique of Idols* London: SCM

Kroeber, A.L. (1948) *Anthropology* New York: Harcourt Brace

Küng, Hans(ed) (1995) *Yes To A Global Ethic* London: SCM

Küng, Hans and Schmidt, Helmut (1997) *A Global Ethic and Global Responsibilities* London: SCM

Küng, Hans (1997) *A Global Ethic for Global Politics and Economics* London: SCM

Kyung, Chung Hyun (1990) *Struggle to be the Sun Again: Introducing Asian Women's Theology* Maryknoll: Orbis

Laclau, E. and Mouffe, C. (1985) *Hegemony and Socialist Strategy: Towards a radical democratic politics* London: Verso

Landau, Paul Stuart (1995) *The Realm of the Word: Language, Gender, and Christianity in a Southern African Kingdom* London: Currey

Larrain, Jorge (1979) *The Concept of Ideology* London: Hutchinson

Lasch, Christopher (1978) *The Culture of Narcissism: American Life in an Age of Diminishing Expectations* New York: Norton

Lash, Nicholas (1973) *Change in Focus* London: Sheed & Ward

Lash, Nicholas (1981) *A Matter of Hope* London: Darton, Longman and Todd

Latouche, Serge (1996) *The Westernization of the World* Cambridge: Polity

Leach, William (1994) *Land of Desire: Merchants, Power and the Rise of a New American Culture* New York: Vintage

Leavis, F.R. and Thompson, D. (1964) *Culture and Environment: The Training of Critical Awareness* London: Chatto and Windus

Lewis, Norman (1989) *The Missionaries* London: Arena

Loades, Ann (1990) *Feminist Theology: A Reader* London: SPCK

Luke, T.W. (1996) 'Identity, Meaning and Globalization: Detraditionalization in Postmodern Space–Time Compression' in Heelas et al(eds) *Detraditionalization* pp.109–133

Luxemburg, Rosa (1970) 'The Junius Pamphlet' (1916) in *Rosa Luxemburg Speaks* ed M.Waters New York: Pathfinder

McCabe, Herbert (1987) *God Matters* London: Geoffrey Chapman

McGrath, John (1990) *The Bone Won't Break: On Theatre and Hope in Hard Times* London: Methuen

McGuigan, Jim (1992) *Cultural Populism* London: Routledge

MacIntyre, Alasdair (1967) *A Short History of Ethics* London: Routledge

MacIntyre, Alasdair (1971) *Against the Self Images of the Age* London: Duckworth

MacIntyre, Alasdair (1985) *After Virtue* London: Duckworth

Mahmood, Tahir(ed) (1993) *Human Rights in Islamic Law* New Delhi: Institute of Objective Studies

Mannheim, Karl (1936) *Ideology and Utopia* London: Kegan Paul

Marx, Karl (1971) *Theories of Surplus Value* 3 vols Moscow: Progress

Marx, K. and Engels, F. (1952)[1848] *The Communist Manifesto* Moscow: Progress

Marx, K. and Engels, F. (1955) *On Religion* Moscow: Progress

Marx, K. and Engels, F. (1975) *Collected Works* Moscow: Progress

Menchu, Rigoberta (1984) *I Rigoberta Menchu* London: Verso

Metz, Johann Baptist (1993) 'The One world: A Challenge to western Christianity' in Regan and Torrance(eds) *Christ and Context* pp.210–223

Meyer, Thomas (2001) *Identity Mania: Fundamentalism and the Politicisation of Cultural Differences* London: Zed

Mies, Maria (1986) *Patriarchy and Accumulation on a World Scale* London: Zed

Mies, Maria, Bennholdt-Thomsen, V. and von Werlhof, C. (1988) *Women: The Last Colony* London: Zed

Milbank, John (1990) 'The End of Dialogue' in D'Costa(ed) *Christian Uniqueness Reconsidered* pp.174–191

Miles, Rosalind (1992) *The Rites of Man: love, sex and death in the making of the male* London: Paladin

Mills, G. and W.(eds) (1948) *From Max Weber* London: Routledge, Kegan and Paul

Moltmann, Jürgen (1977) *The Church in the Power of the Spirit* London: SCM

Moltmann, Jürgen (1999) *God for a Secular Society* London: SCM

Montefiore, Hugh(ed) (1992) *The Gospel and Contemporary Culture* London: Mowbray

Moore, Barrington (1978) *Injustice: The Social Bases of Obedience and Revolt* New York: Sharp

Moore, Stephen (1994) *Poststructuralism and the New Testament* Minneapolis: Fortress

Murray, N. (1996) *A Life of Matthew Arnold* London: Hodder & Stoughton

Mveng, Engelbert (1994) 'Impoverishment and Liberation: A Theological Approach for Africa and the Third World' in Gibellini(ed) *Paths of African Theology* pp.154–165

Myers, Ched (1988) *Binding the Strong Man* Maryknoll: Orbis

Naremore, J. and Brantlinger, P.(eds) (1991) *Modernity and Mass Culture* Bloomington: Indiana University Press

Neill, Stephen (1966) *Colonialism and Christian Missions* London: Lutterworth

Nelson, C. and Grossberg, L.(eds) (1988) *Marxism and the Interpretation of Culture* London: Macmillan

Newbigin, Lesslie (1986) *Foolishness to the Greeks* London: SPCK

Newbigin, Lesslie (1989) *The Gospel in a Pluralist Society* London: SPCK

Newbigin, Lesslie (1990) 'Religion for the Marketplace' in D'Costa(ed) *Christian Uniqueness Reconsidered* pp.135–148

Newbigin, L., Sanneh, L. and Taylor, J. (1998) *Faith and Power: Christianity and Islam in 'Secular' Britain* London: SCM

Niebuhr, H.R. (1951) *Christ and Culture* New York: Harper and Row

Nirmal, A.P. (1991) 'Towards a Christian Dalit Theology' in A.Nirmal(ed) *A Reader in Dalit Theology* Madras: CMS

Nolde, O.F. (1968) *Free and Equal* Geneva: World Council of Churches

Nussbaum, Martha (1997) *Cultivating Humanity* Cambridge(Mass): Harvard University Press

Oduyoye, Mercy Amba (1994) 'Feminist Theology in an African Perspective' in Gibellini(ed) *Paths of African Theology* pp.166–181

Parekh, Bhikhu (2000) *Rethinking Multiculturalism: Cultural Diversity and Political Theory* Basingstoke: Palgrave

Pateman, Carole (1987) 'Feminist Critiques of the Public/Private Dichotomy' in Phillips(ed) *Feminism and Equality* pp.103–126

Petras, James and Veltmeyer, Henry (2001) *Globalization Unmasked: Imperialism in the Twenty First Century* London: Zed

Phillips, Anne(ed) (1987) *Feminism and Equality* Oxford: Blackwell

Pickering, Michael (1982) *Village Song and Culture* London: Croom Helm

Pickering, M. and Green, T. (1987) *Everyday Culture: Popular Song and the Vernacular Milieu* Milton Keynes: Open University Press

Pieris, Aloysius (1988) *An Asian Theology of Liberation* Edinburgh: T&T Clark

Pieris, Aloysius (1989) 'Human Rights Language and Liberation Theology' in M.Ellis and O.Maduro(eds) *The Future of Liberation Theology* Maryknoll: Orbis pp.299–310

Pieris, Aloysius (1993) 'Does Christ Have a Place in Asia? A Panoramic View' in Boff and Elizondo(eds) *Any Room for Christ in Asia?* pp.33–48

Pieris, Aloysius (1996) *Fire and Water: Basic Issues in Asian Buddhism and Christianity* Maryknoll: Orbis

Postman, Neil (1986) *Amusing Ourselves to Death* London: Methuen

Regan, H. and Torrance, A.(eds) (1993) *Christ in Context* Edinburgh: T&T Clark

Ritzer, George (1996) *The McDonaldization of Society* revised edn Thousand Oaks: Pine Forge

Robertson, Roland (1997) 'Social Theory, Cultural Relativity and the Problem of Globality' in King(ed) *Culture, Globalization and the World System* pp.69–90

Rousseau, Jean Jacques (1913) *Social Contract and Discourses* London: Dent

Rowland, Christopher(ed) (1999) *The Cambridge Companion to Liberation Theology* Cambridge: Cambridge University Press

Rowland, C. and Corner, M. (1990) *Liberating Exegesis: The Challenge of Liberation Theology to Biblical Studies* London: SPCK

Rowland, C. and Bradstock, A. (2001) *A Radical Reader* Oxford: Blackwell

Ruether, Rosemary (1983) *Sexism and Godtalk* London: SCM

Rumscheidt, H.M. (1972) *Revelation and Theology: An analysis of the Barth–Harnack correspondence of 1923* Cambridge: Cambridge University Press

Rupert, M. (1995) *Producing Hegemony: The Politics of Mass Production and American Global Power* Cambridge: Cambridge University Press

Rutherford, Jonathan(ed) (1990) *Identity* London: Lawrence and Wishart

Sahgal, Gita and Yuval-Davis, Nira(eds) (1992) *Refusing Holy Orders: Women and Fundamentalism in Britain* London: Virago

Said, Edward (1994) *Culture and Imperialism* London: Vintage

Said, Edward (1995) *Orientalism* Harmondsworth: Penguin

Samuel, Raphael(ed) (1981) *People's History and Socialist Theory* London: Routledge, Kegan & Paul

Sanneh, Lamin (1989) *Translating the Message: The Missionary Impact on Culture* Maryknoll: Orbis

Sanneh, Lamin (1993) *Encountering the West: Christianity and the Global Cultural Process: the African Dimension* London: Marshall Pickering

Sardar, Ziauddin (1998) *Postmodernism and the Other* London: Pluto

Sayyid, S. 'Beyond Westphalia: Nations and Diasporas – the Case of the Muslim Umma' in Hesse(ed) *Un/settled Multiculturalisms* pp.33–50

Schleiermacher, F.D.E. (1958) *Speeches on Religion to its Cultured Despisers* 2nd edn tr J.Oman New York: Harper

Schreiter, Robert (1994) 'Inculturation of Faith or Identification with Culture?' in Greinacher and Mette(eds) *Christianity and Cultures* pp.15–24

Schüssler Fiorenza, Elizabeth (1992) *But She Said: Feminist Practices of Biblical Interpretation* Boston(Mass): Beacon Press

Schüssler Fiorenza, Elizabeth (1993) *Discipleship of Equals* London: SCM

Scott, James (1985) *Weapons of the Weak: Everyday forms of peasant resistance* New Haven: Yale University Press

Scott, Peter (1994) *Theology, Ideology and Liberation* Cambridge: Cambridge University Press

Seabrook, Jeremy (2001) *Freedom Unfinished: Fundamentalism and Popular Resistance in Bangladesh Today* London: Zed

Shorter, Aylward (1975) *African Christian Theology – Adaptation or Incarnation?* London: Chapman

Shorter, Aylward (1988) *Toward A Theology of Inculturation* London: Chapman

Smith, Anthony (1990) 'Towards a Global Culture?' in Featherstone(ed) *Global Culture* pp.171–191

Sobrino, Jon (1984) *The True Church and the Poor* London: SCM

Song, Choan-Seng (1988) *Theology from the Womb of Asia* London: SCM

Spengler, Oswald (1932) *The Decline of the West* London: Allen & Unwin

Spiro, Melford (1987) *Culture and human nature; theoretical papers of Melford S. Spiro* ed B.Kilbane and L.Langness Chicago: Chicago University Press

Spivak, Gayatry Chakravorty (1999) *A Critique of Postcolonial Reason* Cambridge(Mass): Harvard University Press

Stam, R. and Shohat, E. (1994) 'Contested Histories: Eurocentrism, Multiculturalism and the Media' in Goldberg(ed) *Multiculturalism* pp.296–324

Steiner, George (1971) *In Bluebeard's Castle* London: Faber and Faber

Suess, Paulo (1994) 'A Confused Mission Scenario: A Critical Analysis of Recent Church Documents and Tendencies' in Greinacher and Mette(eds) *Christianity and Cultures* pp.107–119

Sugirtharajah, R.S. (2001) *The Bible and The Third World* Cambridge: Cambridge University Press

Surin, Kenneth (1990) 'A "Politics of Speech": Religion in the Age of the McDonald's Hamburger' in D'Costa(ed) *Christian Uniqueness Reconsidered* pp.192–211

Tanner, Kathryn (1997) *Theories of Culture: A New Agenda For Theology* Minneapolis: Fortress

Taylor, J.V. (1963) *The Primal Vision: Christian Presence Amid African Religion* London: SCM

Tenbruck, Friedrich (1990) 'The Dream of a Secular Ecumene' in Featherstone (ed) *Global Culture* pp.193–206

Thistleton, Antony (1995) *Interpreting God and the Postmodern Self* Edinburgh: T&T Clark

Thomas, Keith (1973) *Religion and the Decline of Magic* Harmondsworth: Penguin

Thompson, J.B. (1990) *Ideology and Modern Culture* Cambridge: Polity

Thompson, John (1996) 'Tradition and Self in a Mediated World' in Heelas et al(eds) *Detraditionalization* pp.89–108

Tillich, Paul (1959) *Theology of Culture* New York: Oxford University Press

Tomlinson, John (1991) *Cultural Imperialism* London: Continuum

Tomlinson, J. (1999) *Globalization and Culture* Cambridge: Polity

Townsend, P., Davidson, N. and Whitehead, M.(eds) (1988) *Inequalities in Health* Harmondsworth: Penguin

Trilling, Lionel (1949) *Matthew Arnold* New York: Columbia University Press

Turner, Bryan (1990) 'The Two Faces of Sociology: Global or National?' in Featherstone(ed) *Global Culture* pp.343–358

Turner, Terence (1994) 'Anthropology and Multiculturalism: What is Anthropology that Multiculturalists should be mindful of it?' in Goldberg(ed) *Multiculturalism* pp.406–425

Tylor, E.B. (1958) *Primitive Culture: Researches into the Development of Mythology, Philosophy, Religion, Art and Custom* Gloucester(Mass): Smith

Upkong, Justin (1994) 'Christology and Inculturation: A New Testament Perspective' in Gibellini(ed) *Paths of African Theology* pp.40–61

Villa-Vicencio, Charles (1986) *Between Christ and Caesar* Michigan: Eerdmans

Vroom, Hendrik (1989) 'Syncretism and Dialogue: A Philosophical Analysis' in Gort et al(eds) *Dialogue and Syncretism* pp.26–35

Wallerstein, Immanuel (1990) 'Culture as the Ideological Battleground of the Modern World System' in Featherstone(ed) *Global Culture* pp.31–55

Wallerstein, Immanuel (1997) 'The National and the Universal: Can there be such a thing as World Culture?' in King(ed) *Culture, Globalization and the World System* pp.91–106

Waxman, Chaim(ed) (1965) *The End of Ideology Debate* New York: Funk and Wagnalls

Weil, Simone (1958) *The Need for Roots* London: Routledge

Werbner, Pnina (2000) 'Essentialising Essentialism: Ambivalence and Multiplicity in the Constructions of Racism and Ethnicity' in Werbner and Modood(eds) *Debating Cultural Hybridity* pp.226–254

Werbner, P. and Modood, T.(eds) (2000) *Debating Cultural Hybridity: Multi-Cultural Identities and the Politics of Anti-Racism* London: Zed

Wessels, Anton (1989) 'Biblical Presuppositions For and Against Syncretism' in Gort et al(eds) *Dialogue and Syncretism* pp.52–65

West, Cornel (1993) 'The New Cultural Politics of Difference' in During(ed) *The Cultural Studies Reader* pp.256–270

Wielenga, Bastiaan (1999) 'Liberation Theology in Asia' in Rowland(ed) *Cambridge Companion to Liberation Theology* pp.39–62

Wieviorka, Michel (2000) 'Is it so difficult to be an anti racist?' in Werbner and
    Modood(eds) *Debating Cultural Hybridity* pp.139–153
Williams, Raymond (1961) *Culture and Society 1780–1950* Harmondsworth:
    Penguin
Williams, Raymond (1965) *The Long Revolution* Harmondsworth: Penguin
Williams, Raymond (1976) *Keywords* London: Fontana
Williams, Raymond (1977) *Marxism and Literature* Oxford: Oxford University
    Press
Williams, Raymond (1980) *Problems in Materialism and Culture* London:
    Verso
Williams, Raymond (1985) *The Country and the City* London: Hogarth
Williams, Raymond (1989) *Resources of Hope* London: Verso
Willis, Paul (1978) *Profane Culture* London: Routledge & Kegan Paul
Wilson, K. (1982) *The Twice Alienated: Culture of Dalit Christians* Hyderabad:
    n.p.
Yoder, J.H. (1996) 'How H.Richard Niebuhr Reasoned: A Critique of Christ
    and Culture' in G.Stassen et al(eds) *Authentic Transformation* Nashville:
    Abingdon pp.31–90
Young, Iris Marion (1990) *Justice and the Politics of Difference* Princeton:
    Princeton University Press
Yuval-Davis, Nira (2000) 'Ethnicity, Gender Relations and Multiculturalism'
    in Werbner and Modood(eds) *Debating Cultural Hybridity* pp.193–208
Žižek, Slavov (1999) *The Ticklish Subject: The Absent Centre of Political
    Ontology* London: Verso
Žižek, Slavov (2000) *The Fragile Absolute* London: Verso

Index